The Door of Judgment

By

Stephen T. "Chip" Crosby III

ISBN: 0-7596-8682-3

This book is printed on acid free paper.

1stBooks - rev. 2/22/02

"Behold, the Judge is standing right at the door." James 5:9

Table of Contents

Introduction

The Purpose of this Book

Jesus said that He would come back.

He will come back to raise the dead, judge the world, put an end to evil, and rule in righteousness with the saints for eternity.

For many Christians, the anticipation of His promise is waning. The joy of expectancy has been lost to cynicism. Apathy has replaced readiness. Ignorance of the season has been substituted for watching the "signs of the times."

And it is no wonder. Christians have been "crying wolf" for almost 2,000 years, saying, "The time has come; the signs have been fulfilled!" Believers feel foolish when the promised "signs of his return" never materialize. They feel violated by those who have used prophetic interpretations to manipulate them toward their own selfish ends. Sheepishness has overcome the recipients of the Blessed Hope.

Other Christians have grown discouraged at the slowness of prophetic fulfillment. We have heard again and again that Christ is near, right at the door. Preachers say, "We are only waiting for the rapture of the church." I remember listening to one prominent leader in the "Jesus Movement" as he told his church in the early 1970's that he could not see the world lasting past 1975. Many of my friends took him at his word. (He was, after all, the pastor of one of the largest and fastest growing churches in Southern California.) They delayed their education, or rushed into marriage (or both) on the basis of such misguided belief. Now these same Christians are very reluctant to alter their lifestyles or proclaim the Second Coming to anyone else just because a pastor or teacher says that the Bible prophecies are being fulfilled today.

On the other hand, many saints have developed such a fascination in the Second Coming that it borders upon escapism. They devour popular books devoted to giving the latest news of prophetic fulfillment. For them, millennial fever is rising. Sadly, most of these books offer only shallow and sensationalistic teaching. Thousands of unsuspecting and gullible people have fallen into a false sense of security, thinking that they will simply escape all that lies ahead.

There is a real need for an in-depth and understandable book about the Second Coming of Jesus Christ. In this volume we will examine nearly every Scripture that has to do with prophecies of the end-times. Each chapter has a corresponding compilation of supporting verses located in the appendix. We will fit these together like an elaborate jigsaw puzzle, until a beautiful and complete picture of the Second Coming appears. (All Scriptures quoted in this book are from the New International Version, unless otherwise noted.)

However, since we are dealing with such a complex subject, we need to address some foundational issues first. How are prophecies to be interpreted? Why does Jesus *have* to come back? What is God's plan for the ages? Only after we have answered these questions can we confidently make sense of the "Signs of the Times" and what will take place at the "End of the Age." Finally, we will offer some insights into interpreting the "graduate level" book of prophecy, the "Book of Revelation." Interspersed along the way will be explanations of how current events are fulfilling the prophecies that point to the soon return of our Lord!

The Author's Approach to the Subject

Humility in Interpretation

We need to study this subject both humbly and carefully, remembering that the religious leaders at the time of Christ's first coming had rather dogmatic interpretations about the scriptures dealing with the Messiah. They thought they knew how the Messiah would come. Some of their understandings were even correct. For instance, they knew where He was going to be born (Bethlehem), and they had some ideas about what He would do (like Moses, he would feed the multitudes bread from heaven). Yet, because of their proud rigidity, the religious leaders would not recognize or receive Him as the real Messiah.

Likewise, whenever we deal with things that will take place in the future, we need to remember the Pharisees' poor example lest we, too, miss what God will do. While some prophetic scriptures are quite clear, others can have differing interpretations. Therefore, when we deal with prophetic passages that are certain, I will explain and defend them, but when we deal with scriptures that are less clear, I will admit that as well and offer various possibilities. Finally, when we look into an area that calls for conjecture, I will call it that (interesting though it may be).

Nevertheless, at the end of time, when we will all "know as we have been fully known," no one will be able to say they had all the prophecies figured out perfectly. (Although some may have a better percentage of accuracy than others!) However, just because we cannot say with absolute certainty what will happen in the future does not mean that Jesus never intended us to know *something* about the events at the end of this age. He clearly told us what signs to look for, and to be encouraged by them. We *can* know that Jesus is coming back soon and we *can* know something of what will happen during the end times.

Premillennial in Outlook

It may come as a surprise to many evangelical Christians, but there are differing opinions regarding prophetic questions other than the timing of the rapture! There have been three different theological systems taught by the church concerning eschatology (the study of last things). These systems are known as "Premillennialism," "Amillennialism" and "Postmillennialism."

The proponents of all these systems are godly and intelligent people. Just because they disagree with each other does not make them unspiritual or unbiblical. They all believe in the inspiration of the scriptures. And they all have rational reasons for their conclusions. Their differences arise out of their distinct methods of interpreting the Bible. As we shall see, some of their methods of interpretation may be correct, while their other approaches may be invalid.

Having said all this, this book will take what is called a "Premillennial" perspective as that is, in my reasoned opinion, the best system to harmonize and explain all of the prophetic scriptures. In order to understand what "Premillennial" means, however, we must first look at this and other related terms. Do not skim over the following definitions and explanations, as they are crucial to understanding the wide range of interpretations of prophetic scripture. I must warn the reader, however, that you may have to familiarize yourself with these terms. Otherwise, you may have to keep coming back to these pages in order to fully grasp the important issues involved in prophetic interpretation.

The three eschatological systems are based upon the various interpretations of what is meant by the "Millennium Age," mentioned in Revelation 20:3-5. (Millennium comes from two Latin words, *mille*, meaning thousand, and *annum*, meaning year. The term refers to one thousand years of worldwide peace, instituted by Christ.) *How* Bible interpreters view this key passage also determines how they view the rest of prophetic scriptures. Therefore, the various systems are named after this term. I will briefly define these systems, and then explain why two of them should no longer be considered as valid approaches to eschatological interpretation.

Postmillennialism: Teaches that the Kingdom of God is now being expanded in the world through the preaching of the Gospel and by the power of the Holy Spirit, and that the world will eventually be Christianized. The return of Christ will occur at the close of a long period of righteousness and peace commonly called the "Millennium." Postmillennialism is optimistic in its outlook regarding the influence of Christianity, believing that the world will get better and better due to godly influences of converted people. Postmillennialists believe that the prophetic scriptures dealing with the status of the Jews and Israel are symbolic, and should be applied to the church.

This eschatological position has gained popularity in the latter decades of the twentieth century. It is taught under the names of "Kingdom Now," "Reconstructionism," or "Dominion Theology."

Amillennialism: Believes that the Bible does not predict a literal "Millennium," or period of worldwide peace on this earth. God's kingdom and Satan's kingdom will each continue until the Second Coming of Christ. At that time the resurrection and judgment will take place, followed by the creation of the new heavens and the new earth. Any scriptures that deal with a millennium, as well as the nation of Israel, are believed to be symbolic. They are meant only to describe the age-old conflict between Satan and the Kingdom of God in metaphorical terms.

Premillennialism: Teaches that the Second Coming will be followed by a period of peace and righteousness, during which Christ will reign as King in on this earth for one thousand years. At the end of this period there will be a final rebellion by Satan and mortal humans, followed by the final judgment and the creation of a new heaven and earth. Premillennialists take the word "millennium" literally, as well as other prophecies, unless the context clearly calls for them to be interpreted symbolically. They believe that all of the prophecies concerning the nation of Israel will be fulfilled someday. This view is further subdivided into other categories, based largely over the timing of the prophetic event known as the "rapture:" "Pre-," "Mid-" or "Post-" "tribulation." (We will discuss these views in a later chapter).

Premillennialists do not believe that the world will be totally converted during this age. Although they teach that every nation will have a chance to hear the gospel before the end, they believe that the world will grow progressively worse as people apostatize and rebel against God. This age will be climaxed by the brief rule of the Antichrist, the outpouring of the judgments of God, the Battle of Armageddon, and the visible return of Christ who will resurrect believers to rule for the 1,000 reign of His Kingdom here on earth. Because Premillennialists believe in the literal fulfillment of Biblical prophecies, they teach that the general time of the return of Christ can be known, as certain prophetic signs are fulfilled.

Amillennialsim and Postmillennialism are similar in that they interpret Bible prophecies concerning Israel and the Jews as symbolic or metaphorical. Amillennialism differs from Postmillennialism in that it teaches that the world will not be Christianized before the end comes, and that the world will continue as it is now, with both good and evil in conflict with each other. Postmillennialism is more optimistic in its outlook, emphasizing the transformation of human society by the emergence of the church through the power of the Holy Spirit. While both believe that Christ will return at some point in the future for the resurrection and the final judgment, Postmillennialists deny the possibility of knowing the general time of Christ's return, because they believe these prophecies are all symbolic. Amillennialists do believe in certain definite signs prior to the return of Christ (i.e., the appearance of the Antichrist who will persecute the church, the outpouring of the wrath of God on unbelieving nations, etc.), but they do not stress the possibility of knowing the general time of these events much in advance.

If we study these interpretive systems in light of church history, it becomes easy to see how they arose and why people hold to them so dearly. Understanding this will also enable us to see where some possible errors in interpretation took place.

The early church fathers (the second generation of church leaders, immediately following the Apostles) generally believed in what was called *Chiliasm* (coming from the Greek word *chilias*, also meaning thousand). This system became known as *Historic Premillennialism*. Like modern day Premillennialists, they believed that Christ, at His coming, would set up a one thousand year kingdom on earth. They believed that the Scriptures concerning the Jews, Israel, and Jerusalem would somehow be fulfilled. The early church fathers taught that the church would go through the Tribulation and endure the persecution of the Antichrist. However, today's common understanding of Premillennialism differs from Historic Premillennialism in many respects, notably the timing of the rapture.

After the destruction of Jerusalem in 70 AD and the total exile of the Jews from Palestine in 134 AD, hope for the fulfillment of Scriptures concerning the Jews grew dim. Early church theologians such as Origen, Jerome and Augustine came to interpret prophetic Scriptures in light of the apparent impossibility of their literal fulfillment. They felt that the Jews had forfeited the promises of God's blessing and inheritance because they had rejected their Messiah. The church has now become the new "spiritual" Israel and is the recipient of God's promises. In other words, the Jews were no longer to be considered God's chosen people. This right was given exclusively to the church. (One unfortunate by-product of an extreme form of this position was anti-Semitism.)

Knowing this background, it is now a simple matter to refute Amillennialism and Postmillennialism. Both systems share the same presupposition, namely, a dismissal of God's ability to fulfill His promises to the Jews to return to their land and to their Messiah. Although historical events in the first two centuries made it seem impossible for the Jews to receive these promises, that should not have meant that the Scripture's literal fulfillment could never occur. Jesus said, "the scripture cannot be broken" (John 10:35). He told His followers of His commitment to their fulfillment: "Do not think that I came to destroy the Law *or the Prophets*. I did not come to destroy but to fulfill. For assuredly, I say to you, till heaven and earth pass away, one jot or one tittle will by no means pass from the law till *all is fulfilled*" (Matthew 5:17-18, NKJV).

Why, then, can we dismiss two of the three prophetic systems? Because the scriptures concerning the Jews and Israel *are being fulfilled* in our time, right before our eyes! There is no further need to debate any other issues with Amillennialists or Postmillennialists because the foundations for their symbolic interpretations of scripture have been proven wrong by recent historical events! As we will see throughout this book, prophecies made thousands of years ago are coming to pass with literal accuracy. For instance, the Bible foretold the return of the Jews to their land, with Jerusalem as their capital. Who would have thought this possible even one hundred years ago! Yet, God has glorified His mighty Name with a clear demonstration that He *can* keep His promises. Therefore, it is pointless to continue to hold onto theological systems whose foundations have crumbled.

One other system of prophetic interpretation still needs to be defined and clarified, as it greatly influences modern prophetic understanding among Evangelicals and Pentecostals. In the 1830's, a response to the dominant eschatological systems of Amillennialism and Postmillennialism arose, known today as Dispensationalism. Through the teaching of William Darby, a leader of the Plymouth Brethren and, later, the Scofield Reference Bible, this system evolved into what is the most popular understanding of prophecy today. Although Dispensationalism is Premillennial in its approach to Scripture, it differs in many respects from the Historic Premillennialism of the early church - notably regarding the timing of the resurrection and the rapture of the church.

Dispensationalism teaches that Jesus will secretly return to earth "like a thief in the night" in order to rescue the church through a supernatural event known as the rapture. The rapture will occur prior to a seven-year period of time known as the Great Tribulation. The Antichrist will rule over the entire world for these seven years. During the Great Tribulation, God will begin to accomplish salvation for His chosen people, the Jews. They will endure much persecution at the hands of the Antichrist, leading to the final Battle of Armageddon. At this moment, Jesus will come back again. This return, however, will be visible to all. The Jews will turn to Him as their Messiah and be saved, while the rest of the world will experience His wrath. Following His triumphant return, Christ will institute a period of peace known as the "Millennium."

Like Amillennialism and Postmillennialism, Dispensationalism is based upon some unbiblical assumptions. For instance, at the heart of Dispensationalism lies the supposition that God saved people in different ways in different eras, or "dispensations." These "dispensations" are applied rather arbitrarily, with no clear Scriptural support. There are seven dispensations: Innocence (Genesis 1:28); Conscience (Genesis 3:23); Human Government (Genesis 8:20); Promise (Genesis 12:1); Law (Exodus 19:8); Grace (John 1:17) and, finally, the Millennial Kingdom (Ephesians 1:10). Following the Age of Grace, also known as the Church Age (and after the rapture of the church), God will again deal with the Jews and bring them to salvation through their Messiah. Pentecostals may be surprised to know that one of the beliefs of Dispensationalism is its teaching that the supernatural works of the Holy Spirit ceased at the beginning of the Church Age. Therefore, Dispensationalists do not believe that the gifts of the Spirit are available to the church today.

If the presupposition of a system is in error, the whole system must be suspect. The New Testament does not make distinctions in the key to salvation for anyone in any age; people have always been saved by grace through faith, as Paul made clear in Romans and Galatians. (Noah found grace in the eyes of the Lord; Abraham believed God and it was reckoned as righteousness, etc.) While it is true that God progressively revealed *how* this salvation was going to be worked out through Christ, people have always been saved by believing the truth God has given them. Therefore, if God did not save people in different ways in different dispensations, then perhaps some of the other conclusions of this system may be faulty as well.

Confident in His Soon Return

Many well-meaning Christians, anxious to defuse the debate over the confusing and complex issues of interpretation, throw up their hands and say, "Why all the fuss? We aren't supposed to know the time of Christ's return. Doesn't the Bible say that He would come 'like a thief in the night?' Didn't Jesus say that we won't know the 'day or the hour' of his return?"

While respecting their desire for peace among the brethren, such toleration can result in more harm than good. Jesus chastised the religious leaders of His day for their inability or unwillingness to see the signs of His first coming (Matthew 16:1-4). Just because we debate the issues of prophetic interpretation does not give believers the right to ignore them, nor does the complexity of the issues give us the excuse to uncritically accept the easiest or most popular interpretations.

The fact of the matter is plain: Jesus gave His disciples signs to look for concerning the time of His coming. While it is true that He cautioned us about jumping to quick conclusions, He also said, "When you see *all* these things, you know that it is near, right at the door" (Matt. 24:33). Simply because there are earthquakes, wars, famines, and pestilences taking place in the world, we are not to point at them as *the* definitive signs. But when these occur (as well as other signs which will be explained in the rest of this book), Jesus gave us the comforting word that His return will be near. "When these things begin to take place, stand up and lift up your heads, because your redemption is drawing near" (Luke 21:28).

So, what did Jesus mean when He told His disciples that they were not to know the day or the hour of His return and that He would come "like a thief in the night?"

It is clear that we will not know exactly when Jesus will return, nor should we spend serious time speculating about it. Many Christians have done so in the past, much to their embarrassment. Christians have "cried wolf" so many times that the world considers the possibility of His return about as seriously as the story of the tooth fairy.

The Apostle Peter prophesied about this same attitude as a characteristic of the people who will be alive at the time of the end:

> First of all, you must understand that in the last days scoffers will come, scoffing and following their own evil desires. They will say, 'Where is this 'coming' He promised? Ever since our fathers died, everything goes on as it has since the beginning of creation.' By the same word the present heavens and earth are reserved for fire, being kept for the Day of Judgment and destruction of ungodly men. But do not forget this one thing, dear friends: With the Lord a day is like a thousand years, and a thousand years are like a day. The Lord is not slow in keeping his promise, as some understand slowness. He is patient with you, not wanting anyone to perish, but everyone to come to repentance. But the day of the Lord will come like a thief. The heavens will disappear with a roar; the elements will be destroyed by fire, and the earth and everything in it will be laid bare (2 Peter 3:3-10).

In other words, in the last days people will be dismissing the possibility of the return of Christ simply because He hasn't come back yet!

However, the Bible clearly teaches that we will know the general time of His return. In this same passage above, Peter mentions that Jesus will come "like a thief." In First Thessalonians, Paul uses the same analogy to describe the return of Christ. In both cases, the meaning is the same: a thief relies upon surprise, stealth, and suddenness. But notice that Paul clarifies those to whom the return of the Lord will come as a surprise: "But you, brethren, are not in darkness that the day will surprise you like a thief" (1 Thessalonians 5:4-6; NASB). So, the meaning of Peter's prophecy becomes clearer: the day of the Lord will come like a thief, but *only to scoffers* who have stopped looking for the signs of His return!

Christians will *not* to be surprised by the coming of the Lord! He will not come back as "a thief in the night" for us! Instead, we are commanded to know the "times and the seasons." We should be expecting Him, even while the rest of the world lives in the darkness of deception! That is what this book is about.

As we shall see from the scriptures, we are standing at the Door of Judgment. The Judge of mankind has His hand on the door, ready to enter the courtroom of human history. The signs of Christ's return are being fulfilled. Unfortunately, many people are living their lives like those of Jeremiah's day. Even Christians ignore the prophetic voice that warns of impending disaster. Instead, they call to themselves teachers who tickle their ears with messages of "peace and safety" when there cannot be peace, prosperity, or posterity in this life as it rushes to the end. Like the watchmen of Ezekiel's day, this book will help to sound the alarm and warn people to get ready. Jesus Christ is coming soon!

Part One

The Prophetic Puzzle

Chapter One

The Problem of Mankind

Why must Jesus come back? Why can't the world go on forever as it has been?

The answer to this question begins with the reason He had to come the first time.

Paul explains it in Ephesians 2:1-7:

> 1 As for you, you were dead in your transgressions and sins, 2 in which you used to live when you followed the ways of this world and the ruler of the kingdom of the air, the spirit who is now at work in those who are disobedient. 3 All of us also lived among them at one time, gratifying the cravings of our sinful nature and following its desires and thoughts. Like the rest, we were by nature objects of wrath. 4 But because of His great love for us, God, who is rich in mercy, 5 made us alive with Christ even when we were dead in transgressions - it is by grace you have been saved. 6 And God raised us up with Christ and seated us with Him in the heavenly realms in Christ Jesus, 7 in order that in the coming ages He might show the incomparable riches of His grace, expressed in His kindness to us in Christ Jesus.

In other words, we are all "Sinners" who deserve the righteous wrath of The Creator. But God, out of His great love for us, saved us through the perfect sacrifice of His own Son. Now, those who receive this free gift of mercy will inherit the riches of eternal life. This is the Gospel. Unfortunately, most Christians do not fully understand what it means. They take their salvation lightly, not comprehending what they were saved from!

However, once we know what "Sin" is, the destructive power it wields in our lives, and what Jesus did to redeem us from its power and judgment, we can understand why Jesus *must* come back. His work on our behalf won't be finished until He does.

The Definition and Origin of Sin

The problem with mankind is that everyone is a Sinner (Romans 3:23). God is so angered by our Sin that He calls us "objects of wrath" (Ephesians 2:3). No matter how much we might ignore it, deny it, or blame it on someone else, God calls Sin the cause of our judgment and condemnation into Hell. This very idea is abhorrent to us. Why can't God just ignore us and leave us alone? What is His big deal about Sin?

Therefore, we need to discover what Sin is, and why it is worthy of such a judgment. But at this point, people often get confused and angry, because they are ignorant of what Sin really is. They get upset when Christians call them Sinners because their understanding of Sin means to do something wrong, to be evil, or to break the law. They can accept the fact that people like Hitler, Stalin, or a mass murderer are Sinners. They believe that if there is a Hell, these kinds of people certainly deserve to go there (and what kind of just God would let such people in heaven anyway?) But most people really don't think that they are that bad. They aren't real Sinners. Oh, they may have bad days, or they may do things wrong, but really, everyone makes mistakes. They mean well. Nobody's perfect. Sound familiar?

Unfortunately, most Christians don't really know what Sin is, either. (And it is no wonder. Not one Christian book has been written on the subject in over 150 years! The only book written on it was by a secular psychologist, Dr. Karl Memminger, entitled, appropriately enough, *Whatever Happened to Sin?*) Like non-Christians, believers also tend to define Sin in terms of people's good or bad behavior. Sin is "missing the mark" of God's holy standard. However, this definition is incomplete. It is based upon the results of *being* a Sinner, instead of its root cause.[1]

The reason for this misunderstanding is that the Greek word for Sin, *hamartia*, means "to miss the mark, or bullseye." Since people cannot be good enough to attain the level of God's holiness, they have "missed the mark."

However, the biblical concept of Sin is a Hebrew one, not Greek. When the New Testament was written, *hamartia* was the closest word equivalent to the Hebrew concept, but it still could not express all of the original meaning. Therefore, to really understand it, we need to see how the Bible *uses* the words for Sin. To do this, we must first go back to the origin of Sin, as described in the Old Testament, to get a complete picture of just what it means to be a Sinner. Then we will examine the New Testament to see if its writers had the same Hebrew concept of Sin.

---

[1] This confusion is easy to understand. It must be noted that the Bible *does* use the concept of "sin" in two ways. Most often, it *is* used to describe the breaking of God's commandments. "Everyone who practices sin also practices lawlessness; and sin is lawlessness" (1 John 3:4). But the Bible also describes an inner attitude - almost like a power within us - that is actually the root cause for our breaking the commandments. The Bible uses the word for "sin" to define both this inherent attribute of humanity, and the results being in this state. In order to clarify these differing definitions, I will capitalize the word, Sin, when I am referring to this inner attitude.

The first Sin occurred in the Garden of Eden. Adam and Eve were created to have fellowship with God (Genesis 3:8) and to rule over His creation on earth (Genesis 1:28). God gave them everything they needed for their calling. The only requirement was that they were to be under His ultimate authority. As a sign of this right relationship with their creator and king, they were commanded to obey just one thing: they were not to eat from "the tree of the knowledge of good and evil."

Into this innocent scene came "the serpent of old who is called the devil and Satan, who deceives..." (Revelation 12:9; NASB). We do not know too much about his origin or the events that surrounded his fall (that is his story, not ours). We do know from the Scriptures that at one time he was a beautiful and powerful being in God's heavenly realm. According to Ezekiel 28 and Isaiah 14, he sinned and was cast out of heaven to earth. The essence of his Sin was his desire to "make myself like the Most High" (Isaiah 14:14).

Satan expanded his rebellion upon the earth. He found Adam and Eve in the garden. It is interesting to note that both Adam and Eve were with each other during the temptation. When Eve took the fruit and ate, she then turned and "gave also to her husband *with her*, and he ate" (Genesis 3:6; NASB). Although Adam blamed her for his action, he was right there by her side. The Bible says that Adam was not deceived or tricked by the devil (1 Timothy 2:14); he deliberately chose to listen to his wife instead of God (Genesis 3:17).

How did the devil entice the couple to join his rebellion? We learn from mankind's first temptation just how *all* sin begins. Satan began by attacking the veracity of God's word, "Did God *really* say, 'You must not eat from any tree in the garden'" (Genesis 3:1)? Eve's pitiful response, which innocently added her understanding of God's command, was not corrected by Adam: "...God did say, 'You must not eat fruit from the tree that is in the middle of the garden, and you must not touch it, or you will die'" (Genesis 3:3).

Next, the Deceiver planted the seed of doubt about the nature of God into Adam and Eve's minds, saying (probably as he touched the fruit himself), "You will not surely die, for God knows that when you eat of it your eyes will be opened, and you will be like God, knowing good and evil" (Genesis 3:4-5). In other words, "You're blind and don't know it. God is keeping something important from you. You need to eat this fruit. You need to be like God, so that you can know for yourselves what real wisdom is."

So, we see the devil opened the door to Sin in Adam and Eve by casting doubt into their minds about the truthfulness of God's word and the goodness of God's character. *Sin has at its root <u>unbelief</u> in God's existence, character, or will.*

Mankind's disbelief in God quickly progresses to rebellion against God's rulership. Since we all act upon our deepest beliefs, if we do not believe that

God will rule our lives well, we will look to our own selves to take over - as the rest of the account shows.

The temptation Adam and Eve faced was *not* that they were ignorant about what good or evil was. They already knew! It was actually a simple matter: God had said that everything was good (Genesis 1:31) and only one thing was bad - to eat from the one tree.[2] The nature of the tree was described by its name, "the knowledge of good and evil." In the Hebrew language, to *know* something meant to experience it intimately. The word for knowledge here is the same word the Hebrews used for sexual relations: "Adam *knew* his wife, and she conceived" (Genesis 4:1). So, to eat from this tree meant that they would determine for themselves just what good and evil were. No longer would they live by God's definition of good and evil; they would make the choice themselves. In so doing, they usurped God's role as ruler over them! In other words, *they would be like God*!

Since Adam and Eve did not believe that God's word was true, nor did they trust that God really had their best interests at heart, they took the fruit and ate. They wanted to be like God and control their own destinies. They had become Sinners. Had they broken the Law? Yes, they violated the only one that existed. Had they "missed the mark?" Yes, they had not measured up to God's standard of holiness. But *before* they acted out their sin, *before* they broke the Law, they had already become Sinners in their hearts through unbelief and their desire for self-determination. Only then did they begin to practice other acts of unrighteousness (such as disobedience, lying, accusation, shifting the blame, etc.).

Now we can define what Sin is. Sin begins in our unbelief in the existence, character, and dominion of God. Unbelief results in man's desire to rule over his own life and destiny. Ultimately this inner attitude of self-rule causes him to disobey and rebel against God's will. In short, *Sin is self-rule, caused by unbelief!*[3]

Sin encompasses more than just bad behavior. The Bible declares that even the most righteous among us is still a Sinner. (All of our righteous deeds are like filthy rags, in comparison to God's holiness! - Isaiah 64:6.) Sin goes deeper into

---

[2] God had already provided for Adam and Eve everything they needed for food and for delight for the eyes (the other parts of the temptation). Genesis 2:9 states, "And the Lord God made all kinds of trees grow out of the ground - trees that were pleasing to the eye and good for food. In the middle of the garden were the tree of life and the tree of the knowledge of good and evil." How tragic that they did not avail themselves of what God *had* provided, including the tree of life!

[3] Unbelief is not the same as temptation. Satan can hurl darts of doubt into our minds, as he did with Eve. We can choose to believe him, or we can hold onto God's word and knowledge of His character.

our nature than just missing the standard of God's holiness. In fact, breaking God's Laws is just the *result* of being a Sinner. Self-rulership is at the core of our very being. It is our essence. *It comes from our hearts.* We are, by nature, rebels against God!

If this definition is accurate, we should see this concept of Sin throughout the Bible. And so we do. The moral chaos of Israel during the era of the Judges was summed up as, "In those days there was no king in Israel; *everyone did what was right in his own eyes*" (Judges 21:25, NASB). Jeremiah described the Sin of the people of his day, "*We will continue with our own plans; each of us will follow the stubbornness of his evil heart*" (Jeremiah 18:12). And in the famous Messianic prophecy of Isaiah, God compared the waywardness of mankind to that of a lost sheep, "All we like sheep have gone astray, *each of us has turned to his own way…*" (Isaiah 53:6).

The New Testament also uses this same inner concept of Sin. Jesus tells us that "The pure in heart will see God" (Matt. 5:8). He said that the entire will of God for mankind could be summed up with this, "You shall love the Lord your God with all your heart, and with all your soul, and with all your mind" (Matthew 22:37). But He told the legalistic, self-righteous that, "These people honor Me with their lips, but their hearts are far from Me. They worship Me in vain; their teachings are but rules taught by men" (Matthew15:8-9). He identified the source of humanity's evil: "But the things that come out of the mouth come from the heart, and these make a man 'unclean.' For out of the heart come evil thoughts, murder, adultery," (Matthew 15:18-19).

Paul says in Romans 1 that even people who have never heard the written word of God have seen the existence and attributes of God in nature: "…since what may be known about God is plain to them, because God has made it plain to them. For since the creation of the world God's invisible qualities - His eternal power and divine nature - have been clearly seen, being understood from what has been made, so that men are without excuse" (Romans 1:19-20). An atheistic materialist cannot explain things like love, beauty, or justice on the basis of random chemical reactions. Nor can an evolutionist explain the complexities of the eye or the anatomy of the sexes by the "survival of the fittest" model of evolution. No, God's power, wisdom, creativity and care are all apparent to anyone who chooses to acknowledge them.

However, Paul continues by describing the essence of Sin: "For although they knew God, they neither glorified Him as God nor gave thanks to Him [they refused to believe or subject themselves to what they *did* know of Him], but their thinking became futile and their foolish hearts were darkened. Although they claimed to be wise, they became fools and exchanged the glory of the immortal God for images made to look like mortal man and birds and animals and reptiles" (Romans 1:21-23). In their refusal to worship or submit to the true God, humans always invent a deity to their own liking.

And what are the results of this unbelief and self-rulership?

"They exchanged the truth of God for a lie, and worshipped and served created things rather than the Creator - who is forever praised. Amen. Because of this, God gave them over to shameful lusts...Furthermore, since they did not think it worthwhile to retain the knowledge of God, He gave them over to a depraved mind, to do what ought not to be done. They have become filled with every kind of wickedness, evil, greed and depravity. They are full of envy, murder, strife, deceit and malice. They are gossips, slanderers, God-haters, insolent, arrogant and boastful; they invent ways of doing evil; they disobey their parents; they are senseless, faithless, heartless, ruthless. Although they know God's righteous decree that those who do such things deserve death [just as Adam and Eve also knew the penalty], they not only continue to do these very things but also approve of those who practice them" (Romans 1:25,26,28-32).

Paul sums up the Sinfulness of humanity: "...Jews and Gentiles alike are all under Sin. As it is written: 'There is no one righteous, not even one; there is no one who understands, no one who seeks God. All have *turned away*, they have together become worthless; there is no one who does good, not even one'" (Romans 3:9-10).

Finally, we are warned in the Book of Hebrews, "See to it, brothers, that none of you has a *sinful, unbelieving heart* that turns away from the living God" (Hebrews 3:12).

We are all Sinners. All of us, from the depths of our hearts, have turned away from God and gone our own way. We are self-centered instead of God-centered. Sin permeates our every thought, action and motive. We think about ourselves, we love ourselves, we want to control our lives. We are selfish, self-serving, self-protecting and self-promoting. When we get up in the morning, our first thoughts our usually about ourselves; when we go to bed at night, our last thoughts are usually about ourselves. We do everything with our own self-interest in mind. Even when we love or serve others we often do so out of selfish motives.

Even our language and our culture reflect the extent of Sin's influence. "Look out for number one." "What's in it for me?" "Have it your way!" "The Me decade." "You only go round once in life, so grab all the gusto you can." "I am the captain of my fate, the master of my destiny." And when it is over, we sing, "I did it my way." When we get religious, we want to come to God on our terms, not His. We make up our own theology. We bring God down to our level. "The answer is within." "The force is within you." We find it repugnant to accept God's only way of salvation. "It is too easy," or, "It's too narrow."

The Results of Sin

So what if we *are* all self-oriented rulers of our own lives? Why is that so bad? Well, imagine that the entire world population consists of 50 people living in one large room. The room has enough food, furniture, and all the necessary amenities of life. But every person is a Sinner - each a god unto themselves. How long would it take before conflicts arise between individuals and groups? Despite the abundance of necessities, when would some people acquire more, while some others would go without? When would the first murder occur?

This scenario is exactly what took place after Adam and Eve broke free from God's rulership to try to establish their own. Soon they were at odds with each other. "The eyes of both of them were opened, and they realized they were naked; so they sewed fig leaves together and made coverings for themselves" (Genesis 3:7). They were not suddenly becoming modest. To a Hebrew, nakedness was the supreme embarrassment (c.f. Genesis 9:20-25). All one's faults and imperfections - physical, mental, emotional, and social - are exposed to the awareness of others. Now in control of their own lives, Adam and Eve realized that they were imperfect. So, they covered up. They tried to hide their real selves from each other. They became afraid and insecure.

Even more devastating for mankind was the result of Sin in regards to their relationship with God. Unbelief and rebellion were unacceptable in the presence of their holy Creator. Therefore, the guilty couple hid from God. "I was afraid because I was naked, so I hid" (Genesis 3:10). God knew they had violated His will but He gave Adam the opportunity to confess his guilt. Instead, Adam - still covering up his inability to rule wisely (and thus proving it to Eve!) - shifted the blame, "The woman You put here with me - she gave me some fruit from the tree, and I ate it" (Gen. 3:12). In other words, "It's her fault; and it's Your fault. But it's not *my* fault!" Following her husband's lead, Eve refused her responsibility for her heart-inspired action and put the total blame on the serpent.

God had promised that the consequence for eating the fruit was going to be death: "…for in the day that you eat from it you will surely die" (Genesis 2:17). Did Adam and Eve die that day? Yes and no. No, they did not immediately keel over. But they did die. How? They were now "cut off" from God, the source of life. Death began to work in and through them. Most Americans celebrate Christmas with a Christmas tree in their living room. When we go to select our tree we try to pick the one that is freshest. We set it up, pouring water into a specially designed base. We enjoy its aroma and soft pine needles. Despite all of our efforts to prolong the tree's "life," it withers and "dies" within a couple of weeks. Why? Because it was already dead! It died the moment it was "cut off" from its roots. So it is with humanity. Sin separates us from the Creator, our Life-giver. In fact, one of the Hebrew terms used for death is to be "cut off."

And so we see that death began to work its way backward into the lives of these Sinners. Their relationship with God suffered the death of separation. Their relationship with one another suffered the death of intimacy and partnership and was replaced by fear and competition for each other's roles. Soon, their first-born son killed his brother. How long did it take before Sin and death infected everything God had created and called "good"?

Sin affects man's entire being: his body, his soul, his spirit, his relationships and his society. Physically, death works its way into life through sickness, injury, genetic problems, etc. Our souls feel ill-equipped to handle the pressures of ruling our own lives. With unjustified pride some people boldly and arrogantly assert their wills over others, causing injustice and ruin in the process. Other people, wishing they could be so confident, shrink back into insecurity (which is just the opposite manifestation of pride).[4] All of our mental or emotional problems can be traced back to this one root called Sin. Spiritually, we cannot make our way back to God as long as we persist in our march in the opposite direction. We are blind, deceived, unbelieving, and rebellious. Our best efforts at religion only address our outward behavior, not our inner heart attitude.

When one area of our life is affected by Sin, it touches other areas. We carry our Sin into our society and culture. We can't seem to get along for any length of time. Warfare, slavery, injustice, murder, prejudice, etc. are just some of the results of our collective Sin. If it were not for God's institutions of marriage and government, our Sin would be left completely unchecked. We would end up killing each other. One aspect of Darwinism would be true: only the strongest and fittest would survive.

Sin affects our planet as well. Humanity's desolation of the environment is not a new phenomenon. Greedy, thoughtless people selfishly destroy and devastate this world if it means some kind of advantage: "Your country is desolate, your cities burned with fire; your fields are being stripped by foreigners right before you, laid waste as when overthrown by strangers" (Isaiah 1:7). The Bible says that the "creation waits in eager expectation for the sons of God to be revealed [at the Second Coming of Christ]. For the creation was subjected to frustration, not by its own choice, but by the will of the one who subjected it, in

---

[4] It is interesting to note that many psychologists think the main reason for our society's problems is that people do not have a good, healthy self-esteem. However, now that we know what Sin is, we can see that the answer cannot be teaching people to have a better self-esteem. We consider people who esteem themselves highly as conceited, arrogant, or proud. On the other hand, people with a low self-esteem are called insecure. They wish they were more in control, but are upset or discouraged with themselves for not being self-confident. So, if the answer is not to inflate one's opinion of himself, nor is it to despise one's self, what is it? God's solution is that we be restored to right relationship with Him, and to walk in "*His-esteem!*"

hope that the creation itself will be liberated from its bondage to decay and brought into the glorious freedom of the children of God" (Romans 8:19-22).

Sin also affects the spiritual realm. When man chose to obey Satan rather than God, he did not gain his independence. Instead, Satan became the god of this age (2 Corinthians 4:4). A man is a servant to whomever he obeys. Those in rebellion against God are now captive to their Sin and to the ruler of Sin. It is no wonder that one of the tactics of the devil is to remain hidden from mankind's view. If we really knew that he was controlling our lives through our captivity to Sin, we would probably seek to throw off his shackles ourselves: "...that they will come to their senses and escape from the trap of the devil, who has taken them captive to do his will" (2 Timothy 2:26).

Satan was not alone in his rebellion. The Bible tells us of the existence of other fallen spiritual beings, called demons, devils or unclean spirits. Just as we do not know too much about the pre-fallen state of Satan, we know even less about these demons. There is one passage in the Book of Revelation (Revelation 12:7-9) that implies that these creatures are fallen angels, and that their number was one-third of the angelic host. Nevertheless, we do know that Satan rules over his realm with their help and that they are organized much like human governments. Paul declares that "...our struggle is not against flesh and blood, but against the rulers, against the authorities, against the powers of this dark world and against the spiritual forces of evil in the heavenly realms" (Ephesians 6:12).

These forces of evil take advantage of Sin to rule both individuals and society. Their rule is based upon the same essential lies and deceit their commander practiced in the Garden of Eden: doubting God's word, questioning God's character (or existence) and appealing to our pride and pleasure. According to the Scriptures, these demonic forces can so control sin-trapped individuals that their state becomes "demonized" (Greek—*daimonizomai*) or, in our common usage, "possessed." Jesus said that the devil has come to steal, kill, and to destroy (John 10:10). Mankind's miserable history is the proof of the existence and effect of Sin.

Sin affects our entire being: body, soul and spirit. Its power has reached beyond us into our society, our culture and our environment. Death has followed into each of these areas. This is our unhappy situation.

Mankind's Response to Sin

Ever since the Garden mankind has not dealt adequately with our primary fault. In fact, we have gotten rather adept at not facing up to it. Here are some less than admirable methods we employ:

Hide it - We can't bear the scrutiny of the light of truth on our naked sin. Therefore, we cover up. We try to look good, whether with material things (clothes, cars, money), power (manipulating or controlling others) or the self-righteousness of religion. We cover up because we are afraid of the consequences of our sin, or we are afraid of the rejection or ridicule of our exposure.

Blame it - We really can't help it; it is actually someone else's fault. The devil made me do it. It's a result of my poor childhood. It's society's fault. It's your fault. But it's not my fault! We refuse to take responsibility for our own actions.

Ignore it - We don't really think about it. It's just the way I act in such situations. "Am I my brother's keeper?" Cain replied, insolently ignoring his guilt. We push it under the rug as long as possible. And, we are encouraged to be tolerant of people with sinful lifestyles, as well.

Escape it - We anesthetize its consequences and pain by pursuing other diversions that become addictive: alcohol, drugs, sex, money, power, pleasure, entertainment, etc.

Justify it - We don't think it is really wrong at all. Everybody's doing it. There is no real right or wrong, it all depends upon the situation and circumstances. "Every man did what was right in his own eyes" (Judges 21:25).

Exalt it - We glory in it, boasting, "I am the captain of my fate, the master of my destiny." We begin calling evil good and good evil (Isaiah 5:20). We become proud of our evil deeds, as Lamech boasted to his wives how he killed a man (Genesis 4:23-24).

Worship it - We are really gods. Our society teaches us that if we knew this truth we would be fulfilled and happy. We believe the answer to all our problems lies within. "The Force is with you, Luke."

We will do *anything* but confess it and repent!

Sin is a lie, promising us power, pleasure, and happiness. But its end is always the same. We become trapped in the snares of our own making, leading to death. The Bible declares that our hearts are deceitfully wicked: "The heart is more deceitful than all else and is desperately sick; who can understand it?" (Jeremiah 17:9). We are so good at hiding, justifying, blaming, and escaping that we deceive ourselves. We don't even recognize our own Sin until the results come crashing down upon us. Even then, we often can't or won't admit the truth about ourselves. In exasperation, Jeremiah cried out, "Why then has this people, Jerusalem, turned away in continual apostasy? They hold fast to deceit, they refuse to return" (Jeremiah 8:5).

Why is there Sin?

If God is good, why did He allow evil? This is one of mankind's oldest questions. It is one that unbelievers like to use in order to refute the existence or character of God. The answer comes from the Book of Genesis.

God created man differently from the rest of creation. Genesis 1:26 states, "Let us make man in Our image, according to Our likeness…" When Adam was created, God breathed into him and man became a "living soul" (Genesis 2:7). There is a part of our nature that *is* like God. We *are* special. We *are* different from the rest of physical nature. We have the capacity to know God and to have a relationship with Him. God created mankind in order to share His glory and His love with us, forever. He created us as beings that were never intended to die. Just as God is eternal, so are our souls.

People were created to have a personal and loving relationship with God. In order to make creatures capable of love; God needed to make them capable of not loving Him. Otherwise, He would have simply made robots that would only done what He had created them to do.

Love, by definition, is something that is freely given. It can not spring from coercion or manipulation. Therefore, in order to love, a person has to have the freedom to choose not to love. Free will is necessary for a true and loving relationship. But free will also means the choice not to love becomes a viable alternative.

The question arises, "Couldn't God do otherwise?" "Couldn't God create a world where man would freely choose to have a relationship with his creator and *not* have the opportunity to Sin?"

The answer is no. It is an illogical statement. And just because you append the concept of God to an illogical statement does not make it logical. Once you choose to go one direction, you cannot go the other way at the same time. God chose to give His creation the ability to love Him back - to share in a love relationship. Therefore, the real possibility of not loving had to be present - otherwise the response of man would not truly be love.

And this is precisely our choice today. We still have the choice to love God and follow His will, or we can choose to love ourselves and be our own rulers.[5]

God's Response to Sin: Salvation or Judgment

Now that we know what Sin is and what its awful effects on all of us have been, we can understand more fully why God must judge Sin so thoroughly, and what God's work through Jesus has accomplished.

---

[5] For a more thorough treatment of the subject, see C.S. Lewis' book, *The Problem of Pain*.

Man is responsible for his free choice. Therefore, he is responsible for his Sin. The Bible declares that we will reap what we sow (Galatians 6:7). We have seen that humanity deserves the terrible consequences for Sin. Sin has affected all of life, both individually and corporately. Even nature has reaped the consequences of our selfishness. We have truly earned the promised penalty for Sin: death.

God *must* judge Sin. Mankind's Sin means that there are rulers in the universe other than God. But God, if He is to remain Sovereign, cannot allow the presence of mankind's self-rule to continue forever. There has to come a time when He will judge Sin completely, fully, and forever.

However, because of God's love for His mankind, and for the glory of His Name, He will not allow His highest creation to amount to nothing! He is able to save and redeem anyone who comes humbly before Him. For God so loved the world that He gave His only begotten Son, who became the perfect sacrifice for humanity's Sin.

In His gracious offer of salvation, God made mankind's choice both simple and clear: "For God did not send His Son into the world to condemn the world, but to save the world through Him. Whoever *believes* in Him is not condemned, but whoever does *not believe* stands condemned already because he has not believed in the name of God's only begotten Son" (John 3:17-18). God's plan for salvation is easy. Just as Sin entered the heart of man through unbelief, God begins the end to Sin through our belief!

Notice especially that it is *God's* plan for salvation. Anyone who tries to appease God's wrath any other way is sidestepping the Sin issue![6] Once again, God is giving man a simple, direct choice: "Will you follow God's way, or will you continue to chart your own course?" The essence of Sin must be addressed when one chooses to follow Jesus: accept God's way of salvation, or none at all. There is no other way that can possibly be acceptable to God. He has done all He can do for man, by giving us His Only Begotten Son.

So, Why Must Jesus Return?

Jesus and the early church preached this same message about Sin and salvation. They were clear about the nature and effects of Sin. And their Gospel

---

[6] Even those who are religious and zealous for God can be seeking Him from Sinful motives! Religiously righteous people who do not believe God's plan of salvation through Jesus are still Sinners at their core. Paul writes, "For I can testify about them that they are zealous for God, but their zeal is not based on knowledge. Since they did not know the righteousness that comes from God and sought to establish their own, *they did not submit* to *God's* righteousness" (Romans 10:2-3). To say, then, that other religions are part of God's will becomes an illogical and even blasphemous concept.

14

brought people into the Kingdom Rule of God. Jesus said, "The Kingdom of God is at hand; repent and believe the good news!" He was saying, in effect, "God's rulership is coming. Turn from going your own way and choose to follow Me. Believe that My way is right and good."

Then Jesus demonstrated that the affects of Sin were being overcome by the presence of this rulership of God now at work on earth. Where there was sickness, He healed it. Where there was demon infestation, He cleansed it. Where there was sorrow or turmoil, he brought peace. Where there was Sin, He forgave it. Where there was death, He vanquished it!

Therefore, salvation consists of a complete reversal of the fall of mankind through Sin. We repent of going our own way, and believe in God and His way! When we submit to the rulership of God in our lives, we begin to live as His kingdom representatives here on earth, being re-established in our rightful authority. As we take the Gospel to the world we see others come under His rule. To the degree that this happens, we begin to see other benefits of His rule take place in cultures and societies.

However, Jesus said that we would never completely finish this task. "I tell you the truth, you will not finish going through the cities of Israel before the Son of Man comes" (Matthew 10:23). This world will never fully submit to His rulership until He comes back to put Sin, Satan and death under His feet.

So, why must Jesus come back? According to the Bible, His work is not complete until He does. Jesus came to put an end to Sin, and all its effects: in our souls, in bodies, in our culture, and in the spiritual realm. The Incarnation and the Cross marked only the beginning of the expansion of Kingdom of God into this world. The work of the Kingdom will not be complete until Jesus puts all of God's enemies under His feet at His return. He promised to return, and when He does all heaven and earth will shout, "It is done!" (Revelation 16:17), and "The kingdom of the world has become the kingdom of our Lord and of His Christ; and He will reign forever and ever!" (Revelation 11:15).

Chapter Two

How to Interpret Biblical Prophecy

The Puzzle of Prophetic Interpretation

Interpreting prophecy is much like putting together a complex puzzle. Prophetic Scriptures are spread throughout the Bible. It is our task to uncover them and put them into some kind of sensible order. However, this puzzle is very difficult. Not only does it contain thousands of pieces, but they are mixed together with pieces from other puzzles. Many of the pieces are not easily recognized. And we are even told by Scripture that some of them are missing! (See Rev. 10:4-5, where John was about to write what he had just heard in heaven concerning some prophetic events and was told, "Do not write it down.") It is indeed a difficult task to find the pieces and put them together in an understandable manner.

With such a complex subject, is it any wonder that there are so many different interpretations about the Second Coming of Jesus? Does this mean that interpreting prophecy is just a matter of one's opinion, or is it possible to put the puzzle together with some degree of confidence in its accuracy? Just as there are steps to take in putting a picture puzzle together, so there are principles of interpretation that can help us understand prophecy. So, before we dive into specific Scriptural passages, I need to give some background on the rules of Biblical interpretation in general, and the nature of Biblical prophecy in particular. Then we will attempt to put the puzzle together, first by finding the four corners, then the straight edge pieces, and then we will fill in the inside, subject by subject!

Rules of Biblical Interpretation

The Bible is the Word of God to man. It is inerrent, infallible, and eternal. It is meant to be understood and applied, although its meaning can be hidden from those whose hearts are callused or hard. Jesus promised that one of the tasks of the Holy Spirit is to lead believers into the Truth. This happened, for instance, when Jesus "...opened their minds [the disciples] so that they could understand the Scriptures" (Luke 24.45).

In other words, in order to comprehend the Bible, we need hearts that are willing to believe and obey God. Furthermore, we need to have hearts willing to see the Scriptures from the proper perspective: God's - not man's. When we do study and learn the Word of God, we are able to fulfill Jesus' desire: "Every scribe who becomes a disciple of the Kingdom of Heaven is like a head of a household, who brings forth out of his treasure things new and old" (Matthew 13:52; NASB).

The Bible is fairly straightforward in its style and meaning. It usually interprets itself. If we take its words seriously, bearing in mind that these words can be written in various literary styles (narrative, song, poetry, metaphors, and symbolism), there will not be much trouble in interpretation. The more we read the Bible, the more we will understand it.

However, when confronted with the more difficult or confusing passages, we must remember this important point: the words *did* make sense to those who wrote them! The writers were not trying to deceive or be unclear (cf. Acts 26:26 and 2 Peter 1:16). But the writers lived in different eras and in different cultures than ours. They had different styles of writing. They used different figures of speech. We need to discover what their words meant to them, and why. Only then can their thoughts be understood by our culture. Therefore, we need to use *their* rules of interpretation.

A good example of this rule of interpretation is seen in the Gospel of Matthew's use of the phrase, "The Kingdom of Heaven" and the other Gospels' use of the phrase, "The Kingdom of God." Many "Gentile" interpreters (those coming from a non-Jewish background) have wondered why Jesus used the phrase "Kingdom of God" in some instances and "Kingdom of Heaven" in others. Was He trying to differentiate between two different kingdoms? Dispensational theologians claim that He was. They think that what Jesus said about the "Kingdom of Heaven" was meant to be for one time and realm, while the "Kingdom of God" will be for another. Unfortunately, making this kind of distinction between the concepts is unnecessary. It actually leads to theological error!

Why? If we look at Jewish patterns of speech at the time of Christ, we learn that devout Jews were reluctant to even say the word "God," lest they take His name in vain. Whenever possible, they would use *other* words to convey the concept of deity. So, when Jesus spoke about God's Kingdom, He usually used the Jewish idiom "Kingdom of Heaven," instead. Since the Gospel of Matthew was written primarily to a Jewish audience, Matthew recorded Jesus' words as He spoke them, since they would be clearly understood by his intended readers. However, when Mark and Luke wrote to their largely Gentile audiences, they had to change Jesus words into ones their readers would more easily understand (and to keep clear the actual, original intent of Jesus' words!). The so-called differences between the "Kingdom of God" and the "Kingdom of Heaven" are nonexistent! As a result of this understanding, we can conclude that the Dispensational teaching is in error concerning the concept of two distinct kingdoms.

When we try to interpret prophecy, we need to recognize the differences between our Gentile culture and the ancient Jewish culture. We need to approach

17

the subject of prophecy in a humble manner, learning to interpret it using the Jewish categories of prophecy and styles of writing. Otherwise, we may end up with embarrassing or conflicting interpretations.

The Nature of Prophecy

We are now ready to examine the question, what is Biblical prophecy? When people think of prophecy, they usually understand it to mean, "a prediction of the future." But prophecy is not so simple. The Bible describes many different kinds of prophecy, as well as several styles of prophetic expression.

Many prophecies of the early Hebrew prophets can be classified as **Prescriptive Prophecy**. They would prescribe God's cure for the people's physical, social, or spiritual problems: "Do this and you will live." These kinds of prophecies were not meant to be long-term predictions of future events. Over and over again, the prophets of the Bible said things like, "Even now, declares the Lord, return to Me with all your heart, with fasting and weeping and mourning. Rend your heart and not your garments. Return to the Lord your God, for He is gracious and compassionate, slow to anger and abounding in love, and He relents from sending calamity" (Joel 2:12-13). In this sense, much of the Bible (and Biblically based preaching) can be termed, "prophetic," in that it declares the expressed will of God for people.

Another type of prophecy can be termed **Predictive Prophecy**. It is what most people think about when defining prophecy: God's description of future events. God declared His rule over the affairs of men by telling people what is going to happen in advance. Many of the Bible's prophecies are so accurate and precise that modern skeptics and scholars say that unscrupulous scribes must have added them to the ancient manuscripts *after* the fact. For instance, Isaiah prophesied the very name of the ruler, Cyrus, who would cause Jerusalem to be rebuilt after the Babylonian captivity of the Jews (cf. Isaiah 44:28-45:7). Yet, the text says that God was going to raise up Cyrus "so that you may know that it is I, the Lord, the God of Israel, who summons you by your name" (Isaiah 45:3). That was exactly what happened. When Cyrus found out that the Hebrew Scriptures had foretold his ascension and activities, he gave the Jews great favor in his kingdom! There are many, many other prophecies that clearly show the supernatural works of God!

How did the prophets receive God's word? We usually think of the prophet getting a divine message through the audible voice of God or through an angelic messenger. The prophet would then speak or write, "Thus says the Lord." Although this happened regularly, it was not the only method God used to get His words to mankind. God often showed the prophets a **Vision**, or picture, of His will. The earliest Hebrew prophets were often called "Seers," probably because they could "see" things in the spiritual realm. The prophet would simply report what it was that he saw. Often, he would have to ask God for interpretation or clarification because the vision itself could not be fully comprehended. (See the first chapter of Ezekiel as an example of a vision that definitely needs a fuller explanation!). God also spoke to the prophets through dreams. Like visions, these often needed further clarification or interpretation. Finally, God communicated through events or actions in the physical world. He would then use those events as signs or symbols of His will. For instance, when Ezekiel's wife died, he was told not to mourn for her, as this would be a prophetic picture of what the people of Judah could expect when God's coming judgment fell upon Jerusalem.

Finally, we should also note that because our world is fallen into Sin, the Bible warns us of another kind of prophecy, called **False Prophecy**. Prophets who would speak in the name of God to further their own ends give these prophecies. In order to help people discern between a true prophet and a false one, the Bible gives some guidelines to follow (see Deuteronomy 13:1-3 and Deuteronomy 18:21-22). First, the predictions of a true prophet will be fully accurate. If a prophet said that there was going to be a drought (1 Kings 17:1), then there had better be a drought. Otherwise, he was in danger of being stoned as a false prophet.

Another important criteria for a true prophet was the soundness of their doctrine and obedience to God's morality. A true prophet would teach and prophesy accurately in regard to the nature and character of God, as well as His will for our lives. Although false prophets could be accurate in their predictions, if they led people to worship other gods, or practice sin, their messages were to be rejected.

Prophetic Styles

Biblical prophecy is not just a straightforward, homogeneous collection of messages. Rather, the prophets spoke in different times, in different styles, for different cultures, and even in different languages. All of these elements need to be taken into account in order to interpret each prophecy accurately. Now that we know more of what prophecy is, we can begin to analyze the various styles of Jewish prophecy. Knowing these styles will help us identify what the prophet was trying to convey without misinterpreting him.

Direct Prophecy - By far, this is the most common form of prophecy in the Bible. The prophet announced, "Thus says the Lord...this is going to happen." Jonah, for instance, proclaimed to the city of Nineveh, "Forty more days and Nineveh will be overturned" (Jonah 3:4). Such direct prophecies can be readily identified. Our only difficulty is determining whether a particular prophecy has been fulfilled or not. To do this, all we need to do is compare an individual prophecy with a good history of the ancient Near East.

Prophetic Type, or **Typology** - A few hundred years before the birth of Christ, Jewish scholars began to discover certain allegories within the historical and narrative portions of the Bible. They believed that these allegories, or types, pointed to the coming of the Messiah. It is often said that the Jewish scribes had identified over four hundred prophecies of the Messiah in the Old Testament. Many of these four hundred prophecies are this kind of prophetic type. For instance, when Matthew quoted Hosea 11:1, "Out of Egypt I called my son," as finding its fulfillment in the return of Jesus from Egypt after Herod died, he was not pulling the verse out of its original context. Hosea was originally referring to the initial exodus of the nation of Israel. But the Jews of Matthew's day saw the nation of Israel as a prophetic type of the perfect Son of God, the Messiah. They understood this verse in Hosea to be a prophetic type, representing an event in the Messiah's life.

Other prophetic types have their fulfillment in the New Testament. Jesus, for instance, is described in the Book of Hebrews as being the fulfillment of the perfect sacrifice under the Hebrew sacrificial system. He is also seen as the perfect priest, under the prophetic type known as the Order of Melchizedek (Hebrews 7:11-22).

It must be cautioned, however, that allegorical interpretations can lead into more confusion than light. Unless great care is taken, allegories can be made to mean anything the interpreter wants. At best, we should only use them to support what is already absolutely clear from other places of Scripture.

Prophetic Picture - This is a prophecy that is acted out by the prophet in order to demonstrate God's word, rather than only speaking it. It is said that a picture is worth a thousand words. Often, the visual impact of a demonstration is greater than words alone. For instance, the New Testament prophet Agabus (who was already known for his accurate prophecies concerning a world-wide famine) took the Apostle Paul's belt and tied his own hands and feet with it, proclaiming, "The Holy Spirit says, 'In this way the Jews of Jerusalem will bind the owner of this belt and will hand him over to the Gentiles'" (Acts 21:11). Other examples of prophetic pictures are Jeremiah's burial of his waistband; Ezekiel's lying naked upon his side, and Elisha's request for the king to strike the ground with his arrows.

Jesus prophesied in this fashion, too. At one point, He stated, "I tell you the truth, some who are standing here will not taste death before they see the Son of Man coming in His Kingdom" (Matthew 16:28). The very next passage gives the fulfillment of this prediction, in what is called "the Transfiguration." Peter, James and John saw Jesus glorified, just as He will appear when He comes to take full possession of His Kingdom.

Apocalyptic Prophecy - This is a style of prophecy that began with Daniel. The prophets would describe future events using symbolic pictures or imagery. For instance, the prophet would "see" an object or animal in the spiritual realm and then describe its characteristics or actions. He would ask God what the vision meant and the Lord would reveal the meaning of the picture. From the instances where God interpreted these symbolic pictures, we can deduce the meaning of similar pictures. For instance, the beasts Daniel saw in his visions represented rulers and empires. The similar beast John saw in the Book of Revelation, therefore, also represents a ruler and his empire.

Writers of non-biblical apocalyptic works (such as the Book of Enoch and the Shepherd of Hermas) use similar symbolic pictures in their writings. Occasionally, we can glean from their works just what the Biblical writers might have been meaning as well. For instance, we read in the Book of Revelation that after the opening of the seventh seal there was silence in heaven. Normally, we would think that a very anticlimactic ending following the first six seal judgments! However, the apocryphal book of Second Esdras 7:29-31 tells us that the imagery of silence in heaven means that the works of God are now complete; everything has been accomplished.

Two lesser-known styles of prophecy need to be defined here in order to make this study complete. It is crucial for us to be able to recognize them. If we do not understand them, prophetic interpretation will be very confusing.

Telescopic Prophecy—Prophets often saw pictures or visions of what was going to take place in the distant future. But just as a photo taken with a telescopic lens lacks the perception of depth, some of their prophecies lack the perception of the passing of time. In other words, the prophet describes events that will take place over a long period, but he does not explain *when* each part will be fulfilled.

One of the best examples of this type of prophecy is Ezekiel's description of the judgment of the city of Tyre. We read that God will "bring many nations against you, like the sea casting up its waves" (Ezekiel 26:3). The next verse describes the effects of this judgment: "They will destroy the walls of Tyre and pull down her towers; I will scrape away her rubble and make her a bare rock. Out in the sea she will become a place to spread fishnets" (Ezekiel 26:4,5). This one verse took hundreds of years, several invasions, and the work of sea currents to bring to complete fulfillment. Nebuchadnezzar destroyed the walls and towers of Tyre, but he could not extend his conquest to the part of the city located on an island just off the mainland. It was not until hundreds of years later that Alexander the Great had the rubble of the old city scraped up and thrown into the sea, making a causeway for his armies to destroy the island city of Tyre. This causeway was later filled with silt and sediment, making the location unfit for shipping. Now, only fishermen use the location for the spreading of their nets! The ancient city was never rebuilt (Ezekiel 26:14).

Other prophecies begin to make more sense when viewed from this telescopic perspective. Parts of them have been fulfilled, while other parts have not. The best example of this is Jesus' prophecy of His own Second Coming (cf.

21

Matthew 24, Mark 13, and Luke 21). He clearly prophesied the destruction of both the city of Jerusalem and the Jewish temple. He said that the Jews would be banished from the land and exiled into all nations. However, other elements of the prophecy have clearly not been fulfilled. We have not yet seen the signs of the sun, moon, or stars, nor has the Abomination of Desolation occurred. These are future events, but their fulfillment is as certain as was the fulfillment of the earlier parts of the prophecy.

Eschatological Dualism, or the **Dual Fulfillment of Prophecy** - This is another crucial concept of prophetic interpretation. Eschatological Dualism is a kind of prophecy where there seems to be an initial fulfillment in history, but it is not quite complete in all of the prophetic details. The first and incomplete fulfillment seems to point to a second, more perfect fulfillment. In other words, the prophecy begs a better fulfillment.

The Old Testament writers were familiar with this style of prophecy. For instance, when David received the promise of an everlasting kingdom, the initial fulfillment of the promise was through his son, Solomon (see 2 Samuel 7:12-16). God said that David's descendant would build a house for Him, and establish the throne of His kingdom forever. Although Solomon did build the temple, his kingdom was divided soon after his death, and his dynasty ended at the Babylonian exile. The prophecy's fulfillment in Solomon begged a better fulfillment! However, even before the end of the Solomonic dynasty, the prophets were predicting the eternal fulfillment of the Davidic Promise through the person of the Messiah. Isaiah 9:6-7 reads, "For a child will be born to us, a son will be given to us: and the government will rest on His shoulders; and His name will be called Wonderful Counselor, Mighty God, Eternal Father, Prince of Peace. There will be no end to the increase of His government or of peace, on the throne of David and over his kingdom" (NASB).

Jesus used this type of prophecy at least twice in his ministry. When His disciples asked Him about the necessity for Elijah to come prior to the coming of the Day of the Lord (see Malachi 4:1-6), Jesus replied, "Elijah *is* coming and will restore all things; but I say to you that Elijah *already* came, and they did not recognize him…" (Matthew 17:11-12; NASB). Then, the Scripture says, "…the disciples understood that He had spoken to them about John the Baptist" (Matthew 17:13). The Jews knew the prophecy about Elijah. They expected him to be a forerunner to the Messiah who would prepare the hearts of the people to receive Him (Malachi 3:1). In this sense, John the Baptist was a perfect fulfillment: he appeared in the wilderness (like Elijah) and he prepared the hearts of the people through his message of repentance and belief in the coming Kingdom. However, he was not the literal, flesh and bone Elijah! Nor were the passages in Malachi 4 completely fulfilled which spoke about the final, fiery judgment of the wicked. Therefore, Jesus pointed to an initial fulfillment of Malachi's prophecy in the person of John the Baptist. But He also looked forward to a better, more perfect fulfillment when He predicted, "Elijah *is* coming and will restore all things…" (Matthew 17:11; NASB).

The apostles also used this form of prophetic interpretation.[7] On the Day of Pentecost, Peter quoted the prophet Joel, saying, "But this is what was spoken of through the prophet Joel: 'And it shall be in the last days…that I shall pour forth My Spirit on all mankind'" (Acts 2:16,17; NASB). However, the prophet Joel also prophesied that in these same last days there would be "wonders in the sky above and signs on the earth below, blood and fire, and vapor of smoke. The sun will be turned into darkness and the moon into blood, before the great and glorious day of the Lord shall come" (Acts 2:19,20; NASB). Pentecost fulfilled only the beginning of Joel's prophecy. We eagerly await the more perfect and glorious completion to come!

Knowing how these Jewish styles of prophecy work is especially important when we try to understand Jesus' prophecies about His Second Coming. He used both the Telescopic and Dualistic styles in his great prophetic discourse given on the Mount of Olives. As we shall see, Christ's words begin to make perfect sense when we can read them from this perspective.

In addition to being aware of the Jewish prophetic styles, we also need to understand ancient **Jewish Writing Style**. Although this may be hard for people brought up in our culture to understand, not all cultures think or write in the same manner. We tend to practice the Greek, or Western, method of deductive reasoning and argument. For instance, if "A" equals "B" and "B" equals "C," then "A" equals "C." When we write, we follow accepted forms of logic and reasoning, as follows:

I. First Point
    A.
    B.
    C.

II. Second Point
    A.
    B.
    C.

---

[7] This type of prophetic understanding helps us explain how Matthew could use Isaiah's prophesy of a "young woman" (Heb. *alma*) to be fulfilled in the virgin birth of Jesus. The prophecy given to King Ahaz in Isaiah 7:10-16 had its initial fulfillment in the birth of Isaiah's son through the "prophetess" in Isaiah 8:3-8. Isaiah's wife was the *alma*. But *alma* also was used to describe what every young Jewish woman was, a virgin. Therefore, there was going to be a better fulfillment of the prophecy, where a virgin would conceive and bear a child who would truly be, "Emmanuel" or "God with us!"

The ancient Jews, however, did not reason in this manner. Rather, they used repetition and parallel statements to develop their thoughts. For instance, when a Hebrew wanted to emphasize something, he would write it more than once. A fact was true if it was confirmed by two or three witnesses (Deuteronomy 19:15, Second Corinthians 13:1). The prophet Amos uses this style of repetition in his judgments against the nations in his day: "for three transgressions…and for four". Jesus expected His disciples to understand the deeper significance of the two miraculous feedings of the multitude: "'Why do you discuss the fact that you have no bread? Do you not yet see or understand? Do you have a hardened heart?…Do you not remember, when I broke the five loaves for the five thousand, how many baskets full of broken pieces you picked up?' They said to Him, 'Twelve.' When I broke the seven for the four thousand, how many large baskets full of broken pieces did you pick up?' And they said to Him, 'Seven.' And He was saying to them, 'Do you not yet understand?'" (Mark 8: 17-21; NASB). The two events (which Jesus used as prophetic pictures, by the way) were meant to emphasize or prove something to the hearts of the disciples.

The ancient Jewish writers also used parallel statements to explain or clarify their points. This style is most clearly seen in the Book of Proverbs. There, the author would state a fact in the first part of the verse and then state the same fact in other words in the next line of the verse. Similarly, the author would present a truth in a positive statement and then prove the statement with a contrasting statement. In such a way, the truth is clear, picturesque, and easily remembered.

It is important to remember that, with the exception of Luke, the New Testament writers were Jewish. We can observe their different styles of writing, especially in the epistles. Paul, writing to Gentiles in the Roman Empire, used the form of logic and argument that his readers would understand (and since he was raised as a Roman citizen, he could communicate in both Hebrew and Greek styles). All of Paul's letters followed this Western style: following a brief greeting, he would present an argument from theology, followed by the logical application of that theology in life. Therefore, it is relatively easy to outline a Pauline letter.

However, when we read Peter, James, or John, we cannot outline them in the same manner. Instead, their letters have a different style, one that follows a circular argument, rather than linear logic. They introduce and then repeat their main points over and over. With each repetition, they add to or expand the point. To the person schooled in Western logic, these epistles seem choppy or disjointed. But to the ancient Near Easterner, they were marvelously beautiful.

Why is this important to interpreting prophecy? We usually read the Book of Revelation as if it were a linear narrative with each point following another in time sequence. But this approach is a Greek, not Hebrew, way of interpretation! Instead, the Book of Revelation was written as a series of visions, each of which was meant to give expanded meaning to the other. John expressed these visions using the Hebrew styles of repetition, parallelism, and circular argument. I will demonstrate, for instance, that the judgments of the Seals, the Trumpets, and the Bowls do not follow each other sequentially, but rather, they are merely different views of the same events that will happen on earth.

Putting the Prophetic Puzzle Together

Now that we have analyzed the prophetic puzzle, we can begin to put the pieces together. These are written out in an appendix that contains nearly every Scripture dealing with the Second Coming. They are arranged according to their primary topic (some Scriptures refer to more than one topic, so they are repeated in more than one section). From this collection, we will now begin to put together a fairly complete picture of the Second Coming of Christ.

Chapter Three

God's Plan for the Ages

God was not taken by surprise when mankind rejected His purpose and design through unbelief. He had a plan for mankind's redemption even before the first sin occurred (see 1 Peter 1:20). In our analogy of the prophetic puzzle, this plan for mankind's salvation represents the edge and corner pieces. If we can understand God's plan, it will act as the boundaries of the picture. We can eliminate those pieces that do not fit and arrange those that do with a better perspective. But if we do not know the plan, we can easily get lost in symbolism or allegory, forcing prophetic pieces to fit wherever our whims might take us.

This principle of interpretation is especially important when we discover what God's plans are for the Jews. As I mentioned in the Introduction, the Lord gave many precious promises to these chosen people: a promise of land, posterity, and a kingdom. Many Christians through the ages have given up on the prospect of seeing these promises fulfilled. Instead, they have "spiritualized" them, applying them exclusively to the "new Israel," known now as the church. However, the Bible declares to us that "God's gifts and His call [for the Jews] are irrevocable" (Romans 11:29). In other words, God's prophetic promises will not be set aside. It is to the glory of God to see them all fulfilled!

Therefore, we will see what God's plan is, and how it works in the lives of His people: first to the Jews, and then to the Gentiles.

God's Way of Salvation

God has always reached out to Sinful man, offering a way for him to be restored into fellowship. Right after the Fall, God showed Adam and Eve that He would solve the problems of their Sin and shame. He shed the blood of animals in order for them to be properly covered. (The best they could do about their nakedness was to sew itchy, fragile fig leaves together!)[8] In every age since then, God continued to reach out to mankind and offer people His solution to Sin. How unfortunate it is that people still try to "cover up" the nakedness and shame of Sin using their own efforts. The history of religion is the story of man's attempts to win the favor of God without having to come to God in His way!

---

[8] This is probably why Abel's offering was acceptable, while Cain's was not. Abel offered that which God had shown his parents was acceptable: the shed blood for the covering of Sin; while Cain offered that which God had told his parents was cursed: the fruit of the ground and the sweat of his own labor.

As we learned in the chapter on "The Problem of Mankind," the essence of Sin is unbelief in the existence, character, and will of God for our lives. As a direct result, we seek our fulfillment by going our own way through life instead of following God's path. Salvation is a complete reversal of the Fall: we turn from going our way and believe God's way by following Him. This is the essence of God's plan for salvation for every person in every era.

Whether it was to people before the time of Noah or to the people of our day who have not yet heard the gospel of Jesus Christ, everyone still has to respond in faith to the amount truth and light the Lord gives them. Paul wrote in Romans 1:19-20, "…what may be known about God is plain to them. For since the creation of the world God's invisible qualities - His eternal power and divine nature - have been clearly seen, being understood from what has been made, so that men are without excuse." He continues, "God will give to each person according to what he has done. To those who by persistence in doing good seek glory, honor, and immortality, He will give eternal life. But for those who are *self-seeking* and who reject the truth [through unbelief] and follow evil, there will be wrath and anger" (Romans 2:6-8).

The whole point of Hebrews 11, the "Faith Chapter," is that people have always been saved by faith through their belief in accordance with the revelation they had been given. Even in the earliest years of mankind's history we see that people like Enoch and Noah were commended for their faith, which enabled them to "walk with God" and please Him. Believing God, Hebrews 11:6 says, is the only way to please Him.[9]

---

[9] At this point, we must be clear about the nature of saving faith. Simply giving mental assent to a set of doctrines or ideas is not what the Bible means by faith. Real faith—the kind that brings salvation—involves a deep, heartfelt change of our innermost being. This inner change is summarized by Jesus' first words of the Gospel, as recorded in Mark 1:15: "The time is fulfilled, and the Kingdom of God is at hand; *repent* and *believe* the Gospel."

Repentance and faith are two sides of the same coin. To be genuine, one cannot occur without the other. There are a lot of counterfeit "believers" within the Church today - people who claim to believe in Jesus as Savior, but who have never bowed their hearts to Him as Lord. They claim to believe in Christ's work on the Cross, yet they continue to live their lives their own way. How did this confusion happen? Just as the Church has misunderstood the concept of Sin, so it has also ignored or misapplied the concept of repentance. The Greek word for "repentance" is *metanoia*. Literally, it means "a change of mind." We are to change our minds about how life is to be lived (going our own way by looking out for ourselves), and believe God's way (trust in God's plan for our lives). One cannot happen without the other. For instance, if a person were to say he is going to take a journey from Los Angeles to New York, his trip does not start until he leaves. Likewise, belief in God's way presupposes a change of mind about going our own way.

In order to make the plan of salvation available to all mankind in a way that was both clear and understandable, God called a man who would father a race and become known as the "father of faith." All the saints of the Old Covenant were saved by this same kind of faith. The only difference between the plan of salvation for the Jews and the subsequent revelation of God's plan for the rest of the world is that the Jews had to look forward in faith to the final revelation of God's salvation, while we now only need to look back in faith to see this salvation revealed through Jesus, the Messiah.

Israel's High Calling and Purpose

Why, then, did God begin the revelation process through Abraham and the Jews? Why couldn't he just bring Jesus into the world? If all are saved through faith in God's revelation, what was His purpose for calling the Jews? Did He fail to bring about "Plan A" (the Old Covenant), and had to fall back to "Plan B" (The New Covenant)? Paul addressed this question in Romans 3:1: "What advantage, then, is there in being a Jew, or what value is there in circumcision. Much in every way! First of all, they have been entrusted with the very words of God." In other words, God entrusted the Jews to keep and, as we shall see, to proclaim the words of God to the world, so that the world could more clearly understand whom they were called to believe.

God's purpose for the Jews was revealed for the first time in His promise to Abraham, "I will make you into a great nation and I will bless you; I will make your name great, and you will be a blessing. I will bless those who bless you, and whoever curses you I will curse; and all peoples on earth will be blessed through you" (Genesis 12:2-3). He went on to promise Abraham that his descendants would possess the land (Genesis 17:3-8). In fact, God called this promised land an "everlasting possession." From Abraham on, we see God revealing more and more of His nature and character, promises and faithfulness to these chosen people, who wrote it all down in story, verse, and law so that the world would have a dependable record of God's word.

When Abraham's descendants became numerous, the Lord delivered them out of the bondage of slavery in Egypt. But before God brought them into the

---

When the New Testament was translated into Latin, the word that translators used for *metanoia* was *penetencia*. Unfortunately, some of the full meaning of the original concept was lost in the translation. *Penatencia* means "to be sorry" or "to suffer inner pain." (We get the word "penitentiary" from this Latin word.) Although *metanoia* might include these feelings as part of its work in our hearts, it is not limited to a feeling of emotion. *Metanoia* needs to take place even in a person who has not done anything he needs to feel sorry for. The righteous atheist or the Buddhist monk may not have done anything morally wrong, yet they are still sinners. They need to "change their minds" about the existence, character, and will of the one true God!

Promised Land, He had to take the slavery out of their hearts. First, He gave them a new identity. They were now God's people ("I am the Lord your God, who brought you up out of the land of Egypt"). Next, He gave them two kinds of commandments: *religious* laws (this is how you are to relate to God); and *moral* laws (this is how you are to relate to one another). Finally, He formed them into a community of strong, believing people through the hardships of the desert. As the people of God, they were able to take possession of that which God had promised.

But was this the grand fulfillment of God's purpose for this chosen people - to live in God's land, practicing God's laws and worshipping God's ways? Was God *only* concerned with this relatively small nation? No! His purpose for His people has always gone beyond their nation's borders. Moses told the people:

> 5 See, I have taught you decrees and laws as the LORD my God commanded me, so that you may follow them in the land you are entering to take possession of it. 6 Observe them carefully, for this will show your wisdom and understanding to the nations, who will hear about all these decrees and say, "Surely this great nation is a wise and understanding people." 7 What other nation is so great as to have their gods near them the way the LORD our God is near us whenever we pray to him? 8 And what other nation is so great as to have such righteous decrees and laws as this body of laws I am setting before you today? 9 Only be careful, and watch yourselves closely so that you do not forget the things your eyes have seen or let them slip from your heart as long as you live. Teach them to your children and to their children after them (Deuteronomy 4:5-9; NASB).

And, in another place:

> 1 If you fully obey the LORD your God and carefully follow all his commands I give you today, the LORD your God will set you high above all the nations on earth. 2 All these blessings will come upon you and accompany you if you obey the LORD your God:
> 3 You will be blessed in the city and blessed in the country. 4 The fruit of your womb will be blessed, and the crops of your land and the young of your livestock—the calves of your herds and the lambs of your flocks. 5 Your basket and your kneading trough will be blessed. 6 You will be blessed when you come in and blessed when you go out. 7 The LORD will grant that the enemies who rise up against you will be defeated before you. They will come at you from one direction but flee from you in seven. 8 The LORD will send a blessing on your barns and

on everything you put your hand to. The LORD your God will bless you in the land he is giving you.

9 The LORD will establish you as his holy people, as he promised you on oath, if you keep the commands of the LORD your God and walk in his ways. 10 Then all the peoples on earth will see that you are called by the name of the LORD, and they will fear you (Deuteronomy 28:1-10).

In other words, the grand purpose in God's calling of the Jews was to be His witness to the nations!

Notice, when God's people obeyed Him out of a love and heart-felt faith, He promised to bless them and use this blessing as a witness to the nations:

16 The LORD your God commands you this day to follow these decrees and laws; carefully observe them with all your heart and with all your soul. 17 You have declared this day that the LORD is your God and that you will walk in his ways, that you will keep his decrees, commands and laws, and that you will obey him. 18 And the LORD has declared this day that you are his people, his treasured possession as he promised, and that you are to keep all his commands. 19 He has declared that he will set you in praise, fame and honor high above all the nations he has made and that you will be a people holy to the LORD your God, as he promised (Deuteronomy 26:16-19).

Whenever the Jews followed the Lord, and obeyed His commandments, He blessed them abundantly. He prospered them and made them secure in their land. And, at one time in their history, they actually fulfilled their high calling to be a witness to the nations. We read about this period in 1 Kings 10:1-13:

1 When the queen of Sheba heard about the fame of Solomon and his relation to the name of the LORD, she came to test him with hard questions. 2 Arriving at Jerusalem with a very great caravan—with camels carrying spices, large quantities of gold, and precious stones— she came to Solomon and talked with him about all that she had on her mind. 3 Solomon answered all her questions; nothing was too hard for the king to explain to her. 4 When the queen of Sheba saw all the wisdom of Solomon and the palace he had built, 5 the food on his table, the seating of his officials, the attending servants in their robes, his cupbearers, and the burnt offerings he made at the temple of the LORD, she was overwhelmed.

6 She said to the king, "The report I heard in my own country about your achievements and your wisdom is true. 7 But I did not believe

these things until I came and saw with my own eyes. Indeed, not even half was told me; in wisdom and wealth you have far exceeded the report I heard. 8 How happy your men must be! How happy your officials, who continually stand before you and hear your wisdom! 9 Praise be to the LORD your God, who has delighted in you and placed you on the throne of Israel. Because of the Lord's eternal love for Israel, he has made you king, to maintain justice and righteousness.

10 And she gave the king 120 talents of gold, large quantities of spices, and precious stones. Never again were so many spices brought in as those the queen of Sheba gave to King Solomon.

11 (Hiram's ships brought gold from Ophir; and from there they brought great cargoes of almugwood and precious stones. 12 The king used the almugwood to make supports for the temple of the LORD and for the royal palace, and to make harps and lyres for the musicians. So much almugwood has never been imported or seen since that day.)

13 King Solomon gave the queen of Sheba all she desired and asked for, besides what he had given her out of his royal bounty. Then she left and returned with her retinue to her own country.

History tells us what happened after the queen of Sheba went home. A good number of her subjects committed themselves to the Lord, the God of Israel, and became Jews. The Ethiopian eunuch of Acts 8 who came to worship at Jerusalem was from their tradition. The "Falasha" Jews of today's Ethiopia are their descendants and, as such, are accorded the rights of return which modern day Israel offers every Jew. Imagine what might have happened if ancient Israel had remained faithful to follow God's purpose for them! How many nations would have been influenced?

Although the Lord intended their calling to result in land, prosperity, and witness, the Jews often forsook the Lord and followed after their own ways. In love, God told His people that He would discipline them if they continued in their waywardness and unbelief. This discipline was always meant to be redemptive, so that the people could come back into relationship with the Lord, as we read in 2 Chronicles 6:24-33:

24 When your people Israel have been defeated by an enemy because they have sinned against you and when they turn back and confess your name, praying and making supplication before you in this temple, 25 then hear from heaven and forgive the sin of your people Israel and bring them back to the land you gave to them and their fathers.

26 When the heavens are shut up and there is no rain because your people have sinned against you, and when they pray toward this place and confess your name and turn from their sin because you have afflicted

them, 27 then hear from heaven and forgive the sin of your servants, your people Israel. Teach them the right way to live, and send rain on the land you gave your people for an inheritance.

28 When famine or plague comes to the land, or blight or mildew, locusts or grasshoppers, or when enemies besiege them in any of their cities, whatever disaster or disease may come, 29 and when a prayer or plea is made by any of your people Israel—each one aware of his afflictions and pains, and spreading out his hands toward this temple—30 then hear from heaven, your dwelling place. Forgive, and deal with each man according to all he does, since you know his heart (for you alone know the hearts of men), 31 so that they will fear you and walk in your ways all the time they live in the land you gave our fathers.

32 As for the foreigner who does not belong to your people Israel but has come from a distant land because of your great name and your mighty hand and your outstretched arm—when he comes and prays toward this temple, 33 then hear from heaven, your dwelling place, and do whatever the foreigner asks of you, so that all the peoples of the earth may know your name and fear you, as do your own people Israel, and may know that this house I have built bears your Name.

(Note that this mercy is even extended to the foreigner who has heard of the great name of the Lord!)

However, if the Israelites persisted in going their own way, turning their hearts away from God, they were promised severe chastisement from the Lord. This discipline would culminate in their exile from the land God had promised.

18 Make sure there is no man or woman, clan or tribe among you today whose heart turns away from the LORD our God to go and worship the gods of those nations; make sure there is no root among you that produces such bitter poison. 19 When such a person hears the words of this oath, he invokes a blessing on himself and therefore thinks, "I will be safe, even though I persist in going my own way." This will bring disaster on the watered land as well as the dry. 20 The LORD will never be willing to forgive him; his wrath and zeal will burn against that man. All the curses written in this book will fall upon him, and the LORD will blot out his name from under heaven. 21 The LORD will single him out from all the tribes of Israel for disaster, according to all the curses of the covenant written in this Book of the Law.

22 Your children who follow you in later generations and foreigners who come from distant lands will see the calamities that have fallen on the land and the diseases with which the LORD has afflicted it. 23 The whole land will be a burning waste of salt and sulfur—nothing planted,

32

nothing sprouting, no vegetation growing on it. It will be like the destruction of Sodom and Gomorrah, Admah and Zeboiim, which the LORD overthrew in fierce anger. 24 All the nations will ask: "Why has the LORD done this to this land? Why this fierce, burning anger?"

25 And the answer will be: "It is because this people abandoned the covenant of the LORD, the God of their fathers, the covenant he made with them when he brought them out of Egypt. 26 They went off and worshiped other gods and bowed down to them, gods they did not know, gods he had not given them. 27 Therefore the Lord's anger burned against this land, so that he brought on it all the curses written in this book. 28 In furious anger and in great wrath the LORD uprooted them from their land and thrust them into another land, as it is now" (Deut. 29:18-28)

But was this a final punishment, from which there can be no redemption? Does the historical evidence of God's discipline show us that He has rejected the Jews as His covenant people? NO! Instead, we will see that God will not forget His promise to the Jews. He will glorify His Name when we see His faithfulness and power displayed to these wayward servants!

Israel's Rejection of Her Purpose

Although the Jewish people were notorious for backsliding and spiritual adultery throughout their early history, they did respond to the chastisements of the Lord. When they repented and returned to Him wholeheartedly, He delivered them from judgment and gave them His blessings. However, during the latter period of the monarchy, the people and leaders drifted away more and more. Seldom did they return fully to the Lord (with only a few notable exceptions). In fact the people and rulers of the Northern Kingdom of Israel never repented of their substitute altars to the Lord in Dan and Beersheba.

God sent the prophets to warn the nation again and again, but to no avail. The people became too hardened, too deaf, and too blind to be able to respond to the will of the Lord. Isaiah bemoaned the nation's impending fate in his famous "servant songs." These prophecies identified Israel as a hardened, rebellious servant (Isaiah 48:1-5) who was blind and deaf (Isaiah 42:18-25). The servant, Israel, who had been called by God to be a witness of God's greatness and glory (Isaiah 42:21), needed instead to be saved by God (Isaiah 43:1-3; Isaiah 44:1-5).

In contrast to the sorry state of God's servant of Israel, Isaiah identified a righteous servant who would come and redeem both Israel *and* the nations. Isaiah prophesied:

5 And now the LORD says - He who formed Me in the womb to be His servant to bring Jacob back to Him and gather Israel to Himself, for I am honored in the eyes of the LORD and my God has been my strength - 6 He says: "It is too small a thing for you to be My servant to restore the tribes of Jacob and bring back those of Israel I have kept. I will also make you a light to the Gentiles, that you may bring My salvation to the ends of the earth" (Isaiah 49:5-6).

This savior of the entire world - the one who would save both Jews and Gentiles - was clearly described by Isaiah in the famous "suffering servant" passage of Isaiah 53.

Isaiah even prophesied what people would do to this righteous servant. He cried out plaintively, "Who has believed our message?" (Isaiah 53:1). Isaiah prophesied the contempt, rejection and mocking of the Jews toward God's righteous servant in both Isaiah 53:3 and Isaiah 50:1-11.

But even though God knew the Jews would reject the coming Messiah, His promises for them would never be revoked. Instead, their rejection would only serve to bring the blessings of salvation to the rest of the world, as we shall see.

The Time of the Jews

In one of the most amazing and accurate predictions of the Bible, God revealed to the prophet Daniel not only the exact time the Messiah would come, but also His prophetic plan for the Jews. This text is one of the major keys in understanding the revelation of God's prophetic picture. Therefore, we must give a good deal of attention to this text, as it unlocks our understanding of the future![10]

While praying for his people, Daniel received a revelation through the angel Gabriel about the nation of Israel:

21 while I was still in prayer, Gabriel, the man I had seen in the earlier vision, came to me in swift flight about the time of the evening sacrifice. 22 He instructed me and said to me, "Daniel, I have now come to give you insight and understanding. 23 As soon as you began to pray, an answer was given, which I have come to tell you, for you are highly esteemed. Therefore, consider the message and understand the vision: 24 "Seventy 'sevens' are decreed for your people and your holy city to finish transgression, to put an end to sin, to atone for wickedness, to

---

[10] The following information comes from Josh McDowell's excellent book, *Evidence that Demands a Verdict*, San Bernadino, CA: Here's Life Publishers, 1972, 1979.

bring in everlasting righteousness, to seal up vision and prophecy and to anoint the most holy.

25 "Know and understand this: From the issuing of the decree to restore and rebuild Jerusalem until the Anointed One [Greek, *Christos*], the ruler, comes, there will be seven 'sevens,' and sixty-two 'sevens.' It will be rebuilt with streets and a trench, but in times of trouble. 26 After the sixty-two 'sevens,' the Anointed One will be cut off and will have nothing. The people of the ruler who will come will destroy the city and the sanctuary. The end will come like a flood: War will continue until the end, and desolations have been decreed. 27 He will confirm a covenant with many for one 'seven.' In the middle of the 'seven' he will put an end to sacrifice and offering. And on a wing [of the temple] he will set up an abomination that causes desolation, until the end that is decreed is poured out on him" (Daniel 9:21-27).

In this prophecy, Daniel was told that "seventy 'sevens'" (often translated into English as "weeks")" were decreed for the Jews in order that six things would take place: 1) transgression will be finished; 2) sin will end; 3) wickedness will be atoned for; 4) everlasting righteousness will come; 5) all prophecy will be fulfilled; and 6) the most holy (one) will be anointed (king).

All of this will take place by the end of the seventy "sevens."

What did he mean by this phrase? The Hebrew word for "week" is *shabua*, which literally means "seven." So, are we to understand this phrase to mean 490 days, weeks, or years? The Jews were familiar with using the word "seven" to mean a seven-year period of time. For instance, Leviticus 25:2-4 demonstrates this concept, referring to a "week" of years.

The context of this passage in Daniel demands that we interpret the seventy sevens in terms of years, not weeks or days. Daniel had just been praying about the seventy years the Jews were in captivity in Babylon when he was given this revelation (Daniel 9:1-2). He knew that the length of the Babylonian captivity was based upon the violation of the Sabbatical year (spoken about in the Leviticus passage noted above). Since the Jews were in captivity for 70 years, the Sabbatical year had been violated for 490 years (see Leviticus 26:32-35 and II Chronicles 36:21). Therefore, the context is consistent and only makes sense when we understand the seven "sevens" in terms of years, not weeks or days.

So, what is God saying to us through this revelation? Verse 25 declares that the Messiah would come exactly sixty-nine "sevens" after the city of Jerusalem was decreed to be rebuilt. At the time of Daniel, Jerusalem was lying in ruins. We read of this official decree in Nehemiah 2:1-8, when King Artaxerxes gave the command to restore and rebuild the city of Jerusalem to Nehemiah. We know from Nehemiah 2:1 that this decree was given in the month Nisan, in the twentieth year of King Artaxerxes. Artaxerxes became king in 465 BC. Since there is no specific date mentioned, according to Jewish custom the date would be understood to be the first day of the month, which would be Nisan 1, 444 BC (March 5, 444 BC, according to our calendar).

According to Daniel, the city would be rebuilt in 49 years.

To quote McDowell:

"If Daniel is correct, the time from the edict to restore and rebuild Jerusalem (Nisan 1, 444 BC) to the coming of the Messiah to Jerusalem is 483 years (69 X 7), each year equaling the Jewish prophetic year of 360 days (173,880 days).

"The terminal event of the 69 weeks is the presentation of Christ Himself to Israel as the Messiah as predicted in Zechariah 9:9. H. Hoehner, who has thoroughly researched this prophecy in Daniel and the corresponding dates, calculates the date of this event: 'Multiplying the sixty-nine weeks by seven years for each week by 360 days gives a total of 173,880 days. The difference between 444 BC and AD 33 then is 476 solar years. By multiplying 476 by 365.24219879 or by 365 days, 5 hours, 48 minutes, 45.975 seconds, one comes to 173,855 days, 6 hours, 52 minutes, 44 seconds, or 173,855 days. This leaves only 25 days to be accounted for between 444 BC and AD 33. By adding the 25 days to March 5 (of 444 BC), one comes to March 30 (or AD 33) which was Nisan 10 in AD 33. This is the triumphal entry of Jesus into Jerusalem."[11]

We read in Daniel 9:26 what will happen after the coming of the Messiah. First, the Messiah will be "cut off," which is a Hebrew euphemism for "to be killed." Second, the "people of the ruler who will come" will destroy the city again, as well as the temple.

This prophecy is astounding! Not only does it give the exact date of the coming of the Messiah, but it goes on to reveal the Messiah's death and the subsequent destruction of Jerusalem and the temple in 70 AD!

However, this prophecy was not completely fulfilled. It is an example of what I have defined as a "telescopic" prophecy. It will be fulfilled over a long period of time. The final "seven" has yet to occur. The prophecy declares that "the ruler who will come" will make a covenant with many for that one "seven." During the middle of that seven-year period, this ruler will put an end to sacrifices and offering and will set up an abomination on a wing of the temple. At the end of the seven years, he will be destroyed. Note, this occurs *after* the temple had already been destroyed in 70 AD! Therefore, we can only conclude that the Jews must rebuild another temple. And, in order for them to build a temple, they have to be regathered again into their own land!

Jesus referred to this same Scripture in His description of what would happen after the Jews rejected Him as Messiah. In Luke 13:34-35, He refers to the

---

[11] *Evidence that Demands a Verdict*, p 173.

coming rejection and subsequent judgment upon the Jews, "O Jerusalem, Jerusalem, you who kill the prophets and stone those sent to you, how often I have longed to gather your children together, as a hen gathers her chicks under her wings, but you were not willing! Look, your house is left to you desolate. I tell you, you will not see Me again until you say, 'Blessed is He who comes in the name of the Lord.'" Note that He does imply that the Jews *will* see Him again, but they must first recognize Him as Messiah.

Jesus then told us what would happen when the Jews rejected Him. In so doing, He revealed what would take place between the time of their rejection of His messiahship and the subsequent judgment, and the fulfillment of the last "seven." In Luke 21, Jesus revealed to His disciples what was going to happen to Jerusalem and the Jews:

> 20 "When you see Jerusalem being surrounded by armies, you will know that its desolation is near. 21 Then let those who are in Judea flee to the mountains, let those in the city get out, and let those in the country not enter the city. 22 For this is the time of punishment in fulfillment of all that has been written. [in Daniel 9:26, for instance]. 23 How dreadful it will be in those days for pregnant women and nursing mothers! There will be great distress in the land and wrath against this people. 24 They will fall by the sword and will be taken as prisoners to all nations. Jerusalem will be trampled on by the Gentiles until the times of the Gentiles are fulfilled" (Luke 21: 20-24).

Here, Jesus introduced a new revelation in the plan of God for mankind. It was not a new plan, of course. But it was the revelation of what God was going to do in order to bring *all* nations unto Himself, in accordance with His original intent and plan for the Jews. Remember, Isaiah prophesied, "It is too small a thing for you to be my servant to restore the tribes of Jacob and bring back those of Israel I have kept. I will also make you a light for the Gentiles, that you may bring my salvation to the ends of the earth" (Isaiah 49:6). Since the Jews were going to reject their Messiah, the door of salvation would be opened for the Gentiles. God's judgment upon the Jews would begin the period of time that Jesus called "the times of the Gentiles."

The Apostle Paul explained the "time of the Gentiles" in Romans 11, when he described this "mystery" now revealed to mankind. He wrote, "I do not want you to be ignorant of this mystery, brothers, so that you may not be conceited: Israel has experienced a hardening in part *until* the full number of the Gentiles has come in. And so all Israel will be saved..." (Romans 11:25,26). In other words, the Jewish people have become spiritually blind (at least in a partial way) *until* all of the Gentiles who will come to the Lord will do so. But Paul hastened to make it clear: although the Jews were currently opposed to the Gospel, they are still the recipients of God's promises to their forefathers, the patriarchs, "...for God's gifts and His call are irrevocable" (Romans 11:29).

So, we see that God will not forget His promise and calling to the Jews. They were unbelieving and disobedient, resulting in God's judgment. But their disobedience only served to further God's ultimate plan, by bringing the nations the opportunity to hear the Gospel. And, in the same passage, Paul seems to hint that when the Jews *do* return to the Lord, the whole world will enjoy even "greater riches" (Romans 11:12)! When they return to the Lord, God promises that this will result in "life from the dead" (Romans 11:15)!

The Time of the Gentiles

Jesus said similar things concerning the Jews and Gentiles in His prophecy concerning end-times, known as the "Olivet Discourse:" "This gospel of the Kingdom will be preached in the whole world as a testimony to *all nations*, and then the end will come" (Matthew 24:14). Here, Christ linked the timing of the end to the ability of His disciples to fulfill the Great Commission to "...go and make disciples of all nations..." (Matthew 28:19). Perhaps this is what Peter meant in his second epistle: "as you look forward to the day of God and speed its coming" (2 Peter 3:12). The only thing we can do to hasten the return of Christ is to be faithful to fulfill His command to preach the Gospel to every nation!

It is important to understand just when the "time of the Gentiles" began. Did it begin when the Jewish leaders rejected and crucified Christ? No, not exactly. The Jews were the first to believe in the risen Lord. Paul's ministry to the Gentiles did not really get underway until some 15 years after the resurrection. Even after Paul's ministry was well established, we read that he was known as the apostle to the Gentiles, while Peter was considered to be the primary apostle to the Jews. In other words, there was an overlap between the end of the time of the Jews, and the beginning of the time of the Gentiles.

But by 70 AD (one generation after the resurrection of Christ), the Jews had become highly resistant to the Gospel. Jewish Christians were considered as heretics and were put out of the synagogue. After the destruction of Jerusalem, very few Jews would put their faith in Christ (a pattern that continued up until the latter half of the twentieth century). Therefore, we might conclude that there was an overlapping of one generation between the end of the "time of the Jews" and the beginning of "time of the Gentiles."

Once the Gospel began to be spread among the Gentiles, it expanded throughout the world like a wildfire. It burned quickly throughout the Roman Empire, spreading even to the distant realms of India, through the preaching and martyrdom of the Apostle "Doubting" Thomas, and to black Africa, through the Ethiopian eunuch. (These two penetrations outside the Roman Empire are still with us today, represented by the Mar Thoma Church of India and the Coptic Church of Ethiopia and Egypt, respectively!)

Church history informs us of the steady (though slower) growth of the Christian movement. It survived the persecutions and the political intrigues of the Roman Empire. Eventually, it became the dominant religion of North Africa, Asia Minor, and Europe. After the fall of Rome, the church survived, continuing to grow into formerly pagan areas in Germany, Scandinavia, Ireland, etc.

However, Satan launched several counter-attacks. Where Christianity once flourished, worldliness and nominalism crept in. When this spiritual state takes root, persecution does not always result in a purified church, but an extinct one! This is precisely what happened when the false prophet Mohammed introduced his heretical version of God's will, the Koran. Islam soon replaced nominal Christianity in North Africa and the Near East. The Crusades were the Europeans' response to Islam's encroachment into Spain and the Balkans. For the next few centuries, Christianity resided precariously in Europe in the forms of the Roman Catholic and Eastern Orthodox Churches.

With the Reformation, Christianity enjoyed a period of new vitality, especially in missions. The Gospel was introduced into the Far East and the New World. In the eighteen hundreds, a new missions movement arose among the evangelical segments of Christianity. Mission societies began sending missionaries with greater earnestness than ever before. Brave young men and women gave their lives going into harsh and undiscovered parts of the world in Africa, the South Pacific, and Asia.

But with every new push came a corresponding attempt by the devil to hinder the progress of the church. Since Europe and America were the centers of Christian missions, they were the first to be disrupted - both socially and religiously. New philosophies of Darwinism, Socialism, Communism and religious Liberalism sapped the spiritually vitality out of the church in Europe and America. Today, most European countries have only a remnant of the church left. Less than 3% of Europeans even go to church of *any* kind, much less a Bible-believing one. The present spiritual state of Europe is marked by hedonism, materialism, and worldliness.

The church in America became the primary sender of missionaries in Christendom. Agencies such as Wycliffe Bible Translators and New Tribes Missions, among many others, began sending missionaries to those groups who had had absolutely no Gospel witness in their own languages. They translated the Scriptures so that every man, woman, and child in the world could hear the Gospel in their own native tongue. In the 1970's, it became apparent that the task of reaching every nation could be accomplished. With the knowledge of sociology and anthropology, every tribe, every people, and every nation could be identified and located. It would only be a matter of sending missionaries to them.

Groups such as Ralph Winter's U.S. Center for World Mission, Ed Dayton's Missions Advanced Research and Communication Center (MARC Department) of World Vision International, the Joshua Project, etc. have aided the church world-wide to see that the task could be accomplished. Whole denominations, churches, and even Sunday School classes took this information and began praying, planning, and sending missionaries to reach the unreached.[12]

In February, 1999, the Joshua Project reported that only 1153 people groups in the world did not have at least one church of 100 people among them. (In 1980, the MARC Department of World Vision listed over 16,000 unreached people groups!) Those with no church planting team among them numbered only 626. And of those, all had been claimed by some missionary group in order to send missionaries to them in the near future![13]

The Apostle Peter quoted the second chapter of Joel in his first sermon on the Day of Pentecost:

28 'And afterward, I will pour out my Spirit on all people. Your sons and daughters will prophesy, your old men will dream dreams, your young men will see visions. 29 Even on my servants, both men and women, I will pour out my Spirit in those days. 30 I will show wonders in the heavens and on the earth, blood and fire and billows of smoke. 31 The sun will be turned to darkness and the moon to blood before the coming of the great and dreadful day of the LORD. 32 And everyone who calls on the name of the LORD will be saved; for on Mount Zion and in Jerusalem there will be deliverance, as the LORD has said, among the survivors whom the LORD calls (Joel 2:28-32).

In this prophecy, Peter correctly identifies its initial fulfillment as taking place at that moment. However, the prophecy was not completely fulfilled on Pentecost (the moon and sun did not exhibit any of those signs at that time). But it will have its complete fulfillment as the Day of the Lord draws near!

---

[12] I was privileged to be part of MARC from 1979 to 1982. In addition, the Sunday School class I was part of at Lake Avenue Congregational Church in Pasadena, California, identified the Sundanese people of Indonesia as their project. We sent three couples from the class to minister to the Sundanese. They have planted at least three reproducing churches among them. Imagine, if just a Sunday School class can do it, how long do you think the task will take? One by one, every nation is hearing the gospel.

[13] It must also be pointed out that many of these groups are located in Muslim areas of North Africa or the Middle East - areas where the people at one time *did* have the gospel preached to them. So, in God's view of the whole picture, they may have already been reached in years gone by! (This should not stop us, of course, from making every effort to reach them today, too!)

God *is* pouring forth His Spirit upon all flesh in the last days. Christianity is the fastest growing religion in the world. We don't know exactly when the missionary mandate will be fulfilled, but it is happening faster than could have been imagined just twenty years ago. Furthermore, the number of missionaries being sent by second and third world countries is quickly approaching the total number sent by North American churches. However, this news comes none to soon, because Christianity has entered a period of decline in America. Satan's forces have succeeded in blunting the witness of the American church to its own people. Scandals, political intrigue, materialism, hedonism, and worldliness have made the church the laughingstock of the nation. Will the American church go the way of the ancient North African church or the modern European church and sink into apostasy, while the rest of the Christian world enjoys revival?

The Restoration of the Jews

We seem to be witnessing another overlapping of God's plans for the Jews and the Gentiles. On the one hand, it appears that the "time of the Gentiles" is about to be fulfilled. The task or witnessing to the whole world is almost complete. God is working mightily among those who are hearing the Gospel for the first time. But a great rejection of the Gospel is taking place in those areas that were important centers of Christianity in the past. On the other hand, it seems that God has been preparing His people the Jews for the fulfillment of the "seventieth seven" of Daniel.

What does the Bible say about this restoration of God's promises to the Jews at the end of the age?

God makes plain that even though the Jews were disciplined and exiled for their unbelief, they would never be rejected as His chosen people. Jeremiah recorded God's unchanging will:

> 35 Thus says the Lord, who gives the sun for light by day and the fixed order of the moon and the stars for light by night, who stirs up the sea so that its waves roar; The Lord of hosts is His name: 36 "If this fixed order departs from before Me," declares the Lord, "Then the offspring of Israel also will cease from being a nation before Me forever." Thus says the Lord, "If the heavens above can be measured and the foundations of the earth searched out below, then I will also cast off all the offspring of Israel for all that they have done," declares the Lord (Jeremiah 31:35-36; NASB).

Again, God declared in Deuteronomy 4:26-30, that He would not forget His covenant with Israel's forefathers:

26 "I call heaven and earth to witness against you today, that you will surely perish quickly from the land where you are going over the Jordan to possess it. You shall not live long on it, but will be utterly destroyed. 27 The Lord will scatter you among the peoples, and you will be left few in number among the nations where the Lord drives you. 28 There you will serve gods, the work of man's hands, wood and stone, which neither see nor hear nor eat nor smell. 29 But from there you will seek the Lord your God, and you will find Him if you search for Him with all your heart and all your soul. 30 When you are in distress and all these things have come upon you, in the *latter days* [!] you will return to the Lord your God and listen to His voice. 31 For the Lord your God is a compassionate God; He will not fail you nor destroy you nor forget the covenant with your fathers which He swore to them" (Deuteronomy 4:26-30; NASB).

Note how this return to the Promised Land is also linked to a last days return to their covenant relationship! Moses prophesied this again in Deuteronomy 30:1-6:

1 "So it shall be when all of these things have come upon you, the blessing and the curse which I have set before you, and you call them to mind in all nations where the Lord your God has banished you, 2 and you return to the Lord your God and obey Him with all your heart and soul according to all that I command you today, you and your sons, 3 then the Lord your God will restore you from captivity, and have compassion on you, and will gather you again from all the peoples where the Lord your God has scattered you. 4 If your outcasts are at the ends of the earth, from there the Lord your God will gather you, and from there He will bring you back. 5 The Lord your God will bring you into the land which your fathers possessed, and you shall possess it; and He will prosper you and multiply you more than your fathers. 6 Moreover the Lord your God will circumcise your heart and the heart of your descendants, to love the Lord your God with all your heart and with all your soul, so that you may live" (Deuteronomy 30:1-6; NASB).

Several times throughout the Scriptures, God promised to restore His people to the land of Israel. Only when they are restored will they be given the ability to love Him. Their hearts will be changed. Ezekiel made it clear that this last days restoration was not because they deserved God's blessing, but because God was going to show the nations that He *could* keep His promises to His people. He was going to be glorified in the way He did it!

1 "Son of man, prophesy to the mountains of Israel and say, 'O mountains of Israel, hear the word of the LORD. 2 This is what the Sovereign LORD says: The enemy said of you, "Aha! The ancient heights have become our possession."' 3 Therefore prophesy and say, 'This is what the Sovereign LORD says: Because they ravaged and hounded you from every side so that you became the possession of the rest of the nations and the object of people's malicious talk and slander, 4 therefore, O mountains of Israel, hear the word of the Sovereign LORD: This is what the Sovereign LORD says to the mountains and hills, to the ravines and valleys, to the desolate ruins and the deserted towns that have been plundered and ridiculed by the rest of the nations around you—5 this is what the Sovereign LORD says: In my burning zeal I have spoken against the rest of the nations, and against all Edom, for with glee and with malice in their hearts they made my land their own possession so that they might plunder its pastureland.' 6 Therefore prophesy concerning the land of Israel and say to the mountains and hills, to the ravines and valleys: 'This is what the Sovereign LORD says: I speak in my jealous wrath because you have suffered the scorn of the nations. 7 Therefore this is what the Sovereign LORD says: I swear with uplifted hand that the nations around you will also suffer scorn.

8 "'But you, O mountains of Israel, will produce branches and fruit for my people Israel, for they will soon come home. 9 I am concerned for you and will look on you with favor; you will be plowed and sown, 10 and I will multiply the number of people upon you, even the whole house of Israel. The towns will be inhabited and the ruins rebuilt. 11 I will increase the number of men and animals upon you, and they will be fruitful and become numerous. I will settle people on you as in the past and will make you prosper more than before. Then you will know that I am the LORD. 12 I will cause people, my people Israel, to walk upon you. They will possess you, and you will be their inheritance; you will never again deprive them of their children.

13 "'This is what the Sovereign LORD says: Because people say to you, "You devour men and deprive your nation of its children," 14 therefore you will no longer devour men or make your nation childless, declares the Sovereign LORD. 15 No longer will I make you hear the taunts of the nations, and no longer will you suffer the scorn of the peoples or cause your nation to fall, declares the Sovereign LORD.'"

16 Again the word of the LORD came to me: 17 "Son of man, when the people of Israel were living in their own land, they defiled it by their conduct and their actions. Their conduct was like a woman's monthly uncleanness in my sight. 18 So I poured out my wrath on them because they had shed blood in the land and because they had defiled it with their

idols. 19 I dispersed them among the nations, and they were scattered through the countries; I judged them according to their conduct and their actions. 20 And wherever they went among the nations they profaned my holy name, for it was said of them, 'These are the LORD's people, and yet they had to leave his land.' 21 I had concern for my holy name, which the house of Israel profaned among the nations where they had gone.

22 "Therefore say to the house of Israel, 'This is what the Sovereign LORD says: It is not for your sake, O house of Israel, that I am going to do these things, but for the sake of my holy name, which you have profaned among the nations where you have gone. 23 I will show the holiness of my great name, which has been profaned among the nations, the name you have profaned among them. Then the nations will know that I am the LORD, declares the Sovereign LORD, when I show myself holy through you before their eyes.

24 "'For I will take you out of the nations; I will gather you from all the countries and bring you back into your own land. 25 I will sprinkle clean water on you, and you will be clean; I will cleanse you from all your impurities and from all your idols. 26 I will give you a new heart and put a new spirit in you; I will remove from you your heart of stone and give you a heart of flesh. 27 And I will put my Spirit in you and move you to follow my decrees and be careful to keep my laws. 28 You will live in the land I gave your forefathers; you will be my people, and I will be your God. 29 I will save you from all your uncleanness. I will call for the grain and make it plentiful and will not bring famine upon you. 30 I will increase the fruit of the trees and the crops of the field, so that you will no longer suffer disgrace among the nations because of famine. 31 Then you will remember your evil ways and wicked deeds, and you will loathe yourselves for your sins and detestable practices. 32 I want you to know that I am not doing this for your sake, declares the Sovereign LORD. Be ashamed and disgraced for your conduct, O house of Israel!

33 "'This is what the Sovereign LORD says: On the day I cleanse you from all your sins, I will resettle your towns, and the ruins will be rebuilt. 34 The desolate land will be cultivated instead of lying desolate in the sight of all who pass through it. 35 They will say, "This land that was laid waste has become like the garden of Eden; the cities that were lying in ruins, desolate and destroyed, are now fortified and inhabited." 36 Then the nations around you that remain will know that I the LORD have rebuilt what was destroyed and have replanted what was desolate. I the LORD have spoken, and I will do it.'

37 "This is what the Sovereign LORD says: Once again I will yield to the plea of the house of Israel and do this for them: I will make their people as numerous as sheep, 38 as numerous as the flocks for offerings at Jerusalem during her appointed feasts. So will the ruined cities be filled with flocks of people. Then they will know that I am the LORD" (Ezekiel 36:1-38).

Finally, we read in Daniel, The Book of Revelation, and the Book of Zechariah (among other places) that this regathered nation will become a problem to the rest of the world community. "It will come about in that day that I will make Jerusalem a heavy stone for all the peoples; all who lift it will be severely injured. And all the nations of the earth will be gathered against it" (Zechariah 12:3; NASB). We will see in subsequent chapters that it is to this nation, and at that time, that Jesus will return. The "Seventieth Week" of Daniel will culminate in the return of the Jews to their Messiah. Zechariah's prophecy says:

9 "And in that day I will set about to destroy all the nations that come against Jerusalem. 10 I will pour out on the house of David and on the inhabitants of Jerusalem, the Spirit of grace and of supplication, so that they will look on Me whom they have pierced; and they will mourn for Him, as one mourns for an only son, and they will weep bitterly over Him like the bitter weeping over a firstborn" (Zechariah 12:9-10; NASB).

It is clear that God is able to fulfill all of His will for His people. We are now standing at the threshold of the "Door of Judgment." The signs of the return of Jesus Christ are being fulfilled before our eyes, as we will see in the following chapters.

Chapter Four

The Picture of the Second Coming

What have we discovered about our prophetic puzzle thus far? The overall picture describes the redemption of mankind from all the effects of Sin. God gave people everything they need to know about Him, His character, and His will. He gave us His Word. He gave us the Word made flesh, who took our penalty of Sin upon Himself. He gave us His Spirit as the down payment of our future inheritance. And He gave us His promise to return and put a complete end to Sin and all its effects. We have seen how this grand plan has unfolded throughout human history. Our knowledge of this plan gives us the outer perimeter of the puzzle, into which we can carefully arrange the other pieces.

We have also taken the necessary step of describing the prophetic styles in the Bible; thereby helping us identify and understand the various prophecies concerning the end-times. Having accomplished this, now we can turn over all the pieces, see them for what they are, and begin to arrange them.

But how can we possibly arrange the individual pieces? We need some kind of authoritative guide. If we do not have an outline to follow, one person's interpretation may be just as good as another. To use our puzzle analogy, we need to see the picture on the box! I believe we can find this broad outline in the Bible from none other than the words of Jesus concerning His Second Coming. His words are the most important source of prophetic information in the Bible. After all, He is the Son of God. His Father had shown Him "all things" (John 16:30). He told His disciples that there was only one thing the Father had not revealed to Him - the exact day and hour of His return to Earth in power and glory: "But of that day and hour no one knows, not even the angels of heaven, nor the Son, but the Father alone" (Matthew 24:36; NASB).

Therefore, we will use Jesus' own description of His Second Coming as our ultimate guide. We will be able to fit all other prophetic Scriptures onto His framework, subject by subject. Then, by paying attention to prepositions such as "after," "when," "then," etc., we will be able to arrange the events of the Second Coming into chronological order.[14]

The most in-depth teaching Jesus gave concerning His return is found in Matthew 24, Mark 13, and Luke 21. This teaching is called, "The Olivet Discourse," because Jesus gave it while He and the disciples were sitting on the Mount of Olives, east of the City of Jerusalem. Jesus and His disciples had just walked past the beautiful Jewish temple on their way outside the city. The disciples were awed by its beauty and majesty, and they shared their enthusiasm

---

[14] These words will be highlighted in the text in order to make the chronology clearer.

with Him. He replied, "As for what you see here, the time will come when not one stone will be left on another; every one of them will be thrown down" (Luke 21:6). Taken aback by this statement, they asked Jesus some important questions - questions that gave Jesus the opportunity to tell them more about the events that would follow.

However, when we read Matthew and Luke (Mark's version is similar to Matthew's longer one), we discover that their accounts are not exactly alike. Although they are similar in many ways, using the same words, thoughts, and subject order, they seem to emphasize different things and different timetables. I do not believe they contradict one another, or even confuse what Jesus meant to say. I believe we are seeing the sovereign hand of God in the compilation of Scripture. Instead of contradicting one another, Matthew and Luke recorded Jesus' words in ways that provide a *complete* picture for us - a picture that enables us to put together the entire prophetic puzzle!

The differences in Matthew and Luke are derived from the way the two writers recorded the disciples' questions to Jesus. If we read them carefully, we notice that Luke's and Matthew's accounts contain slightly different questions.

Luke recorded the disciples' questions as follows:

Question 1: "When will these things happen?"
Question 2: "What will be the sign that they are about to take place?"

Luke arranged Jesus' words in order to answer these questions, both of which focused upon the impending destruction of the temple and the judgment upon the Jews for rejecting Him.

However, while Matthew also recorded the disciples' first question, he left out their second one. Instead, Matthew recorded an additional question the disciples had asked Jesus. It was this third question which prompted Jesus to speak about a more distant fulfillment regarding His coming:

Question 1: "When will this happen?"
Question 3: "What will be the sign of your coming and the end of the age?"

As we examine both passages, we will see examples of both the telescopic and dual fulfillment styles of prophecy. Jesus clearly foretold God's judgment upon the Jews, the capture of Jerusalem, and the destruction of the temple. But His words also pointed to a future judgment upon the entire world, after the Gospel had been preached to all the nations.

Therefore, we will examine what Jesus said in both major passages. As we do, a complete picture of end-time events will unfold in the *order* of their occurrence. We will discover just how Jesus' words have been fulfilled both in ancient and modern history, as well as the unmistakable signs Jesus gave which announce His soon return. We will have a complete overview of all the events that will usher in the final chapter of human history. From this outline, we will be able to confidently piece together the rest of the prophetic puzzle in the subsequent chapters of this book!

The Picture in Luke

Luke's picture is based upon these two questions the disciples asked Jesus:

(1) When will the temple be destroyed?
(2) What will the sign of the temple's destruction be?

5 And while some were talking about the temple, that it was adorned with beautiful stones and votive gifts, He said, 6 "As for these things which you are looking at, the days will come in which there will not be left one stone upon another which will not be torn down"

7 And they questioned Him, saying, "Teacher, **when** therefore will *these things* be? And what will be the sign when *these things* are about to take place?" (Luke 21:5-7; NASB).

Luke focused Jesus' answer on God's judgment upon Jerusalem, which signaled the beginning of the Times of the Gentiles.

An outline for Luke's account is as follows:

I. The Time of the Judgment upon the Jews

    A. False Christs and False Prophets (Luke 21:8)
    B. Human Suffering (Luke 21:9-11)
    C. Persecution of believers (Luke 21:12-19)
    D. Jerusalem Occupied by Gentile Nations until the Time of the End (Luke 21:20-24)

II. The Time of the End

    A. The Judgment of God (Luke 21:25-26)
    B. Christ's Coming in Glory (Luke 21:27)

III. Our Response

    A. Recognize the Signs of the Times (Luke 21:28-33)
    B. Be ready for His return (Luke 21:34-36)

I. The Time of the Judgment upon the Jews

A. False Christs and False Prophets (Luke 21:8)

   8 And He said, "See to it that you be not misled; for many will come in My name, saying, 'I am He,' and, 'The time is at hand'; do not go after them'" (Luke 21:8; NASB).

In light of the numerous warnings Jesus gave about jumping to conclusions concerning His Second Advent, it is surprising how often Christians have done just that! Over and over Jesus told us not to be so misled. However, even the early Christians suffered from this confusion. Paul's church in Thessalonica mistakenly wondered whether the Day of the Lord had already come. In reply, Paul wrote, "...we ask you, brothers, not to become easily unsettled or alarmed by some prophecy, report or letter supposed to have come from us, saying that the day of the Lord has already come" (2 Thessalonians 2:1-2). He then gave them some signs to look for in order to identify exactly when the time of the end arrived, one of them being the appearance of the "man of lawlessness," commonly known by his other name, the "Antichrist."

B. Human Suffering (Luke 21:9-11)

   9 "And when you hear of wars and disturbances, do not be terrified; for these things must take place **first**, *but the end does not follow immediately.*
   10 Then He continued by saying to them, "Nation will rise against nation, and kingdom against kingdom, 11 and there will be great earthquakes, and in various places plagues and famines; and there will be terrors and great signs from heaven" (Luke 21:9-11; NASB).

How often throughout church history have Christians looked at the distresses of their era and concluded that Jesus would soon come back? Yet, Jesus warned us not to interpret every war, famine, earthquake, plague, or even cosmic occurrences as the definitive signs of His soon arrival! This word should have warned the early Christians, as well as Christians of every age, not to "cry wolf!" These are *not* the signs we are to look for because they are common with every age of mankind. They are, for the most part, by-products of our sinful world. However, Jesus did give us more definite signs to observe - signs that unmistakably point to the immanence of His return, as we shall soon read.

C. Persecution of Believers (Luke 21:12-19)

12 "But **before** all these things, they will lay their hands on you and will persecute you, delivering you to the synagogues and prisons, bringing you before kings and governors for My name's sake. 13 It will lead to an opportunity for your testimony. 14 So make up your minds not to prepare beforehand to defend yourselves; 15 for I will give you utterance and wisdom which none of your opponents will be able to resist or refute. 16 But you will be delivered up even by parents and brothers and relatives and friends, and they will put some of you to death, 17 and you will be hated by all on account of My name. 18 Yet not a hair of your head will perish. 19 By your endurance you will gain your lives" (Luke 21:12-19; NASB).

Up to this point, Luke recorded warnings to Christians not to "jump the gun" just because people point to world events as the signs of Christ's return. Jesus made it clear that these kinds of things are not what we are to look for. He knew a judgment was coming upon the Jews, and that His disciples might misinterpret the warfare and turmoil of that time of judgment as a sign of His return. He warned them not to be alarmed when the conflict came.

However, before this judgment would come upon the Jews, Jesus told His disciples to get ready for persecution. "Before these things," in this context can only refer to the increasing persecution Jewish believers experienced at the hands of their countrymen. Jewish believers were being put out of their synagogues and ostracized from Jewish society prior to the judgment on Jerusalem in 70 AD. The Jewish elders even introduced anti-Christian responsive readings into their synagogue worship in order to discover any secret believers among them.

Jesus warned His followers in advance not to take this persecution as a sign of the end, but as an expected price for those destined for eternal life! He promised, "In the world you will have tribulation, but be of good cheer, I have overcome the world" (John 16:33). The Apostle Paul stated categorically that persecution is the mark of the Christian: "All who desire to live godly lives in Christ Jesus *will be* persecuted" (2 Timothy 3:12).

D. Jerusalem will be Occupied by the Gentile Nations until the Time of the End (Luke 21:20-24)

20 "But **when** you see Jerusalem surrounded by armies, then recognize that her desolation is at hand. 21 Then let those who are in Judea flee to the mountains, and let those who are in the midst of the city depart, and let not those who are in the country enter the city; 22 because

these are days of vengeance, in order that all things which are written may be fulfilled.

23 "Woe to those who are with child and to those who nurse babes in those days; for there will be great distress upon the land, and wrath to this people, 24 and they will fall by the edge of the sword, and will be led captive into all the nations; *and Jerusalem will be trampled under foot by the Gentiles **until** the times of the Gentiles be fulfilled"* (Luke 21:20-24; NASB).

Here, Jesus answered the disciples' second question, "What would be the sign of the destruction of the temple?" He had warned them not to be deceived by wars, famines, or persecutions. "But when" they saw Jerusalem surrounded by armies, they were to get out of town fast. At this sign, the faithful were to recognize that God's judgment upon the Jews was coming. Jesus' prophecy against the temple would soon be fulfilled.

Jesus then described what would happen to the Jews: most would be killed and the remnant would be taken captive into all the nations. Just as the rebellious and stubborn Jews had to be exiled in 586 BC for their sins, they would be forced out of their country again. And, just as God foretold the length of the Jews' first exile (70 years), Jesus also prophesied an end to their second exile. Jerusalem would be ruled over by the Gentiles, *until* the time of the Gentiles was fulfilled. In other words, when God's plan for the salvation of the Gentiles was finished, the Jews would once again rule the city of Jerusalem.

We need to review the history of the Jews from the time of Christ until the present day in order to see how wonderfully God has fulfilled His promises to the Jews.

As mentioned earlier, by 65 AD most Jews were resistant to the Gospel. They were expelling any Jewish believers from both the synagogue and their social life. In 66 AD, the Pharisees joined the Zealots in their revolt against Rome. They succeeded in driving the Romans out of Jerusalem and, eventually, out of Judea and Galilee. The emperor Nero sent his best general, Titus Vespasian, with three legions to put down the rebellion. By 67 AD, Galilee had been retaken. In 68 AD, a major revolt broke out against Nero in Gaul and Spain. Seeing his cause was lost, Nero committed suicide. During the next year, Vespasian suspended the warfare in Judea, after isolating the fighting to Jerusalem. In the spring of 70 AD, Vespasian ascended to the throne of Rome. He then sent Titus, his son, to complete the conquest of Jerusalem. By August 6, 70 AD, the temple sacrifices were ended and, on the ninth of Ab (August 28), the Temple itself was entered and burned. By the decree of Titus, the people of Jerusalem were taken captive and all its buildings were leveled to the ground. Jewish Christians had already left the city on the eve of the siege, taking refuge at Pella beyond the Jordan.

Although the city was destroyed in 70 AD, the Jews were allowed to continue living in their land. In 132 AD, a Jewish false messiah who called himself Bar Kochba ("Son of the Star") began another rebellion against Roman rule. He claimed to be the fulfillment of Balaam's prophesy in Numbers 24:17: "I see him, but not now; I behold him, but not near; A star shall come forth from Jacob, a scepter shall rise from Israel, and shall crush through the forehead of Moab, and tear down all the sons of Sheth." For two years his forces held the Roman legions back, but Bar Kochba was finally killed and his rebellion crushed in 134 AD. By now, the Romans had had enough of these rebellious people. Over a million Jews were slaughtered throughout the land. The remaining captives were transported to the nearest slave markets in Egypt.

The Romans turned Jerusalem into a Gentile city, renaming it Aelia Capitolina. They forbade any Jew from entering the city and erected a temple to Jupiter over the site of the destroyed Herodian temple. From this point on, the Jews were completely exiled from their land.

All of this was but another example of the fulfillment of ancient prophecy. Moses had predicted this very event in Deuteronomy 28:62-68:

> 62 "Then you shall be left few in number, whereas you were as numerous as the stars [!] of heaven, because you did not listen to the voice of the Lord your God. 63 It shall come about that as the Lord delighted over you to prosper you, and multiply you, so the Lord will delight over you to make you perish and destroy you; and you will be torn from the land where you are entering to possess it. 64 Moreover, the Lord will scatter you among all peoples, from one end of the earth to the other end of the earth; and there you shall serve other gods, wood and stone, which you or your fathers have not known. 65 Among those nations you shall find no rest, and there will be no resting place for the sole of your foot; but there the Lord will give you a trembling heart, failing of eyes, and despair of soul. 66 So your life shall hang in doubt before you; and you will be in dread night and day, and shall have no assurance of your life. 67 In the morning you shall say, 'Would that it were evening!' And at evening you shall say, 'Would that it were morning!' because of the dread of your heart which you dread, and for the sight of your eyes which you will see. 68 The Lord will bring you back to Egypt in ships, by the way about which I spoke to you, 'You will never see it again!' And there you will offer yourselves as male and female slaves, but there will be no buyer'" (Deuteronomy 28:62-68; NASB).

Amazingly, this prophecy was fulfilled exactly! The Jews, once as numerous as the stars, were slaughtered when they followed the false messiah, "Son of the

Star." The remnant of the Jews was taken to Alexandria, Egypt in ships to be sold into slavery. However, no one would buy these rebellious people! The Jews were scattered throughout the earth. They found themselves living in every country under heaven. However, wherever they went the Jews faced the awful specter of persecution.

Despite their exile, the Jewish people remained distinct as a race, being unified through their religion. Only a handful of Jews eventually were allowed to return to Jerusalem. Meanwhile, because of neglect and a remarkable change of weather patterns, their ancient homeland land turned into an ecological wasteland - "an object of hissing and horror" (Jeremiah 29:18).

For nineteen hundred years, the Jews endured persecution and mistreatment by the Gentiles. It is indeed a sad and unfortunate fact that much of this was at the hand of so-called Christians. Nevertheless, late in the nineteenth century a movement arose among the Jews known as Zionism, under the leadership of a visionary named Theodore Hertzl. Russian Jews had just witnessed yet another round of deadly "pogroms," or persecutions. European Jews had seen the unjust trial and conviction of a Alfred Dreyfus, a French army officer who was Jewish. Hertzl began to encourage Jews to return to their land in what was then called Palestine.

At that time, Palestine was a part of the Turkish Ottoman Empire. It was a place of disease-ridden swamps along the coast, and denuded, desert-like hills in the interior. The few hardy Jews who responded to Hertzl's message were able to buy some of this worthless land from its Arab inhabitants.

These pioneers discovered that God had already gone before them and was preparing the way. One of the reasons the land of Palestine had become a waste place was because the normal patterns of rainfall had been interrupted. In biblical times, rain fell primarily during two times of the year. The rainy seasons were called the "early" and "latter" rains. The early rains fell during the spring, giving water for the seeds, while the latter rains began in September and October, allowing the crops to grow to maturity. Sometime after the Jews were exiled, the latter rains became inconsistent and even ceased altogether. People were no longer able to live in much of the land as a result. However, in fulfillment of yet another prophecy, the latter rains returned with regularity to the land at the end of the nineteenth century! "So rejoice, O sons of Zion [!], and be glad in the Lord your God; for He has given you the early rain for your vindication. And He has poured down for you the rain, the early and latter rain as before" (Joel 2:23; NASB).

World War I brought about more monumental changes for the Jews. On November 2, 1917, the British Prime Minister, Arthur James Balfour, issued what became known as the Balfour Declaration. In gratitude for Jewish support of Great Britain during World War I, Balfour promised British support for a

Palestinian homeland for the Jews after the war was over.[15] Because the Ottoman Empire had fought with the Germans against the Allies, their empire was partitioned among the victors. The British were awarded the mandate to govern Palestine in 1920.

Jewish immigration into Palestine remained at a trickle. Most Jews were content with life in Europe, Russia, and the United States. But with the rise to power of Adolph Hitler in the 1930's, this trickle became a stream, as Jews sought to escape the growing anti-Semitism of Germany. The increased immigration caused the first real signs of strain between the Jews, the Arabs, and the British rulers of Palestine. In response, the Jews began to organize an underground defense force.

The horrors of the Nazi holocaust drove home this inescapable conclusion to the entire world: the Jews needed a homeland. Zionism had birthed the idea, but the murder of more than six million Jews convinced the victorious allies. It is interesting that several sites for a homeland had already been suggested. One potential site was located in eastern Africa while another place was in Siberia. But by the end of World War II, the homeless European Jewish remnant had set their hope upon Palestine, their promised land. A modern day Exodus began, despite the antagonism and opposition of the British, who were still trying to maintain an impossible balance of power between the Jews and Arabs. Jews and Arabs, alike, armed themselves and trained for war.

The newly organized United Nations stepped into the situation. In 1947, the land of Palestine was partitioned between the Jews and Palestinians. The Arab League attempted to stop the partition by invading Israeli-held lands. The fledgling Israeli army successfully resisted and, on May 14, 1948, the Jews proclaimed the formation of the modern state of Israel. Many Jews and evangelical Christians saw this event as the fulfillment of prophecy, including Isaiah's word, "Who has ever heard of such a thing? Who has ever seen such things? Can a country be born in a day or a nation be brought forth in a moment? Yet no sooner is Zion in labor than she gives birth to her children" (Isaiah 66:8). Beginning with the Soviet Union, country after country recognized this new nation. For the first time in over 2,000 years, the Jews ruled their own nation!

From its beginning, Israel faced the threat of annihilation from its neighbors. They have had to fight four full-scale wars: the War for Independence in 1948, the Suez War against Egypt in 1956, 1967 Six-Day War, and the Yom Kippur War in 1973. But it was during the miraculous Six-Day War that prophecy was again fulfilled. Following the partition of Palestine by the United Nations, the Old City of Jerusalem (including the location of the temple) was allocated to the Palestinians. During the Jewish War for Independence, the Kingdom of Jordan

---

[15] Among other things, Jewish scientists discovered a process that stabilized TNT, for use in high explosive artillery shells.

annexed the Palestinian lands on the West Bank of the Jordan River and the Old City of Jerusalem. During Israeli's amazing victory in June of 1967, the Old City was taken. Jerusalem was no longer trodden under foot by the Gentiles. For the first time since 70 AD, Jerusalem was now Jewish territory!

It is this indisputable, historical fulfillment which unmistakably tells us that we are living in the last days. Jerusalem is no longer trodden under foot by the Gentiles. It became a Jewish-controlled city in 1967. The Times of the Gentiles are at an end.[16]

And, when the Time of the Gentiles is fulfilled, the judgment of God will soon come!

II. The Time of the End

A. The Judgment of God (Luke 21:25-26)

25 "And there will be signs in sun and moon and stars, and upon the earth dismay among nations, in perplexity at the roaring of the sea and the waves, 26 men fainting from fear and the expectation of the things which are coming upon the world; for the powers of the heavens will be shaken"
(Luke 21:25-26; NASB).

Here is an example of a telescopic prophecy. In a telescopic prophecy, the events are written in a way where they seem to occur one right after another. However, there can be great gaps of time between their actual fulfillments. Verse 24 tells us that the temple would be destroyed and Jerusalem would be occupied by the nations. Almost 1900 years passed before the prophecy was completely fulfilled! In verse 25, Jesus briefly describes what will happen next in the world.[17]

Simply because end-time events are only summarized here in this passage, the details are still important and should be remembered. This is an important puzzle piece as it serves to join many other prophecies to this period of time. We must take note of the fact that just prior to the end there will be cosmic disturbances of such magnitude that men will be in dread over the hopelessness of their situation. We should also remember for further reference the inclusion of the phrase, "roaring of the sea and the waves." Something will cause a shaking

---

[16] Remember, we read in the last chapter how the gospel witness to the Gentile nations is nearly complete.

[17] It is noteworthy to recognize that Matthew's account presents the destruction of Jerusalem as a dualistic prophecy - one that has an initial but incomplete fulfillment which will be fulfilled in its entirety in the Last Days.

of both the heavenly bodies and the ocean depths. We will see these events described in other prophetic Scriptures when we examine the final judgment of God's wrath in a subsequent chapter.

B. Christ's coming in glory (Luke 21:27)

"**And then** they will see the Son of Man coming in a cloud with power and great glory" (Luke 21:27; NASB).

After these signs in the sky which cause such dismay and fear among the nations, Jesus will come back. He will be seen by all, in His majesty as King of kings and Lord of lords! Luke recorded the ascension of Jesus in the Book of Acts. There, Jesus ascended into the clouds to heaven. The angels told those who witnessed the event that Jesus would return to the earth in a similar manner.

III. Our Response

A. Recognize the Signs of the Times (Luke 21:28-33)

28 "But **when these things begin to take place**, straighten up and lift up your heads, because your redemption is drawing near." 29 And He told them a parable: "Behold the fig tree and all the trees; 30 as soon as they put forth leaves, you see it and know for yourselves that summer is now near. 31 Even so you, too, *when you see these things happening, recognize that the kingdom of God is near.*
32 "Truly I say to you, *this generation will not pass away* **until** *all things take place.* 33 Heaven and earth will pass away, but My words will not pass away" (Luke 21:28-33; NASB).

Although Jesus had warned His disciples not to jump to the conclusion that His return was imminent just because there was turmoil or persecution on the earth, He did not intend for us to be taken by complete surprise either. We are to look for the correct signs of His return, and we are to be encouraged when we see them being fulfilled!

From Luke 21 we have learned one of the two definitive signs of Christ's return: the status of Jerusalem. (We already examined the other definitive sign in the last chapter: "And this gospel of the kingdom shall be preached in the whole world for a witness to all the nations, and then the end shall come.") Jerusalem would be judged, the temple destroyed, and the city given over to Gentile rule - *until* the time of the Gentiles was fulfilled. When this happened, Jesus said that the generation that saw it would not pass away until *all* things He had prophesied would take place. Since Jerusalem is now a Jewish city, and the gospel has just about been proclaimed in every nation, isn't it logical to expect the end to come sometime soon?

Many evangelical, Bible-believing Christians were excited by the formation of the nation of Israel. Modern premillenialists had been predicting it for years.[18] Since a biblical generation is 40 years, many Christians sincerely expected Jesus to return around 1988. There was even a book published entitled, "Eighty-eight Reasons Why Jesus Will Return in 1988." Since the Old City of Jerusalem was not really in the possession of the Israeli's until 1967, we can anticipate a similar expectancy among Christians in 2007.

Though we may enjoy speculating, we do not really know with certainty exactly when "this generation" will be fulfilled. It may be forty years from 1967, or it may even be 40 years after a new temple has been built. It must be noted that it was about 40 years after Jesus spoke these words that Jerusalem was destroyed. This may very well be another example of an eschatological dualism. There was a forty-year overlap when the Time of the Jews was ending and the Time of the Gentiles was beginning. We may be seeing the same process in reverse: the Time of the Gentiles is winding down while the Jews are being prepared for the last seven years of Daniel's prophecy.

B.   Be Ready for His Return (Luke 21:34-36)

34 *"Be on guard*, that your hearts may not be weighted down with dissipation and drunkenness and the worries of life, and *that day come on you suddenly* like a trap; 35 for it will come upon all those who dwell on the face of all the earth.

36 "But keep on the alert **at all times**, praying in order that you may have strength to escape all these things that are about to take place, and to stand before the Son of Man" (Luke 21:34:36; NASB).

A common theme in all end-time prophecy is the call to stay awake, to be alert, and to keep watch. Why? Not only is it human nature to ignore unpleasant things, but we often hide from them. We tend to make life in this temporal world our only source of hope or joy. Jesus said that the time of the end would be hard, for the believer and unbeliever alike. The prophet Amos warned us, "Woe to you who long for the day of the Lord! Why do you long for the day of the Lord? That day will be darkness, not light. It will be as though a man fled from a lion only to meet a bear, as though he entered his house and rested his hand on the wall only to have a snake bite him. Will not the day of the LORD be darkness, not

---

[18] For instance, I own a pamphlet written by Evangelical Christians in the 1930's that gives the biblical reasons why the Jews had to be re-established in Israel before Jesus could return.

light - pitch-dark, without a ray of brightness?" (Amos 5:18-20; NASB). It will be tempting to ignore the signs of the end and put Jesus' coming out of our minds. People will be saying that it can't really be happening (2 Peter 3:3-4). But Jesus encourages us to pray, be on guard, and to be strong in thc faith - because we will certainly need all our spiritual resources in order to make our way through its awesome events!

The Picture in Matthew

We now turn to examine Matthew's account of the Olivet Discourse. He approaches it differently than Luke, putting more of an emphasis on the answer to the disciple's third question, "What will the signs of the end be?"

> 1 And Jesus came out from the temple and was going away when His disciples came up to point out the temple buildings to Him. 2 And He answered and said to them, "Do you not see all these things? Truly I say to you, not one stone here shall be left upon another, which will not be torn down."
> 3 And as He was sitting on the Mount of Olives, the disciples came to Him privately, saying, "Tell us, **when** will these things [the temple's destruction] be, and what will be the sign of Your coming, and of the end of the age?" (Matthew 24:1-3; NASB).

We will see how Matthew arranged the words of Christ so they effectively answered the question of what the end-time events would be like. Not understanding God's sovereignty in the writing of Matthew and Luke has confused many interpreters. Instead of trying to reconcile each verse with its corresponding verse, we will discover how these two passages serve to complement one another, providing a full picture of end-time events. Whereas Luke arranged the words of Jesus to focus upon the judgment of the Jews; Matthew described events which will happen *after* the Gospel is preached to the whole world (the Time of the Gentiles). By using the Jewish style of prophecy that points to a dual fulfillment, Matthew tells us what will take place just prior to the return of Christ. By combining Matthew and Luke, we are able to piece together the chronological sequence of the events of the end!

Matthew's outline looks like this:

I. The Time of the Gentiles

    A. False Christs and False Prophets (Matthew 24:4-5)
    B. Birth Pangs (Matthew 24:6-8)
        1. Wars and rumors of wars

      2. Plagues and famines

      3. Earthquakes

  C. Persecution of Believers (Matthew 24:9-13)

  D. Gospel Preached to the Whole World (Matthew 24:14)

II. The Time of the End

  A. Antichrist and the Abomination of Desolation (Matthew 24:15-20)

  B. The Great Tribulation (Matthew 24:21-22)

  C. Religious Deception (Matthew 24:23-28)

  D. God's Judgment on Earth (Matthew 24:29)

III. The Coming of Christ

  A. Christ's Coming in Glory (Matthew 24:30)

  B. The Resurrection and Rapture of the Saints (Matthew 24:31)

IV. Our Response

  A. Recognize the Signs of the Times (Matthew 24:32-36)

  B. Be Ready for His Return (Matthew 24:37-44)

I. The Time of the Gentiles

A. False Christs and False Prophets (Matthew 24:4-5)

4 And Jesus answered and said to them, "See to it that no one misleads you. 5 For many will come in My name, saying, 'I am the Christ,' and will mislead many" (Matthew 24:4-5; NASB)

As in Luke's account, Jesus warned His disciples about false messiahs who would mislead the spiritually gullible. We will discuss the delusion and deception of the last days in more detail in the section, "The Kingdom of the Antichrist."

B. Birth Pangs (Matthew 24:6-8)

6 "And you will be hearing of wars and rumors of wars; see that you are not frightened, for those things must take place, but **that is not yet the end**. 7 For nation will rise against nation, and kingdom against

kingdom, and in various places there will be famines and earthquakes. 8 *But all these things are merely the beginning of birth pangs"* (Matt. 24:6-8; NASB).

Again, as in Luke, Jesus warned the disciples against making rash pronouncements concerning the fulfillment of the end-times just because there are wars, famines or earthquakes. However, Matthew includes Jesus' statement which uses an interesting metaphor to describe the approach of the end. He likened wars and other human calamities to "birth pangs." Birth pangs are an apt description of the events that will lead to the climactic end of human history. Just as labor pains begin as mild discomforts that increase in frequency and intensity, so these wars, famines and earthquakes will increase in frequency and ferocity as the end-times approach. But these are not definitive signs. Just as labor pains can be mistaken by what is called "false labor," so prophetic interpreters have often been confused. Zealous Christians have proclaimed the end was near just because of some horrible but localized war or natural disaster.

However, real labor does progress over time to a climatic end. It must be pointed out that the twentieth century has been the most violent and destructive time in human history. Modern warfare probably began with the American Civil War. More effective methods of killing, such as the repeating rifle and the machine gun, were first used in this war, resulting in more deaths in single battles than at any other war up to that time. By the time of World War I, human inventiveness had developed such killers as poison gas, high explosive shells, and the airplane. The destruction was so horrifying that people wishfully termed that Great War as "The War to End All Wars." This was not to be. Just twenty years later, the world was afflicted with another war - the most costly one in human history, with over 30 million deaths. World War II launched mankind into the nuclear age with the first use of atomic weapons. For the next 60 years, conflicts between the superpowers brought us wars in Korea, Vietnam, Afghanistan, and numerous smaller regional battles. It has been estimated that over 200 million people were killed by warfare in the twentieth century alone!

But war was not the only terror that mankind has faced in the twentieth century. Genocide and political purges have killed nearly as many people as open conflict. Stalin killed 20 million Ukrainians; Chairman Mao killed 30 million Chinese; Hitler killed 8 million Jews and other "undesirables;" and Pol Pot killed some two million Cambodians. The century began with the ethnic cleansing of more than a million Armenians, and it finished with genocide in places like the Sudan, Rwanda, and Kosovo.

War, climatic abnormalities, injustice, and overpopulation have all contributed to the specter of famine. The Sahara Desert has been expanding southward at a rate of several miles per year. Former agricultural areas are receding, leaving starvation in its wake. The city of Timbuktu (yes, there really is a place by that name) is all but a ghost town. Bangladesh, located at the fertile mouth of the Ganges River, is so overpopulated that the threat of famine is only a cyclone away. With its enormous amounts of land and resources, the world can probably support three times its six billion people. But that number is unlikely to be reached, given mankind's selfishness, greed, and injustice.

Disease and pestilence have also taken their toll upon mankind in the twentieth century. Great advances in medicine have cut the mortality rate throughout the world. But new diseases have replaced old pestilences. The most alarming disease afflicting mankind is probably the AIDS epidemic. Though this killer could be exterminated in one generation simply by a change of lifestyle, it continues to expand its deadly reach throughout the world. There are some countries in Africa, for instance, that may have 40% of their populations infected with the HIV virus.

In light of the evidence of the twentieth century, it seems that we are witnessing a steady progression from one birth pang to the next. Even false labor must give way to actual labor. Humanity's ever increasing birth pangs remind us that the true event is approaching!

C. Persecution of Believers (Matthew 24:9-13)

9 "**Then** they will deliver you to tribulation, and will kill you, and you will be hated by all nations on account of My name. 10 And **at that time** many will fall away and will deliver up one another and hate one another. 11 And many false prophets will arise, and will mislead many. 12 And because lawlessness is increased, most people's love will grow cold. 13 *But the one who endures to the end, he shall be saved"* (Matthew 24:9-13; NASB).

Whereas Luke's gospel warned early Christians about persecution, Matthew's message is for believers in the last days. His placement of this passage after the beginnings of labor pains, and his warning to endure to the end, despite the lawless society all around, puts its context into the time just prior to Christ's return.

One of the characteristics of the labor pains of the end-times will be an increased atmosphere of persecution toward the church. The twentieth century has produced more Christian martyrs than at any other time in history. It has recently been estimated that over 200,000 believers were killed for their faith throughout the world in one year (1998). Persecution has a purifying effect upon the church. People will not risk their temporal lives for something they really do not believe.

But, the turmoil and pain of society will also produce hatred, deception, and lawlessness. Everyone will "do what is right in his own eyes," because peoples' lives will not be grounded upon anything eternal or lasting. This social chaos will serve to give rise to mankind's final ruler: a man non-Christians will look to for their earthly salvation. But the believer who endures - who is looking for a salvation from above - will alone be saved.

D. Gospel Preached to the Whole World
    (Matthew 24:14)

"And this gospel of the kingdom shall be preached in the whole world for a witness to all the nations, and **then the end shall come**" (Matthew 24:14; NASB).

Here, Jesus gives us the other distinct and unmistakable sign of His soon coming: the Gospel must be preached in the whole world before the end will come. As we mentioned in our last chapter, this task has almost been completed. It is possible for any person in the world to tune into Gospel radio broadcast from a number of Christian short-wave radio transmitters. There are Christians living in every country of the world (though some must remain as "secret" believers, living in danger of their lives). However these facts do not fulfill this prophecy completely. The Greek word for nation is *ethne*, from which we get our term, "ethnic" group. As I noted in the last chapter, there are still a handful of ethnic groups that have not yet had the direct opportunity to hear the gospel. The Book of Revelation tells us that there will be representatives from "every tribe, tongue, and nation" who will celebrate the final victory of King Jesus (Revelation 7:9).

The Great Commission will soon be fulfilled. This fact, coupled with the city of Jerusalem being under Jewish rule, gives us clear indication that the climax of human history is near. Jesus is coming back in our day!

II. The Time of the End

A. The Antichrist and the Abomination of Desolation
    (Matthew 24:15-20)

15 "Therefore **when** you see the Abomination of Desolation which was spoken of through Daniel the prophet, standing in the holy place (let the reader understand), 16 then let those who are in Judea flee to the mountains; 17 let him who is on the housetop not go down to get the things out that are in his house; 18 and let him who is in the field not turn back to get his cloak. 19 But woe to those who are with child and to those who nurse babes in those days! 20 But pray that your flight may not be in the winter, or on a Sabbath;" (Matthew 24:15-20; NASB).

Up to this point, we might suppose that Jesus was still referring to prophetic events leading up to the initial destruction of Jerusalem and the judgment upon the Jews, just in the same way Luke recorded the prophecy. We have read about the same warnings not to be misled, the same kind of reference to wars, famines, and earthquakes, the same encouragement through persecution, and the same kind of reference to the Gospel being spread among the Gentiles. But at this point (verses 15-20), Jesus seemed to shift the focus to a point of time in the future - a time far beyond the destruction of Jerusalem in 70 AD. How did He do this, and not contradict what Luke recorded Him as saying?

What we see in this passage is an example of a dualistic prophecy. To review, a dualistic prophecy is one that has an initial fulfillment in history that does not seem to be a complete fulfillment. The initial fulfillment only points to a more perfect one at some future date. Matthew often used this form of prophetic interpretation. He used it to explain how Jesus was the perfect virgin-born Emmanuel (see chapter 2). Matthew pointed to the Exodus of the Israelites in Egypt as a prophetic type which had its perfect fulfillment in the return of the baby Jesus from Egypt (Matthew 2:15). Jesus used this style of prophecy when He referred to John the Baptist as Elijah who had prepared the way of the Lord. But Jesus then told His disciples that "Elijah comes and will restore all things" (Matthew 17:11-12).

So, there on the Mount of Olives, Jesus prophesied the coming destruction of Jerusalem in a way that applied both to its initial destruction in 70 AD, and also to a time in the future. How do we know He was not referring only to what took place at the end of the Jewish War of 66-70 AD? Because that war did not have anything in it that resembled the Abomination of Desolation. Matthew even inserted a parenthetical reminder to his readers: you need to understand what the Abomination of Desolation is. So, in order to understand the Abomination of Desolation, we need to examine the Book of Daniel where the concept first originated.

Daniel referred to an Abomination of Desolation three times in his prophetic work. The first occurrence is in chapter 9, in the same context where the "seventy sevens" are mentioned. During the last "seven," the "ruler who is to come" will "...confirm a covenant with many for one 'seven.' In the middle of the 'seven' he will put an end to sacrifice and offering. And on a wing [of the temple] he will set up an abomination that causes desolation, until the end that is decreed is poured out on him" (Daniel 9:27).

The second reference to the Abomination of Desolation is in Daniel 11:30-32: "Ships of the western coastlands will oppose him, and he will lose heart. Then he will turn back and vent his fury against the holy covenant. He will return and show favor to those who forsake the holy covenant. His armed forces will rise up to desecrate the temple fortress and will abolish the daily sacrifice. Then they will set up the abomination that causes desolation. With flattery he will corrupt those who have violated the covenant, but the people who know their God will firmly resist him."

The last mention of the Abomination of Desolation is in the final words of the Book of Daniel: "From the time that the daily sacrifice is abolished and the abomination that causes desolation is set up, there will be 1,290 days" (Daniel 12:11).

Here we are given yet another example of a dualistic prophecy. These prophecies were fulfilled in part during the period of time between the end of the writing of the Old Testament and the beginning of the New Testament. After the Jews returned from the Babylonian exile, they rebuilt the city of Jerusalem and the temple. The Jews lived under the rule of the Persians and, later, the Greek empire of Alexander the Great. After Alexander died, his realm was divided among his four top generals.

It was during this era (around 200 BC), that Greek (or, "Hellenistic") influences began to seep into Jewish life. Some Jews began to speak Greek, dress in Grecian robes, and even changed their names to Greek ones. Some even accepted Greek religious philosophies. Other, more devout Jews rejected these influences and withstood this growing apostasy, or falling away from their faith. They feared the Greek rulers would try to make them worship Greek gods.

Their fears were well founded. In 175 BC, a new ruler came to power in Syria, named Antiochus Epiphanes. His title, "Epiphanes," means "the god manifest." He tried to unify his realm by forcing everyone, including the Jews, to adopt Greek customs. His exploits, and the political situation of his era, are described in such accurate detail in Daniel 11 that Biblical critics claim that these passages must have been written after the fact and then attributed to Daniel.

In 168 BC, Antiochus invaded Egypt (the "king of the South," of Daniel 11:25), but was forced by the threats of Rome (Daniel 11:30) to return home. On his way, he sent his commander, Apollonius, to Jerusalem to enforce his orders for the Hellenization of the Jews (Daniel 11:31). Apollonius entered the city as if invading an enemy fortress. He butchered many civilians and took many others into slavery. He destroyed part of the city and tore down some of the city wall. Then, he erected a military garrison next to the temple. Finally, he issued an edict making the city of Jerusalem a polis - a Greek city, under Grecian laws and customs. This meant that the temple ceased to be the property of the Jewish people. Seeing further resistance by faithful Jews, Antiochus forbade the practice of Judaism, put an end to the sacrifices, and ordered the destruction of all copies of the Torah. Pagan altars were established throughout the land, and Jews were forced to eat swine's flesh under penalty of death. In December, 167 BC, an alter to Zeus was set up in the temple, and a sacrifice of pigs was made upon it. This was the first Abomination of Desolation. The Jews, under the leadership of Judas Maccabeus, resisted and were able to defeat the Syrians (verse 33). In December, 164 BC, the Maccabeans (as they were called) were able to cleanse and rededicate their temple. For the next 80 years, the Jews enjoyed independence.

Therefore, it appears that the reference to the Abomination of Desolation in Daniel 11 was fulfilled through Antiochus Epiphanes. But Jesus told us that another Abomination of Desolation would occur. As we have already seen in our explanation of Daniel 9:24-27, there will be a complete fulfillment of this prophecy in the last seven years of Jewish history. Another ruler, similar to Antiochus Epiphanes, will set himself up in the temple and proclaim himself a god. He will put an end to sacrifices and offerings, and will persecute believers. Here in Matthew 24, Jesus is saying that this man would come to power *after* the gospel had been preached to all nations. The apostle Paul told us in 2 Thessalonians 2:4 about this same man, who would "take his seat in the temple of God, displaying himself as being God."

It is interesting that Jesus predicted at the same time both the destruction of the temple ("not one stone will be left upon another" - Matthew 24:2) and the necessity for its rebuilding at some later date, so that the Abomination of Desolation could occur there!

Many devout Jews living in Israel today are planning for the time when the temple will be constructed. But there is a major obstacle that must be dealt with before the temple can be rebuilt. Islam's third holiest shrine, the Mosque of Omar, is located right on the traditional site of the original Jewish temple. The Israeli government has no intention of tearing it down, as the "Mother of All Holy Wars" would be the inevitable result! However, archeological studies have been made which suggest that the original Jewish temple was located in a different location on the Temple Mount. Though there are conflicting theories (one locates the temple to the north of the mosque, while the other puts it to the south), the rebuilding of the temple is now a distinct possibility.

To summarize, we have seen that while Luke recorded Jesus' words concerning Jerusalem in a way that clearly spoke of its impending judgment and destruction, followed by the Time of the Gentiles, Matthew placed the Gospel being preached to all the Gentile nations first, followed by the Abomination of Desolation in a rebuilt temple in the future!

B. The Great Tribulation (Matthew 24:21-22)

21 "for **then** there will be a *great tribulation*, such as has not occurred since the beginning of the world until now, nor ever shall. 22 And unless those days had been cut short, no life would have been saved; but for the sake of the elect those days shall be cut short" (Matthew 24:21-22; NASB).

These verses present us with another good example of why we should use Jesus' words as our guide for prophetic events, instead of the common Dispensational teaching. Most evangelicals have been taught that the Bible calls the last seven years of human history (the Seventieth Week of Daniel) the "Great Tribulation." But, according to Jesus, the "Great Tribulation" will not begin until *after* the Abomination of Desolation has happened. We learned that Daniel prophesied the Abomination of Desolation will occur halfway through the last seven years (Daniel 9:27). This means that the Great Tribulation will last for three and one half years, not seven. Dispensational teaching is clearly in error on this point.

Nevertheless, these three and a half years will be the worst time in all of human history. As we shall see in greater detail in subsequent chapters, the wrath and judgment of God will be poured out upon mankind. Those last days will be so cataclysmic that unless Jesus returned to put them to an end, all humanity will be wiped out.

Note the reason Jesus gave for shortening the time period of judgment: "for the sake of the elect." Dispensationalists make an arbitrary interpretation concerning the identity of "the elect" mentioned here in Matthew 24. The Greek term, *eklectos*, is used throughout the New Testament to refer to all believers in Jesus the Messiah. (For instance, Romans 8:33 uses the term for *all* Christians: "Who will bring a charge against God's elect? God is the one who justifies.") However, in order to bend Jesus' order of events to fit their understanding of the resurrection and the rapture of the church, they have to assume that Jesus was only talking about *Jewish* believers in this chapter. There is no internal evidence from this passage to support such a view. It is a gross violation of the rules of biblical interpretation. A literal interpretation would simply take the standard usage of the word in the New Testament and apply it here: the elect are all believers, both Jewish and Gentile.

C. Religious Deception (Matthew 24:23-28)

23 "Then if anyone says to you, 'Behold, here is the Christ,' or 'There He is,' do not believe him. 24 For false Christs and false prophets will arise and will show great signs and wonders, so as to mislead, if possible, even the elect. 25 Behold, I have told you in advance. 26 If therefore they say to you, 'Behold, He is in the wilderness,' do not go forth, or, 'Behold, He is in the inner rooms,' do not believe them. 27 For just as the lightning comes from the east, and flashes even to the west, so shall the coming of the Son of Man be. 28 Wherever the corpse is, there the vultures will gather" [a Jewish proverb, similar in meaning to our modern saying, "Where there's smoke, there's fire."] (Matthew 24:23-28; NASB).

A common warning in prophecy is our need to beware of demonic deception in the last days. Although we will address this important topic in more detail in a later chapter, we note here that Jesus said this deception would reach its height during the time of the Great Tribulation.

The apostle Paul also linked the coming of the Antichrist with a powerful delusion that will be believed by the vast majority of the world population. He said that the coming of the "man of lawlessness" would be in "accordance with the work of Satan displayed in all kinds of counterfeit miracles, signs and wonders, and in every sort of evil that deceives those who are perishing. They perish because they refused to love the truth and so be saved. For this reason God sends them a powerful delusion so that they will believe the lie and so that all will be condemned who have not believed the truth but have delighted in wickedness" (2 Thessalonians 2:9-12).

John also warned us of the spirit of the Antichrist, which was already at work in his time, deceiving people within the church to believe false doctrines and teachings: "This is the spirit of the Antichrist, which you have heard is coming and even now is already in the world" (1 John 4:3b). That spirit of deception has always been in the world, deluding people into following their Sin. However, John clearly stated in this passage that the Antichrist "is coming." When he does, the Book of Revelation tells us, he will perform "great and miraculous signs, even causing fire to come down from heaven to earth in full view of men. Because of the signs he was given power to do on behalf of the first beast, he deceived the inhabitants of the earth" (Revelation 13:13-14). His lies will have an effect upon the visible church. Some who claim to be Christians will follow, or even propagate these doctrines of demons. However, true believers - the elect - will not be so deceived. A shepherd's sheep will not respond to the voice of a stranger (John 10:4-5). We look to heaven for our salvation, not to the temporal salvation the world may try to offer. And from heaven we shall see the sudden and glorious coming of Son of Man, a coming Jesus likened to the bright, sky-splitting flash of lightning!

D. God's Judgment on Earth (Matthew 24:29)

> 29 "But **immediately after** the tribulation of those days 'the sun will be darkened, and the moon will not give its light, and the stars will fall from the sky, and the powers of the heavens will be shaken,'" [this is a quote from Isaiah 13:9-13] (Matthew 24:29; NASB).

This verse is similar to Luke 21:25-26: "And there will be signs in the sun and moon and stars, and upon the earth dismay among nations, in perplexity at the roaring of the sea and the waves, men fainting from fear and the expectation of the things which are coming upon the world; for the powers of the heavens will be shaken" (NASB). Both mention signs in the sun, moon, and stars. Some cataclysmic event will occur which will cause the sun to appear darkened, hide the moon from view, and result in a severe meteor shower. (This can be the only meaning of "stars will fall from the sky." We still use the phrase "shooting star" today to mean a meteor, not a literal star.)

Jesus was very, very clear about when these cosmic signs would occur in relation to other end-time events. He said that they will occur "immediately after" the Great Tribulation. Most Christians have assumed that the wrath of God will be poured out throughout the last seven years. But this is not what Jesus taught us. Therefore, we must interpret the puzzle pieces of the Book of Revelation using Jesus' outline to guide us, not the other way around. As we shall see in our chapter on the Day of the Lord, the Book of Revelation also reveals that the judgment and wrath of God will come as a rapid, earth-shattering event at the very end of the last seven years.

III. The Coming of Christ

A. Christ's Coming in Glory (Matthew 24:30)

> 30 "and **then** the sign of the Son of Man will appear in the sky, and then all the tribes of the earth will mourn, and they will see the Son of Man coming on the clouds of the sky with power and great glory" (Matthew 24:30; NASB).

Only after these cosmic events occur will Jesus come back. As in Luke, Matthew stressed the fact that His return will be visible worldwide. The Book of Zechariah gives us a picture that fits into this same scenario very well. Chapters 12 and 14 of Zechariah describes a battle where all the nations have gathered against the Jews and Jerusalem. In the midst of the battle, when it seems all is lost, "then the Lord my God will come, and all the holy ones with Him" (Zechariah 14:5). "On that day His feet will stand on the Mount of Olives" (Zechariah 14:4). But what is most revealing is that when He returns to earth, Zechariah prophesied, "And I will pour out on the house of David and the inhabitants of Jerusalem a spirit of grace and supplication. They will look on Me, the one they have pierced, and they will mourn for Him as one mourns for an only child, and grieve bitterly for Him as one grieves for a first born son" (Zechariah 12:10-11). There will be mourning of repentance among the Jews, in fulfillment of Daniel's Seventieth Week, when they will accept Jesus Christ as their Messiah!

B. The Resurrection and Rapture of the Saints (Matthew 24:31)

> 31 "And *He will send forth His angels with a great trumpet and they will gather together His elect* from the four winds, from one end of the sky to the other" (Matthew 24:31; NASB).

Jesus referred to the Book of Daniel again and again in the Olivet Discourse. He mentioned the Abomination of Desolation and He called Himself the "Son of Man" (Daniel's title for the Messiah in Daniel 7:13). Here, Jesus referred to the passage in Daniel 12:1 that foretold the resurrection of the dead. This same passage in Daniel tells us that the resurrection would occur after a "time of distress such as never occurred since there was a nation until that time" (Daniel 12:1; NASB). Clearly, Jesus intended us to interpret this verse in that context: when He returns to earth in the clouds, there will be a great trumpet blast and all the elect (all the saints, not just some of them) will be resurrected.

As we shall discover in the chapter "The Resurrection and the Rapture," these same phenomena (angels, trumpet blast, and resurrection) are all mentioned whenever the rapture occurs.

IV. Our Response

A. Recognize the Signs of the Times (Matthew 24:32-36)

> 32 "Now learn the parable from the fig tree: when its branch has already become tender, and puts forth its leaves, you know that summer is near; 33 even so you too, when you see all these things, recognize that He is near, right at the door. 34 Truly I say to you, this generation will not pass away until all these things take place. 35 Heaven and earth will pass away, but My words shall not pass away. 36 But of that day and hour no one knows, not even the angels of heaven, nor the Son, but the Father alone" (Matthew 24:32-36; NASB).

Even though only God the Father knows the exact time He will send Jesus back to earth, Jesus did say that we will know the approximate time. Just as the blooms of spring precede the heat of summer, when we see these signs being fulfilled we will know that Jesus is standing at the door, ready to bring judgment upon the earth. As I mentioned in our first chapter, Christians who are spiritually awake and alert will be aware of the fulfillment of these signs. It seems from verse 34 that there will be a generation of believers who will know Christ's return will soon take place. It will not be a surprise to them; Jesus' promise will come to pass.

B.   Be Ready for His Return (Matthew 24:37-44)

37 "For the coming of the Son of Man will be just like the days of Noah. 38 For as in those days which were before the flood they were eating and drinking, they were marrying and giving in marriage, until the day that Noah entered the ark, 39 and they did not understand until the flood came and took them all away; so shall the coming of the Son of Man be. 40 Then there shall be two men in the field; one will be taken, and one will be left. 41 Two women will be grinding at the mill; one will be taken, and one will be left.

42 "Therefore be on the alert, for you do not know which day your Lord is coming. 43 But be sure of this, that if the head of the house had known at what time of the night the thief was coming, he would have been on the alert and would not have allowed his house to be broken into. 44 For this reason you be ready too; for the Son of Man is coming at an hour when you do not think He will.

45 "Who then is the faithful and sensible slave whom his master put in charge of his household to give them their food at the proper time? 46 Blessed is that slave whom his master finds so doing when he comes. 47 Truly I say to you, that he will put him in charge of all his possessions. 48 But if that evil slave says in his heart, 'My master is not coming for a long time,' 49 and shall begin to beat his fellow slaves and eat and drink with drunkards; 50 the master of that slave will come on a day when he does not expect {him} and at an hour which he does not know, 51 and shall cut him in pieces and assign him a place with the hypocrites; weeping shall be there and the gnashing of teeth" (Matthew 24: 37-51; NASB).

Here, Jesus admonished His disciples to be always ready for His return. He used three analogies to describe the spiritual state of those who will be surprised by His coming because of their disregard of the prophetic signs. First, just as the people of Noah's day chose to ignore the large ark he was building in his backyard (which, along with his preaching, was a prophetic picture the coming judgment), so people in the last days will continue with normal life without regarding the prophetic warnings from believers. Right up until the time of the rapture (verses 40-41), the possibility of the return of Jesus will be rejected (cf. 2 Peter 3:3-9).

Second, Jesus' coming will be like the break-in of a thief. Jesus did not mean that His coming will be a secret event, however, as most modern evangelicals believe (see page 11). No, Jesus had just made clear that His return and the rapture would be seen by all (verses 30-31).[19] The emphasis on this verse is on its surprise to unsuspecting unbelievers. The head of the house was ignorant of the thief's impending arrival and was unprepared for it.[20] Likewise, the Apostle Paul used this same reference to the thief in 1 Thessalonians 5:4-7. There, he admonished believers to be ready for the return of Christ. If we are not looking for His return, we would be just like those in the darkness to whom Jesus would come "like a thief."

Finally, Jesus warned His servants to live as if He were coming back. Once again, the emphasis here is on the contrast between those who are ready and expecting His return and those who are not. Those servants who don't really believe He will return will be surprised when He does arrive. In fact, because these servants demonstrated their true unbelieving hearts through their actions, they will be assigned the same judgment as the rest of the unrepentant sinners (verse 51). In other words, a true Christian is one who loves Jesus and always welcomes Him into his or her world.

Summary of Christ's Chronology of the Second Coming

Now that we have put both the Matthew and Luke passages together, we have a complete picture of Christ's chronology of the end-time events. Using this outline, we can now place all other prophetic Scriptures into this coherent and understandable order:

A. The judgment upon the Jews and their exile from Israel in 70 AD
B. The Time of the Gentiles and the evangelization of the nations
C. The regathering and restoration of the Jews into their land
D. The Antichrist and the Abomination of Desolation
E. The signs in the sky and the wrath of God's judgment
F. The return of Christ and the resurrection and rapture
G. The admonition to believers: Be ready for Christ's return

This is Christ's picture of prophetic events. From it we can fill in most of the puzzle pieces. Since we have covered the first three points in the last two

---

[19] Perhaps this misinterpretation is what Jesus was referring to when He stated in verse 44, "for the Son of Man is coming at an hour you do not think He will." Most Christians think He is coming secretly to rapture believers away from the persecution of the Great Tribulation. We will discuss this at much greater detail in the chapter, "The Resurrection and the Rapture."

[20] It is important to understand the difference between a "secret" and a "surprise." A secret is something that is hidden from people; a surprise is something that is revealed. In this parable, the thief's deed is not secret, but the discovery of his activity was a surprise to the unsuspecting household!

chapters, we will fill in the rest of our prophetic puzzle using this chronology as our guide. Subsequent chapters will deal with the kingdom of the Antichrist, the characteristics of social and religious life in the last days, the Day of the Lord, the return of the Lord, when the rapture and resurrection will occur, and how to be ready for Christ's return.

Part Two

The Last
Evil
Empire

Chapter Five

The Antichrist

The Next Event on the Prophetic Calendar

We have put together the basic outline of events in the prophetic puzzle. What will happen next? We have learned that the two undeniable signs of Christ's imminent return are being fulfilled in our time. The Jewish people have been regathered into their ancient homeland, occupying their traditional capital, Jerusalem; and, the Great Commission is nearly complete. Only a handful of ethnic groups have yet to hear the gospel.

The next event, according to Christ's chronology, will be the appearance of the Antichrist. The beginning of the end will be heralded by the Antichrist's act of the Abomination of Desolation (Matthew 24:15). This same scenario is repeated by the Apostle Paul in Second Thessalonians:

> 1 Now we request you, brethren, with regard to the coming of our Lord Jesus Christ and our gathering together to Him, 2 that you not be quickly shaken from your composure or be disturbed either by a spirit or a message or a letter as if from us, to the effect that the day of the Lord has come. 3 Let no one in any way deceive you, for it will not come unless the apostasy comes first, and the man of lawlessness is revealed, the son of destruction…(2 Thessalonians 2:1-3; NASB).

Paul told the Thessalonian believers what would take place *before* the return of the Lord and the rapture ("the coming of our Lord Jesus Christ and our gathering together to Him"). First, he warned them about deceptive teachings on this subject. The events of the Day of the Lord will not occur until two things happened: the apostasy and the revelation of man of lawlessness. In other words, the return and rapture will take place *after* the Antichrist appears and a great falling away from Christianity takes place!

How do Dispensationalists ignore this clear chronology? They do so by translating the Greek word for "apostasy" (*apostasia*) as "departure," which they then interpret to mean "the departure of the church from earth." In the Greek language used during the Classical Period, *apostasia* occasionally had this meaning. However, Classical Greek was spoken five hundred years before Paul wrote his epistles. Paul wrote in a form of the language known as *koine*, or "common" Greek. Over time, words often fall into disuse or their meanings can change. For us to interpret the word *apostasia* using its ancient (and rare) meaning would make as much sense as trying to communicate to modern

Americans using the English of Chaucer's "Canterbury Tales." Therefore, it is highly unlikely that Paul would reach back to Classical Greek to use an obscure word for "departure" when he could more easily employ the commonly used *koine* words for "departure," *exodus* or *analusis*, instead.

Furthermore, Paul's use of the word *apostasia* was full of meaning for any person with an understanding of Jewish history. *Apostasia* was the word used by the Macabbeans to describe what many Jews did during the persecution by Antiochus Epiphanes: they apostatized from Judaism rather than fight for their faith. Therefore, it is much more certain that this was Paul's meaning here. Just as Antiochus Epiphanes (a prototype of the Antichrist) caused many to fall away from their faith, the Antichrist will cause many believers to apostatize as well.

Finally, the early church had the same understanding as Jesus and Paul. The early church fathers taught that Christians would both see the Antichrist and face his persecution. Justin Martyr wrote, "The man of apostasy [the Antichrist]...shall venture to do unlawful deeds on the earth against us the Christians..." (*Trypho*, cx). Irenaeus wrote, "And they [the ten kings] shall...give their kingdom to the beast, and put the church to flight" (*Against Heresies*, V, 26,1). In the same work, he also wrote, "But he [the Apostle John] indicates the number of the name [Antichrist, 666] now, that when this man comes we may avoid him, being aware of who he is" (*Against Heresies*, V, 30, 4).

Since it is clear from Scripture that Christians will recognize the time of the end and will meet the Antichrist, our study of this subject is more than academic. We need to know what the Antichrist will do, and what his kingdom will be like.

The Biblical Concept of "The Antichrist"

Although Christians usually refer to the end-time ruler as the "Antichrist," this term appears only four times in Scripture - all of them penned by the Apostle John. In his clearest reference to *the* Antichrist, he wrote, "Dear children, this is the last hour; and as you have heard that the Antichrist is coming, even now many antichrists have come. This is how we know it is the last hour" (1 John 2:18). In this passage, he pointed to the Antichrist as one who will come, but at the same time he referred to other "antichrists" at work in the world of his day. In fact, the other three references carry this latter meaning (c.f. 1 John 2:22; 1 John 4:3; and 2 John 7). The reason for this dual meaning is found in 1 John 4:3: "This is the spirit of the Antichrist, which you have heard is coming and even now is already in the world." The spirit of Antichrist is always in the world working to deceive and to destroy mankind. We have seen this spirit at work through world despots such as Napoleon, Stalin, and Hitler. This spirit of the Antichrist will have its full manifestation in the end-time ruler.

The term, "antichrist," comes from two Greek words: *anti* and *christos*. *Christos*, means "anointed one" or "messiah." While *anti* means "against" in our modern usage, its primary meaning in *koine* Greek was "instead of," or "in place of." Therefore, the word "antichrist" literally means "instead of Christ." A better understanding of this man's character and his appeal to the world comes from this original meaning of the word, *anti*. While the Antichrist will certainly oppose the work of Christ and His church, the world will receive him as their ruler "instead of Christ." They will turn to him as their savior "instead of Christ." They will worship him as lord "instead of Christ." He will be the devil's counterfeit messiah. All of the world's hopes, dreams, and future will be centered upon him and his kingdom, not the Kingdom of God. The world will have a choice: will mankind serve the god of this world and his temporal kingdom, or will they serve the God of the Universe and His eternal kingdom? People's choice of allegiance will clearly expose their hearts' desire.

Just as Jesus has many titles that describe His character and work, so the Antichrist is called by many other names. Daniel called him "a little horn," "beast," and "the ruler who is to come." Paul described him as "the man of lawlessness" and "the son of perdition." These terms come from the passages that clearly describe this end-time ruler and his realm: Daniel 2, 7, 9 and 12; Revelation 12-13; Matthew 24, and 2 Thessalonians 2.[21] Although these passages are few in number, they are central pieces in our prophetic puzzle. We will examine each of them, giving us a complete picture of this man's activity and character.

The End-Time Empire (Daniel 2: 1-49)

1 In the second year of his reign, Nebuchadnezzar had dreams; his mind was troubled and he could not sleep. 2 So the king summoned the magicians, enchanters, sorcerers and astrologers to tell him what he had dreamed. When they came in and stood before the king, 3 he said to them, "I have had a dream that troubles me and I want to know what it means."

4 Then the astrologers answered the king in Aramaic, "O king, live forever! Tell your servants the dream, and we will interpret it."

5 The king replied to the astrologers, "This is what I have firmly decided: If you do not tell me what my dream was and interpret it, I will have you cut into pieces and your houses turned into piles of rubble. 6 But if you tell me the dream and explain it, you will receive from me

---

[21] Some interpreters think they see references to the Antichrist in other passages, but they are so obscure or debatable that I will not deal with them here.

gifts and rewards and great honor. So tell me the dream and interpret it for me."

7 Once more they replied, "Let the king tell his servants the dream, and we will interpret it."

8 Then the king answered, "I am certain that you are trying to gain time, because you realize that this is what I have firmly decided: 9 If you do not tell me the dream, there is just one penalty for you. You have conspired to tell me misleading and wicked things, hoping the situation will change. So then, tell me the dream, and I will know that you can interpret it for me."

10 The astrologers answered the king, "There is not a man on earth who can do what the king asks! No king, however great and mighty, has ever asked such a thing of any magician or enchanter or astrologer. 11 What the king asks is too difficult. No one can reveal it to the king except the gods, and they do not live among men."

12 This made the king so angry and furious that he ordered the execution of all the wise men of Babylon. 13 So the decree was issued to put the wise men to death, and men were sent to look for Daniel and his friends to put them to death.

14 When Arioch, the commander of the king's guard, had gone out to put to death the wise men of Babylon, Daniel spoke to him with wisdom and tact. 15 He asked the king's officer, "Why did the king issue such a harsh decree?" Arch then explained the matter to Daniel. 16 At this, Daniel went in to the king and asked for time, so that he might interpret the dream for him.

17 Then Daniel returned to his house and explained the matter to his friends Hananiah, Mishael and Azariah. 18 He urged them to plead for mercy from the God of heaven concerning this mystery, so that he and his friends might not be executed with the rest of the wise men of Babylon. 19 During the night the mystery was revealed to Daniel in a vision. Then Daniel praised the God of heaven 20 and said: "Praise be to the name of God for ever and ever; wisdom and power are his. 21 He changes times and seasons; he sets up kings and deposes them. He gives wisdom to the wise and knowledge to the discerning. 22 He reveals deep and hidden things; he knows what lies in darkness, and light dwells with him. 23 I thank and praise you, O God of my fathers: You have given me wisdom and power, you have made known to me what we asked of you, you have made known to us the dream of the king."

24 Then Daniel went to Arioch, whom the king had appointed to execute the wise men of Babylon, and said to him, "Do not execute the wise men of Babylon. Take me to the king, and I will interpret his dream for him."

25 Arioch took Daniel to the king at once and said, "I have found a man among the exiles from Judah who can tell the king what his dream means."

26 The king asked Daniel (also called Belteshazzar), "Are you able to tell me what I saw in my dream and interpret it?"

27 Daniel replied, "No wise man, enchanter, magician or diviner can explain to the king the mystery he has asked about, 28 but there is a God in heaven who reveals mysteries. He has shown King Nebuchadnezzar what will happen in days to come. Your dream and the visions that passed through your mind as you lay on your bed are these:

29 "As you were lying there, O king, your mind turned to things to come, and the revealer of mysteries showed you what is going to happen. 30 As for me, this mystery has been revealed to me, not because I have greater wisdom than other living men, but so that you, O king, may know the interpretation and that you may understand what went through your mind.

31 "You looked, O king, and there before you stood a large statue— an enormous, dazzling statue, awesome in appearance. 32 The head of the statue was made of pure gold, its chest and arms of silver, its belly and thighs of bronze, 33 its legs of iron, its feet partly of iron and partly of baked clay. 34 While you were watching, a rock was cut out, but not by human hands. It struck the statue on its feet of iron and clay and smashed them. 35 Then the iron, the clay, the bronze, the silver and the gold were broken to pieces at the same time and became like chaff on a threshing floor in the summer. The wind swept them away without leaving a trace. But the rock that struck the statue became a huge mountain and filled the whole earth.

36 "This was the dream, and now we will interpret it to the king. 37 You, O king, are the king of kings. The God of heaven has given you dominion and power and might and glory; 38 in your hands he has placed mankind and the beasts of the field and the birds of the air. Wherever they live, he has made you ruler over them all. You are that head of gold.

39 7"After you, another kingdom will rise, inferior to yours. Next, a third kingdom, one of bronze, will rule over the whole earth. 40 Finally, there will be a fourth kingdom, strong as iron—for iron breaks and smashes everything—and as iron breaks things to pieces, so it will crush and break all the others. 41 Just as you saw that the feet and toes were partly of baked clay and partly of iron, so this will be a divided kingdom; yet it will have some of the strength of iron in it, even as you saw iron mixed with clay. 42 As the toes were partly iron and partly clay, so this kingdom will be partly strong and partly brittle. 43 And just as you saw

the iron mixed with baked clay, so the people will be a mixture and will not remain united, any more than iron mixes with clay.

44 "In the time of those kings, the God of heaven will set up a kingdom that will never be destroyed, nor will it be left to another people. It will crush all those kingdoms and bring them to an end, but it will itself endure forever. 45 This is the meaning of the vision of the rock cut out of a mountain, but not by human hands—a rock that broke the iron, the bronze, the clay, the silver and the gold to pieces. "The great God has shown the king what will take place in the future. The dream is true and the interpretation is trustworthy."

46 Then King Nebuchadnezzar fell prostrate before Daniel and paid him honor and ordered that an offering and incense be presented to him. 47 The king said to Daniel, "Surely your God is the God of gods and the Lord of kings and a revealer of mysteries, for you were able to reveal this mystery."

48 Then the king placed Daniel in a high position and lavished many gifts on him. He made him ruler over the entire province of Babylon and placed him in charge of all its wise men. 49 Moreover, at Daniel's request the king appointed Shadrach, Meshach and Abednego administrators over the province of Babylon, while Daniel himself remained at the royal court.

Daniel was one of the first of the Jews to be taken to Babylon by King Nebuchadnezzar. He and his friends were of royal, or noble blood (Daniel 1:1-3). Although they were to be trained for the king's service in his administration, their presence in Babylon was also intended to help keep Nebuchadnezzar's puppet government in Jerusalem in line.

Nebuchadnezzar's reign over Babylon had scarcely begun by this time. He had assumed the throne after his father, Nabopolassar, died. According to Babylonian accounts, Nabopolassar was a man of humble origins. Since he was not from the ruling aristocracy, there undoubtedly was a great deal of envy and jealousy among those who formally held power. Knowing this, one can understand Nebuchadnezzar's suspicion of his counselors and advisors.

In the second year of his reign, King Nebuchadnezzar had some dreams that greatly troubled him. He discerned that their origin was from the spiritual realm. Therefore, he called upon his advisors, the magicians and sorcerers who had served the royal court under his father's reign to help him. This dream also gave him an opportunity to test both their abilities and their loyalties. He demanded that they tell him his dream and its correct interpretation. If they failed to do so, he would have all of these counselors killed and he would start over with new ones. The conjurors, magicians, sorcerers, and Chaldeans were unable to solve this mystery, saying only the gods could give such an answer. So, they were sentenced to death.

Though Daniel and his friends did not practice occultic arts, they were listed as among the wise men in service of the king. Therefore, they were also rounded up for the same punishment. When he heard of the reason for their fate, Daniel appealed for time to solve the king's challenge. After praying with his friends, the Lord revealed both the king's dream and its correct interpretation.

Daniel was ushered into the king's presence, where he declared that "there is a God in heaven who reveals mysteries, and He has made known to King Nebuchadnezzar what will take place *in the latter days*" (Daniel 2:28, NASB). Literally, the Hebrew for "latter days" is even more specific, meaning "the end of the days." What Daniel was about to reveal would have its fulfillment in the last days.

Daniel proceeded to repeat the king's dream. He had dreamt of a large statue, the head of which was cast of gold, its breast and arms of silver, its belly and thighs of bronze, and its legs of iron, and its feet a mixture of iron and clay. In the dream, Nebuchadnezzar saw a stone, fashioned without the use of human hands, which struck the statue at its feet. This small stone caused the whole statue to fall, crushing every part of its form into such small particles that they blew away. Meanwhile, the stone grew to become a huge mountain that filled the entire earth (Daniel 2:31-35).

This dream is an example of the apocalyptic style of prophecy. The future is given in the form of a picture. Just as Nebuchadnezzar could not understand or interpret the picture without an accurate God-given interpretation, neither can we. However, the Bible reveals to us those parts of the picture's interpretation we need to know. In this case, God revealed the picture's meaning immediately.

First, Daniel assured King Nebuchadnezzar that the almighty God had given the entire kingdom into his dominion (Daniel 2:36-38). His was the head of gold. It is interesting in light of Nebuchadnezzar's own future, that God told him that his rule included that of the "beasts of the field" (verse 38), for that is where his proud response to this dream would lead him.

Nevertheless, Babylon's golden rule would be followed by a series of other kingdoms of lessor value. Two subsequent kingdoms, composed of silver and bronze, would each rule over the earth in turn (Daniel 2:39).

Next, a kingdom that was of the least intrinsic value would follow them: one made only of iron. This iron kingdom is described in greater length and detail than all the others. It would "crush and shatter" all the previous kingdoms into pieces (verse 40).

Finally, Daniel described the last part of the statue: the feet of iron and clay. The feet are related to the legs in that they are partially composed of iron, but they are weak appendages in that they had the brittleness of baked clay pottery. Whereas the kingdom of the iron legs had great power in order to crush all opposition, the clay feet only appeared strong. Daniel's revelation of this final kingdom shows that the empire's people will only appear to be unified. They will not adhere to one another any more than iron and pottery do.

However, this kingdom's rule will ultimately be crushed and shattered by a rock "cut out, but not by human hands." This rock will strike the statue at its feet, crushing and pulverizing it into particles so fine that it will blow away. In its place, the rock will grow to become a mountain that will encompass the whole earth.

We know from the context of this revelation that the kingdom of gold was the Babylonian Empire. History identifies the remaining kingdoms. The silver arms and chest is the Medo-Persian Empire, which conquered Babylon. The belly and thighs represent the Grecian Empire, which arose when Alexander the Great conquered the world. The Greek Empire succumbed to the Romans who, interestingly, used iron as a symbolic description of their strength and power.

It was during the rule of the Roman Empire that a small, seemingly insignificant event occurred in a manger in Bethlehem of Judea. The virgin-born Son of God grew up to be "the stone the builders rejected" (Matthew 21:42). Christ was the "rock," whose appearance was not called into existence by the act of humanity, but by the will of God. He came, announcing the advent of a new empire, the Kingdom of God. In one sense, this new empire has already encompassed the whole earth, in that its subjects are now counted from every tribe and nation. But in another sense, the Kingdom of God will not be complete until Christ returns to put an end to the kingdoms of this world.

Just as Christ's rule will be fully established through two stages (His first and second advents), so the end-time empire to which He comes also has two manifestations. Daniel's interpretation of the dream described a strong, powerful empire and a similar, but weaker empire. The legs were of iron, but its feet were of iron and clay. In this apocalyptic vision, history progresses as we move downward on the statue's body. We can conclude that the feet and toes represent the latter part of the iron kingdom's influence. We see here that the "rock" will strike the statue in its feet, at the last manifestation of the iron kingdom's rule. Jesus came to earth the first time during the rule of the kingdom of iron; He will return to rule forever during a second manifestation of that iron-like kingdom.

This apocalyptic picture accurately portrayed the future of mankind. These four kingdoms did arise. The fourth kingdom, the Roman Empire, still influences modern civilization. But Daniel has much more to say about the nature of this fourth kingdom, as well as its final ruler.

The End-Time Ruler (Daniel 7: 1-28)

1   In the first year of Belshazzar king of Babylon, Daniel had a dream, and visions passed through his mind as he was lying on his bed. He wrote down the substance of his dream.

2   Daniel said: "In my vision at night I looked, and there before me were the four winds of heaven churning up the great sea. 3   Four great beasts, each different from the others, came up out of the sea.

4   "The first was like a lion, and it had the wings of an eagle. I watched until its wings were torn off and it was lifted from the ground so that it stood on two feet like a man, and the heart of a man was given to it.

5   "And there before me was a second beast, which looked like a bear. It was raised up on one of its sides, and it had three ribs in its mouth between its teeth. It was told, 'Get up and eat your fill of flesh!'

6   "After that, I looked, and there before me was another beast, one that looked like a leopard. And on its back it had four wings like those of a bird. This beast had four heads, and it was given authority to rule.

7   "After that, in my vision at night I looked, and there before me was a fourth beast—terrifying and frightening and very powerful. It had large iron teeth; it crushed and devoured its victims and trampled underfoot whatever was left. It was different from all the former beasts, and it had ten horns.

8   "While I was thinking about the horns, there before me was another horn, a little one, which came up among them; and three of the first horns were uprooted before it. This horn had eyes like the eyes of a man and a mouth that spoke boastfully.

9   "As I looked, "thrones were set in place, and the Ancient of Days took his seat. His clothing was as white as snow; the hair of his head was white like wool. His throne was flaming with fire, and its wheels were all ablaze. 10   A river of fire was flowing, coming out from before him. Thousands upon thousands attended him; ten thousand times ten thousand stood before him. The court was seated, and the books were opened.

11   "Then I continued to watch because of the boastful words the horn was speaking. I kept looking until the beast was slain and its body destroyed and thrown into the blazing fire. 12   (The other beasts had been stripped of their authority, but were allowed to live for a period of time.)

13   "In my vision at night I looked, and there before me was one like a son of man, coming with the clouds of heaven. He approached the Ancient of Days and was led into his presence. 14   He was given

authority, glory and sovereign power; all peoples, nations and men of every language worshiped him. His dominion is an everlasting dominion that will not pass away, and his kingdom is one that will never be destroyed.

15 "I, Daniel, was troubled in spirit, and the visions that passed through my mind disturbed me. 16 I approached one of those standing there and asked him the true meaning of all this.

"So he told me and gave me the interpretation of these things: 17 'The four great beasts are four kingdoms that will rise from the earth. 18 But the saints of the Most High will receive the kingdom and will possess it forever—yes, for ever and ever.'

19 "Then I wanted to know the true meaning of the fourth beast, which was different from all the others and most terrifying, with its iron teeth and bronze claws—the beast that crushed and devoured its victims and trampled underfoot whatever was left. 20 I also wanted to know about the ten horns on its head and about the other horn that came up, before which three of them fell—the horn that looked more imposing than the others and that had eyes and a mouth that spoke boastfully. 21 As I watched, this horn was waging war against the saints and defeating them, 22 until the Ancient of Days came and pronounced judgment in favor of the saints of the Most High, and the time came when they possessed the kingdom.

23 "He gave me this explanation: 'The fourth beast is a fourth kingdom that will appear on earth. It will be different from all the other kingdoms and will devour the whole earth, trampling it down and crushing it. 24 The ten horns are ten kings who will come from this kingdom. After them another king will arise, different from the earlier ones; he will subdue three kings. 25 He will speak against the Most High and oppress his saints and try to change the set times and the laws. The saints will be handed over to him for a time, times and half a time.

26 "'But the court will sit, and his power will be taken away and completely destroyed forever. 27 Then the sovereignty, power and greatness of the kingdoms under the whole heaven will be handed over to the saints, the people of the Most High. His kingdom will be an everlasting kingdom, and all rulers will worship and obey him.'

28 "This is the end of the matter. I, Daniel, was deeply troubled by my thoughts, and my face turned pale, but I kept the matter to myself."

Daniel's description of the four world kingdoms occurred in the early years of his service to King Nebuchadnezzar. Much later in life, Daniel received further revelation concerning them. He had a dream which greatly distressed him, in much the same way that Nebuchadnezzar was disturbed by the content of his dream about the end-times. Just as Nebuchadnezzar's dream outlined the history of human empires, so this dream followed the same course. There are enough similarities in this vision's imagery with Nebuchadnezzar's dream that we can conclude that they are meant to complement one another

In this dream, Daniel saw four beasts, coming up out of the sea. The first was like a winged lion. Its wings were plucked out and it was lifted up from the ground and made to stand on two feet. This beast was then given a human heart. Here, Daniel's dream described the Babylonian kingdom and Nebuchadnezzar's life. The national symbol of the Babylonian kingdom was a lion with wings on its back. This symbol can still be seen at the ruins of ancient Babylon. The Book of Daniel tells us what happened to Nebuchadnezzar after his dream. In addition to erecting a golden statue of a man, in honor of his "golden" rulership, he lifted himself up in the arrogance of his power and accomplishments. Although he was warned by Daniel of the consequences of pride, he continued in this attitude until God struck him with madness. He crawled around like an animal for a period of seven years (probably protected from public disclosure by his close advisors). At the end of this time, he repented in humility and recognized the Lord as the true ruler over all. In response, God returned his senses to him. It may be that King Nebuchadnezzar experienced salvation from the Lord (see Daniel 4).

The second beast was described as a bear, raised up and with three ribs crushed in its mouth. Following Nebuchadnezzar's death, several Babylonian kings reigned in short successions. Babylon's last king was known as Nabonidus. After stabilizing his rule, Nabonidus, for some reason, decided to live in the city of Tema rather than Babylon. He set up his son, Belshazzar as co-regent. For this reason, Daniel recognized Belshazzar as the last king of Babylon. While Nabonidus was out of direct government affairs, Cyrus II began his rise to power. He was the king of Anshan, a vassal state of Astyages, the ruler of Media. The first "rib" Cyrus crushed was Media. Having conquered Astyages, he became heir to the Medo-Persian Empire. Three years later he devoured Croesus, the king of Lydia, thereby gaining control of Asia Minor. Finally, he attacked Babylon in 539 BC. His army engineers diverted the Euphrates River several miles upstream, enabling his troops to march under the city walls in the dry riverbed. He crushed the third "rib" with hardly a fight, and conquered the mighty Babylonian Empire.[22]

The third beast Daniel described was a leopard with four wings like a bird. This beast is then shown as also having four heads. Here we see one of the characteristics of Jewish apocalyptic style: fluid shifts in imagery. The changing

---

[22] The Jewish historian, Josephus, wrote that Cyrus read where Isaiah the prophet had prophesied about his rise to power some 140 years before his time (Isaiah 44:27-45:7). He was so impressed that the God of the Jews called him by name that he freed them from their captivity and assisted them in resettling in their land!

pictures describe various aspects of this empire. We know from history that the next empire to arise after Persia was from Macedonia, under the rulership of Alexander the Great. With leopard-like speed and agility, his armies conquered the entire civilized world in just a few short years.

Alexander's father, Philip, had succeeded in uniting Greece through conquest in 338 BC. He instilled in his son a love and admiration for Hellenistic culture. When Philip defeated the Greeks, he reorganized their armies and combined them with his Macedonian troops. He than began to plan an invasion of the mighty Persian Empire in Asia Minor. However, he was murdered shortly before the invasion was to begin.

Alexander was only twenty years old when he ascended his father's throne in the year 336 BC. After putting down internal rivalries and revolts, he left the Macedonian capital of Pella in April, 334 BC with an army of 35,000 men. He never returned. He defeated the first Persian army in Asia Minor and continued his conquest south, taking the city of Tyre in January, 332 BC. By November of 332 BC he conquered Egypt without a fight. In 331 BC, Alexander marched through Mesopotamia to defeat the Persian ruler, Darius, at Gaugamela. He continued on through Persia, reaching the Hyphasis river at the border of India in the summer of 326 BC. There, his army refused to go further. It is reported that Alexander sat down and wept, because there were no other realms to conquer. Three years later, at the age of 33, Alexander died in the city of Babylon.

Alexander did not appoint any heir to his throne. As he was dying, his generals asked him who be his successor. He responded that the kingdom would go to the strongest. For the next twenty years his generals competed for power. Finally, they agreed to divide the kingdom into four realms, as Daniel foresaw.

In just 13 years, Alexander accomplished not only the conquest of many diverse nations and cultures, but succeeded in uniting them under the culture of Greece. Alexander learned his military prowess through his father, but he learned to love and appreciate the superiority of the Greek culture through his tutor, Aristotle. As Alexander conquered territories, he established colonies and built cities modeled after those in Greece. Usually, he was hailed as a liberator, not a conqueror. In Egypt, he crowned himself Pharaoh and established the new city of Alexandria where Greek culture and learning were introduced and spread throughout the world. In Babylon, he was venerated because he revived their former institutions. In Persia, he was worshipped as a god. People saw his rule as the gateway of a new world, espousing the common civilization, culture, and language of Greece. So great was Grecian influence that this period of time was known as the "Hellenistic Age."

As we shall see in the Book of Revelation, the end-time ruler will embody many of the elements of previous rulers and empires (Revelation 13:2). In this respect, Alexander's conquests and rule provides us with some interesting clues to some of the attributes of the Antichrist.

Like Alexander, the Antichrist's rise to power will be rapid (2 Thessalonians 2:3 says that he will be "revealed," or "uncovered" to the world). Second, he will unite the world by political skill, intrigue, and, if necessary, overwhelming force. Third, he will unite the world under one government. Fourth, he will be seen as savior by the peoples and will desire to be worshipped as such. Finally, he will accomplish his feats even though he is still only a young man.[23]

The last beast Daniel saw is described as a horrible, dreadful and exceedingly strong one, with large iron teeth. It crushed and devoured all those who were before it. Once again, the apocalyptic picture Daniel gave us is fluid and it describes a development over time. The Roman Empire truly "crushed and devoured" its enemies. Rome ruled with an iron fist.

But just as the leopard had four heads, which were the four kingdoms evolving out of Alexander's empire, so this beast has ten horns coming up out of its head. In Jewish understanding, a horn represents power or rulership. It is a good assumption that these ten horns represent ten rulers who will arise out of this beast's empire.

This passage is clearly giving us a further development of the puzzle pieces describing the end-time ruler's kingdom, his actions, and his ultimate judgment.

While Daniel was pondering the meaning of the last beast and its horns, he saw another horn, a little one, arise against the ten and pull out three of them by their roots (Daniel 7:8). He described this small horn as having eyes like a man and a mouth that uttered great boastful words.

While this little horn was exalting himself, Daniel saw the Lord take His seat in preparation for the judgment. Just as Revelation 20:4 shows us that many thrones will be set up at the time of judgment, here we see them being set up before the Lord's presence. Likewise, Revelation tells us of the Books of Judgment being opened at that time, so we see those Books opened here (Daniel 7:10).

Daniel's attention was drawn back to the insolent little horn that kept boasting against the Almighty. He then saw its judgment: it was killed and its body was thrown into the burning fire (Daniel 7:11). Once again, we see similarities in this judgment with the one planned for the beast and the false prophet in the Book of Revelation. There, they are slain and thrown into the Lake of Fire (Revelation 19:20).

Again, what happened next in Daniel's vision seems to parallel the events in the Book of Revelation. The other beasts (the three other empires Daniel had seen represented by different animals) were allowed to continue for "an appointed period of time" (Daniel 7:12). We see in the Book of Revelation that

---

[23] Admittedly the following is conjecture, but just as Alexander conquered the entire world by the time he was 33, Jesus also conquered the kingdom of this world by that age. Will the devil try to mimic Jesus with a young Antichrist?

after the kingdom of the Antichrist is destroyed and he is thrown into the Lake of Fire, the peoples of the earth will continue to live on earth under the dominion of Christ and the resurrected saints (Revelation 20:1-10). This period of time is known to us as "The Millennium,"which will be described in a later chapter.

Daniel was still disturbed by these night visions. He continued watching them and saw "one like a Son of Man" who was presented before the Lord, standing before the "Ancient of Days." This "Son of Man" was given eternal authority over all peoples and nations - a kingdom that will never end (Daniel 7:13-14). Jesus used this same title to describe who He was. He quoted this passage in the Olivet Discourse, as recorded in Matthew 24:30: "And then the sign of the Son of Man will appear in the sky, and then all the tribes of the earth will mourn, and they will see the Son of Man coming on the clouds of the sky with power and great glory." He quoted the same passage again when He was being tried by the high priest. There was no doubt in the high priest's mind about who Jesus was claiming to be: "Then the high priest tore his robes and said, 'He has blasphemed! What further need do we have of witnesses? Behold, you have now heard the blasphemy!'" (Matthew 26:65; NASB).

Still seeking understanding, Daniel asked what this all meant (Daniel 7:15-16). An angel (we assume this from the context) told him that the four beasts represented four kings who would arise from the earth. (Daniel 7:23 tells us that the interpretation of the image of a beast can also stand for the kingdom over which they rule. In fact, the Hebrew word for "king" is interchangeable for the word "kingdom." Its translation depends upon the context.) After being assured that God's kingdom will triumph and that the saints of the kingdom will receive and possess that kingdom forever (Daniel 7:18), Daniel wanted to know more about the dreadful beast with the iron teeth, as well as the meaning of the little, boastful horn.

In answer to these queries, Daniel saw that the little horn was waging war against the saints of God and overpowering them (v.21). This is the first clear indication in Scripture that the time of the Day of the Lord will be exceedingly difficult for God's people. Unfortunately for end-time saints, this theme keeps recurring throughout God's subsequent revelation. There is no ambiguity about it in the Bible: the saints will suffer such widespread persecution that it will seem that the people of God have been beaten. Jesus called this time of the Antichrist's persecution "the Great Tribulation." Jesus also spoke of this time of darkness when He said in John 9:4, "We must work the works of Him who sent Me, as long as it is day; night is coming, when no man can work" (NASB).

Although we joyfully anticipate the return of Christ, we also need to be realistic about the difficulties those who live during that time will have to endure. In one of his visions, the apostle John was told to eat a scroll on which was written the events of the end. It was sweet in his mouth, but turned bitter in his stomach (Revelation 10:9-10). Likewise, we look forward to that Final Day with both a sweet expectation and an apprehensive dread.

The Book of Revelation is quite clear in its description of the persecution of the saints by the Antichrist. "He was given power to make war against the saints and to conquer them...If anyone is to go into captivity, into captivity he will go. If anyone is to be killed with the sword, with the sword he will be killed. This calls for patient endurance and faithfulness on the part of the saints" (Revelation 13:7,10). Admittedly, the picture we are examining is not a pretty one. No one likes to suffer. No one likes to hear discouraging reports. We search for ways not to believe the messenger of bad news. But the Bible is clear: just as Jesus suffered in the flesh at the hands of God's enemies, the Body of Christ will suffer at the hands of the devil's henchman. The good news is just as Christ rose victoriously to claim His Kingdom, so the church - the Body of Christ - will be resurrected into victory with new bodies fit for eternal rule!

This victorious stance is repeated to Daniel in verse 22: the Ancient of Days came and rendered judgment against the little horn, giving the Kingdom to the saints!

The details of the little horn's reign are given in verses 23 to 25. Ten kingdoms (symbolized by the ten horns) will arise out of the kingdom of the fourth beast. These ten horns remind us of the ten toes spoken of earlier in Nebuchadnezzar's dream. These ten toes were part of the latter part of the reign of the fourth kingdom symbolized by the statue. Therefore, what we are about to discover is more detail in the prophetic picture of the last-days kingdom.

To try to identify each of the nations or empires that the ten horns represent is pure conjecture - not enough information is given here or elsewhere in Scripture. All we know is that these kings or kingdoms will arise out of the dreadful and powerful fourth kingdom. For this reason, most interpreters believe that the center of the Antichrist's kingdom will be in Europe. Others see the empire arising out of the oil-rich Muslim world in the Near East (which was also a part of the Roman Empire). We do know that these ten kingdoms will still be in existence when the little horn rises to power. We know this fact because these verses tell us that the little horn will subdue three of the other horns, hence, they must be in existence at the same time.

The little horn's realm will, in some respects, encompass the entire world. We have learned from Daniel 2 that this realm will include all nations, but that it will not have an internal adhesion. In other words, it will appear to be strong and cohesive, but will not be able to remain united under pressure. We see from other Scriptures that the kingdom of the Antichrist is one that is very strong militarily. The whole world will be afraid to rebel against his rule because of the threat of retaliation. (Revelation 13:4 asks, "Who can make war against him?)

Very important information about the activities of the little horn is found in Daniel 7:25. His opposition to the things of the Lord will not only cause him to blaspheme God and persecute the church, but it will extend into the political, economic, and social structure of society. The first advent of Christ has been considered the most important event of human history.   Its influence has permeated throughout the entire world.   This is reflected in our calendar. Although some societies still use other dating systems, the entire world recognizes the Christian calendar as the international standard. Is it any wonder that the Antichrist would seek to change this standard system, which records every year with the words, *anno domini* - "in the year of our Lord?"[24]

Another aspect of social and political life the little horn will attempt to change is the system of law. As we will see when we examine one of the Antichrist's other titles, the "lawless one," mentioned in 2 Thessalonians 2, he will attempt to change the whole basis upon which law in society is founded. Once again, it is important to note that he will not succeed completely in accomplishing all his goals as mentioned here in Daniel 7:25. But in his attempts to bring about the complete restructuring of time and law he will persecute and ridicule the old order.

Finally, Daniel 7:25 gives us the length of time the persecution of the Antichrist will last. The saints will be under his power for "a time, times, and a half of time." This phrase is repeated several times in Scripture, three times in Daniel alone. We will examine it and more of the political intrigues of the Great Tribulation in the next passage, Daniel 9:20-27.

Despite the repeated warnings about the persecution of the saints in this passage, there are more encouraging words for those who have to endure that time. Verses 26 and 27 again repeat the fact that God will judge the insolent little horn. He will be destroyed forever. And when he is vanquished, the saints will be given the everlasting Kingdom of God. All rule, power, authority, and dominion will belong to the eternal Son of Man, Jesus Christ!

The Last Seven Years of This Age (Daniel 9: 20-27)

20 While I was speaking and praying, confessing my sin and the sin of my people Israel and making my request to the LORD my God for his

---

[24] We remember the cost and complexities involved in fixing the "Millennium Bug." This computer problem originated when programmers shortened the enumeration of the "year of our Lord" into just two digits, rather than the full four digits. But since the cost of changing over to the full four digits was so expensive and time consuming, it is difficult to imagine the world ever trying to change the dating system again, once programmers have already fixed it! It is possible that the Antichrist may not try to redo the whole system, but will adopt a calendar system which would operate concurrently. Or, he could simply insist upon using the designation, "CE" meaning "Common Era" as so many archeologists are doing today. Daniel says that he will only "try" to change the times, not necessarily that he would succeed in doing so.

holy hill—21 while I was still in prayer, Gabriel, the man I had seen in the earlier vision, came to me in swift flight about the time of the evening sacrifice. 22 He instructed me and said to me, "Daniel, I have now come to give you insight and understanding. 23 As soon as you began to pray, an answer was given, which I have come to tell you, for you are highly esteemed. Therefore, consider the message and understand the vision:

24 "Seventy 'sevens' are decreed for your people and your holy city to finish transgression, to put an end to sin, to atone for wickedness, to bring in everlasting righteousness, to seal up vision and prophecy and to anoint the most holy. 25 "Know and understand this: From the issuing of the decree to restore and rebuild Jerusalem until the Anointed One, the ruler, comes, there will be seven 'sevens,' and sixty-two 'sevens.' It will be rebuilt with streets and a trench, but in times of trouble. 26 After the sixty-two 'sevens,' the Anointed One will be cut off and will have nothing. The people of the ruler who will come will destroy the city and the sanctuary. The end will come like a flood: War will continue until the end, and desolation's have been decreed. 27 He will confirm a covenant with many for one 'seven.' In the middle of the 'seven' he will put an end to sacrifice and offering. And on a wing [of the temple] he will set up an abomination that causes desolation, until the end that is decreed is poured out on him." (NASB)

We have already examined this passage in terms of its fulfillment in the first coming of Christ. We showed that the only interpretation of the Hebrew concept of the "sevens" which made historical sense was that they were literal numbers of years. We saw that Jesus came exactly 483 Jewish years after the decree to rebuild Jerusalem had been issued. This leaves us the remaining seven-year period that has yet to be fulfilled.

Furthermore, we saw that this prophecy would be fulfilled over time. In other words, there was going to be period of time between the fulfillment of the 483 years and the final seven-year period. We know this from the context: verse 26 states that the city of Jerusalem and the temple would be destroyed, but verse 27, which describes the time period of the last "seven" has the temple rebuilt and offerings being given.

What new picture does this puzzle piece give to us about the nature and character of the rule of the Antichrist?

First, it identifies him as being part of the same empire that crucified Jesus. Note verse 26: the Messiah would be killed by "the people of the ruler who will come." We have seen that Jesus came during the reign of the fourth beast, the kingdom of iron. The ruling people of this empire were the Romans. Therefore, the "ruler who will come" will in some way be related to the kingdom of the

Roman Empire. Now, this fact only narrows our focus. We do not have to look for the Antichrist to come forth from any other nation except one that had been a part of the Roman Empire. However, the Roman Empire stretched from England to Mesopotamia and from Germany to North Africa. Therefore, this "ruler who will come" will arise out of this geographical region. Many scholars are convinced that he will arise out of Europe, as that was the center of the Roman Empire. But at this point, we cannot say this with absolute certainty.

Second, this picture tells about the world political situation in the era of the Antichrist. The "ruler who will come" will begin the last seven-year period of Jewish history with a "covenant" made between nations, probably in the form of a peace treaty. We cannot assume, however, that his reign in power will begin at that same time. The Bible is only identifying for us when the last seven-year period for the Jews will begin, not the actual beginning of the reign of the Antichrist. We know from Daniel 7 that he will consolidate his worldwide power by overthrowing three other major rulers. But we do not have enough information to identify just how or how long his ultimate ascension to world dominion will take place.

Nevertheless, the Antichrist's crowning achievement for the world political system will be the introduction of world peace. The world has always longed for "peace on earth, good will toward men." Jesus offered this peace through the introduction of His kingdom, the Kingdom of God. However, the world has had plenty of opportunities to receive Christ's peace - and the offer has been rejected. Instead, people want their own kingdom, based upon their own notions of good and evil. As we will see, the revelation of the Antichrist will come when Sin comes to its fruition, without God's restraining power upon it.

In what way will this "human" peace come? Daniel tells us here: a covenant will be made between Israel and the ruler. Since I have already shown that we are in the last days, and that those days began when Jerusalem was "no longer trodden under foot by the Gentiles," we can look at modern Middle Eastern politics in the light of the prophetic Scriptures. The Book of Zechariah and the Book of Revelation both describe the world's consternation and anguish over the nation of Israel in the end-times. In the same prophetic passage that declares the return of the Jews to their Messiah, when they will "look on me, the one they have pierced," Zechariah described Jerusalem as "an immovable rock for all the nations. All who try to move it will injure themselves" (Zechariah 12:3).

The current problems in the Middle East are unsolvable. The Jews claim that the land is theirs by historical and theological rights. It was given to Abraham, they dwelt in it for over fifteen hundred years, and they won it back after World War II at the price of six million victims of the Holocaust. Jerusalem is their city. It is the site of their holiest place. However, millions of Palestinians and their Arab neighbors strongly dispute the Jews' claim to the land, especially their occupation of the old city of Jerusalem. They have lived in the land for over fifteen hundred years. Jerusalem is one of their holiest cities, as well. Although Israel now holds the stronger hand militarily, the Palestinians will not willingly cede their rights to the Jews.

The Middle East is a dangerous political quagmire. Leaders who have tried to solve the dilemma are often targeted themselves by the warring parties. Anwar Sadat, Yitzack Rabin, and Count Bernadotte are just a few of the many who have been assassinated trying to bring about a compromise for peace. Israel is currently pursuing a policy of trading land for peace. Anwar Sadat, Menachem Begin, and Jimmy Carter worked out a separate peace treaty between Egypt and Israel. In return for its recognition of Israel's right to exist, Egypt received back the Sinai Peninsula, captured by Israel in the 1967 Six-Day War. The Palestinians, under Yassar Arafat, are being granted a measure of self-rule in the Gaza Strip and parts of the West Bank of the Jordan River, with the long-term goal of a separate Palestinian state.

The status of the city of Jerusalem makes these peace efforts pointless. Neither side is willing to give up their claim to an inch of the city's land. And without an acceptable settlement, conflict is inevitable. The 1973 Arab-Israeli War taught the industrialized nations that any problem in the Middle East affects the whole world. When the Arab oil producing nations shut off their oil to the West in solidarity with their Arab brothers in the conflict, the world economy suffered the worst recession since the Great Depression.[25]

The Antichrist will broker a political deal that will appear to solve the problem once and for all. Amazingly, the Bible seems to describe just what the solution will be, if we look at all those puzzle pieces having to do with this last seven years of human history. The solution is hinted at in this passage. We read that "the people of the ruler who will come" will destroy the city and the temple. This happened when the Roman army captured Jerusalem in 70 AD. However, the next verse tells us that the "ruler who will come" will broker a covenant that will last three and one half years - the middle of the seven-year period. At that time, he will put an end to the sacrifices and offerings. We have already seen that this act is called elsewhere in Scripture "the Abomination of Desolation." Therefore, we have to conclude that the Jewish temple will be rebuilt in order for the Antichrist to commit this act of desecration!

How can the Jews rebuild their temple, given today's political and religious climate in the Middle East? Such an act would surely spark a major Arab/Israeli war! Yet the Bible is clear: the temple will be in existence in the last days. Jesus spoke of the Abomination of Desolation taking place in the city of Jerusalem (Matthew 24). Paul spoke of the man of lawlessness taking his seat in the temple and declaring himself God (2 Thessalonians 2:4). And, the Book of Revelation

---

[25] It was the fear of another economic disaster that prompted the United States and the rest of her allies to go to war with Iraq after Saddam Hussein invaded Kuwait in 1990.

describes a rebuilt temple, during the ministry of two powerful prophets in the last forty-two months (Revelation 11:1-13).

Since these puzzle pieces concerning the last day's temple obviously are referring to the same events, we can look at them closely and discover some interesting facts. The passage in chapter 11 of the Book of Revelation gives us some fascinating details about this end-times temple. John was told to measure the temple. He found that it was not complete. The outer court could not be built because it had been "given to the Gentiles" (Revelation 11:2). Why would the Jews, who have just regained the city in 1967 from the nearly 1,900 years of Gentile-domination, give back the city (or at least the Temple Mount) to the Gentiles when the temple is rebuilt?

One way to reconcile these seemingly conflicting Scriptures (and not go into meaningless symbolism) is the following scenario. We have already seen that real, lasting peace in modern Israel cannot be achieved until the status of Jerusalem is settled. However, Jerusalem is the holiest city on earth, with sacred sites for Jews, Muslims, and Christians. The Jews and the Muslims will fight to the death should their claims on the city be taken away. Who will rule the city, the Jews or the Muslims? The answer the Antichrist will propose is this: *neither*! Since the city is sacred for the people of the whole world, the city will become an international city, under the administration of the world governing body (such as the United Nations).[26]

And what guarantee will Israel have that her rights to the city will never be violated again? The Antichrist will allow the Jewish people to rebuild their temple on the Temple Mount. This will be the international recognition of their right to exist in peace with their Muslim neighbors.[27] Once all factions agree upon this covenant, the world will enjoy the peace and assurance of prosperity it so longs for. The Middle Eastern powderkeg will be defused! The leader who brought all the parties together will be hailed as a hero - no, a savior!

One of the major obstacles for the rebuilding of the Jewish temple on the Temple Mount is the traditional site for the temple is now occupied by the Islamic holy shrine, the Dome on the Rock. It cannot be removed without a major religious war. The Temple Mount measures approximately 45 acres in extent. It lies topographically just below the peak of Jerusalem ridge system

---

[26] This solution has already been proposed as far back as the original partition between Israel and Palestine in 1948!

[27] This will also be in answer to a prayer from the Jewish Prayer Book: "Because of our sins we were exiled from our country and banished from our land. We cannot go up as pilgrims to worship Thee, to perform our duties in Thy chosen house, the great and Holy Temple which was called by Thy name, on account of the hand that was let loose on Thy sanctuary. May it be Thy will, Lord our God and God of our fathers, merciful King, in Thy abundant love again to have mercy on us and on Thy sanctuary; rebuild it speedily and magnify its glory."

known as Mount Moriah. Mount Moriah is the same place where Abraham was told to sacrifice his son, Isaac (Genesis 22:1-2). Both the First and Second Temples were built on the same foundations, at the same location somewhere on the Temple Mount. The new temple, therefore, has to be built upon the same foundation. Furthermore, the original site had to be on consecrated ground that had not been previously used for tombs and that had not been used as for pagan worship. Since the site of the first temples had to be so consecrated, the new temple cannot be built on the same site as the Dome on the Rock, because it would be considered a "pagan" house of worship! Obviously, another alternative must be found.

Some archeologists who have been studying the Temple Mount since Israel regained the city in 1967 think they have found some possible solutions to this problem. Although the traditional site of the Jewish Temple is now occupied by the Dome on the Rock, these archeologists have found rather convincing proof that the original temple was not on that same site after all. However, the archeologists are still disputing the exact location. Some put it about three hundred feet north of the Dome on the Rock, while other arguments are being made for a location to the south of the Muslim structure. However, either location has enough room to build a Jewish temple. But neither location has enough room for the outer Court of the Gentiles because of the proximity of the Muslim places of worship![28]

Many Jews in Israel today are praying for and working toward the rebuilding of their temple. While some sincerely believe that the temple cannot be rebuilt by anyone but the Messiah, others, who are part of the Jewish "Temple Mount Faithful Movement" are already preparing. The temple designs have been drawn; the implements and tools have been crafted; the priests are recruited and trained; and some parts of the building are said to have been prefabricated. Many of these people were greatly encouraged when a red heifer was born in Israel late in 1996. A red heifer is a cow with red hair, which the Bible says must be used in the purification of the temple. Such cows are so very rare that many people see this as just another sign that we are very close to the rebuilding of the temple.

Therefore, the Antichrist may be able to bring about a peace settlement between the Jews and Arabs, based upon the internationalization of the city of Jerusalem. In exchange for their power to administer the city, the Jews will receive the new temple as a symbol of their nation's right to exist. Meanwhile, the Arabs will get their city out of the control of the Zionists. Everyone will be satisfied; yet as with any compromise, no one will get all that they want.

---

[28] Ehud Barak, the Israeli Prime Minister in 2000, offered the Palestinians control of parts of the Old City of Jerusalem in return for the right for the Jews to build a Jewish house of worship in the northwest corner of the Temple Mount (Source: *Newsweek*, November 19, 2000).

For the first three and one-half years of the treaty, all will go well for the kingdom of the Antichrist. It will go so well and his pride will be so lifted up that he will claim divine wisdom and power, as did some of the emperors of ancient Rome. Since the temple's construction will take some time, it might not even be dedicated and used before the Antichrist comes to Jerusalem to set himself up as the savior of the world. He will be the messiah many religious Jews are looking for today - the one who will give them their temple!

Daniel's revelation of the activities of the last seven years fit in perfectly with other Scriptures concerning the end-time ruler. In Daniel 9:27, we see that the Abomination of Desolation occurs halfway through the seven year period, or at the three and one-half year mark. We have already noted that the "little horn" who blasphemes and opposes God will oppress and overpower the saints for a "time, times, and half a time" (Daniel 7:25). Does this phrase refer to the same amount of time? I believe it does, and is proved both linguistically and scripturally.

First, the Hebrew language has the ability to give not only the plural form of a noun (where many objects are meant) but also to give a form of plurality where only two objects are numbered. While other modern languages allow for this, English does not have this ability. The only word that conveys what the Hebrew form of duality can do is our word, "both." For instance, if someone said, "I had my friends over to dinner last night," we would only know that some people came over to the speaker's house for dinner. However, we would not know how many friends the person had. But, if he said, "I had my friends over for dinner last night, both of them," we would immediately understand that this person had two people over. Likewise, the Hebrew for "time" is singular, while the word for "times" denotes this type of speech. Only two "times" are understood. Therefore, the total number of "times, time and half a time" is what we would call "three and one-half."

Second, the Book of Revelation links this Hebrew figure of speech together with a definite period of time. In Revelation 12:14, John is shown a vision of Israel being cared for in the wilderness for a period of a "time, times, and half a time." In Revelation 12:6, John described the same event, saying that Israel would be cared for a period of one thousand two hundred and sixty days, or forty-two months, or three and one-half years.

Therefore, we can examine all the puzzle pieces that mention this same period of time in order to discover more about the Antichrist and his kingdom.

Daniel 7:25 tells us that the saints will be given into the hand of the Antichrist for a "time, times, and half a time."

In Daniel 9:27, the Antichrist will make a covenant with Israel for seven years. In the middle of that period (three and one-half years), he will set up the Abomination of Desolation in the rebuilt temple.

In Daniel 12:6,7, Daniel asked how long the "great distress" coming upon Israel will last. He was told, "...that it would be for a time, times, and half a time; and as soon as they finish shattering the power of the holy people, all these events will be completed."

Revelation 13:5 says, "...authority to act was given to him [the beast] for forty-two months." Revelation 13:7 says, "...and it was given to him to make war with the saints and to overcome them; and authority over every tribe and people and tongue and nation was given to him."

Finally, Revelation 11:1-13 describes the status of the rebuilt temple and the ministry of two witnesses for God. The city will be given into the authority of the nations, this time for a period of forty-two months. Meanwhile, God will grant authority to His two witnesses for 1,260 days. "And when they have finished their testimony, the beast that comes up out of the abyss will make war with them, and overcome them, and kill them" (Revelation 11:7).[29]

In each of these passages the theme is the same: the Antichrist will persecute the saints and overcome them. And in each case the amount of time of the persecution is also the same: three and one-half years. We can conclude that the actual length of time of the Great Tribulation is not the entire seven years of Daniel's vision, but only three and one-half years.

Christ's Description of the Great Tribulation (Matthew 24:15-31)

15 "So when you see standing in the holy place 'the abomination that causes desolation,' spoken of through the prophet Daniel—let the reader understand—16 then let those who are in Judea flee to the mountains. 17 Let no one on the roof of his house go down to take anything out of the house. 18 Let no one in the field go back to get his cloak. 19 How dreadful it will be in those days for pregnant women and nursing mothers! 20 Pray that your flight will not take place in winter or on the Sabbath.

21 "For then there will be great distress, unequaled from the beginning of the world until now—and never to be equaled again. 22 If those days had not been cut short, no one would survive, but for the sake of the elect those days will be shortened. 23 At that time if anyone says to you, 'Look, here is the Christ!' or, 'There he is!' do not believe it. 24 For false Christs and false prophets will appear and perform great signs

---

[29] This passage may be referring to the first three and one-half year period of the last seven years. After the Abomination of Desolation, the Jews will probably realize the deception of the Antichrist and will reassert their control over the city of Jerusalem. Admittedly, this is conjecture, but it does explain why Israel would need to be protected in the wilderness for the final three and one half-year period.

and miracles to deceive even the elect—if that were possible. 25 See, I have told you ahead of time.

26 "So if anyone tells you, 'There he is, out in the desert,' do not go out; or, 'Here he is, in the inner rooms,' do not believe it. 27 For as lightning that comes from the east is visible even in the west, so will be the coming of the Son of Man.

29 "Immediately after the distress (tribulation) of those days "'the sun will be darkened, and the moon will not give its light; the stars will fall from the sky, and the heavenly bodies will be shaken.'

30 "At that time the sign of the Son of Man will appear in the sky, and all the nations of the earth will mourn. They will see the Son of Man coming on the clouds of the sky, with power and great glory. 31 And he will send his angels with a loud trumpet call, and they will gather his elect from the four winds, from one end of the heavens to the other.

Although we have already studied this passage, we can now see more detail regarding the "abomination that causes desolation." Matthew reminded us to piece together all the Biblical descriptions of this event in order to get a clear picture of the whole time period. Again, note that the Great Tribulation does not begin until *after* the Abomination of Desolation occurs. Therefore, I must repeat, Jesus implied that the Great Tribulation will last three and one half years, not seven.

Jesus also indicated that the judgment upon the kingdom of the Antichrist would begin during these three and one half years. Verse 22 tells us that if the time extended beyond three and one half years, no one would be left alive. So great will be the judgment of God that "Men will faint from terror, apprehensive of what is coming on the world, for the heavenly bodies will be shaken" (Luke 21:26). Just as Daniel was assured that the final victory belonged to the Son of Man, Jesus reminds us, "At that time the sign of the Son of Man will appear in the sky, and all the nations of the earth will mourn. They will see the Son of Man coming on the clouds of the sky, with power and great glory. And he will send his angels with a loud trumpet call, and they will gather his elect from the four winds, from one end of the heavens to the other" (Matthew 24:30-31).

The Restrainer of the "Man of Lawlessness" (2 Thessalonians 2:1-12)

1 Concerning the coming of our Lord Jesus Christ and our being gathered to him, we ask you, brothers, 2 not to become easily unsettled or alarmed by some prophecy, report or letter supposed to have come from us, saying that the day of the Lord has already come. 3 Don't let anyone deceive you in any way, for that day will not come until the rebellion occurs and the man of lawlessness is revealed, the man doomed

to destruction. 4 He will oppose and will exalt himself over everything that is called God or is worshiped, so that he sets himself up in God's temple, proclaiming himself to be God.

5 Don't you remember that when I was with you I used to tell you these things? 6 And now you know what is holding him back, so that he may be revealed at the proper time. 7 For the secret power of lawlessness is already at work; but the one who now holds it back will continue to do so till he is taken out of the way. 8 And then the lawless one will be revealed, whom the Lord Jesus will overthrow with the breath of his mouth and destroy by the splendor of his coming. 9 The coming of the lawless one will be in accordance with the work of Satan displayed in all kinds of counterfeit miracles, signs and wonders, 10 and in every sort of evil that deceives those who are perishing. They perish because they refused to love the truth and so be saved. 11 For this reason God sends them a powerful delusion so that they will believe the lie 12 and so that all will be condemned who have not believed the truth but have delighted in wickedness.

We have already examined the first three verses of this passage regarding the timing of the events of the end. We have also discussed Paul's description of the Abomination of Desolation referred to in verse four. We will now focus upon the force that is now restraining the Antichrist, and how he will win over the allegiance of the world when he does appear.

In verse five, Paul reminded his Thessalonian church about something he had taught them in his brief time of ministry with them (Acts 17:1-9 states that he may have been with them for as few as three weeks). It is fascinating that Paul seems to have informed new believers so thoroughly about prophecy, given the fact that he was only with them for such a short period of time. He asked them to remember that he had already given them the complete picture of what was going to happen. They should not have been so easily deceived by false hopes or doctrines because they would still have to face the Antichrist before the coming of the Lord and the resurrection and rapture.

However, he went on to jog their memories about what it is that is holding back the Antichrist. Unfortunately for us, the Thessalonians may have remembered what it was he was referring to, but he did not include that information in this letter! We can only guess, and whole volumes have been written by Christian scholars about what it might be. Therefore, we can conclude that no firm conclusion can be made.

What we do know from this passage is that the restrainer of the Antichrist is both a principle and an entity. Paul wrote, "And now you know *what* is holding him back…" (verse 6). The Greek word translated "what" in this passage is in the neuter form, meaning it is a thing, an object, or a principle. However, in verse seven, Paul says, "...but the *one* who now holds it back will continue to do so until *he* is taken out of the way." Here, Paul is clearly referring to a person or an entity. The problem arises, how can the restrainer be both a person and an object?

As a result, interpreters have focused upon either one or the other. The most common interpretation today comes from the popular Dispensational theology. It teaches that the Holy Spirit in the church is the restrainer of the Antichrist. When the church is raptured during the secret coming of Jesus prior to the "Seven Year Tribulation," the Holy Spirit will be taken out of the world, making way for the appearance of the Antichrist.

This scenario is clearly wrong. I have already shown that the Antichrist will be revealed *before* our "gathering together" to Jesus. But in addition to this obvious error, I must also point out that the Bible teaches that there will be saints who are alive during the Tribulation. Dispensationalists claim that these saints are Jewish people who will become believers during the Great Tribulation, as well as some Gentiles who missed the Rapture but got saved afterwards. Now if the Holy Spirit is gone, how can anyone be reborn? How can any miracles or prophecy occur? According to Jesus, only the Holy Spirit can convict and convince people in order to be saved (cf. John 16:8).

If the restrainer cannot be the Holy Spirit, what is it and who is he? I believe the best alternative interpretation is hinted at here in this passage. Paul described the Antichrist and the character of his kingdom in two ways. First, he wrote, "the secret power of lawlessness is already at work." Second, he described the result of that power of lawlessness: "the lawless one will be revealed." What we see in his description is both a principle (the power of lawlessness) and a person (the lawless one). In the same manner, he described "what is holding him back" as a principle, and the "one who holds it back until he is taken out of the way" as a person. Paul clearly intended the parallelism in his description of these concepts, as noted in the following chart:

A Godly Principle	An Ungodly Principle
"what is holding him back"	"secret power of lawlessness is...at work"

A Godly Entity	An Ungodly Entity
"one who holds it back will continue until he is taken out of the way"	"lawless one will be revealed"

A "Godly principle" is holding back the secret power of lawlessness. This principle restrained the full expression of lawlessness in Paul's day, and is still doing so in our own time. However, the restraining principle seems to be administered by either a person or an entity. When this entity is taken out of the way (at God's command, by implication), then the lawless one, who is the embodiment of the spirit of lawlessness, will be allowed to come upon the world scene.

Is there any scriptural indication as to the identity of is the powerful principle that restrains lawlessness and what Godly entity administers that power of law? Yes, there is.

The Law of God - both the written law and the law written on people's consciences—restrains the full expression of evil in the world. In Chapter 1, I described the natural progression of Sin when people do not acknowledge the Creator, who has revealed Himself through that creation. According to Romans 1:18-32, people who ignore the revelation of God will eventually become dishonored and destroyed by their self-centered waywardness. Yet, Romans 2:15 tells us that everyone has a God-given ability to listen to their conscience. Even though different cultures and societies may have slightly different standards of right and wrong, they all have morals and they all agree that they must obey them. However, their consciences also bear witness to the fact that no person is able to live perfectly, no matter what rules are followed. Men who have never heard of God's written law will be judged by whether they obey the law of their conscience.

The Bible says that God gave mankind the Law because of our transgressions (Galatians 3:19). Therefore, we can know for certain just what God's will is for our relationships with Him and each other. God never intended us to measure up to the Law. He knew we could not. However, we find that we have to depend upon His mercy for forgiveness. This was the proper use of the Law: to restrain our natural inclination toward evil, and to lead us to salvation through God's Son, Jesus Christ. The rest of Galatians 3:19-24 says exactly this:

> 19 What, then, was the purpose of the law? It was added because of transgressions until the Seed to whom the promise referred had come. The law was put into effect through angels by a mediator. 20 A mediator, however, does not represent just one party; but God is one. 21 Is the law, therefore, opposed to the promises of God? Absolutely not! For if a law had been given that could impart life, then righteousness would certainly have come by the law. 22 But the Scripture declares that the whole world is a prisoner of sin, so that what was promised, being given through faith in Jesus Christ, might be given to those who believe. 23 Before this faith came, we were held prisoners by the law,

locked up until faith should be revealed. 24 So the law was put in charge to lead us to Christ that we might be justified by faith.

It is important to note just *how* the Law was given to mankind: "The law was put into effect through angels *by a mediator*"(verse 20). Paul was referring to the fact that the Law was given to mankind through the agency of a spiritual mediator. In other words, the mediator is a being! Here we see both the principle which restrains the lawless one (the Law), and the entity who "holds it [lawlessness] back." The restrainer is the angelic mediator of the Law! This angelic mediator of the Law will remain "until he is taken out of the way!"

The question arises, are angels capable of restraining other evil beings? We see a picture of this kind of spiritual warfare in Daniel 10:13, 20-21, where the angel Gabriel does battle against the spiritual forces over Persia in order to bring a message from God to Daniel. In the Book of Revelation we read about four angels who are bound up at the River Euphrates (Revelation 9:14-15), as well as a single angel who will bind up the Devil (Revelation 20:1-2). So, Paul's reference to an angelic restraint of the evil one is not a foreign concept to the Scriptures.

Therefore, the most likely interpretation of Paul's meaning here in 2 Thessalonians is that the Law of God is restraining mankind's inclination toward lawlessness. This Law is administered by an angelic force that will restrain the full revelation of the Antichrist until the time of the end.

This interpretation makes the best sense historically as well. Since the time of Constantine, Christianity has been the primary religious influence in society, including its legal system. Western civilization has been based upon the precept that God is the ultimate lawgiver and judge. All of Western world's morality is derived from God's standards of right and wrong, as expressed through the Bible. The concept of Absolute Truth, sought after by poets, philosophers, and lawmakers of all cultures, now has its full revelation to mankind. Through the work of the missionary activity of the church, the knowledge of the Law of God has covered the globe.

Why is this so important? What difference does it make that God's law and the angelic mediator of the Law are restrainers of the Antichrist? Because, just as the Law has gone forth into the entire world and restrained mankind's evil inclinations, so the spirit of lawlessness has always been at work in society. We can look at history and see what happens when a culture or civilization throws off the restraint of God's moral law. Every great society on earth began its descent into oblivion when its people no longer lived by the standards they once held.

Usually, when a culture or a country experiences this rebellion, a powerful ruler steps in to restore order. Napoleon rose to power following the anarchy of the French Revolution. Hitler filled the moral vacuum of the defeated Germany following World War I and the worldwide Great Depression. These godless and brutal leaders became "types" of the Antichrist - the result of the spirit of lawlessness already at loose in the world.

Paul states in 2 Thessalonians 2:8 that this breakdown of law and morality in society will open the way for the deception of the Antichrist. After the Antichrist is revealed, Paul tells us that he will perform many miraculous signs and wonders (verse 9). He will not only be a great political leader, but a spiritual one as well. Humans are incurably religious. We are born to worship. If we do not worship our creator, we will find some other more powerful or awesome being to worship. Hence, idolatry is found in every age and every society. (Even our materialistic society worships "greed," which Paul says in Colossians 3:5 is the same thing as idolatry.) The people of the end-time kingdom will worship this man who will appear to bring salvation to the world.

There will be no spiritual middle ground. People will either turn to God for salvation through the truth of the Gospel, or they will believe the lies of the devil's "savior." Our world is already being set up to receive the "deluding influence" God will send upon them. According to Daniel 7:25, the Antichrist will even try to change the set times and laws. In his hatred and opposition to all that is related to Christ, the Antichrist will try to do away with the Judeo-Christian system of morality (as well as the Christ-based calendar).

Over the last few centuries, the philosophical basis our culture has turned away from the belief in a knowable Absolute Truth. Instead, truth has become a matter of subjective relativism. Truth is now whatever story is beneficial for the moment. To say that someone is wrong or that their way of life is evil is seen as being intolerant. Christians who proclaim that "God so loved the world that He gave His only begotten Son, that whosoever believes in Him will not perish but have everlasting life" are branded as hate-mongering bigots. How dare Christians say that people who do not follow Jesus are damned to Hell! That belief is intolerant of other "truths" people might have. Christians who speak the loving message of salvation will not be tolerated. We will be persecuted for our belief in the truth.

Jesus said that what people did with the truth will be the basis for their judgment: "This is the judgment, that the Light has come into the world, and men loved the darkness rather than the Light, for their deeds were evil. For everyone who does evil hates the Light, and does not come to the Light for fear that his deeds will be exposed. But he who *practices the truth* comes to the Light, so that his deeds may be manifested as having been wrought in God" (John 3:19-21). Today, people won't even tolerate the truth. It is an undefined, unknowable subject, just as it was to Pontius Pilate, the Roman procurator who sentenced Jesus to death, who sarcastically asked Jesus, "What is truth?" (John 18:38).

Sin, rebellion, and lawlessness will have their fullest manifestations during the kingdom of the Antichrist. There will be nothing to hinder their full expressions. Every man will be able to do "what is right in his own eyes" (Judges 21:25).

The Heavenly Battle (Revelation 12: 1-17)

1 A great and wondrous sign appeared in heaven: a woman clothed with the sun, with the moon under her feet and a crown of twelve stars on her head. 2 She was pregnant and cried out in pain as she was about to give birth. 3 Then another sign appeared in heaven: an enormous red dragon with seven heads and ten horns and seven crowns on his heads. 4 His tail swept a third of the stars out of the sky and flung them to the earth. The dragon stood in front of the woman who was about to give birth, so that he might devour her child the moment it was born. 5 She gave birth to a son, a male child, who will rule all the nations with an iron scepter. And her child was snatched up to God and to his throne. 6 The woman fled into the desert to a place prepared for her by God, where she might be taken care of for 1,260 days.

7 And there was war in heaven. Michael and his angels fought against the dragon, and the dragon and his angels fought back. 8 But he was not strong enough, and they lost their place in heaven. 9 The great dragon was hurled down—that ancient serpent called the devil, or Satan, who leads the whole world astray. He was hurled to the earth, and his angels with him.

10 Then I heard a loud voice in heaven say: "Now have come the salvation and the power and the kingdom of our God, and the authority of his Christ. For the accuser of our brothers, who accuses them before our God day and night, has been hurled down. 11 They overcame him by the blood of the Lamb and by the word of their testimony; they did not love their lives so much as to shrink from death. 12 Therefore rejoice, you heavens and you who dwell in them! But woe to the earth and the sea, because the devil has gone down to you! He is filled with fury, because he knows that his time is short."

13 When the dragon saw that he had been hurled to the earth, he pursued the woman who had given birth to the male child. 14 The woman was given the two wings of a great eagle, so that she might fly to the place prepared for her in the desert, where she would be taken care of for a time, times and half a time, out of the serpent's reach. 15 Then from his mouth the serpent spewed water like a river, to overtake the woman and sweep her away with the torrent. 16 But the earth helped the woman by opening its mouth and swallowing the river that the dragon had spewed out of his mouth. 17 Then the dragon was enraged at the woman and went off to make war against the rest of her

offspring—those who obey God's commandments and hold to the testimony of Jesus.

Who are the characters in this apocalyptic description? John uses images from the Old Testament to describe the spiritual battle between the kingdom of darkness and the Kingdom of God. Verse one reveals to us that "the woman" of the passage is the nation of Israel, using the same terms that Joseph used to describe his father, Israel, and his twelve sons (c.f. Genesis 37:9). This woman gave birth to a son who will "rule all the nations with a rod of iron" (verse five). This is a reference to Psalm 2, where the Lord's anointed one (*christos*, in the Greek Septuagint translation of the Hebrew Scriptures) is called God's Son. He will rule the nations with "a rod of iron." It is clear that the son of the woman is Jesus Christ, the Son of God!

John's vision describes the opposing forces in this spiritual war. An enormous and powerful red dragon with seven heads and ten horns stood before the woman in order to devour, or kill, the infant king at his birth. Verse nine identifies for us the exact identify of this beast: he is known as the devil, Satan, the tempter in the Garden and the accuser of the brethren. In league with the devil are "a third of the stars" in heaven (v. 4). We often hear in popular teaching that one third of the angels fell with Satan in his rebellion against God. This is the only passage that hints of this figure. We assume that these "stars" are the same angelic beings described later in verse seven, where Satan and his angels are defeated by Michael and his heavenly army of angels, but it is only an indirect inference.

We can identify the dragon's attempt on the life of the woman's newborn son with Satan's initial attack against the baby Jesus when King Herod ordered the murder of the innocent babies of Bethlehem. Clearly, Satan tried to "devour her child the moment it was born" (v. 4).

John's vision then describes how the woman fled to the desert, where she could be protected for 1,260 days (v. 6). More information about this is found in verses thirteen through seventeen. After the dragon was defeated by the heavenly hosts, he took his frustration and wrath out upon the woman. But she is protected by "the wings of a great eagle" who allow her to flee out of the serpent's reach for three and a half years ("time, times, and half a time"). Another of the serpent's attacks will be thwarted when the earth itself swallows up the "river that the dragon had spewed out of his mouth." We do not know enough about the imagery in this case to be able to make a clear interpretation of exactly what will happen to Israel. But we do know that the length of the attacks is a definite time period. John uses two ways to describe the same length of time, both of which are referred to in the Book of Daniel as being at the end of the age. Some commentators understand this passage as being symbolic of the Church Age, between Christ's first and second advents. However, this interpretation does not fit historically or theologically. Israel has experienced severe persecution from the devil from the time of God's judgment in 70 AD to the present. In no way could we honestly say the Word of God in this passage has been fulfilled, because Israel has not been "taken care of." No, we must look to a future fulfillment of this prophecy. When we recognize the significance of the exact nature of the time period involved, we see that this prophecy can only be fulfilled in the last half of Daniel's "Seventieth Week."

Another point of debate from this passage is the timing of Satan's fall from heaven, described in verses seven through twelve. We cannot really understand why Satan would be allowed into the throne room of God in the first place. We know from the first chapters of Job that he had this kind of access, but how or why this could happen is beyond our limited ability to comprehend. Nevertheless, we know from this passage that Satan will be thrown down to earth in one final battle. But, once again, we do not know just when this happens. Jesus told His disciples that He "saw Satan falling like lightning from heaven" (Luke 10:18). Was Jesus speaking of an event which occurred before His first advent, at that very moment, or at some point in the future? We cannot know for sure, nor is it really important to speculate.

What we do learn from Revelation 12 is the victory of the Kingdom of God whereby the accuser of the brethren is cast down to earth, out of the presence of God forever. No longer does he have the right to point his finger at our guilty stains of sin. Instead, we can overcome him through our trust in the work of Christ on the Cross. We can overcome his works of darkness by our testimony of God's truth in our lives. And we can overcome the temptations of this world by dying to ourselves daily.

The good news of our eternal victory is tempered by the reality of Satan's presence on earth. He knows his time will soon end. Satan's kingdom will not be allowed to co-exist with God's kingdom forever. In wrath, he will lash out at both the Jews of Israel, as well as the rest of the woman's offspring. Who are the other offspring of the women? The answer is quickly given: they are all those who hold to the testimony of Jesus. They cannot be the Jews, for Israel is represented by the "woman." They can only be those Christians who will be living at the same time that Israel is being pursued by the Antichrist.

The "Seventieth Week" of Daniel points to the hope of the ultimate restoration of the Jews to their calling. We have seen that God's promises to the Jews will be fulfilled. They will be grafted back into the olive tree. This last seven-year period will witness the greatest revival among the Jews in all of history. The Book of Revelation is clear: God will work in the last days to restore His covenant people back to Himself. This does not mean that He will suddenly give up on His work to the Gentiles. Just as we saw the overlapping of God's work at the beginning of the Time of the Gentiles with His work among the Jews, so we will see a continued work among the nations, while God once again deals with the Jews.

The "Beast" (Revelation 13:1-13)

1 And the dragon stood on the shore of the sea. And I saw a beast coming out of the sea. He had ten horns and seven heads, with ten crowns on his horns, and on each head a blasphemous name. 2 The beast I saw resembled a leopard, but had feet like those of a bear and a mouth like that of a lion. The dragon gave the beast his power and his throne and great authority. 3 One of the heads of the beast seemed to have had a fatal wound, but the fatal wound had been healed. The whole world was astonished and followed the beast. 4 Men worshiped the dragon because he had given authority to the beast, and they also worshiped the beast and asked, "Who is like the beast? Who can make war against him?"

5 The beast was given a mouth to utter proud words and blasphemies and to exercise his authority for forty-two months. 6 He opened his mouth to blaspheme God, and to slander his name and his dwelling place and those who live in heaven. 7 He was given power to make war against the saints and to conquer them. And he was given authority over every tribe, people, language and nation. 8 All inhabitants of the earth will worship the beast—all whose names have not been written in the book of life belonging to the Lamb that was slain from the creation of the world.

9 He who has an ear, let him hear. 10 If anyone is to go into captivity, into captivity he will go. If anyone is to be killed with the sword, with the sword he will be killed. This calls for patient endurance and faithfulness on the part of the saints.

11 Then I saw another beast, coming out of the earth. He had two horns like a lamb, but he spoke like a dragon. 12 He exercised all the authority of the first beast on his behalf, and made the earth and its inhabitants worship the first beast, whose fatal wound had been healed. 13 And he performed great and miraculous signs, even causing fire to come down from heaven to earth in full view of men. 14 Because of the signs he was given power to do on behalf of the first beast, he deceived the inhabitants of the earth. He ordered them to set up an image in honor of the beast who was wounded by the sword and yet lived. 15 He was given power to give breath to the image of the first beast, so that it could speak and cause all who refused to worship the image to be killed. 16 He also forced everyone, small and great, rich and poor, free and slave, to receive a mark on his right hand or on his forehead, 17 so that no one

could buy or sell unless he had the mark, which is the name of the beast or the number of his name.

18 This calls for wisdom. If anyone has insight, let him calculate the number of the beast, for it is man's number. His number is 666.

This is one of the most intriguing and complex passages in the Bible concerning the Antichrist and his end-time empire. Its accurate interpretation requires extensive use of Old Testament prophecy, as well as a careful analysis of the arrangement of the text itself. The difficulties of interpretation come from the confusion over the identities of the beast, the head that appeared to have a fatal wound, the mouth of the beast, and the other beast who was able to perform miraculous signs. Yet, it is from this difficult passage that most of the scenarios of end-time books and movies have been derived.

The passage consists of two visions (or two parts of the same vision). The first part (verses 1-10) describes a beast coming up out of the sea to rule over the world. It concludes with a word of wisdom for believers who witness this beast's arrival. The second vision begins with verse eleven, when John wrote, "Then I saw another beast..." This second vision builds upon the information from the first. And, like the first vision, John concludes with another word of wisdom for end-time believers, this one helping them identify who the other beast is.

Most commentators have interpreted this passage as describing two different people, who they identify as the Antichrist and the False Prophet. They say that the Antichrist will suffer a grievous head wound - perhaps even rising from the dead. His pseudo-resurrection will so amaze the world that people will fall at his feet in worship. The second beast (verses 11-17) is identified by these same commentators as the False Prophet - a type of John the Baptist who makes the world ready to receive the Antichrist. However, a careful reading of the text shows us that John is not describing two different people. Instead, he is giving us detailed information about both the kingdom of the Antichrist (the first beast), as well as the Antichrist himself (the second beast).

According to verse one, the devil will oversee the establishment of the last-days empire. John saw a beast coming up out of the sea. The apocalyptic symbols used here are the same we saw in Daniel 7:2, where the four great beasts came up out of the sea. Daniel 7:17 identifies each beast as representing an empire, while the sea represents the people of the world. The beast of Revelation 13 is the final representation of the fourth, terrifying beast of Daniel 7. Daniel's fourth beast also had ten horns, representing ten kings or kingdoms that would arise out of the fourth beast's empire. The symbolism of the heads is more difficult to identify, as they can mean two different things. They are interpreted for us in Revelation 17, where they are symbolic of a city built on seven hills (everyone of John's day would know this meant the City of Rome), but we are told that they also represent seven kings (Revelation 17: 9-10).

We remember that the fourth beast of Daniel 7 crushed and devoured all the previous empires. Likewise, Revelation 13:2 tells us that this final beast has parts of the other empires in its nature. It was swift like a leopard, powerful like a bear, and roaring like a lion. This beast is awesome and fearful in its manifestations. The people of the world will give obedience to it because they fear its military might (Revelation 13:4).

The beast John is referring to in this first part of the vision is an empire, not an individual. Just as Daniel's four beasts represented empires, so this one should be understood as the last-days empire of the Antichrist. But if this is so, who or what is the identity of "one of the heads of the beast" which "seemed to have a fatal wound, but the fatal wound had been healed" (Revelation 13:3)? The context of this passage gives us a clue: verse twelve tells us that the world's inhabitants will worship this beast, "whose fatal wound had been healed." Verse fourteen describes an image or idol set up in honor of the beast "who was wounded by the sword and yet lived." Note, that they are worshipping the beast, not one of the heads. The focus of these two references is toward the *beast* that came up out of the sea rather than just the one head, or ruler. Therefore, it is not possible to state definitely that the wounded head represents an assassination attempt against the Antichrist. Rather, it would make more sense to understand the wounding of the beast's head to represent a military blow struck against the empire (or a at least a part of it).

Revelation 13:5-8 tells us about the "mouth" of the beast. Once again, the symbolism of Daniel 7 helps us conclusively identify who the "mouth" is. In Daniel 7, the last empire is ruled by "a little horn who had a mouth that spoke boastfully" (Daniel 7:8). This person will wage war against the saints and defeat them for a "time, times and half a time" (Daniel 7:21,25). Just as Daniel spoke of both the end-time empire and its ruler, Revelation 13:5-8 is referring to the same thing. The beast's mouth will "utter proud words and blasphemies and exercise his [the empire's] authority for forty-two months." Like the little, boastful horn of Daniel 7, this man will be given the ability to make war against the saints and overcome them (Revelation 13:7). Daniel 7:23 tells us that the authority of the end-time empire will be over the whole earth. Revelation 13:8 says the same thing, adding the fact that everyone who has not looked to God for salvation through Jesus Christ will instead worship the empire.

So great is the persecution against the body of Christ by the Antichrist and his empire that John is given a word of encouragement for end-time believers. Revelation 13:10 tells us that God's sovereignty will extend even into these troubled times. Yes, Christians will be captured and even killed, but they will have the ultimate victory when the Son of Man appears. The parallel passage in Daniel 7:26-27 encourages the saints in much the same way: even though the saints will be handed over to the boastful horn "for a time, times and half a time," the heavenly court will sit [in judgment], and his power will be taken away and completely destroyed forever. Then the sovereignty, power and greatness of the kingdoms under the whole heaven will be handed over to the saints, the people of the Most High." If we endure to the end, despite the prospect of physical death, we will be saved. Jesus told us not to be afraid of the one who could kill us, but to fear the One who could both kill and send people to Hell.

In the next section, John describes another beast. From his description, we can identify it as another view of the Antichrist. This beast looks like a lamb, but speaks like the devil (verse 11). He will perform great and miraculous signs, including causing fire to fall from heaven as Elijah the prophet did. In this sense, we may add to his list of biblical names the one of the "false prophet." We read about the false prophet in Revelation 16:13, where three evil spirits came out of the mouths of the dragon, the beast, and the false prophet. It is usually assumed that the "other beast" of Revelation 13:11 is this false prophet mentioned in Revelation 16 and 19:20. But the false prophet and the Antichrist are not two different people - they are one and the same. Why? Because we read that this "other beast" will deceive the people of the earth by performing signs and wonders. This is exactly the same as Paul's description of what the Antichrist will do, recorded in 2 Thessalonians 2:9-10.[30]

The Antichrist will use the empire's might and authority to cause people to worship the state (verses 14 - 15). Worship of the state is not a new phenomenon on the earth. The Roman Caesars and the Egyptian Pharaohs encouraged a form of emperor worship. However, these practices were but an extension of polytheism, using the power of the divine ruler to assure the loyalty of their subjects. With the Judeo/Christian basis of law denied in today's post-Christian philosophical environment, godless humanity still needs a motivating force to inspire people to the obedience of law and morality. The logical extension of the teaching of evolution is the "survival of the fittest" in matters of sociology in addition to biology. If we have no final judge to stand before and give an account of our lives, then what difference does it make how we live as long as we are happy? And who is to judge what a person should or should not do to be happy? The only reason a godless society can give for living a moral lifestyle is to appeal to the greater good of the state. Placing a government (even a democratically elected one) in the position of determining what is right or wrong

---

[30] Revelation 19:20 states that the beast and the false prophet will both be captured and thrown into the Lake of Fire. From this passage, most commentators assume that they are two different people: the Antichrist and his prophet. However, the beast spoken of here is more likely the same as the fourth empire of Daniel 7. In the Daniel passage, both the fourth beast *and* the little horn (the empire and its ruler) are judged. Daniel 7:11 states that the beast will be thrown into the blazing fire. So, it is biblically possible to understand the beast of Revelation 19:20 to be the empire, while the false prophet is just another name for the Antichrist.

is simply making the Sin of the people collective. The state has becomes the arbiter of absolute morality, rather than God. (On the other hand, our U.S. Constitution is based upon the granting of certain inalienable rights to man by God. The state's authority is limited by these rights from God. The state cannot infringe upon them.) We have seen this "deification" of the state several times in this century through communism, fascism, and totalitarianism. We have also seen how these systems inspire people to "religious" fervor when their leaders are worshipped as supermen: Lenin, Hitler, Mao, and Saddam Hussein.

The passage in Revelation 13:15 is not as mysterious as it appears. This false prophet for the worship of the end-time government will set up an image by which this empire can be identified. Just as Christians rally around the symbol of the cross, so godless humanity will have a unifying symbol. John is hearing the image, or picture, of the beast speak. This is not necessarily a supernatural phenomena, especially in today's world of video special effects. George Orwell's book, *1984,* gave us a hauntingly similar image of the power of a government "Big Brother." In his story, television was what we would now call "interactive entertainment." The state used it to keep the population under control, constantly watching for any signs of disloyalty among the people. This invasion of our privacy is available here today. It is possible (and currently being done by both government and private industry) to examine any person's e-mail and world-wide-web usage without their knowledge!

The Antichrist will extend his power into the lives of ordinary people through economic means as well. He will force everyone to receive a mark on their hand or forehead, without which they cannot engage in any economic activity (vv. 16-17). This type of coercion is not new either. The first century Jews ostracized messianic believers from the community life, forcing them to either recant their faith or face starvation.

Today, a diabolical ruler can completely control the lives of everyone. Advancements in computer science and communication make it theoretically possible for nearly every human being to be identified and traced. Computer chips powered by a person's own body energy can be implanted just under the skin. These mini-computers can even be used to track someone by the Global Positioning Satellite System. There are, however, some places in the world where conditions are so primitive that it may not ever be possible to include everyone in the modern banking system. Nevertheless, wherever modern technology has been introduced, this kind of control can be a reality.

The idea of a universal identification system is not an invention of the computer age. When the Social Security system of the United States was first being debated, one of the primary arguments used against it was the biblically-based revulsion against giving every citizen an identification number whereby they could be more easily traced and controlled by the government. The original Social Security Act specifically prohibited the use of the individual's number from being used for identification purposes. This stipulation has been conveniently forgotten, even though it has never been repealed. However, to this day, ministers and priests may voluntarily opt out of the Social Security system based upon their conscientious objection.[31]

Our computer-age society is ready for a cashless society, based upon a universal numbering system. Admittedly, there are many economic and social advantages in favor of a cashless economy. Crime would be reduced. The government could control the drug trade, prostitution, illegal gambling, etc. Common thieves and muggers would have little to steal and nowhere to fence their booty. People would have to pay their taxes, as every dollar could be accounted for electronically. Not only would crime rates go down, but the economy could be more precisely controlled to assure continued prosperity. Finally, people would appreciate the convenience of never running short on cash; their money would always be available to them.

One can also see the negative aspects of such a scheme in regards to personal liberty. The government would have the power to control the economic life of everyone. If it chose to do so, a government could make it impossible for a targeted individual or group to live in society. And that is exactly what the Antichrist will do to anyone who opposes his rule.

Would anyone stand up in protest over such an abuse of power and the trampling of inalienable rights? Who would be able to? Their financial life would be held hostage. Furthermore, who would really want to oppose such a wonderful system which promised economic prosperity and social order? Christians who oppose the system based upon their religious principles would be labeled as reactionaries or, worse yet, traitors to the new order.

We are already seeing the development of a cashless society. The vast majority of economic activity in the developed world takes place electronically, rather than with hard currency. In fact, anti-drug laws have made it inconvenient or even illegal to pay for expensive items with cash. Banks are discouraging the use of paper checks, in favor of electronic funds deposits and payments. The wide spread use of the Internet as a means of commerce is forcing the development of fool-proof electronic shopping. Bank card companies are developing ways of conclusively identifying people using their retinas or fingerprints. How ironic (and prophetic) that the two areas on the human body that are absolutely unique to each individual are located on the hand and the forehead, as identified by John the Apostle in Revelation 13:16![32]

---

[31] Officially they must object to the belief in a government-sponsored retirement program.

[32] In the mid-1990s, Master Card ran a TV commercial announcing the development of a new experimental personal identification system, which they called, "The Mark." After running the ad for a few weeks, they were forced by public pressure to change the ad,

Some form of the cashless system will probably be in effect some time before it is required for all people (a transitional period would be a logical way of introducing the benefits and working out the problems of a new system). What will believers do when something like "The Mark" is required? Would it be possible for a believer to take the mark of the beast accidentally? No, Revelation 14:9 tells us that people will be amply warned that their allegiance to the Antichrist is tied into their receiving of the Mark.

Could the Mark of the Beast cause people to fall away from Christ? Certainly the prospect of losing all one's worldly goods and livelihood would separate the true believers from those who would only use God as a means to increase their personal wealth! How many churches or parachurch ministries would be willing to shut down before they agreed to take electronic "flesh" transfers!

The Number of the Beast: 666

One of the most intriguing mysteries of the Bible is the reference in Revelation 13:18 to the number of the beast. According to the verse, a person with insight or wisdom will be able to identify who the Antichrist is by using a mathematical calculation. And many people have tried throughout Christian history! The label of "Antichrist" has been pinned to leaders like Caesar Nero, various Popes, Adolph Hitler, and even the Secretary of State during the Nixon presidency, Henry Kissenger.

The common understanding of the type of mathematical formula to be used to solve the mystery comes from the Hebrew practice of using their alphabet for numbers. (Aleph equals one; Bet is two; Yod is ten, etc.) Therefore, every Hebrew letter in a word or a person's name can be added together to come up with a numeric value. A person who knows Hebrew could easily transliterate a person's name into Hebrew and then determine if it added up to 666.[33] The text is clear: the Beast's name will be recognizable to those with wisdom. The rest of the world's population, though they may become aware of this ruler's identification with this number, will only shrug it off as an interesting coincidence.

---

dropping the reference to "The Mark." They did not, of course, drop the development of this system!

[33] Someone has noted that when the "www" used to denote the World Wide Web is transliterated into Hebrew, it becomes "vav, vav, vav" - the Hebrew number used for the letter 6 repeated three times, or "666." Interesting, but not a fulfillment...

Summary: Putting the Puzzle Pieces Together

What have we been able to understand about the Antichrist and his kingdom in this section? By examining the various prophetic pieces, we have discovered the following:

A. The End-Time Empire (Daniel 2:31-45)

Gold	=	Babylon
Silver	=	Persia
Bronze	=	Greeks
Iron	=	Romans
Iron & Clay	=	Kingdom of antichrist
Little Rock	=	Kingdom of God comes

B. The End-Time Ruler (Daniel 7:2-28)

Lion with wings	=	Babylon
Powerful Bear	=	Persia
Swift Leopard	=	Greece
Terrifying Beast	=	Rome
with a Little Horn	=	End-Time Ruler

The characteristics of the "little horn:"

- He will wage war against the saints and defeat them (v. 21).
- He will devour the whole earth (v. 23).
- He will speak against God (v. 25).
- He will oppress the saints (v. 25).
- He will change the calendar (v. 25).
- He will be able to persecute the saints for 3 1/2 years (v. 25).
- The Son of Man will come and put an end to his rule and set up the Kingdom of God, with the saints in charge (v. 13).

C. The Last Seven Years of this Age (Daniel 9:24-27)

The "ruler to come" will:

- Make a covenant (peace treaty) with Israel for seven years.

- Half way through (3 1/2 years), he will end the temple worship and set up the Abomination of Desolation (v. 27).
(See Daniel 8:10-12 and Matthew 24:15 for more detail of this.)

D. The Man of Lawlessness (II Thessalonians 2:1-12)

- He will oppose and exalt himself over God (v. 4).
- He will set himself up in God's temple, proclaiming himself to be God (v. 4).
- He will perform deceiving signs and wonders (v. 9)
- He will deceive those who do not love the truth (v. 10).
- He is being restrained by both an angelic administrator of God's Law and by the working of God's law and justice in society.
- Jesus will defeat him with the breath of His mouth and the splendor of His coming. (v. 8).

E. The Beasts of Revelation (Revelation 13)

1. The End-Time Empire (v 1-10)

- It has all the characteristics of the previous empires (v 2).
- Part of the empire suffered grievously from war (vs. 3,14).
- The recovery of this particular "head" will astonish the world (v3).
- The beast will be very powerful militarily; no other nation would consider making war with it. (v4)
- The beast reigns with total authority on earth for 42 months (3 1/2 years) (v 5).
- The beast will be given the ability to persecute and conquer the saints (v7).
- All nations will be in some way in subjection to the beast (v 7).
- All inhabitants of the world will worship this beast (v 8).

2. The End-Time Ruler (The Antichrist) (v 11-18)

- This is the Empire's "mouth" (compare verses 5 and 12).
- He appears like a lamb! (v 11)
- He makes the inhabitants of the earth worship the Empire (compare verses 4,8,12,).
- He performs miraculous signs to deceive people (v 14).
- All who refuse to worship the beast will be killed (v15).

- All who give allegiance to the beast must receive a mark on their hand or forehead, without which they will be unable to live in society (vs16-17).

The saints are warned not to take the mark of the beast, according to Revelation 14:9-12. Life will *not* go on as usual for saints (nor for anyone else for that matter). The difference between the two groups will be that one seeks its hope and salvation in God, while the other finds it in the Antichrist.

Chapter Six

The Kingdom of the Antichrist

We have examined those pieces of the puzzle that describe the Antichrist himself. It is important to remember that he will not come to power without the full support of the world's population. Most people will receive him as their hero and savior. At the same time, the world will throw off the restraints that God has placed into the social order to keep sin and lawlessness in check. Persecution of believers in the one true God will increase. How do we know all this? There are many prophetic puzzle pieces that give us the background of what mankind will be like in the last-days. These Scriptures describe the religious, philosophical, social, political and economic climate of the society that will welcome the Antichrist with open arms. Some of the most instructive are found in Paul's final letters, written at the end of his ministry.

Religious and Philosophical Life in the Last Days

1 But the Spirit explicitly says that in later times *some will fall away from the faith, paying attention to deceitful spirits and doctrines of demons*, 2 by means of the hypocrisy of liars seared in their own conscience as with a branding iron, 3 men who forbid marriage and advocate abstaining from foods, which God has created to be gratefully shared in by those who believe and know the truth.
(1 Tim. 4:1-3; NASB)

1 But realize this, that in the last days difficult times will come. 2 For men will be lovers of self, lovers of money, boastful, arrogant, revilers, disobedient to parents, ungrateful, unholy, 3 unloving, irreconcilable, malicious gossips, without self-control, brutal, haters of good, 4 treacherous, reckless, conceited, lovers of pleasure rather than lovers of God; 5 *holding to a form of godliness, although they have denied its power;* and avoid such men as these. (2 Tim. 3:1-5; NASB)

3 For the time will come when they will not endure sound doctrine; but *wanting to have their ears tickled, they will accumulate for themselves teachers in accordance to their own desires*; 4 and will turn away their ears from the truth, and will turn aside to myths. (2 Tim. 4:3-4; NASB)

These Scriptures point to a massive shift of philosophical and religious thinking in the latter years. Although people may still claim to believe in God, their understanding of His will and character will be so warped that it will have little resemblance to the God of the Bible.

We are witnessing the breakdown of the Judeo-Christian system in the world today. It is being replaced by a materialistic and relativistic society where belief in God has no real relevance. Judge Robert Bork, in his book, *Slouching Towards Gomorrah*, traces the slow, but steady descent of religious life in Western culture. His insights are very pertinent to our discussion of the society which will welcome the absolute rule of the "lawless one." He identifies two new core values in modern thinking:

"...radical egalitarianism (the equality of outcomes rather than of opportunities) and radical individualism (the drastic reduction of limits to personal gratification). These may seem an odd pair, for individualism means liberty and liberty produces inequality, while equality of outcomes means coercion and coercion destroys liberty. If they are to operate simultaneously, radical egalitarianism and radical individualism, where they would compete, must be kept apart, must operate in different areas of life. That is precisely what we see in today's culture.

"Radical egalitarianism reigns in areas of life and society where superior achievement is possible and would be rewarded but for coercion towards a state of equality. Quotas, affirmative action, and the more extreme versions of feminism are the most obvious examples...Radical individualism is demanded when there is no danger that achievement will produce inequality and people wish to be unhindered in the pursuit of pleasure. This finds expression especially in the areas of sexuality and the popular arts.

"Sometimes the impulses of radical individualism and radical egalitarianism cooperate. Both, for example, are antagonistic to society's traditional morality...When egalitarianism reinforces individualism, denying the possibility that one culture or moral view can be superior to another, the result is cultural and moral chaos, both prominent and destructive features of our time." [This seems to be the philosophical basis for the modern value of "toleration."]

"Radical egalitarianism necessarily presses us towards collectivism because a powerful state is required to suppress the differences that freedom produces. That raises the sinister and seemingly paradoxical possibility that radical individualism is the handmaiden of collectivist tyranny.

"But why [have these forces come to dominate modern society] now? Liberalism has been with us for centuries; why should it become modern liberalism in the latter half of this century? The desire for self-gratification, which underlies individualism, has been around since the human species appeared [I have identified this trait as 'Sin']; why should it become radical individualism in our time? The desire for equality, in large part rooted in self-pity and envy, is surely not a new emotion; why has it recently become the menace of radical egalitarianism?

"Men were kept from rootless hedonism, which is the end stage of unconfined individualism, by religion, morality, and law. These are commonly cited. To them I would add the necessity for hard work, usually physical work, and the fear of want. These constraints were progressively undermined by rising affluence [of post World War II society]. The rage for liberty surfaced violently in the 1960s, but it was ready to break out earlier and was suppressed only by the accidents of history. It would be possible to make a case that conditions were ripe at the end of the nineteenth century and the beginning of the twentieth but that the trend was delayed by the Great War. The breaking down of restrictions resumed in the Roaring Twenties. But that decade was followed by the Great Depression, which produced a culture whose behavior was remarkably moral and law-abiding. The years of World War II created a sense of national unity far different from the cultural fragmentation of today. The generations that lived through those times of hardship and discipline were not susceptible to extreme hedonism, but they raised a generation that was.

"Affluence reappeared in the late 1940s and in the decade of the 1950s and has remained with us since…Affluence brings with it boredom. Of itself, it offers little but the ability to consume, and a life centered on consumption will appear, and be, devoid of meaning. Persons so afflicted will seek sensation as a palliative, and that today's culture offers in abundance…With the time and energy of so many individuals freed from the harder demands of work, the culture turned to consumerism and entertainment. Sensations must be steadily intensified if boredom is to be kept at bay.

"A culture obsessed with technology will come to value personal convenience above almost all else, and ours does. Among the consequences, however, is impatience with anything that interferes with personal convenience. Religion, morality, and law do that, which accounts for the tendency of modern religion to eschew proscriptions and commandments and turn to counseling and therapeutic sermons, of morality to become relative and of law, particularly criminal law, to become soft and uncertain. Religion tends to be strongest when life is hard, and the same may be said of morality and law. A person whose main difficulty is not crop failure but video breakdown has less need of the consolations and promises of religion." [34]

Bork's analysis shows us how society is ripe for the Antichrist.[35] A people who have thrown off the shackles of God's law will eventually reap the

---

[34] Bork, Robert H., *Slouching Toward Gomorrah*, New York: Harper Collins Publications, 1996, selections from pp. 5-9.

[35] C.S. Lewis foresaw and wrote about these same forces at work in Western culture over fifty years ago. He wrote about them in his popular fictional work, "That Hideous Strength," and his more scholarly treatise, "The Abolition of Man." Francis Schaeffer warned Christians in the 1970's of the progress of anti-Christian humanism in his book,

consequences of that rebellion, both individually and socially. When internal checks upon people's actions have broken down (such as conscience and religion), people will seek the security of government control to maintain peace and prosperity. Affluence and technology have given us a society addicted to ever increasing levels of pleasure and convenience. We have become a people who "are lovers of themselves, lovers of money…, and lovers of pleasure rather than lovers of God" (2 Timothy 3:2,4). Even many "Christians" living in the last days will want their "ears tickled" rather than face the fact of their Sin, and the necessity to repent and live for God. In a society where safety, security and convenience are the most important values, people have little felt need for the promises of salvation or judgment in some distant afterlife.

Christian pollster, George Barna, echoes Bork's dismal summary of modern culture. Barna's social research reveals a society that is "post-Christian" in attitudes and practices, holding to a form of Christianity but living much differently. In his book, *The Second Coming of the Church* (Word Publishing, 1998), Barna summarizes these alarming social values and trends in American society and the church:

- Among American Christians, "fewer than 10 percent actually possess a biblical worldview, a perceptual filter through which they see life and its opportunities. Lacking this filter, most Christians make important decisions on the basis of instinct, emotion, assumptions, past experience, external pressure, or chance" (p. 23).
- Although 86 percent of Americans call themselves Christian, one-third of adults describe their god as "the total realization of personal, human potential;" or "a higher consciousness that a person may reach;" or "everyone is God" (p.26).
- Most non-Christians don't care to discuss their salvation because "they believe they already have their eternal security sewn up. A majority of Americans believe they are going to heaven after they die; most of the people who are not relying on Christ's atonement for their sins are relying instead on their own good deeds, their good character, or the generosity of God. Research indicates that the evangelistic efforts of Christians are viewed as insensitive and unnecessary" (p. 28).

Barna's sad report card for the health of the American church does not mean that there are no places where people are spiritually hungry and churches are healthy and growing. However, he also notes another disturbing trend: the large

---

"How Then Shall We Live." Chuck Colson and Dr. James Dobson are among our modern day prophets, standing against the tide of popular thought, and warning us of society's coming demise.

"mega-churches" are growing only at the expense of the decline of numerous smaller churches. Pointing to the few large churches does not mean that the overall state of the American church is healthy or vibrant. Rather, it signals a pulling back of the overall witness of the church.

Americans are no longer living in a society dominated by Judeo-Christian biblical values. Instead, most Americans follow the values and principles of existentialism, or post-modernism. Barna summarizes these values as follows:

- "There is no grand purpose to life. The reason for living is to achieve comfortable survival. Success is defined as the absence of pain and sacrifice, and the experience of happiness.
- "There is no value to focusing on or preparing for the future. Every person must live in the moment and for the moment.
- "There are no absolutes. All spiritual and moral principles are relative to the situation and the individual.
- "There is no omnipotent, all-knowing deity that guides reality. We must lean on our own vision, competencies, power, and perceptions to make the most of life" (p.59).

Barna feels the most dangerous social trend in America (and the Western world) is the belief that there is no such thing as absolute moral truth. His research shows that "only one out of every four adults - and even fewer teenagers - believe that there is such a thing as absolute moral truth. The Bible is relegated to nothing more than a book of riveting stories and helpful suggestions. Human reason and emotion become the paramount determinants of all that is desirable and appropriate" (p. 62).

The spiritual and social implications of this mind-set are frightening. Barna concludes, "This cultural perspective hardens the hearts and deafens the ears of those who embrace it. Without absolute moral truth, there can be no right and wrong. Without right and wrong, there is no such thing as sin. Without sin, there can be no such thing as judgment and no such thing as condemnation. If there is no condemnation, there is no need for a Savior. This progression renders the death and resurrection of Jesus Christ historically unique - and eternally meaningless" (p. 62).

Instead of needing a savior from Sin, people living in the end-times will willingly and enthusiastically embrace anyone who can promise them their affluence and convenience. Anyone who opposes such a political "savior" will be branded as an intolerant fool. Just prior to His arrest and crucifixion, Jesus told His disciples that, "We must work the works of Him who sent Me, as long as it is day; night is coming, when no man can work" (John 9:4; NASB). The twilight hours are upon us.

There will come a time in the future where the church will be scattered by the onslaughts of the beast. Both the prophets Daniel and John warn believers to expect a massive persecution which, for a season, will overpower the saints. Life in the last days will not be pleasant.[36]

Most American Christians are expecting a great world-wide revival, quoting Joel 2:28 and Acts 2:17 where God promises to pour out His Spirit on all flesh in the last days. I hope and pray that America will be part of such a revival. As a pastor and a teacher, I ache over the general apathy of believers. But two things need to be understood. First, the promised revival *has* been going on - since the turn of this century! The expansion of world missions and the return of the supernatural gifts of the Holy Spirit have born witness of the fulfillment of God's promise. Second, the Antichrist will come to a society that will be willing to accept him, "instead of" Christ. Therefore, there has to be a large number of people who will have already rejected Christianity. This is precisely what is taking place today. We live, whether we are brave enough to admit it or not, in the post-Christian society that will embrace the Antichrist.

Social and Economic Life in the Last Days

"...the Day of the Lord will come like a thief in the night. *While people are saying, 'Peace and safety,'* destruction will come upon them suddenly..." (1 Thessalonians 5:2-3)

"And there will be a time of distress such as never occurred since there was a nation until that time; and at that time your people, everyone who is found written in the book, will be rescued...But as for you, Daniel, conceal these words and seal up the book until the end of time; *many will go back and forth, and knowledge will increase*" (Daniel 12:2,4; NASB).

"And at that time many will fall away and will deliver up one another and hate one another...And *because lawlessness is increased, most people's love will grow cold*" (Matthew 24:10,12; NASB).

In addition to the religious and philosophical deceptions of the last days, people will be lulled into a sense of well being by the dream of attaining a utopian society of peace, prosperity, and knowledge. We have seen the greatest intellectual and economic achievements in the history of mankind in the last one

---

[36] Jeremiah's message of the coming judgment in his day was not enthusiastically received by his contemporaries either. No one wants to be the bearer of sad news. Nor do people willingly receive it if they do not want to repent. The similarities between the religious people of Jeremiah's day and the so-called Christians who only want a God who brings them comfort and prosperity are astounding, as we shall see in a later chapter.

hundred years. In the days of Benjamin Franklin, a person could learn nearly everything there was to know by reading an encyclopedia. It is estimated today, however, that the accumulated amount of human knowledge is doubling every five years! Advances in transportation and communications have made the world a vast interconnected web of neighborhoods. Advances in medicine and biology are knocking on the door of eternal physical life. Economic science and global corporations have done away with the boundaries of nations.

Yet, while all the material progress is being made, the spiritual core of society is decaying. Justice is being trampled down by those who can afford the highest priced lawyers. Corruption reigns in the highest offices and courts. A higher law no longer restrains the conscience of mankind. The morality of "getting away with it" has filtered into all levels of society.

Paul outlines the progressive nature of Sin in the first chapter of his letter to the Romans. Because the truth has been suppressed and ignored (verses 18 and 28), God will give society over to all the evil and wicked vices of sin. He uses words like "depraved," "ruthless," "God-hating," "heartless," and "inventors of evil" to describe a society which has totally rejected God. The natural inclinations of mankind will be turned upside down. This is especially true in the area of our sexuality. The homosexual lobby hates what Paul said in this passage: "...God gave them over to shameful lusts. Even their women exchanged natural relations for unnatural ones. In the same way the men also abandoned natural relations with women and were inflamed with lust for one another. Men committed indecent acts with other men, and received in themselves the due penalty for their perversion" (Romans 1:26-27). Homosexuals try to assert that theirs is but an alternative lifestyle; they are born with that sexual orientation. It escapes their notice that if their activities were "natural," natural selection and evolution would have made human bodies capable of "safe" sex. Instead, sodomy has always been know to destroy those who practice it through many different fatal diseases - even before the introduction of the AIDS virus into the human community.

The effects of Sin will eventually eat away at any temporary gains humanity has made through the applications of technology and economic theory. We have seen this at work already in our inner cities. Social rot is spreading throughout our society. Prosperity is limited. The gap between the rich and poor, educated and uneducated is progressively widening. Family structure has broken down, along with the social stability that comes with it. Gangs, drugs, violence and apathy are now problems even in the most unexpected places. Today's children are reaping the consequences of two or three generations of parental neglect or ignorance.

In order to maintain social order, more and more laws must be passed which limit our freedom. People who have no inner restraint of right or wrong will have to be controlled by the threat of force. As more and more of our children grow up and find themselves morally unable to cope with society, people will have to turn to the force of government in order to maintain law and order. Yes, there will be "peace and safety," but at the expense of true freedom.

Our world is ready for the Antichrist. People of all nationalities, cultures, and religions are longing for someone who has the wisdom and power to bring the world together. Humanists, Muslims, Jews, and liberal Christians are all looking for a savior who will unite the whole world. Most people have rejected the need for the Savior of the Bible, Jesus Christ. Instead, they want someone who will give them continued peace and prosperity in the face of life's uncertainties. All that is necessary is some global crisis that will provide the excuse to elevate a world leader above the sovereignty of individual nations.

Part Three

The Judgment
of
God

Chapter Seven

God's Judgments in the Past

"When your judgments come upon the earth, the people of the world learn righteousness" (Isaiah 26:9).

God has judged mankind many times throughout human history. The Bible records several instances of the wrath of God being poured out upon sinful man. God used these judgments to teach people about the penalty for Sin as well as the blessing of righteousness. When we walk with God and follow His ways we enjoy His provision and protection, but when we follow the lusts of our sinful nature, we reap what we sow. God will not and can not let us continue to rebel. He must judge - both to uphold His glory and to bring us to our knees in repentance. "Those whom I love, I rebuke and discipline…" Revelation 3:19.

In addition to their immediate impact upon mankind, God's judgments of the past serve as prophetic pictures of the Final Judgment. We can learn much about the Day of the Lord by examining how and why He judged people in the past. In this chapter we will examine five of the major judgments found in the Bible: the Fall, the Flood, the Tower of Babel, Sodom and Gomorrah, and the Exile. They will give us insight into the social and religious attitudes that resulted in the necessity for God's judgment to come. From them, we can gain prophetic insights about the future.

The Fall: Redemption in the Midst of Judgment

We have already covered the cause of humanity's problem in Chapter One. Now we will examine God's judgment for the first Sin in more detail, because in doing so we will see how God's redemption works even in the midst of judgment. God not only promises salvation for fallen man, but He will even reverse the effects of the judgment at Christ's coming.

God warned Adam (and Eve, through Adam) about the results of eating the fruit of the tree of the knowledge of good and evil: "…in the day you eat from it you will surely die" (Genesis 2:17; NASB). And when Adam and Eve sinned, death was introduced to mankind, with all of its ugly facets. Some of the effects of Sin are simply the natural consequences of its presence in the world. These consequences are not direct judgments from God. Rather, they are simply the results of the death working its way backwards into life.

For instance, the first consequence of Sin occurred immediately after the rebellious act. Sin opened Adam and Eve's eyes to their own guilt and shame. Quickly, they sought to hide their flaws from one another with crude and uncomfortable coverings. No longer could they be completely intimate, lest the insecurities and failures of their imperfect self-rule become exposed (Genesis 3:7). God did not ordain our guilt, shame or insecurity. These traits are simply the direct results of Sin.

Another natural human consequence of Sin was Adam and Eve's fear of God's presence. Even though God sought them out, calling to them, "Where are you?;" they hid from Him. Instead of confessing and repenting of their Sin, they tried to hide it. And being confronted with their Sin, they attempted to blame it on someone else. Sin was already working to bring about its destructive results. The first couple was beginning to reap what they had sown. In the same way, God does not have to bring a direct judgment upon most of sinful humanity. He simply lets Sin work its natural course, bringing death of relationships, hopes, and, ultimately, life itself. People's sins still cause all manner of suffering in this present evil age.

However, God *did* bring His judgment upon the guilty parties in more direct ways. Though these judgments were hard, they also served to work a measure of redemption for mankind. First, God dealt with the ultimate cause of the temptation: the serpent. In a word with prophetic hope, God declared that the seed of the woman would some day bruise (or crush) the head of the serpent. This was the first prophecy of Jesus, who, being conceived by the Holy Spirit in the womb of the virgin Mary, grew up to bring victory over Satan.

Next, He turned His attention to the one who gave ear to the devil's temptation, the woman. Originally, she was created to be Adam's partner - "a helper corresponding to him" (Genesis 2:18; NASB). In other words, she was to be a complementary partner to her husband. Together, (and not separately) they reflected the complete image of God (Genesis 1:27). Where he was weak, she would be strong; and where she was weak, he would be strong. Together, they would rule over the world.[37]

This original role of the woman was altered by God's judgment. First, she would have increased pain in childbirth. Her ability to conceive and form other human beings who were made in the image of God was supposed to be a reflection of the creative work of God. (Compare Genesis 5:3: Seth was "made in [Adam's] likeness, according to his image;" with Genesis 1:27: "God created man in His own image, in the image of God He created them; male and female He created them.") Now this glorious work of creating new life would not be easy. Those created to glorify God would enter into life through suffering. Yet, even this part of God's judgment points to the final redemption. The apostle Paul wrote, "For we know that the whole creation groans and suffers the pains of

---

[37] It is an unfortunate misunderstanding of the King James' Old English that perpetrates the assumption that God always intended for the woman to be subservient to men. The words, "an help-mete" does *not* mean "a helper." Rather, it also means "someone who is perfect for another."

childbirth together until now...waiting eagerly for our adoption as sons, the redemption of our body"(Romans 8:22-23; NASB).

The second judgment upon the woman dealt with the role she had with her husband. Because the man was created first, and because the woman was the first to obey the tempter, God placed her role under that of her husband. This is the meaning of the last part of Genesis 3:16: "Yet your desire (Hebrew: *teshuqah*) will be for your husband, and he will rule over you." Here, "desire" has nothing to do with sex or procreation, as one might imply from our English understanding of the word, as well as the previous statement about having pain in childbirth. Rather, the Hebrew word is referring to desiring the husband's place of leadership in the family unit. In other words, "You will long to assert your will over your husband, but he will be responsible for ruling the family."

Yet again, we can see God's redemption even in judgment. Because of the destructive forces of Sin let loose in the world, God ordained a structure for the family that would hinder the full manifestation of Sin in society. The family - a husband and wife working to provide a safe and secure environment for each other and for the raising of children - provides the building blocks for true social security.[38] This is what Paul meant in 1 Timothy 2:13-15: "For it was Adam who was first created, then Eve. And it was not Adam who was deceived, but the woman being deceived fell into transgression. But women will be saved through the bearing of children if they continue in faith and love and sanctity with self-restraint" (NASB). In other words, "If you maintain your role (which requires your faith, love and self-restraint), you will be kept safe."

However, the role of man was not ignored in the judgment. Whereas he had been the recipient of the blessings of Paradise, now he would have to eke out an existence for his family through toil and sorrow. The work of his hands would never result in complete security. Just as the woman would have to trust her husband to lead (an act of faith), her husband would have to trust God to provide, despite the thorns and thistles of life.

Another act of redemption in the midst of judgment was God's covering of Adam and Eve's nakedness. Their own attempts of clothing were feeble and ineffectual (not to mention uncomfortable). God shed the blood of innocent animals in sacrifice for the well being of His beloved people. This was but another prophetic picture of our eventual redemption through "the blood of the Lamb!"

---

[38] The breakdown of the family in our society is illustrated by our inability to decide as a culture just what *is* a family. In years past everyone would agree that it was a father, mother, children and close blood relatives. Today, thanks to decades of "no-fault" divorce and millions of children born out of wedlock, a "family" is becoming any grouping of people who have strong, mutual affection - no matter how temporary it may be.

These examples show us that God always works toward mankind's redemption, even in the midst of judgment. We see this theme over and over again throughout the Bible. The Book of Revelation tells us that even in the last days, God calls out to mankind through the plagues of wrath and the witness of His saints, urging people to repent. Who knows how many souls will be snatched from the fire in the last moments?

Sinful mankind, however, has tried to circumvent their dependence and need for God. God in His mercy has allowed us to alleviate some of the effects of these judgments. But simply because we can develop labor saving devices does not free people from toil, pain, and slavery to work. Anesthesia and birth control do not free women from their role in relation to their husbands. Yet, modern society would give the impression that society *is* free from the effects of this judgment. The modern feminist movement and the sexual revolution, spawned by the availability of effective birth control, has tried to overturn God's redemptive order for the family. Women no longer see themselves as wives and homemakers, but as co-laborers with their husbands. Men no longer see themselves as providers or protectors, but as equals with women - in the work place and even on the battlefield. Sexual roles are in turmoil. Men and women are experimenting with all manner of immorality, including homo- and bi-sexuality. In the name of "freedom," we have thrown off the God-given restraints to Sin, and we will reap the consequences - eventually. A society that purposefully turns away from God will have to experience God's wrath, so that they will re-learn righteousness.

Another lesson this passage teaches us concerning the impending judgment of the end is found in God's statement concerning the banishment of Adam and Eve from Eden. "Then the Lord God said, 'Behold, the man has become like one of Us, knowing good and evil; and now, he might stretch out his hand, and take also from the tree of life, and eat, and live forever' - therefore the Lord God sent him out from the garden of Eden..." (Genesis 3:22-23; NASB). God knows that Sinful man cannot live forever in his state of Sinfulness. He has become like God in the sense that he rules his own life. If mankind found some way of living eternally, he would wreak the havoc of Sin throughout God's creation! Therefore, God could not allow man to take from the Tree of Life at his own discretion. Eternal life could only come as a gift to those people who repented and believed in God's way through the real Tree of Life, the Cross of Jesus!

However, Sinful man is pursuing the complete elimination of the judgment of the Fall. Scientists have discovered the mysteries of the basic building blocks of life. The Human Genome Project, sponsored by the U.S. government, has used supercomputers to map the entire DNA structure of the human gene. Scientists may soon be able to use bio-technology to alter or heal every disease or malady known to mankind. One of the byproducts of this research is the ability to clone, or duplicate, exact replicas of living beings. (Thankfully, no one has yet tried this process upon a human being, though many scientists would not have any ethical qualms about doing so. Would a person's clone have a soul?) Another interesting result of the DNA and cloning research is the discovery of the gene that apparently causes a cell to divide only a fixed number of times. Once the gene's controlled number of divisions has been reached, the organism dies. Scientists hope that they can someday reprogram the gene to duplicate indefinitely. If this can be achieved, mankind will truly be said to be able to "...stretch out his hand, and take also from the tree of life, and eat, and live forever."

Just as God did not allow mankind to attain his own eternal life the first time Sin appeared in the Garden, He will not allow us to create our own immortality. The kingdom of the Antichrist may promise mankind their own eternal life through the wonders of technology, but the arrogance of mankind will not be allowed to continue unchallenged or unjudged by the true Creator of Life.

The Flood: The Inherent Wickedness of Mankind

The first worldwide judgment against sinful mankind occurred during the flood of Noah, recorded in Genesis 6-8. Peter referred to the flood as a warning to the unbelief and complacency of the last generation:

> 3 "Know this first of all, that in the last days mockers will come with their mocking, following after their own lusts, 4 and saying, 'Where is the promise of His coming? For ever since the fathers fell asleep, all continues just as it was from the beginning of creation.' 5 For when they maintain this, it escapes their notice that by the word of God the heavens existed long ago and the earth was formed out of water and by water, 6 through which the world at that time was destroyed, being flooded with water. 7 But by His word the present heavens and earth are being reserved for fire, kept for the day of judgment and destruction of ungodly men" (2 Peter 3:3-7; NASB).

Jesus also said that the end-times would be similar to the time of Noah: "As it was in the days of Noah, so it will be at the coming of the Son of Man" (Matthew 24:37). What was so corrupt and abominable about that society to cause such a complete and catastrophic judgment?

> 5 The LORD saw how great man's wickedness on the earth had become, and that every inclination of the thoughts of his heart was only evil all the time. 6 The LORD was grieved that he had made man on the earth, and his heart was filled with pain (Genesis 6:5-6).

In this passage we see what kind of attitudes and activities force God to judge mankind. We also discover just how God feels when He has to punish his creation so severely. A study of the Hebrew words used in this passage will help us understand the depth of the depravity of this society. The Lord saw that every inclination and thought of mankind was evil continually. The word for "every" is inclusive; stressing that every single one of man's thoughts fell into this category. The word for "inclination" represents the intangible thoughts, while the word for "thoughts" is used for concrete thinking. In other words, every time they thought a thought it was bent toward evil and every time they put it into practice it was to carry out that evil. Again, God emphasized that they were evil "all the time," literally meaning "all the whole day."

God's heart was grieved when He observed mankind's character and activities. The Hebrew word used is *nacham*, which means "to sigh or breathe deeply." It speaks of the extreme emotional impact upon a person's physical being when overcome with sadness. (i.e., like the emotional breathing of a child after a spanking). God was stabbed with pain (Hebrew root - "to carve out") because of mankind's rebellion. He hurts over our Sin. Jesus showed the same feeling when He lamented over His wayward people, "O Jerusalem, Jerusalem, you who kill the prophets and stone those sent to you, how often I have longed to gather your children together, as a hen gathers her chicks under her wings, but you were not willing" (Matthew 23:37). It's as if God's heart toward man cries, "Why, oh why won't you repent and enjoy my goodness? How often I have longed to bless you, but you would not have me…" It is certainly not God's will that people fall into condemnation. Rather, Peter tells us that the Lord "…is patient toward you, not wishing for any to perish but for all to come to repentance" (2 Peter 3:9; NASB).

The Tower of Babel: The Pride of Mankind's Strength and Ability

Following the first world-wide judgment of mankind's evil, the pride and arrogance of Sinful man arose again. This time, they worked together trying to build an ordered, permanent society.

1 Now the whole world had one language and a common speech. 2 As men moved eastward, they found a plain in Shinar and settled there. 3 They said to each other, "Come, let's make bricks and bake them thoroughly." They used brick instead of stone, and tar for mortar. 4 Then they said, "Come, let us build ourselves a city, with a tower that reaches to the heavens, so that we may make a name for ourselves and not be scattered over the face of the whole earth.

5 But the LORD came down to see the city and the tower that the men were building. 6 The LORD said, "If as one people speaking the

same language they have begun to do this, then nothing they plan to do will be impossible for them. 7 Come, let us go down and confuse their language so they will not understand each other.

8 So the LORD scattered them from there over all the earth, and they stopped building the city. 9 That is why it was called Babel—because there the LORD confused the language of the whole world. From there the LORD scattered them over the face of the whole earth" (Genesis 11:1-9).

This account shows us how Sinful man thought, and still thinks today. The key phrase is, "Let us make a name for ourselves, lest we be scattered" (Genesis 11:4). Rather than seeking God for their blessing, provision, and protection, they relied upon their own strength for their preservation and glory. Fallen man seeks fulfillment not by trusting God, but by relying upon his own intellect and abilities to make a name for himself. Here, they did it by building a city and a tower whose top would reach into heaven. This tower, most biblical scholars agree, represents the earliest attempt by man to control his destiny through the practice of astrology and the occultic arts. Archeologists have discovered numerous similar towers in the area of ancient Babylon. Throughout the Bible, including the Book of Revelation, Babylon is regarded as the representative of mankind's proud rebellion against God. This proud arrogance had its beginning with the building of the Tower of Babel.

It is interesting to note some of the similarities between the first Tower of Babel and today's humanistic society. First, they both have a common language. Today, if anyone wants to conduct international business, they must use the standard international trade language, English. Furthermore, the use of computers, satellites, and the Internet has made our world one large "village" where people can easily and instantly communicate with others across the globe.

Second, God described the people of Babel as being united. With a common goal and language, God declared that mankind could do anything. Today's world is increasingly becoming united as well. The concept of national sovereignty is giving way among our world's leaders, in favor of the concept of globalism.[39] International banks and multinational corporations have made national boundaries nearly obsolete. Scientific and technological knowledge is rapidly spread throughout the world.

Third, the people of Babel used their united strength and abilities to build a way to "reach to the heavens." Admittedly, their "reaching" consisted in tapping into the forbidden spiritual realm of the occult, including astrology and even "astral-projection." Although today's secular humanists reject the spiritual

---

[39] Strobe Talbot, Undersecretary of State in the Clinton Administration, predicted the elimination of national sovereignty by the middle of the twenty-first century.

realm, mankind is still reaching into the heavens. In a little over a generation mankind has made space travel a relatively common practice. We have reached into the farthest corners of our solar system. Three of our space probes (Pioneer 1, Pioneer 2, and Voyager) have flown beyond the orbit of Pluto. Each of these spacecraft has an interesting attachment on its side: a plaque containing information about mankind and the planet earth. Should some space alien somehow discover these deep space travelers, he would be able to ascertain who we are and where we are located. One of the plaques has a picture of a naked man and woman - like an Adam and Eve - with the man waving a greeting to some extraterrestrial friend!

C.S. Lewis, the noted Oxford scholar and Christian apologist, wrote a science fiction trilogy that exposed some of this modern-day arrogance against God. In the first of the series, *Out of the Silent Planet*, he described a visit to the planet Mars (this was written before we really knew if other planets could support life or not). The earthlings discovered a planet in complete harmony with its creator. The creatures were ruled over by gentle angelic-like guardians of the planet. The creatures were happy, peaceful, and intelligent. Sin and rebellion were absent, until the men from earth came and inflicted their disease of Sin upon the inhabitants. In the story, the only righteous space traveler of the group was deserted and marooned by his wicked companions. He learned the language and ways of the gentle creatures, even being introduced to the angelic "eldils." He was told that Earth was known in the solar system as "The Silent Planet." God forbade any creature from going there, because our "eldil" was "bent."

It is an interesting concept. We usually assume that any extraterrestrial visitor would come here to take over and destroy us. In reality, *we* are the evil, bent creatures of the universe. Given the opportunity, *we* would exploit and enslave the creatures of other planets in order to further our own selfish ends! Since we are currently attempting to reach to the heavens through space travel, it is not unlikely that God would come to put a stop to our efforts, lest we infect the universe with our deadly Sin!

God's response to the tower of Babel was to scatter these proud people. God had to judge this attitude, not because He wants mankind to suffer from the results of sin, but because men were not turning to God for their strength. God can be trusted to give help, sustenance and a heritage whenever people come to Him in humility. He showed this over and over again to His children throughout the Bible. But He cannot allow us to glory in our own pride and self rule. In mercy, He will knock down whatever tower we build against His benevolent rulership.

Sodom and Gomorrah: The Perversion of Sin

Jesus drew our attention to two judgments of the past as examples of the time of the Second Coming: the Flood and the destruction of Sodom and Gomorrah. He said,

> 26 Just as it was in the days of Noah, so also will it be in the days of the Son of Man. 27 People were eating, drinking, marrying and being given in marriage up to the day Noah entered the ark. Then the flood came and destroyed them all.
> 28 It was the same in the days of Lot. People were eating and drinking, buying and selling, planting and building. 29 But the day Lot left Sodom, fire and sulfur rained down from heaven and destroyed them all (Luke 17:26-29).

We have discussed the wickedness of the people of Noah's day. God judged the world because the earth was full of violence and every thought and inclination of the hearts of men were bent toward evil. But what were the people of Sodom like, to deserve the fiery wrath of God? What was their sin? How is their example a warning to our world today?

The Book of Genesis gives us the important details surrounding the destruction of Sodom and Gomorrah. It tells us, "Now the men of Sodom were wicked exceedingly and sinners against the Lord" (Genesis 13:13). Nevertheless, Abraham's nephew, Lot, chose to live there. Although he was grieved and tormented in his soul by the lawless deeds of the inhabitants (2 Peter 2:7-8), he stayed to become an important person in that city. (Lot is one of the people who "sat at the gate of the city" - a place where the town's rulers and merchants gathered to conduct city business.)

Though Lot had some influence in Sodom, he could not change the hearts of the people through reason, legislation or economic means.[40] God tried to warn these wicked people as well. They had recently been defeated in warfare by a numerically inferior force (Genesis 14). Lot had to be rescued by his uncle Abraham who, with a few hundred men, was able to defeat the coalition forces of the four kings who had conquered and plundered the armies of the five kings of Sodom, Gomorrah, Admah, Zeboiim and Zoar. Apparently, this defeat did not

---

[40] We can assume that he may have tried to do so. The only record we have is his last, feeble attempt to compromise and bargain with the wicked crowd at his door: "Please, my brothers, do not act wickedly. Now behold, I have two daughters who have not had relations with man; please let me bring them out to you, and do to them whatever you like; only do nothing to these men, inasmuch as they have come under the shelter of my roof" (Genesis 19:7-8).

cause these wicked people to reflect upon their own lives, nor did their salvation through a tiny band of Abraham's men cause them to turn to the God of Abraham and Lot.

The next time we read about Sodom and Gomorrah is just prior to the outpouring of God's wrath upon these cities. In a passage that reveals as much about the character of God's mercy as upon His judgment, we read how He informs Abraham of what He is about to do:

> 17 And the Lord said, "Shall I hide from Abraham what I am about to do, 18 since Abraham will surely become a great and mighty nation, and in him all the nations of the earth will be blessed? 19 For I have chosen him, in order that he may command his children and his household after him to keep the way of the Lord by doing righteousness and justice; in order that the Lord may bring upon Abraham what He has spoken about him."(Genesis 18:17-19; NASB).

Because Abraham was chosen and beloved, God wanted to reveal His will and His character to him. Likewise, God has given us many evidences of the coming judgment today.

When Abraham heard what God planned for Sodom, he began to intercede on behalf of his righteous nephew. Again, God's response is revealing: He would spare the city if He could find even a tiny number of righteous people living there. If there is a remnant of people who are able to share His message of repentance, and if there are sinful people who are willing to turn from their selfish ways, then God will continue to be patient with them, not wishing that any should perish, but that all should come to eternal life. But this was not so in Sodom and Gomorrah. Nor will it be the case today, when God determines that sinful mankind will not listen to His word or His people any longer.

How sinful were Sodom and Gomorrah? God sent two angels to give these people one last chance to show any spark of righteousness. Genesis 19 tells the story of the angels' visit. Instead of welcoming the strangers, the men of Sodom tried to sexually abuse them.[41] Lot rescued them (though they needed no human protection), and he was delivered from the fire and brimstone that rained down from heaven upon Sodom, Gomorrah, Admah and Zeboiim (Zoar was spared because Lot asked if he could flee to that tiny town.)

It is clear from Genesis 19 that the wickedness of Sodom did not consist of being inhospitable (as some homosexuals claim today). Rather, their Sin had so overwhelmed their lives that they were consumed with deviant passion.

The Bible is very clear about homosexuality. It is a perversion of God's created order for mankind. "God created man in His own image,…male and

---

[41] We get the word "sodomy" from this biblical story.

female He created them. God blessed them; and God said to them, 'Be fruitful and multiply...'" (Genesis 1:27, 28a). God made men and women capable of reproduction through their separate and unique reproductive systems. And each time a child is born as a result of sexual union, another person is created "in God's image." The very act of giving birth becomes a holy, sanctified moment! Yet, homosexuality precludes this possibility. Instead, it seeks selfish sexual pleasure in ways God never intended or designed.[42]

Homosexuality is also a perversion of God's design for male and female relationships. The "one flesh" union between a man and a woman signifies more than the sexual act. It is the process of two different genders becoming complete in one another. Men and women are different in more than just their physical attributes and reproductive systems.[43] They think and act differently.[44] This was by God's design: Only together do they reflect the fullness of the image of God! Only by denying their own selfish, self-centered ways will they grow to recognize the strengths and blessings God has put into one another. God ordained the lasting covenant of marriage in order to keep a man and a woman together long enough to learn that they are better together than apart!

---

[42] Even evolutionists, or people who claim that homosexuality is a genetic condition, fail to see the fallacy of their arguments. If our genetic pool is shaped by the law of "the survival of the fittest," then homosexuality would soon cease to exist (if it could ever exist at all) because homosexuals would not naturally choose to reproduce! Furthermore, the human body has never adapted (a process evolutionists employ to explain change over eons) to the homosexual act of sodomy. God created male and female sexual organs for one another. They are designed for reproduction and for sexual pleasure. However, the rectum was only designed for expelling human waste. Sodomy is unhealthy and destructive. Homosexual sex destroys the rectum's thin tissue walls and opens the way for bacteria and disease to penetrate the body. This fact was recognized even in ancient society. Paul wrote (concerning homosexuality), "...men with men committing indecent acts and receiving in their own persons the due penalty of their error" (Romans 1:27b; NASB).

[43] Though common sense is all it takes to prove this fact, scientific studies have finally showed our politically correct society the same results. Those who deny the obvious are only engaging in wishful thinking.

[44] One difference that is important in understanding the perversion of homosexuality is the different avenues of sexual response between men and women. Men are primarily visually motivated while women are usually emotionally motivated (the romance and security of loving relationship). In order to have a fulfilling sexual relationship with his wife, a husband needs to meet her emotional needs. Otherwise, she will find it difficult or impossible to enjoy his sexual advances. Likewise, since a man is more visually stimulated, his wife should strive to maintain her appearance if she would want to please her husband. Therefore, *both* the husband and wife are called upon by God's natural design to lovingly deny themselves for the benefit of the other. But when they do, sex is great!

A society that allows or condones open homosexual behavior as an acceptable, alternative lifestyle has denied God's plan for human relationships. The Apostle Paul writes in the first chapter of Romans that when a society thoroughly rejects God's created order, the Lord will "give them over to every kind of degradation, including blatant homosexuality. The judgment of God upon such people will quickly follow. Just as fire and sulfur came burning down upon the people of Sodom and Gomorrah, so the fiery judgment of God will soon descend upon our world today!

Jerusalem and the Babylonian Exile: The Prototype of the Day of the Lord

We have seen how Jesus used the judgment upon Jerusalem in 70 AD as a prophetic picture of what the world would be like prior to His Second Coming. But this was not the first time God used Jerusalem's fate in that way. In 586 BC, the Babylonians captured Jerusalem and led the surviving people into exile. Looking ahead, the prophets Zephaniah, Joel, Isaiah, Jeremiah and Ezekiel saw so many similarities between Jerusalem's judgment and the Day of the Lord that they described both judgments in similar terms.

For instance, in what is often described as his "mini-apocalypse," Isaiah prophesies about the coming world-wide judgment: "See, the Lord is going to lay waste the earth and devastate it; He will ruin its face and scatter its inhabitants…" (Isaiah 24:1). After describing its destruction, he shows the similarity between the coming judgment upon Jerusalem and that of the whole world: "The ruined city lies desolate; the entrance to every house is barred. In the streets they cry out for wine; all joy turns to gloom, all gaiety is banished from the earth. The city is left in ruins; its gate is battered to pieces. So will it be on the earth and among the nations…"(Isaiah 24:10-13a).

The first chapter of Zephaniah is even clearer:

1 The word of the LORD that came to Zephaniah son of Cushi, the son of Gedaliah, the son of Amariah, the son of Hezekiah, during the reign of Josiah son of Amon king of Judah:

2 "I will sweep away everything from the face of the earth," declares the LORD.

3 "I will sweep away both men and animals; I will sweep away the birds of the air and the fish of the sea. The wicked will have only heaps of rubble when I cut off man from the face of the earth," declares the LORD.

4 "I will stretch out my hand against Judah and against all who live in Jerusalem. I will cut off from this place every remnant of Baal, the names of the pagan and the idolatrous priests—5 those who bow down on the roofs to worship the starry host, those who bow down and swear

by the LORD and who also swear by Molech, 6 those who turn back from following the LORD and neither seek the LORD nor inquire of him. 7 Be silent before the Sovereign LORD, for the day of the LORD is near. The LORD has prepared a sacrifice; he has consecrated those he has invited. 8 On the day of the Lord's sacrifice I will punish the princes and the king's sons and all those clad in foreign clothes. 9 On that day I will punish all who avoid stepping on the threshold, who fill the temple of their gods with violence and deceit. 10 "On that day," declares the LORD, "a cry will go up from the Fish Gate, wailing from the New Quarter, and a loud crash from the hills. 11 Wail, you who live in the market district; all your merchants will be wiped out, all who trade with silver will be ruined. 12 At that time I will search Jerusalem with lamps and punish those who are complacent, who are like wine left on its dregs, who think, 'The LORD will do nothing, either good or bad.' 13 Their wealth will be plundered, their houses demolished. They will build houses but not live in them; they will plant vineyards but not drink the wine.

14 "The great day of the LORD is near—near and coming quickly. Listen! The cry on the day of the LORD will be bitter, the shouting of the warrior there. 15 That day will be a day of wrath, a day of distress and anguish, a day of trouble and ruin, a day of darkness and gloom, a day of clouds and blackness, 16 a day of trumpet and battle cry against the fortified cities and against the corner towers. 17 I will bring distress on the people and they will walk like blind men, because they have sinned against the LORD. Their blood will be poured out like dust and their entrails like filth. 18 Neither their silver nor their gold will be able to save them on the day of the Lord's wrath. In the fire of his jealousy the whole world will be consumed, for he will make a sudden end of all who live in the earth." (Zeph. 1:1-18)

Note how Zephaniah shifted his focus between the immediate judgment upon Jerusalem and the final "great day of the Lord." This principle occurs so often in the writings of the Prophets that we can see many of the events described by Jesus, Paul and the Book of Revelation in them. We have quoted these passages in the appendix for the reader's further study.

However, one aspect of the Babylonian judgment upon Jerusalem that is worthy of further explanation concerns the religious attitudes of the people, as described by Jeremiah. From him, we can learn much more about the deception and apostasy of the last-days.

The Church's "Jeremiah Ministry"

Jeremiah lived through the terrible last days of the Kingdom of Judah. He began his ministry at the time of a great religious revival during the reign of the righteous king, Josiah. But during this time of religious fervor, he noticed an appalling fact: the hearts and lives of the people were only superficially touched. Although Josiah was deeply moved to follow the Lord, the vast majority of the people only gave lip service to God: "And although they say, 'As the Lord lives,' surely they swear falsely" (Jeremiah 5:2; NASB). Jeremiah spent the remaining years of his life trying to influence the people to turn to the Lord with all their hearts, but with little success.

One of the reasons for the deafness of the people to his plea was their choice to believe religious leaders who would "tickle their ears" with what they wanted to hear, rather than the truth about their hypocrisy. Concerning these false prophets, Jeremiah said, "An appalling and horrible thing has happened in the land: the prophets prophesy falsely, and the priests rule on their own authority; and My people love it so! But what will you do at the end of it?" (Jeremiah 5:30-31; NASB).

These popular prophets would assure the people that God was pleased with them, no matter how they were living. He would never judge them because they were the chosen people, His beloved possession. But Jeremiah countered, "They have lied about the Lord and said, "Not He; misfortune will not come on us, and we will not see sword or famine" (Jeremiah 5:12; NASB).

One of the motives for the lack of backbone in the priesthood was financial. If the prophets and priests really confronted the people over their hypocrisy, they might lose their source of income. Josiah's reforms had led to a resurgence in the fortunes of the priesthood. They were not about to lose their "favor" among the people by telling them to change their wicked ways. Therefore, they allowed financial considerations to take priority over God's will: "For from the least of them even to the greatest of them, everyone is greedy for gain, and from the prophet even to the priest everyone deals falsely. They have healed the brokenness of My people superficially, saying, 'Peace, peace,' but there is no peace" (Jeremiah 6:13-14; NASB).

Nevertheless, the people chose to believe the lies about God's nature and His ways, rather than turn back to the Lord. The people became deaf to God's plea through His prophet: "To whom shall I speak and give warning that they may hear? Behold, their ears are closed and they cannot listen. Behold, the word of the Lord has become a reproach to them; they have no delight in it" (Jeremiah 6:10; NASB).

Not only did they not want to hear Jeremiah (they once tried to get rid of him by throwing him into a well), but they stubbornly refused to return to the ways of God and walk with Him: "Thus says the Lord, 'Stand by the ways and see and ask for the ancient paths, where the good way is, and walk in it; and you will find rest for your souls. But they said, 'We will not walk in it'" (Jeremiah 6:16; NASB).

Finally, God told Jeremiah not to even pray for the people; they had gone too far in their apostasy and would be given over to judgment (Jeremiah 7:16 and Jeremiah 11:14). The Lord explained, "Therefore, thus says the Lord, 'Behold I am bringing disaster on them which they will not be able to escape; though they will cry to Me, yet I will not listen to them'" (Jeremiah 11:11; NASB).

The similarities between the judgment of Judah and the final judgment are sobering.

Jeremiah's message needs to be heard by the church today. False prophets who promise peace and prosperity surround us. People go to their churches and have their ears tickled with soothing words of good times and happy feelings. "God wants you rich," they say glibly. "Give to this ministry, and you will reap one hundred-fold!" they promise. And what is most amazing is that thousands of people flock to them in order to be fleeced!

Jeremiah's words summarize the state of much of the visible church in America. We are a consumer-oriented people. We like a comfortable, non-confrontive church that entertains us and meets our needs for socialization. We want a large church with the most modern facilities, inspiring orators and professional musicians. All we are required to do is attend somewhat regularly (once a month is good) and drop a few hundred dollars in the offering plate once in a while to help pay for the show.

We still want to go to heaven when we die, so we will raise our hands, or walk the aisle, and ask Jesus into our hearts (whatever that means). We readily believe only half the Gospel. God is a God of love. He doesn't judge people anymore. We're saved by grace, so we can do anything we want and still go to heaven. Jesus is coming back soon, but we don't have to worry about persecution by the Antichrist because we will be all raptured out of here anyway. (And those who say otherwise simply do not believe the "plain and literal Word of God!")

The popular understanding of Christianity is so insipid and weak that the world doesn't take it seriously. Jesus said that we are to be the "salt of the earth" and "light of the world." If we do not wake up and revive what remains we may find ourselves "trampled underfoot by men."

The true believers in the last-days will find themselves repeating Jeremiah's ministry, warning people who are complacent in their faith and deceived in their understanding of God's ways. Despite our weeping, our compassion, our acts of kindness and generosity, we may only see a few sparks of revival among such spiritually hardened people. Like the people of Jeremiah's day, they only seek God in order to get Him to do something beneficial for them. They are attracted to false gospels with counterfeit signs and wonders. They will be ripe for the deception of an Antichrist. Just as there were only a few who responded to Jeremiah's message of repentance in his day, so we will see fewer and fewer people truly being saved today. Admittedly, this is not a popular analysis. No one wants to report bad news. But it *is* what is happening in our increasingly secular world.

Chapter Eight

The Day of the Lord

We are now ready to discuss the final chapter in human history, referred to in the Bible as "The Day of the Lord." It is the time when God will pour out His judgment upon unbelieving, sinful mankind in a final, cataclysmic demonstration of His divine power and wrath. Using the prophetic puzzle we have put together thus far as our framework, we will see how the Book of Revelation and other related passages describe the Day of the Lord for us.

But first we need to know how to interpret the Book of Revelation. It is not easy to understand, as it requires an extensive knowledge of the Bible, Jewish culture, Bible prophecy, and world history. One might say that it is the "Ph.D. level" of Biblical interpretation. Therefore, before I attempt to give my interpretation of its description of the Day of the Lord, we must learn some essential background information.

The Book of Revelation was written in the Jewish literary style known as "Apocalyptic Literature." This form of prophecy began to be used during the time of the prophets Daniel and Zechariah. Apocalyptic prophecies differed from other Jewish prophetic styles in that they primarily used metaphors or symbols to describe prophetic events, rather than the straightforward approach, "Thus says the Lord…," which the earlier Hebrew prophets usually used.

In order to interpret apocalyptic symbolism, we must first recognize the difference between what is to be taken as symbolic and what is to be understood as literal. Generally, the best way to tell what is symbolic is to allow the Bible to interpret itself. For instance, the context of the passage often reveals to us what the symbolism means. A good example of this is found in Revelation 1:20 where the meaning of John's vision of Jesus among the lampstands is explained: "…the seven stars *are* the angels of the seven churches, and the seven lampstands *are* the seven churches."

We can also discover a symbol's meaning from other books of the Bible. For instance, we have seen that the Book of Daniel describes one of the "beasts" in Revelation 13 as symbolic of an empire. In the Book of Revelation, the Apostle John draws our attention to many other Old Testament passages by using symbols and ideas drawn from them. Our task is to correctly match the corresponding prophetic puzzle pieces in order to get the best picture!

Next, we need to recognize that John was seeing visions of two realms: the spiritual realm - that which transpires in heaven; and the physical world - that which takes place on earth as a result of God's judgments. John was literally seeing and hearing things that will occur in heaven and earth in the last days. However, he could not describe them adequately because they were beyond his understanding. His impairment is easy to understand using the following illustration. Suppose a time traveler went back 2,000 years ago and brought someone back to this century for a short visit. How would that person describe what he saw here in this century to people living in his time? What words or concepts would he use in order to describe a modern invention such as a light bulb? He might say that it was a "burning crystal" or "a fire that doesn't consume." But however he said it, his description would sound mysterious to our modern ears. It is obvious that John was having this same kind of linguistic difficulty. He simply did not have the understanding or the vocabulary to adequately describe the visions he was seeing. And, we must humbly admit that even our own account of the heavenlies would sound as mysterious as John's was if we, too, were called upon to describe such divine scenes! Our woeful attempt might sound something like apocalyptic literature, too!

Another helpful clue for understanding the Book of Revelation is to realize that the people who will be alive during the time of the Tribulation will only see the Book of Revelation from their earthly, physical point of view. They won't hear or see the judgments of the seals, trumpets, or bowls as they occur in heaven. They will only experience the results of those judgments upon the earth. So, if we concentrate our study upon what those judgments will be like for earth dwellers, we will be able to determine how they might happen.

Finally, we need to see the Book of Revelation as a whole before examining its individual parts. Many people get confused about this book because they read it as if it was a simple narrative, telling the story from beginning to end in chronological order. They do not realize that John wrote this book using a characteristically Jewish style of writing that requires a different interpretive approach. We need to be aware of these styles. Otherwise we will "read into" John's message things that he did not mean.

In the Western world we are used to expressing ideas in the framework of a logical outline. When we tell a story or describe an event, we expect it to be told as a narrative, with a linear progression of ideas from beginning to end. ("This happened, then this happened, then this happened next, and finally, this happened.") However, the Jewish writers did not always write in this manner. Although they could tell a story in narrative form (the historical books of Kings and Chronicles are good examples of historical narratives), they had other styles of writing as well.

The Jewish culture delighted in painting word pictures in order to describe or illustrate truths. They wanted to be able to "experience" or "feel" the truth, rather than just understand it. The Apostle Paul noted this cultural difference in I Corinthians 1:22 where he contrasted the learning styles of the Jews and the Greeks: "Jews demand a sign; Greeks search for wisdom."

In order to create these word pictures, Jews often used a "repetitive" form of writing (also known as "parallelism"), where subjects were repeated over and over again in order to paint the complete word picture of the topic. (See pages 33-35 for a full explanation.)

For instance, the Book of Proverbs is a good example of this Jewish writing style. The sage would present a particular truth in the first line ("Trust in the Lord with all your heart") and then repeat or expand upon that truth in the next line ("And lean not on your own understanding.") Taken together, both lines give the full picture of what is meant. However, the picture is still not complete. The writer intends the reader to look at *all* the references to the subject in his book. Hence, the Book of Proverbs was not categorized subject by subject (as we would want to do with our Western, logical educational styles). Rather, each subject (such as wisdom, the tongue, work ethics, etc.) is presented from different perspectives over and over again throughout the whole book!

In the New Testament, the letters of Peter, James, and John also follow this repetitive pattern. For instance, John's first letter talks about love over and over again, interspersed with other topics like fellowship, sin and forgiveness, etc. (which are also repeated again and again).

On the other hand, Paul used the Greek, or Western, style of writing. Though he was trained as a Jewish rabbi and could understand the Jewish manner of expression, he was also schooled in the Greek and Latin cultures. He was the perfect person for God to use in order to make the bridge between the Jewish way of expressing God's truth and the Western world's method of learning. Therefore, we can see why Paul's letters are easy for us to outline. They follow a logical sequence of thoughts. We can also see why it is impossible for us to make such sequential outlines of James or 1st John.

Why is this important? Because the Book of Revelation should be interpreted with the perspective of this Jewish form of writing! Otherwise, it will not make much sense. Contrary to most interpretations, I will demonstrate that the Book of Revelation does not follow a strict sequential format. Instead, it is the written account of a series of John's visions. It is only our Western-based assumption that causes us to think that each vision is followed sequentially by the events described in the next vision!

For instance, most readers see the seals, trumpets and bowls in chapters 4-19 as a timeline of events that will happen one after the other, as the following chart shows:

One Period of Time:	A Subsequent Period of Time:	The Final Period of Time:
7 SEALS	7 TRUMPETS	7 BOWLS

Followed by:

THE RETURN OF CHRIST

However, this system of interpretation presents us with many impossible and irreconcilable contradictions within the text. For instance, chapters 4—19 describe Jesus as coming back to earth in triumphant glory at least two different times! (And this number does not count the pretribulation interpretation of a secret coming in order to rapture the church before the Great Tribulation even begins!) We read that "The kingdom of this world *has* become the kingdom of our Lord and of His Christ..." at the blowing of the last trumpet in Revelation 11:15. However, we also see Jesus returning again at the Battle of Armageddon in Revelation 19:11-20.[45] All kinds of explanations are given by interpreters in order to avoid this "contradiction." However, if we understand the Jewish style of expression in the book, there is no need to have Jesus could come back secretly, or to stop temporarily on His way back in the mid-heaven, or to come back at the middle of the so-called "seven year tribulation," in order to reconcile these passages.

Another difficulty in interpreting the seals, trumpets and bowls as consecutive events is seen in the very nature of their effects upon the earth! How could such catastrophes take place in rapid succession without severely affecting the economic and political life of the end-time kingdom of the Antichrist? We have shown that this kingdom will be one where the people praise their secular savior because he has brought them final peace and prosperity. People will be exclaiming, "Peace and safety!" (1 Thes-salonians 5:3a). Such a statement cannot be made when the sixth seal, for example, has the sky "rolling up like a scroll" near the beginning of the "seven-year tribulation;" or the sixth trumpet has one-third of mankind involved in a major world war!

A better way of understanding the Book of Revelation is to see the seals, trumpets, and bowls as all describing different aspects of the same time period - the Great Tribulation, as follows:

One Period of Time:

SEALS - one prophetic vision of that time
TRUMPETS - a second prophetic vision of that time
BOWLS - a third prophetic vision of that time

---

[45] In fact, the primary reason many people believe in a mid-tribulation rapture (half way through the so-called "seven-year tribulation") is because they interpret the passage in Revelation 11:15 as the same last trumpet that Paul refers to in 1 Corinthians 15:52 when Jesus comes to resurrect the dead and rapture those who are remaining alive on earth.

Following the Jewish repetitive style, each of these apocalyptic pictures builds upon the previous one, and thereby gives us a complete view of God's judgment. This interpretation will be made perfectly clear in our discussion of the individual judgments later in this chapter.

What makes the Book of Revelation even more complicated, however, is the fact that within each section concerning the judgments of the seals, trumpets and bowls are even more visions. These visions give expanded details of what life on earth will be like during the judgments. It would have been better if John could have put parenthesis marks around these visions so that we could follow his train of thought more easily! For instance, after the sixth seal is opened in Revelation 6:17, the kings of the earth respond, "...the great day of their wrath has come, and who is able to stand?" This question is then answered in one of these "parenthetical" visions. The whole next chapter tells us that God will seal two groups of people for their protection and ultimate deliverance: 144,000 Jews and a great multitude of people from every tribe, nation, and tongue. Then, after this explanation, the primary vision concerning the seals resumes with the opening of the seventh seal in Revelation 8:1. This same pattern is repeated in the visions of the trumpets and the bowls, adding greater confusion for those who take a sequential approach to the book!

However, if we recognize how the Jewish repetitive style works, we will see that each parenthetical vision (also called an "interlude" or an "excursus" by commentators) builds upon the previous one. With each elaboration, we are given more details about end-time events and characters. We are introduced to the Devil, the Beast, the False Prophet, mystery Babylon, etc. Each interlude builds upon the information we have been given in the previous one.

For instance, we have just seen how the first parenthetical vision introduces us to the two groups of people who will be sealed by God in order to be able to stand before Him at the judgment (the Jewish believers in one group and the Gentile believers from every nation in the other). The next interlude occurs between the blowing of the sixth and seventh trumpets (Revelation 10:1 - 11:14). Here, we are given more information about the work of evangelism among the Jews in the last days (Rev. 11:1-14). Following the blowing of the last trumpet in Revelation 11:15-19, we have another parenthetical vision before the vision of the bowls is described. This interlude gives further elaboration of what will happen during the last three and one-half years of human history to the two groups of people. It describes God's protection of the Jews from Satan's wrath (Revelation 12:1-16) and the devil's persecution of the rest of God's children who believe in Jesus (Revelation 12:17). Next, we are given more information about the kingdom of the Antichrist (referred to in passing as "Babylon the great" in Revelation 14:8) and those who will receive his mark (Revelation 12 - 14). Finally, the last interlude gives more detail regarding the judgment upon this end-time kingdom of Babylon (Revelation 17-18). So, we see that each new interlude builds upon the previous ones, describing life on earth in the last days in greater and greater detail. Like the seals, trumpets, and bowls, these interludes are not meant to be taken sequentially. Rather, they all describe different aspects of the same period of time, thereby giving us the complete picture.

An Overview of the Book of Revelation

Now we can look at the Book of Revelation from a better perspective. We can organize and group our puzzle pieces in a manner where they will all fit together! Instead of trying to arrange them into a single line, we have shown that they fit better in groups! As we have noted, Revelation is a compilation of a series of visions. These visions describe three main scenes: (1) Jesus, the Lord of His Church; (2) Jesus, the Returning King; and (3) Jesus, the Lord over All. The first section deals with John's vision of Jesus as Lord over His Church. The second section is a series of visions that describe in scene after scene the judgment of God upon sinful man and the climatic return of Christ. The final section gives us a brief glimpse of Jesus as He institutes His Kingdom.

Chapters 1-3   Jesus, Lord of His Church

1	The Vision of Jesus
2-3	Jesus' Words to His Church

Chapters 4-19 Jesus, the Returning King

Chapters 4-8:1 The Seven Seals

4-5	Jesus, Worthy to Open the Seals
6	The First Six Seals
7	(Elaboration, answering the question, "Who is able to stand, when the great day of God's wrath has come?")
8:1	The Seventh Seal

Chapters 8:2-14 The Seven Trumpets

8:2-9	The First Six Trumpets
10-11:14	(Elaboration concerning events taking place in heaven and on earth during this time.)
11:15-19	The Seventh, or Last, Trumpet
12-14	(More elaboration concerning last time events in heaven and on earth.)

Chapters 15-19 The Seven Bowls of God's Wrath

15	The Introduction of the Bowls
16	The Bowls poured out
17-18	(Elaboration by an angel of Bowls about the judgment of God upon the end-time kingdom of the Beast.)
19	The Return of Christ

Chapter 20-22 Jesus, Lord Over All

| 20 | The Heavenly Rewards and Hellish Punishments |
| 21-22 | The New Heaven and the New Earth |

Now we are ready to unlock some of the mysteries of the Book of Revelation!

Jesus, Lord of His Church

In the first chapter of the Book of Revelation, we read that John has been exiled to the island of Patmos because of a severe persecution of the church (during the reign of the Emperor Domitian). There, he received the first of a series of visions that make up the entire Revelation.[46] In this first vision, he saw the glorified Jesus standing in the midst of seven golden lamp stands. Jesus told him to "Write...what you have seen, what is now and what will take place later" (Revelation 1:19). The rest of the Book of Revelation is the result of John's obedience to that command.

Most commentators organize the Book of Revelation around this verse. Chapter one describes what John has seen: the vision of the glorified Jesus. Chapters two and three contain seven messages to the seven churches of Asia Minor where John was the overseer. The rest of the Book of Revelation (chapters 4-21) is a prophetic message of the future.

Surprisingly, despite Jesus' plain language describing *how* these chapters are to be considered, interpreters have often violated His intent! No one seems to have much of a problem with the vision of "what you have seen." All recognize it as being a vision of Jesus. However, interpreters have several opinions regarding the meaning of the second part, "what is now." And there are widely

---

[46] This is another reason we should not take the book as a simple chronological narrative. When John wrote, "after this, I saw..." (which he does at least five times throughout the book), we should not understand him to mean, "After this thing happens, then that will take place next," but rather, "After I finished seeing this vision, then I saw the next vision."

diverse and contradictory interpretations over the meaning of the last statement, "what will take place later."

Once again, we see that an interpreter's presuppositions will influence his or her conclusions regarding the Biblical text. Those people who do not give much credence to God's ability to give prophetic revelation will interpret much of the Book of Revelation as either a symbolic portrayal of the spiritual conflict between the kingdom of Satan and the Kingdom of God (called the "Idealist" view) or that John was writing about the clash between Rome and the first century church (called the "Preterist" view). Others view the Book of Revelation as an inspired prophecy of church history, from the first century until the Second Coming (called the "Historical" view). Finally, those interpreters who see the Book of Revelation as a prophetic forecast of history just prior to the Second Coming are called "Futurists." The most popular version of the "Futurist" school of interpretation is called "Dispensationalism." However, the Dispensational interpretation of the Book of Revelation is not the *only* view that sees the book as futurist prophecy (as I am demonstrating in this book).

We can dismiss the first two interpretive systems - the "Idealist" and the "Preterist" positions - because of their anti-supernatural bias. As Revelation 1:19 implies, Jesus meant that the visions were to be prophetic, not symbolic of events of the first century. The "Historical" school cannot be taken seriously because when words are taken symbolically of historical events they loose their meaning, as they can now stand for anything an interpreter wishes!

Dispensational theologians use Revelation 1:19 as a formula for interpreting the whole book. They see the letters to the seven churches as representing seven successive ages of church history. There are enough similarities between those letters and the various stages of church history to make some general comparisons between them. The church at Ephesus (Revelation 2:1-7) symbolizes the early church of the apostolic fathers: doctrinally sound but beginning the slide into mediocrity. The church in Smyrna (Revelation 2:8-11) represents the church persecuted by the Roman emperors. The early Roman Catholic Church and the introduction of idolatry into worship is symbolized by the church at Pergamum (Revelation 2:12-17). The corrupt and abusive power of the Roman Catholic Church during the Middle Ages is seen in the message to the church of Thyatira (Revelation 2:18-29). Hints of the Reformation and the Protestant Church are given in the message to the church of Sardis (Revelation 3:1-6). The church of Philadelphia was a loving, powerful church. Dispensationalists see themselves as the fulfillment of this church in the Church Age. Finally, the apostate and lukewarm Laodicean church is symbolic of the "liberal" denominations today that have denied the inerrancy of the Word of God and the fundamentals of the faith.[47]

However, there are numerous problems with this Dispensationalist understanding about Christ's messages to the seven churches. First, Jesus told John to write about "what is *now*." The letters were addressed to churches already in existence at that time. Jesus was speaking directly to them about their individual problems or issues. An interpreter has to make a huge assumption that the seven churches symbolize all of church history in chronological order! There is nothing in the text itself to suggest the idea seven separate stages of church history.

Second, there are obvious historical contradictions using the Dispensationalist view of successive ages of the church. During the apostolic era, the church was also living under constant threat of persecution. So, we have to admit that the first two church ages (represented by Ephesus and Smyrna), were in existence simultaneously. We should also note that the third and fourth churches (Pergamum and Thyatira) both represent the Catholic Church - one in its early development and the other in its latter manifestation. Yet, the fifth church (Sardis) has to represent the Protestant Reformation only in its final stage of apostasy! But it was the Reformation that brought new life into the church and ultimately spawned the modern missionary movement! Only within the last century can anyone say that the Reformation-era church has become "dead!" Finally, if we are living in the last days (as Dispensationalists believe), then we should be seeing the apostate, lukewarm church. Yet, they claim to be the manifestation of the "Philadelphia" church. In other words, their system must allow for more than one manifestation of the stages of the church to be in existence at the same time! Therefore, even Dispensationalists cannot insist upon a rigid chronological order.

But does this mean that John's letters to the seven churches have no significance to us today? Absolutely not! The number "seven" does have symbolic meaning in apocalyptic literature. It represents "completeness." It is the number of God's "perfection." In this context, we can assume that these letters are intended for the "whole" or "complete" church - meaning the church at any time or in any place. When we look at *any* period of church history, we can see elements of *all* these seven churches in existence at that time. In other words, every century of church history had churches that were loving, evangelical, powerful, and faithful; or immoral, idolatrous, or dead, and even some that were

___

[47] Dispensational teaching also presupposes that the supernatural gifts of the Holy Spirit (tongues, prophecy, healing, miracles, etc.) passed out of existence after the apostolic church ended. They fail to connect the prophecy of Joel 2: 28 ("In the Last Days I will pour out My Spirit upon all flesh...") with the mighty outpouring of the Holy Spirit taking place during these Last Days!

persecuted. Certainly this is true today. While admitting the danger of over-generalization, today we find that the European church is "dead" (Sardis), the American church is lukewarm (Laodicean) or legalistic (Ephesus), and the Chinese church is persecuted (Smyrna). Numerous African churches struggle with idolatry and immorality (Pergamum and Thyatira). Yet there are examples of loving, powerful, and faithful churches throughout the world (Philadelphia)! So, whatever the time or the place, Jesus still speaks the same last seven messages to His church. Whatever problems face us, we can - through the obedience of faith - overcome them!

Jesus - the Returning King!

The next section of the Book of Revelation begins in chapter four with the words, "After these things I looked, and behold, a door standing open in heaven, and the first voice which I had heard, like the sound of a trumpet speaking with me, said, 'Come up here, and I will show you what must take place after these things'" (Revelation 4:1; NASB). Immediately, John is shown God's throne room in heaven.

Dispensationalists see a pretribulation rapture implied by this verse. They understand it to mean the following: After the church age (symbolized by the seven churches), John is beckoned into heaven where he witnesses the final judgment of God. The phrase, "after these things" is understood to mean, "after the Church Age." They note that the word "church" does not occur in the Book of Revelation after this point. Therefore, since the organized church is not mentioned during the tribulation period, they conclude that it has been raptured into heaven. This verse is often used by Dispensationalists in their arguments in favor of the pretribulation rapture.

However, their argument is one of implication and assumption. It rests upon the validity of their interpretation of chapters two and three, which we have just shown to be a gross generalization at best. Furthermore, their assertion that the church is not mentioned in the rest of the Book of Revelation is also in error. For instance, Jesus said that the entire book was intended "for the churches" (Revelation 22:16). Just because the word, "church" is not mentioned per se, it does not follow that the church is not present. Certainly "the saints" and "believers" are spoken of several times. It is an example of circular reasoning when Dispensationalists conclude that these tribulation believers are saints who became Christians *after* the rapture.

A better explanation of this verse is that John is now simply moving on to the next series of visions. This verse introduces us to the second section Jesus spoke about in Revelation 1:8. "After these things" means: after these visions about "what is now" he was given more visions about "what will take place later."

An Overview of the Seals, Trumpets, and Bowls

It is the thesis of this chapter that the seals, trumpets, and bowls are different visions covering the same events upon the earth. The common interpretation today is that these judgments will occur in chronological order, as popularized by Hal Lindsey's *The Late Great Planet Earth* and Tim LaHaye's *Left Behind* series. Their understanding is that, after a secret rapture of the church, the world will enter a seven-year period of rule by the Antichrist. During this time, God will begin His judgments with the seven seals, after which come the seven trumpets, which are followed by the seven bowls of wrath, and finally, the triumphant and visible return of Christ.

This scenario does not make sense - logically or biblically. As mentioned above, the Bible says that the Antichrist will be heralded as a savior because he will bring about world peace and prosperity. He will proclaim himself as god when he defiles the rebuilt Jewish temple three and one half years into the last seven years of history. Therefore, we must conclude that there has to be peace and prosperity at least up until that time! However, the common Dispensational teaching says that the seven seal judgments (at least) have been unleashed upon the earth by then. These seven judgments include worldwide war, famine, persecution, and horrifying cosmic events (including the sky rolling back like a scroll, the sun and moon turning blood-red, and the visitation of the "wrath of the Lamb").[48] How could anyone on earth not be affected by such calamities? How would anyone conclude that their world-ruler had ushered in a time of unparalleled peace, prosperity, and safety with all these catastrophic events taking place?

Personally, it was this illogical and unlikely scenario which caused me to rethink the popular evangelical system of eschatology. Clearly, a different approach was necessary. I began to study the events that would take place on earth when each of the seven seals, trumpets and bowls occurred. Since we will not hear or know when the seals, trumpets, or bowls will be unleashed in heaven, we will only feel their effects upon the earth. And, since there is no "time" as we know it in heaven ("A day is as a thousand years, and a thousand years are like a day"), we cannot be sure when the heavenly cause will have its direct effect upon the earth. Therefore, the only thing people on earth will know is the end result of the judgment. As I focused upon the earthly effects, I noticed some amazing similarities among the visions, as the following chart shows:

---

[48] Technically, it is not correct to label the seven seals as judgments at all. The fifth seal describes the persecution of believers. How can anyone honestly call that a judgment of God? Rather, a better way of looking at the seven seals is to see them as a broad outline of end-time events, as I will prove.

Comparison Chart of the Seals, Trumpets, and Bowls

Seals -   Revelation 5-6, (7 is elaboration)
                       Revelation 8:1 - seventh seal

1	2	3	4	5	6	7
war	war	famine	war: 1/4 earth involved	martyred saints	earthquake: sun like sack- cloth, moon red, stars fall; The wrath of the Lamb (v.16)	silence in heaven

Trumpets -   Revelation 8:2-9, (10-11:14 is elaboration)
                       Revelation 11:15-19 - the last trumpet

1	2	3	4	5 (1st Woe)
hail & fire fall to earth; earth burned	a "great mountain" falls into the sea	great star falls into sea, waters bitter	1/3 of sun and moon and stars darkened	star falls; opens pit of Hell; "locusts" inflict painful sores upon people who do not have God's seal

6 (2nd Woe)	7 (3rd Woe)
final war Euphrates River mentioned	kingdom comes; dead judged, saints rewarded

Bowls of Wrath -   Revelation 15-16 (17-18 is elaboration)
                       Revelation 19

1	2	3	4	5
sores on those who worship beast	sea becomes like blood	rivers, waters like blood	sun scorches with fire	darkness upon the beast

6	7
War at Armageddon, Euphrates River dries up	"It is done" Great earthquake; judgment upon Babylon Return of Christ during Battle of Armageddon

Based upon these observations, I will show the following:

- The seals, the trumpets, and the bowls each conclude with the return of Christ, proving that they are meant to be understood as complementary pictures of the Day of the Lord rather than consecutive events of the tribulation period.
- The seven seals follow Christ's chronology of events as He outlined them for us in the Olivet Discourse.
- The sixth seal is the outpouring of the wrath of God upon mankind.
- The first five trumpets and the first five bowls describe the sixth seal in greater detail. (They describe the "First Woe" of mankind.)
- The sixth trumpet and the sixth bowl describe the events leading up to and including the Battle of Armageddon. (They describe the "Second Woe" of mankind.)
- The Seventh Trumpet and the Seventh Bowl both describe what will happen to mankind when Christ returns. (They describe the "Third Woe" of mankind.)

The Return of Christ in the Seals, Trumpets, and Bowls

The first obvious similarity I noticed in this chart concerned the seventh trumpet and the seventh bowl. Both declare the culmination of this age with the return of Christ. As the seventh bowl is poured out, a loud voice declares, "It is done!" (Revelation 16:17), followed by a description of the judgment upon mystery Babylon and the return of Christ at the Battle of Armageddon (Revelation 17-19). At the seventh trumpet, loud voices in heaven declare, "The kingdom of the world has become the kingdom of our Lord and of His Christ; and He will reign forever and ever" (Revelation 11:15). This statement is immediately followed by the testimony of the twenty-four elders who say, "...the nations were enraged, and Your wrath came, and the time came for the dead to be judged, and the time to reward Your bond-servants the prophets and saints and those who fear Your Name, the small and the great, and to destroy those who destroy the earth" (Revelation 11:18; NASB). In other words, the seventh bowl and the seventh trumpet both declare that the end has come - God's wrath has been poured out upon unbelievers and God's reward has been given to believers![49]

---

[49] Remember that both Jesus and Paul tell us that the Second Coming will be attended by a loud voice, a trumpet call, and the resurrection and/or rapture of the righteous. All of these elements are present in the seventh trumpet - in other words, the Last Trumpet!

Seeing this pattern, I wondered, "Does the seventh seal represent a similar finale?" The seventh seal seems like a rather anticlimactic ending to what had just taken place in the first six seals: "And there was silence in heaven for a half an hour" (Revelation 8:1). What does this mean? How can there be a "half an hour" in a timeless place? Commentators struggle with this verse. The usual interpretation is that it describes a period of readiness prior to the next series of judgments (using the popular subsequent/consecutive system of interpretation). But the seventh seal is not really a judgment at all if it is interpreted in that manner. It is just a pause before more judgments are released.

There is a better way of looking at the seventh seal. Remember, John was using apocalyptic language - a style of Jewish prophecy that was common in his day. Many of the symbols he used were not unique the Book of Revelation. These symbols often had standard meanings in apocalyptic literature. Can the meaning of "silence in heaven" be discovered from other Jewish apocalyptic writings? It can. The apocryphal book of 2 Esdras 7:29-31 speaks of a time of silence at the time of the final judgment and the introduction of the new creation:

"And after these years my son the Messiah shall die, and all who draw human breath. And the world shall be turned back to primeval silence for seven days, as it was at the first beginnings; so that no one shall be left. And after seven days the world, which is not yet awake, shall be roused, and that which is corruptible shall perish."

The point here is not to endorse the eschatological interpretation of an apocryphal book, but to show that the metaphor of silence at the last judgment was at least understood in John's day as symbolic of the end of human history, prior to the creation of the new heavens and new earth!

Therefore, I believe that the seventh seal represents the very same ending as that of the trumpets and bowls: the return of Christ and the end of this age. If this is the case, we *must* interpret the seals, trumpets and bowls as being different views of the same events because they all end at the same point - the Second Coming of Christ!

Christ's Chronology and the Seven Seals

Jesus gave us the authoritative description of how the end-time events will unfold in the Olivet Discourse. Using such words as "when," "after," and "then," He presented us with a broad outline of the events leading to His return. Therefore, it is probably wiser to fit the events of the Book of Revelation into Jesus' chronology rather than trying to do it the other way around. What did Jesus say about what was going to happen, and how do the seals, trumpets, and bowls fit into His scenario?

To review, Jesus warned us not to be fooled by the "birth pangs" of the approach of the Day of the Lord. He said that there would be wars, rumors of wars, earthquakes, famines, pestilences, and diseases. They are not the definitive signs of His soon coming. But just as birth pangs increase in severity and frequency, so the wars, famines, earthquakes, etc. will grow worse as the time of the end draws near.

Jesus also said that believers can expect ferocious persecution - both in His day and throughout church history. This persecution will reach its zenith during the reign of the Antichrist. Jesus said, "When you see the Abomination of Desolation…standing in the Holy place…flee!" (Matthew 24:15,16).

The key signs signaling the imminence of the end are: (1) the return of Jerusalem to Jewish sovereignty; and (2) the completion of the church's witness to all the nations. After this, the Antichrist will rise to power, proclaim himself a god, and persecute true believers. Jesus called this final period the "Great Tribulation." It would be so severe that, "Unless those days had been cut short, no life would have been saved…" (Matthew 24:22; NASB).

After this tribulation, Jesus said that calamitous cosmic signs would wreak havoc upon the earth: the sun would turn red, the moon would turn the color of blood, stars (meteorites) would fall from the sky, the seas would roar and toss, and people would be in great distress and fear over their destiny (c.f., Matthew 24:29; Luke 21:25-26).

Finally, after this great judgment upon mankind, Jesus said that He would return with a mighty shout, a trumpet call, the resurrection of the dead, and the gathering together of His elect (Matthew 24:30-31).

How do the seals, trumpets, and bowls fit into this framework? Perfectly, if each of these visions is describing the same events of God's judgment. But upon what internal evidence is this interpretation based?

As we look at the opening of the first six seals, we see the same outline of events Jesus gave us! The first four seals describe the "birth pangs:" wars, conquests, famine, and plague; while the fifth seal announces the persecution of Christians.

When are the seals broken open in heaven? It is pointless to ask; we cannot know. But what we do know is that the birth pangs of the 20th century have been both strong and frequent! It is very possible that our world is now experiencing the consequences of the breaking of the first five seals!

All we are waiting for is the Antichrist to rise to power, where he will broker a Middle East peace treaty and unify the world in a post-Christian empire. (These events are spelled out in progressive detail in the interlude sections of the Book of Revelation, which I wrote about in the chapter, "The Last Evil Empire.)

After the Antichrist's persecution of Christians, the sixth seal will be broken:

12 I watched as he opened the sixth seal. There was a great earthquake. The sun turned black like sackcloth made of goat hair, the whole moon turned blood red, 13 and the stars in the sky fell to earth, as late figs drop from a fig tree when shaken by a strong wind. 14 The sky receded like a scroll, rolling up, and every mountain and island was removed from its place.

15 Then the kings of the earth, the princes, the generals, the rich, the mighty, and every slave and every free man hid in caves and among the rocks of the mountains. 16 They called to the mountains and the rocks, "fall on us and hide us from the face of him who sits on the throne and from the wrath of the Lamb! 17 For the great day of their wrath has come, and who can stand? (Revelation 6:12-17)

This is exactly what Jesus said would happen "immediately after the tribulation of those days" (Matthew 24:29; NASB). *Therefore, we must conclude that the seven seals represent a general outline of the events of the last days*!

The Sixth Seal: The Outpouring of God's Wrath!

Let's look more closely at the events described by the sixth seal. These events are called "the wrath of the Lamb" and "the great day of their wrath" (Revelation 6:16,17). There will be a great earthquake, causing every mountain and island to be moved from their place. This earthquake is also described in the passage of the Book of Isaiah, known as Isaiah's Apocalypse: "The earth is broken up, the earth is split asunder, the earth is thoroughly shaken. The earth reels like a drunkard, it sways like a hut in the wind; so heavy upon it is the guilt of its rebellion that it falls never to rise again" (Isaiah 24:19-21). The quake will not be just a localized magnitude 10 on the Richter scale (large as that would be). It will cause the whole earth to wobble and sway. Even mountains and islands will be destroyed! In addition, the sixth seal tells us about cataclysmic events taking place above the earth. The sky will roll back like a scroll, the sun will appear as black as sackcloth, the moon will turn the color of blood red, and the stars will fall to the earth. Everywhere, people will try to protect themselves from this calamity by hiding in caves or mountains.

Jesus said that, unless He cut these days short, no life would remain on earth. The sixth seal seems to be describing just such an event of life-threatening magnitude. To suppose that two more separate series of judgments (the trumpets and bowls) can occur after the worldwide destruction of the sixth seal is hardly possible.

The Complementary Nature of the Trumpets and Bowls

I believe that after John saw the general outline of events through the opening of the seven seals, he saw two more, complementary visions that describe the horrible destruction of the sixth seal. After the seventh seal was opened, he saw seven angels with the seven trumpets of God. One by one the angels blow their trumpets. With the possible exception of the last trumpet (which Jesus and Paul said would be heard), earth dwellers will not hear them as they are blown. But the earth will certainly feel their effects. Notice the similarities between the effects of the sixth seal and those of the first five trumpets:

Rev. 8:7 The first angel sounded his trumpet, and there came hail and fire mixed with blood, and it was hurled down upon the earth. A third of the earth was burned up, a third of the trees were burned up, and all the green grass was burned up.

8 The second angel sounded his trumpet, and something like a huge mountain, all ablaze, was thrown into the sea. A third of the sea turned into blood, 9 a third of the living creatures in the sea died, and a third of the ships were destroyed.

10 The third angel sounded his trumpet, and a great star, blazing like a torch, fell from the sky on a third of the rivers and on the springs of water—11 the name of the star is Wormwood. A third of the waters turned bitter, and many people died from the waters that had become bitter.

12 The fourth angel sounded his trumpet, and a third of the sun was struck, a third of the moon, and a third of the stars, so that a third of them turned dark. A third of the day was without light, and also a third of the night. 13 As I watched, I heard an eagle that was flying in midair call out in a loud voice: "Woe! Woe! Woe to the inhabitants of the earth, because of the trumpet blasts about to be sounded by the other three angels!"

Rev. 9:1 The fifth angel sounded his trumpet, and I saw a star that had fallen from the sky to the earth. The star was given the key to the shaft of the Abyss. 2 When he opened the Abyss, smoke rose from it like the smoke from a gigantic furnace. The sun and sky were darkened by the smoke from the Abyss. 3 And out of the smoke locusts came down upon the earth and were given power like that of scorpions of the earth. 4 They were told not to harm the grass of the earth or any plant or tree, but only those people who did not have the seal of God on their foreheads. 5 They were not given power to kill them, but only to torture them for five months. And the agony they suffered was like that of the sting of a scorpion when it strikes a man. 6 During those days men will seek death, but will not find it; they will long to die, but death will elude them. 7 The locusts looked like horses prepared for battle. On their heads they wore something like crowns of gold, and their faces resembled human faces. 8 Their hair was like women's hair, and their teeth were like lions' teeth. 9 They had breastplates like breastplates of iron, and the sound of their wings was like the thundering of many horses and chariots rushing into battle. 10 They had tails and stings like scorpions, and in their tails they had power to torment people for five months. 11 They had as king over them the angel of the Abyss, whose name in Hebrew is Abaddon, and in Greek, Apollyon.

12 The first woe is past; two other woes are yet to come. (Revelation 8:7 - 9:12)

Here we have descriptions of judgments from above, wreaking havoc and destruction upon the earth. The sixth seal describes stars falling from the sky, the atmosphere rolling up like a scroll, the sun and moon obscured from view, and people hiding from these cataclysmic effects by digging holes in the ground. The first five trumpets seem to give us more descriptive elements about this judgment.

The first trumpet unleashes a torrent of fiery ice upon the earth, burning all of the grass and one-third of the rest of the vegetation. The second trumpet describes a mountain-sized object striking the ocean, resulting in the immediate death of one-third of the sea life and the loss of one-third of the world's ships. The third trumpet tells us about a blazing shooting star that pollutes of one-third of the fresh water supply. The fourth trumpet reveals that the sun, moon, and stars are obscured from view for one-third of their course across the sky. Finally, the fifth trumpet's blast gives added details to what had just taken place, saying that the star that "had fallen from the sky to the earth" opened up a large hole ("the abyss").[50] The smoke from this impact will ascend into the atmosphere and block the sun, moon, and stars from view. And, as much as we may find the Bible's cosmology strange to our modern scientific understanding, the hole in the earth's crust will break open the inner part of earth where demonic creatures have been trapped since the time of their fall (c.f., Jude 6). These creatures will be released to torment the people who do not have the protective seal of God with painful sores and afflictions for a period of five months.

Now, observe the similarities between the first five trumpets and the first five bowls of wrath:

---

[50] It appears from this description of the fifth trumpet that all the trumpets may be referring to different aspects of the very same event. Here, the fifth trumpet is simply telling us of added dimensions to the second and fourth trumpet blasts.

1 Then I heard a loud voice from the temple saying to the seven angels, "Go, pour out the seven bowls of God's wrath on the earth."

2 The first angel went and poured out his bowl on the land, and ugly and painful sores broke out on the people who had the mark of the beast and worshiped his image.

3 The second angel poured out his bowl on the sea, and it turned into blood like that of a dead man, and every living thing in the sea died.

4 The third angel poured out his bowl on the rivers and springs of water, and they became blood.

8 The fourth angel poured out his bowl on the sun, and the sun was given power to scorch people with fire. 9 They were seared by the intense heat and they cursed the name of God, who had control over these plagues, but they refused to repent and glorify him.

10 The fifth angel poured out his bowl on the throne of the beast, and his kingdom was plunged into darkness. Men gnawed their tongues in agony 11 and cursed the God of heaven because of their pains and their sores, but they refused to repent of what they had done. (Revelation 16:1-4, 8-11)

Although the events are listed in a different order of occurrence, they seem to be referring to the same things. The fifth trumpet describes demonic creatures that sting only those people who do not have the protective seal from God. They are tormented with pain for several months. The first bowl tells us that these sores will afflict only those who have taken the mark of the beast and worshipped him. The second trumpet describes the impact of a mountainous object into the ocean. The second bowl tells us that it will eventually kill all sea life. The third trumpet describes the pollution of the earth's fresh water. Likewise, the third bowl tells us that the water will become undrinkable, just as the Nile River turned to blood when Moses struck it with his staff. The fourth and fifth trumpets describe the atmospheric effects of the impact of the "falling star." The fourth and fifth bowls tell us that weather patterns will be adversely affected, resulting in extremes in heat and darkness.

No one on earth will know what has just taken place in heaven concerning the trumpets or bowls. The trumpets will be blown and the bowls will be poured out, but people will only see their effects upon the earth. Therefore, it does not matter to us in what order they occur in heaven. But it does seem that their effects upon earth will happen concurrently.

Yet, despite all these cataclysmic judgments, mankind will still refuse to see the hand of God in them. They will continue to refuse to repent from their sins (Revelation 16:11). Why won't people see the judgment of God in all these things? Sadly, they will interpret them as natural events, rather than supernatural ones.

The Sixth Seal: Described by the Trumpet and Bowl Judgments

Until recently, it has been difficult for Bible scholars to determine just what will cause the destruction described by the sixth seal, the trumpets, and the bowls. Some interpreters thought that they were first century attempts at describing nuclear warfare, global warming, and/or environmental pollution. These kinds of interpretations are based upon the assumption that the judgments are the results of mankind reaping the consequences of our sin against each other and the environment. However, these interpreters fail to take into account that the judgments are described as coming *down* from heaven. Therefore, the judgments should not be understood as the consequences of our sins. Rather, they are God's direct judgment upon Sin!

If the judgment is coming down from above, what could it possibly be? What instrument will God use to bring about the worldwide cataclysm that John describes? Recent scientific discoveries may have given us a clue. It is a distinct possibility that the tool God will use for His judgment upon the earth will be what the ancients called, "the Sword of the Lord." The only thing that can cause the kind destruction described by the Book or Revelation is the impact of a comet upon the earth!

How can we be sure of this conclusion? Evidence from earth's past gives us good evidence for this hypothesis! Our planet has been struck numerous times in its history by comets or asteroids, leaving huge craters in the surface (most of which have been eroded into near obscurity). But it wasn't until 1978 when four scientists, trying to discover why there was a mass extinction of dinosaurs some 65 million years ago, came upon crucial information about the effects of comet and asteroid collisions upon life on earth. Geologists have long known that there was an unusual gap in the fossil record. In rock strata older than 65 million years, certain species of dinosaurs lived. But at a certain layer (known as the Cretaceous Period), these dinosaurs suddenly became extinct. Just as suddenly whole new species of animals came into being, beginning what is called the Tertiary Period. The scientists (physicist Luis Alvarez, chemists Frank Asaro and Helen Michel, and geologist Walter Alvarez) discovered abnormal amounts of the element iridium in the thin layer of clay that separates the two strata of rock (known as the "KT boundary").

In his report, "The Search for the KT Crater," Walter Alvarez writes:

"Iridium is very rare throughout the solar system and is even more depleted in the Earth's crust because it alloys with iron; consequently, most of the Earth's original allotment of iridium is probably stored in the

Earth's iron core. After several years of additional measurements and debate, the research team concluded that the anomalous iridium had reached the Earth as a small fraction of a large asteroid or comet that struck the planet 65 million years ago. The team suggested that this impact would have lofted so much [iridium-rich] dust into the atmosphere around the planet that the surface would have become very dark for some months, stopping photosynthesis and producing mass extinction among the animals by starvation."

"During the 1980s researchers discovered many lines of evidence that supported the impact theory for the KT mass extinction. Paleontologists studying the fossil record showed that the extinction in many groups of animals and plants was extremely abrupt. Tiny rock spherules were found in the KT boundary layer around the world and were shown to have originated as droplets of rock melted by the heat of the impact, ejected through the atmosphere in a giant impact fireball, and scattered in ballistic trajectories outside the atmosphere. Grains of quartz sand from the KT boundary were shown to have features produced only by great shock pressures, which occur in nature only during impact events. Finally, these features - iridium anomalies, impact-melt spherules, and shocked-quartz grains - were found worldwide in the KT boundary but were absent elsewhere in the record of Earth's history except as markers for a handful of other impact events."[51]

The impact point for this powerful collision was identified as the Chicxulub formation, which straddles the Yucatan Peninsula and the Caribbean Sea. To quote Alvarzez's report again,

"A comet or asteroid hitting the Earth, the Moon, or another planet or satellite is traveling at a very high velocity (between 11 and 80 kilometers per second in the case of the Earth). At this velocity it has enormous kinetic energy. On hitting the Earth, it penetrates many kilometers below the surface as it is slowing down, and in the process of slowing down much of its kinetic energy is converted to heat. This heat causes a gigantic explosion. In the case of the KT impactor, the explosion probably released 10,000 times as much energy as is contained in all the present nuclear arsenals (though it must be remembered that in the case of an impact, this is not nuclear energy but just the energy of

---

[51] The Search for the KT Crater, Dr. Walter Alvarez, Department of Geology and Geophysics, University of California, Berkeley, from the Encyclopedia Britannica Yearbook of Science and the Future, 1993, p. 90.

motion of a big rock moving fast). The result is an enormous explosion centered perhaps 10 or 20 kilometers below the Earth's surface, the depth to which the impactor has penetrated. Such an explosion produces a circular crater regardless of whether the impact is oblique - circular because it is blown out rather than scooped out."

"The estimate of a crater 150 kilometers in diameter is derived partly from calculations of the energy of the impact explosion and partly from observations of the known craters on the Earth. Craters on the Earth that are up to 100 kilometers in diameter do not seem to have produced mass extinctions, and so something bigger would be needed to explain the KT extinction."[52]

Further evidence for the destructive power of a comet impact came on July 16, 1994, when the Shoemaker-Levy Comet (named after its discoverer's Eugene and Carolyn Shoemaker and their collaborator, David Levy) struck the planet Jupiter. Apparently, the comet had been captured by the massive planet's gravity as it traveled in toward the sun. Its icy nucleus broke apart into at least 21 pieces as it swung around Jupiter on its first orbit. The largest of the pieces was only two miles in diameter. Their next orbit brought them on a collision course with the 90,000 mile-wide target. One by one, traveling at 37 miles per second, they struck the planet with such force that they literally blew earth-sized holes into the Jovian atmosphere, each 8,000 miles in diameter!

On a much smaller scale, our own planet was struck by a cosmic visitor early in the twentieth century. On June 30, 1908, a small comet blew up as it entered the atmosphere over the Tunguska area of Siberia. The shock wave of the explosion decimated the Siberian forest in a butterfly-shaped pattern some 85 square miles in area. Since no traces of celestial rock or iron have ever been found, it is theorized that the explosion was most likely made when the icy nucleus of the comet exploded when it hit the atmosphere. Fortunately, the area was sparsely populated and few, if any, people were killed. However, what is eerie about this occurrence is that no one even saw it coming!

What would happen to earth if a large comet struck the earth? Astronomer David Levy wrote about the consequences of a comet impact in the May 10, 1998 issue of Parade Magazine:

"The end comes swiftly. The comet breaks through the upper atmosphere, destroying the Earth's protective ozone layer. There is a deafening sonic boom. Seconds later, with the force of 100 million hydrogen bombs, the comet slams into the Pacific Ocean just off the coast of Los Angeles. Virtually every rock within 5 miles of ground

---

[52] Ibid., p. 94

zero is instantly vaporized. The Earth trembles as a force-12 quake topples any animal trying to stand up. In less than a minute, a mighty shock wave gouges out a crater 100 miles wide and 25 miles deep. Another shock wave tears the comet apart, and its remnants vaporize as they plow into the Earth.

"Mile-high tsunamis rush upward from the point of impact and speed across the Pacific, flooding coastal cities from Los Angeles to Tokyo. The force of impact generates enormous heat, and a fireball of hot gas, visible for thousands of miles, rises high into the atmosphere. Millions of tons of rocky debris and dust billow upward in a gigantic cloud. All over the Earth, storms of heavy rocks - the debris dredged up by the impact - strike the ground with enough violence to tear it up. Anyone outdoors feels temperatures as high as an oven set to broiling. Ground fires ignite and quickly spread around the world.

"That's just the overture. As the world wide fires burn for months, fine dust thickens high in the Earth's atmosphere. The sky becomes black as a darkroom, and for more than six months there is no sunlight anywhere on Earth. Cooling rains fall, but they are poisoned with sulfuric acid. After more than a year of darkness, the sky finally clears, and temperatures begin a slow rise as the Earth turns into a giant greenhouse.

"What a scenario for Armageddon this is!"

Little did Dr. Levy know that he had inadvertently described the judgment of God, as revealed to us in the Book of Revelation!

John saw something like a "great mountain burning with fire" thrown into the sea. Why do I believe that this will be a comet and not an asteroid? First, Dr. Shoemaker, in an article, "The Collision of Solid Bodies," (*The New Solar System*, third edition, 1990) states that a comet - even though it is made of ice - would cause just as much destruction as an asteroid, because its velocity is much greater. Second, it is much easier to discover a comet. It announces its arrival into the solar system with the growth of a "tail." The tail is formed when the solar radiation warms the comet, ejecting icy material from its nucleus. As the comet nears the sun, the tail grows longer. Interestingly, the tail does not "follow" the comet around the sun. Instead, the "solar wind" blows the tail away from the sun. Therefore, as the comet departs from the sun the tail goes ahead of it.

Why is this important? The Bible seems to imply that people on earth will see the disaster coming. Jesus described "...men fainting from fear and the expectation of the things coming upon the world; for the powers of the heavens will be shaken" (Luke 21:26). It is quite possible that astronomers will discover the comet as it approaches the sun and will then calculate when it will impact the earth some months in the future. People will have some time to prepare, by digging holes or caves in the mountains for protection. Revelation 6:15 tells us that, "the kings of the earth and the great men and the commanders and the rich…hid themselves in the caves and among the rocks of the mountains…"

The final reason for supposing that the judgment will be a comet is the fact that the Bible describes the impact as "hail and fire, mixed with smoke" (Revelation 8:7). Until the last few decades, astronomers did not even know what made up a comet. Now, we know that it consists primarily of ice. It is quite possible that our earth will encounter the comet's tail first, before the nucleus, causing this icy meteor shower. Imagine what would happen if thousands of Tunguska-sized chunks of ice hit the earth just prior to the main body of the comet!

When the comet enters the earth's atmosphere, the initial shock wave will push the atmosphere away with such force that it would look like the sky was "rolled back like a scroll" (Revelation 6:14; Isaiah 34:4). No one who witnesses this will be able to live to tell about it. Anyone able to watch the comet enter the atmosphere would be pulverized by the blast.

The comet will strike the earth in the ocean, according to Revelation 8:8: "…a great mountain burning with fire was thrown into the sea; and a third of the sea became blood." The comet will explode deep within the earth's crust, under the sea, sending mountainous volumes of ejecta back into the atmosphere. The impact will force walls of water into mile-high tsunamis that will rush back and forth throughout the world's oceans, destroying nearly everything on the surface of the ocean and for tens of miles inland.[53] Jesus said that there would be, "…dismay among nations, in perplexity at the roaring and tossing of the sea" (Luke 21:25; NASB).

The vast amounts of dust in the atmosphere will change weather patterns severely. The Bible says that the sun, moon, and stars will be obscured for one-third of the time. We have seen how volcanic eruptions blow tons of dust into the atmosphere. The famous Krakatoa eruption actually caused a "mini-ice age" for several years because the debris from that one island blocked so much sunlight from reaching the earth. Imagine what an effect a crater one hundred miles wide would cause! John saw that darkness covered the kingdom of the Antichrist. The fallout from this dust will pollute all the fresh water on the planet. Rainfall will become caustic for plants and animals alike. The Bible seems to imply that this dust cloud will trap surface temperatures and turn the planet into a hot house (see Revelation 16:8).

---

[53] When the island of Krakatoa blew up in the 19th century, its huge tsunamis made their way throughout the world. Ripples from those waves were felt even up the Thames River in London, as docks and buoys were seen violently bobbing up and down.

Our world has been warned. We have witnessed what can happen to our world if a comet should hit. Some astronomers are even saying that such a collision is inevitable and that we should prepare some kind of space defense plan to detect and destroy any comet or asteroid coming our way. We have even been entertained with this scenario in two block-buster summer movies, "Deep Impact" and "Armageddon!" So when the wrath of God is visited upon the Earth in this way, people will just say it is just our bad luck. It has happened in the past; but we will somehow overcome.

After the comet impact, the Bible says that there will be at least five months before the visible return of Christ (Revelation 9:5). Despite the torment from the demonic creatures coming forth from the crater, the survivors will attempt to rebuild something of civilization. What they will do next will usher in the end of this present evil age.

The Sixth Trumpet and Sixth Bowl: the Battle of Armageddon

The fifth trumpet ends the first Woe to mankind (the comet impact). It warns of two more Woes to come (Revelation 9:12). The second Woe is described by the sixth trumpet. Again, we see amazing similarities between what takes place at the sixth trumpet and the events heralded by the sixth bowl. *Both* of them mention a large army crossing the Euphrates River in order to invade the Holy Land.

> 13 Then the sixth angel sounded, and I heard a voice from the four horns of the golden alter which is before God, 14 one saying to the sixth angel who had the trumpet, "Release the four angels who are bound at the great river Euphrates." 15 And the four angels, who had been prepared for the hour and day and month and year, were released, so that they would kill a third of mankind. 16 The number of the armies of the horsemen was two hundred million; I heard the number of them" (Revelation 9:13-16).
>
> 12 The sixth angel poured out his bowl on the great river, the Euphrates; and its water was dried up, so that the way would be prepared for the kings from the east [lit. "rising of the sun"]. 13 And I saw coming out of the mouth of the dragon and out of the mouth of the beast and out of the mouth of the false prophet, three unclean spirits like frogs; 14 for they are spirits of demons, performing signs, which go out to the kings of the whole world, to gather them together for the war of the great day of God, the Almighty. 15 ("Behold, I am coming like a thief. Blessed is the one who stays awake and keeps his clothes, so that he will not walk about naked and men will not see his shame.") 16 And they

gathered them together to the place which in Hebrew is called Har-Magedon (Revelation 16:12-16).

These Scriptures are not speaking about two different invasions. Both passages refer to the Euphrates River as the location of the invasion route of large armies coming from the east. The first tells us that one-third of mankind will perish in that war. The second passage tells us that the war will have its culmination at Har-Magedon (or in modern terminology, Armageddon).

This final battle in human history is also described in other parts of the Bible. The best account is found in chapters 12 and 14 of the Book of Zechariah. Let's look more closely at the details of this, the Second Woe, as told to us by Zechariah:

"I am going to make Jerusalem a cup that sends all the surrounding peoples reeling. Judah will be besieged as well as Jerusalem. 3 On that day, when all the nations of the earth are gathered against her, I will make Jerusalem an immovable rock for all the nations. All who try to move it will injure themselves. 4 On that day I will strike every horse with panic and its rider with madness," declares the LORD. "I will keep a watchful eye over the house of Judah, but I will blind all the horses of the nations. 5 Then the leaders of Judah will say in their hearts, 'The people of Jerusalem are strong, because the LORD Almighty is their God.'

6 "On that day I will make the leaders of Judah like a firepot in a woodpile, like a flaming torch among sheaves. They will consume right and left all the surrounding peoples, but Jerusalem will remain intact in her place. 7 "The LORD will save the dwellings of Judah first, so that the honor of the house of David and of Jerusalem's inhabitants may not be greater than that of Judah. 8 On that day the LORD will shield those who live in Jerusalem, so that the feeblest among them will be like David, and the house of David will be like God, like the Angel of the LORD going before them. 9 On that day I will set out to destroy all the nations that attack Jerusalem.

10 "And I will pour out on the house of David and the inhabitants of Jerusalem a spirit of grace and supplication. They will look on me, the one they have pierced, and they will mourn for him as one mourns for an only child, and grieve bitterly for him as one grieves for a firstborn son. 11 On that day the weeping in Jerusalem will be great, like the weeping of Hadad Rimmon in the plain of Megiddo. 12 The land will mourn, each clan by itself, with their wives by themselves: the clan of the house of David and their wives, the clan of the house of Nathan and their wives, 13 the clan of the house of Levi and their wives, the clan of

Shimei and their wives, 14 and all the rest of the clans and their wives (Zechariah 12:2-14).

From this passage we can see that the pseudo-peace of the Antichrist will not hold together, particularly after the stress of the recent comet impact. All the nations of the earth will come against the nation of Israel. We know that in the spirit realm, the devil will have three demonic beings incite the kings of the east to invade the land (Revelation 16:13,14). However, we are not given any earthly reason. We can only speculate as to their justification for war. Perhaps Israel will be protected from most of the consequences of the First Woe. Just as God protected the Israelites from most of the effects of the ten plagues in Egypt, He will also shield the land of Israel from the comet's initial destruction and the subsequent adverse weather patterns. It is very possible that the reason the large numbers of people from the East will make their way across the dry Euphrates River bed is because there will be nothing left to live for in their homeland![54] These people will be desperately seeking a place of safety.

Whatever the reason, all the nations of the earth will join against little Israel in this showdown between the Kingdom of God and kingdoms of this world. It appears that the armies of Israel will be able to withstand the initial assault (verses 6-8). But this success will not last. Israel will be overwhelmed by the shear numbers of the invaders. Her modern, well-equipped armies will soon run out of supplies and munitions. According to the following parallel passage, Jerusalem will be besieged, captured, and ransacked:

A day of the LORD is coming when your plunder will be divided among you. 2 I will gather all the nations to Jerusalem to fight against it; the city will be captured, the houses ransacked, and the women raped. Half of the city will go into exile, but the rest of the people will not be taken from the city.

3 Then the LORD will go out and fight against those nations, as he fights in the day of battle. *4 On that day his feet will stand on the Mount of Olives*, east of Jerusalem, and the Mount of Olives will be split in two from east to west, forming a great valley, with half of the mountain moving north and half moving south. 5 You will flee by my mountain valley, for it will extend to Azel. You will flee as you fled from the

---

[54] It is very possible that the comet will hit somewhere in the Pacific or Indian Oceans. Admittedly, this is speculation, but it is based upon some rational possibilities. First, the chances are greater that the comet will strike one of these two bodies of water because together they make up half the world's surface. Second, since Israel is not affected by the resulting tsunami, it has to be some distance away.

earthquake in the days of Uzziah king of Judah. Then the LORD my God will come, and all the holy ones with him. (Zechariah 14:1-3).

But both passages in Zechariah include fantastic messages of hope and victory! The Lord, Himself, will come to fight against the enemies of Israel. When He does, the Spirit of God will work mightily among the people, bringing about conviction of Sin and repentance toward God. His grace will be poured out upon the chosen people of God. They will look upon Jesus, the one whom their ancestors rejected and pierced, and they will receive Him as their long-awaited savior!

When Jesus ascended into heaven from the Mount of Olives, two angels told the amazed disciples that Jesus would return again in the same way He had just left. Zechariah 14:4 tells us that at the moment when the battle for Jerusalem is lost, Jesus Christ will return to the Mount of Olives, splitting it apart with the weight of His glorious presence!

If Jesus is returning to Jerusalem, why does the Book of Revelation mention the final Battle of Armageddon? Actually, it does not mention a battle at Armageddon at all. Revelation 16:16 simply reports that the forces arrayed against Israel will be gathered together at Armageddon. Why would the armies gather there? Armageddon is located in the Plain of Jezreel, just north of the Judean hills. This area has been the site of numerous invasions into Israel for millennia. It makes a perfect staging area for mounting attacks into the southern and eastern parts of the country. Therefore, as the bulk of the fighting will be taking place in Jerusalem, the plain of Jezreel will become the rear area, used as the headquarters and supply center.

The Seventh Trumpet and the Seventh Bowl: The Return of Christ

To those who are fighting against Him, Christ's return will become their Third Woe. The Apostle John referred to the passage in Zechariah 12 earlier in the Book of Revelation: "Look, he is coming with the clouds, and every eye will see him, even those who pierced him; and all the peoples of the earth will mourn because of him. So shall it be! Amen" (Revelation 1:7). What could be the worst news for the devil and his sinful allies but the sound of the Last Trumpet announcing the triumphant return of Jesus Christ! There will be mourning indeed, but theirs will not be the sorrow of repentance!

In a last act of desperation, the armies of the world will turn their useless and feeble weapons upon Christ and the armies of heaven! The one-side massacre is described in Revelation 19:11-21:

11 I saw heaven standing open and there before me was a white horse, whose rider is called Faithful and True. With justice he judges and

makes war. 12 His eyes are like blazing fire, and on his head are many crowns. He has a name written on him that no one knows but he himself. 13 He is dressed in a robe dipped in blood, and his name is the Word of God. 14 The armies of heaven were following him, riding on white horses and dressed in fine linen, white and clean. 15 Out of his mouth comes a sharp sword with which to strike down the nations. "He will rule them with an iron scepter." He treads the winepress of the fury of the wrath of God Almighty. 16 On his robe and on his thigh he has this name written: KING OF KINGS AND LORD OF LORDS.

17 And I saw an angel standing in the sun, who cried in a loud voice to all the birds flying in midair, "Come, gather together for the great supper of God, 18 so that you may eat the flesh of kings, generals, and mighty men, of horses and their riders, and the flesh of all people, free and slave, small and great."

19 Then I saw the beast and the kings of the earth and their armies gathered together to make war against the rider on the horse and his army. 20 But the beast was captured, and with him the false prophet who had performed the miraculous signs on his behalf. With these signs he had deluded those who had received the mark of the beast and worshiped his image. The two of them were thrown alive into the fiery lake of burning sulfur. 21 The rest of them were killed with the sword that came out of the mouth of the rider on the horse, and all the birds gorged themselves on their flesh.

The prophet Joel says much the same thing, describing the gathering of all the nations against Israel, the concurrent darkening of the sun and moon, and the trampling of the grapes of wrath!

1 'In those days and at that time, when I restore the fortunes of Judah and Jerusalem, 2 I will gather all nations and bring them down to the Valley of Jehoshaphat. There I will enter into judgment against them concerning my inheritance, my people Israel, for they scattered my people among the nations and divided up my land.

9 Proclaim this among the nations: Prepare for war! Rouse the warriors! Let all the fighting men draw near and attack. 10 Beat your plowshares into swords and your pruning hooks into spears. Let the weakling say, 'I am strong!' 11 Come quickly, all you nations from every side, and assemble there. Bring down your warriors, O LORD!

12 'Let the nations be roused; let them advance into the Valley of Jehoshaphat, for there I will sit to judge all the nations on every side. 13 Swing the sickle, for the harvest is ripe. Come, trample the grapes, for

the winepress is full and the vats overflow—so great is their wickedness!'

14 Multitudes, multitudes in the valley of decision! For the day of the LORD is near in the valley of decision. 15 The sun and moon will be darkened, and the stars no longer shine. 16 The LORD will roar from Zion and thunder from Jerusalem; the earth and the sky will tremble. But the LORD will be a refuge for his people, a stronghold for the people of Israel.

17 'Then you will know that I, the LORD your God, dwell in Zion, my holy hill. Jerusalem will be holy; never again will foreigners invade her.

18 'In that day the mountains will drip new wine, and the hills will flow with milk; all the ravines of Judah will run with water. A fountain will flow out of the LORD's house and will water the valley of acacias. 19 But Egypt will be desolate, Edom a desert waste, because of violence done to the people of Judah, in whose land they shed innocent blood. 20 Judah will be inhabited forever and Jerusalem through all generations. 21 Their bloodguilt, which I have not pardoned, I will pardon.' The LORD dwells in Zion! (Joel 3:1-2, 9-21).

Why would anyone try to resist this divine display of power and might? Why would people aim their weapons upward toward the armies of heaven? The answer may be that modern man has been primed to believe an unbelievable lie. As far-fetched as it sounds, people may be deceived enough into thinking that the coming heavenly Savior is an invading alien instead! Certainly our modern society has been primed to believe such rubbish! Through books, such as *The Chariots of the Gods*, and movies, such as *2001, A Space Odyssey*, many people believe that superior alien beings have visited our planet in the past. Ancient people were so entranced by their power that they worshipped these space visitors as gods. Today, vast numbers of people believe that these intelligent beings are still watching over the development of our planet and are even visiting us from other solar systems, as evidenced by UFO sightings!

However, it is impossible for UFOs to travel from other star systems. According to Einstein's Theory of Relativity, no physical object can exceed the speed of light. Furthermore, if anyone is able to approach this speed, time slows down, in relation to those people the traveler has left behind. The obvious conclusion is that it would be impossible for beings to travel the great distances in space between the stars. Our nearest celestial neighbor is Alpha Centari, over four light years in distance from our solar system. If we were to send a space ship to this star (assuming there would even be an earth-like planet to visit there), it would have to be self-contained and self-supporting for a journey that might take one or two generations in length (depending upon the spacecraft's ultimate speed). And, if we *could* get a spacecraft to travel at warp speed (whatever *that* is), there would still be no way to communicate with it because the farther it got from our planet, the older the Earth's residents would become. If they traveled to a star one hundred light years away, the space travelers would have to send communications back to their great-great-grandchildren!

In other words, as entertaining as shows like Star Wars and Star Trek are, they are impossible according to the physical laws of this universe. Space aliens cannot come here any more than we could go there, as long as we are limited by our mortal bodies in this space-time continuum!

Yet, for decades, we have been looking to the heavens for extra-terrestrial life! We think that by such a discovery we would somehow solve many of the mysteries of the universe (Are we alone? What is our destiny?). Science fiction writers such as Arthur C. Clarke, Jules Verne and H.G. Wells have stretched our imaginations with tales of space travel, exotic worlds, and weird alien races. Vast numbers of gullible and scientifically ignorant people already believe that aliens from more advanced worlds could and have traveled to Earth. Many so-called modern thinkers believe that our religious stories of miracles and powerful encounters with angels were actually the results of alien visitations in the past. Some New Age adherents believe that these alien races are still here with us, leading and guiding us toward our cosmic goal. These beings are bodiless "ascended masters" who have evolved past their need for mortal bodies.

Meanwhile, Hollywood produces fantastic hi-tech films about invasions from outer space by horrible-looking monsters that want to eat people for dinner. *From War of the Worlds* to *Independence Day*, the plot is the same: mankind rallies together, fights off the aliens, and unites to form a wonderful peaceful world in the end. So is it any wonder that the armies of the world will unite in their last ditch attempt to keep the King of kings from taking His rightful throne?

The Bible says that the slaughter in that day will be tremendous. John describes the destruction of the Antichrist and his kingdom in two visions found in Revelation 14:9-20. The first (verses 9-13) offers comfort for those believers who will be persecuted unto death by the Antichrist and his henchmen:

> 9 A third angel followed them and said in a loud voice: "If anyone worships the beast and his image and receives his mark on the forehead or on the hand, 10 he, too, will drink of the wine of God's fury, which has been poured full strength into the cup of his wrath. He will be tormented with burning sulfur in the presence of the holy angels and of the Lamb. 11 And the smoke of their torment rises for ever and ever. There is no rest day or night for those who worship the beast and his image, or for anyone who receives the mark of his name." 12 This calls for patient endurance on the part of the saints who obey God's commandments and remain faithful to Jesus. 13 Then I heard a voice

from heaven say, "Write: Blessed are the dead who die in the Lord from now on." "Yes," says the Spirit, "they will rest from their labor, for their deeds will follow them." (Revelation 14:9-13).

The people who take the mark of the Beast will have to drink of the "wine of the wrath of God." They will be tormented in the same pit into which the Beast and the Devil will be thrown.

In the second vision, John is shown the magnitude of the judgment when the harvest of the grapes of wrath is taken:

14 I looked, and there before me was a white cloud, and seated on the cloud was one "like a son of man" with a crown of gold on his head and a sharp sickle in his hand. 15 Then another angel came out of the temple and called in a loud voice to him who was sitting on the cloud, "Take your sickle and reap, because the time to reap has come, for the harvest of the earth is ripe." 16 So he who was seated on the cloud swung his sickle over the earth, and the earth was harvested.

17 Another angel came out of the temple in heaven, and he too had a sharp sickle. 18 Still another angel, who had charge of the fire, came from the altar and called in a loud voice to him who had the sharp sickle, "Take your sharp sickle and gather the clusters of grapes from the earth's vine, because its grapes are ripe." 19 The angel swung his sickle on the earth, gathered its grapes and threw them into the great winepress of God's wrath. 20 They were trampled in the winepress outside the city, and blood flowed out of the press, rising as high as the horses' bridles for a distance of 1,600 stadia (Revelation 14:14-20).

In language reminiscent of Joel's prophecy of the day of the Lord, John graphically tells us that the blood of those slain at that time will flow for a distance of two hundred miles (1,600 stadia—a stadia is a Roman measurement approximately 600 feet long).

The Third Woe is completed. The kingdom of this world will have become the Kingdom of our Lord and of His Christ! What will happen at the return of Jesus for those who believe? That is the subject of the next two chapters.

A Summary of Prophetic Events

Christ's Chronology of Prophetic Events:

- Birth Pangs
- The Antichrist, the Abomination of Desolation, and the Tribulation
- God's Judgment upon the Earth

• The Return of Christ

Revelation's Chronology of Prophetic Events:

The Seven Seals summarize Christ's chronology, and are elaborated upon by the Seven Trumpets and the Seven Bowls.

Seals 1-4:   Birth Pangs
Seal 5:   Antichrist's Persecution and Tribulation of the Saints
Seal 6:   God's Judgment upon the Earth and the Day of the Lord

   • Trumpets 1-5; Bowls 1-5 describe the judgment upon the earth by a comet (the First Woe)
   • Trumpet 6 and Bowl 6 describe the last great world war (the Second Woe)

Seal 7:   The Return of Christ

   • Trumpet 7 and Bowl 7 describe Christ's return at the height of the last battle (the Third Woe).

Part Four

The
Blessed
Hope

Chapter Nine

The Resurrection and the Rapture

Everyone wants to live forever. Indeed, God has "set eternity in the hearts of men" (Ecclesiastes 3:11). From the moment when God graciously covered the nakedness of Adam and Eve with the skins of animals He had slain on their behalf, people have longed for complete restoration of their eternal relationship with God. The Bible gives us enough information about it to give us assurance and hope. However, we cannot know the full picture. It is incomprehensible in its fullness. The Bible admits that "No eye has seen, no ear has heard, no mind has conceived what God has prepared for those who love him" (I Corinthians 2:9).

People of all faiths and cultures believe in some form of an afterlife. Is it any wonder that there are so many wildly different ideas about what eternal life will be like? But because it begins after death, we can only rely upon God's revelation to know what it will truly be like. Jesus alone has come from God and knows the things of God. He said, "In my Father's house are many rooms; if it were not so, I would have told you. I am going there to prepare a place for you. And if I go and prepare a place for you, I will come back and take you to be with me that you also may be where I am" (John 14:2-3). Therefore, let us look at the prophetic puzzle pieces having to do with the nature of the resurrection and eternal life.

In what many scholars believe to be one of the oldest books of the Bible, Job declares his hope and faith in God's plan for him after death: "I know that my redeemer lives, and that in the end He will stand upon the earth" (Job 19:25). King David also spoke of this joyous hope in Psalm 16:9-11:

9 Therefore my heart is glad and my tongue rejoices; my body also will rest secure,

10 because you will not abandon me to the grave, nor will you let your Holy One see decay.

11 You have made known to me the path of life; you will fill me with joy in your presence, with eternal pleasures at your right hand.

David tells us in another passage that not only will there be "eternal pleasures" for the righteous, but that the wicked (whose hope and joy are only in this life) will be brought low:

13 Rise up, O LORD, confront them, bring them down; rescue me from the wicked by your sword.

14 O LORD, by your hand save me from such men, from men of this world whose reward is in this life. You still the hunger of those you cherish; their sons have plenty, and they store up wealth for their children.

15 And I—in righteousness I will see your face; when I awake, I will be satisfied with seeing your likeness. (Psalm 17:13-15).

Daniel reiterates this belief, revealing that both the righteous and the wicked will be resurrected - but with different ends:

"Multitudes who sleep in the dust of the earth will awake: some to everlasting life, others to shame and everlasting contempt" (Daniel 12:2).

We have God's promise that He will vanquish the power and fear of death for us, as the prophet Hosea writes (and quoted by Paul in 1 Corinthians 15):

"I will ransom them from the power of the grave; I will redeem them from death. Where, O death, are your plagues? Where, O grave, is your destruction?" (Hosea 13:14).

The Nature of the Resurrection

The world's religions have different and contradictory beliefs of what eternal life will be like. For the Hindu, every living thing must endure an endless series of reincarnations until the soul achieves perfect "karma." At that point, the soul will be freed from the cycle and will become one with the impersonal universe - no longer having any concept of its individual existence.[55] Some Muslims (and even the Mormons) believe that sexual relations are included in David's reference to "eternal pleasures." Even Christians are confused regarding the nature of the resurrection. They may be surprised to discover that there are not "seven levels" of heaven. That concept comes from Jewish apocryphal (not apocalyptic) thought, and was made popular in the Middle Ages by the poet Dante. Some are even confused over the resurrection itself, supposing that Christians will dwell in heaven forever (playing harps on clouds, perhaps?).

What does the Bible say about the nature of the resurrection? The Apostle Paul addressed this subject in 1 Corinthians 15. As the Apostle to the Gentiles, he knew about Greek thought on the issue. The Greeks felt that the soul was kept in bondage due to the evil and imperfect nature of the body. The idea that God

---

[55] It is amazing how Western versions of reincarnation ignore the possibility of one's coming back in another incarnation as something ignoble as a mosquito or a slug. No one ever claims to have been a milk cow in a former life!

would resurrect the human body as the vessel for eternal life seemed ludicrous to them. That is why Paul was mocked by the Greek philosophers on Mars Hill in Athens when he proclaimed the gospel of Christ's resurrection (cf. Acts 17:31). For the Greeks, eternal life was supposed to be a bodiless, spiritual existence.

As Paul corrected the Corinthian's misconception, he gave us much needed insight into the nature of the resurrection for the believer:

20 But Christ has indeed been raised from the dead, the firstfruits of those who have fallen asleep. 21 For since death came through a man, the resurrection of the dead comes also through a man. 22 For as in Adam all die, so in Christ all will be made alive. 23 But each in his own turn: Christ, the firstfruits; then, when he comes, those who belong to him. 24 Then the end will come, when he hands over the kingdom to God the Father after he has destroyed all dominion, authority and power. 25 For he must reign until he has put all his enemies under his feet. 26 The last enemy to be destroyed is death. 27 For he "has put everything under his feet." Now when it says that "everything" has been put under him, it is clear that this does not include God himself, who put everything under Christ. 28 When he has done this, then the Son himself will be made subject to him who put everything under him, so that God may be all in all.

35 But someone may ask, "How are the dead raised? With what kind of body will they come?" 36 How foolish! What you sow does not come to life unless it dies. 37 When you sow, you do not plant the body that will be, but just a seed, perhaps of wheat or of something else. 38 But God gives it a body as he has determined, and to each kind of seed he gives its own body. 39 All flesh is not the same: Men have one kind of flesh, animals have another, birds another and fish another. 40 There are also heavenly bodies and there are earthly bodies; but the splendor of the heavenly bodies is one kind, and the splendor of the earthly bodies is another. 41 The sun has one kind of splendor, the moon another and the stars another; and star differs from star in splendor.

42 So will it be with the resurrection of the dead. The body that is sown is perishable, it is raised imperishable; 43 it is sown in dishonor, it is raised in glory; it is sown in weakness, it is raised in power; 44 it is sown a natural body, it is raised a spiritual body. If there is a natural body, there is also a spiritual body.

45 So it is written: "The first man Adam became a living being"; the last Adam, a life-giving spirit. 46 The spiritual did not come first, but the natural, and after that the spiritual. 47 The first man was of the dust of the earth, the second man from heaven. 48 As was the earthly man, so are those who are of the earth; and as is the man from heaven, so also

are those who are of heaven. 49 And just as we have borne the likeness of the earthly man, so shall we bear the likeness of the man from heaven.

50 I declare to you, brothers, that flesh and blood cannot inherit the kingdom of God, nor does the perishable inherit the imperishable. 51 Listen, I tell you a mystery: We will not all sleep, but we will all be changed—52 in a flash, in the twinkling of an eye, at the last trumpet. For the trumpet will sound, the dead will be raised imperishable, and we will be changed. 53 For the perishable must clothe itself with the imperishable, and the mortal with immortality. 54 When the perishable has been clothed with the imperishable, and the mortal with immortality, then the saying that is written will come true: "Death has been swallowed up in victory."

55 "Where, O death, is your victory? Where, O death, is your sting?"

56 The sting of death is sin, and the power of sin is the law. 57 But thanks be to God! He gives us the victory through our Lord Jesus Christ. (I Corinthians 15:20-28; 35-57).

Here Paul reveals several important facts about the resurrection. First, just as Jesus was raised from the dead, so shall we be raised. His resurrection has become the hope and the promise of our own. That is what is meant by saying that Christ's resurrection represented the "first fruits" of the resurrection. The Jewish concept of first fruits came from its sacrificial system of offerings. As a sign that the farmer trusted God for the bounty of his crops, he sacrificed the very first of his field's produce. In this sense, our own resurrection will be like Christ's. Jesus not only made the way for us to have eternal life through His sacrificial atonement, but He showed us what kind of life it will be like - with a resurrection body!

Second, Paul addresses the next logical question: "What kind of body will we have?" To answer this, he uses nature as an analogy. There are many different kinds earthly bodies, skins, and states of being. We do not think it strange when we plant a seed and see a plant or a tree sprout from the soil. Likewise, when we are "planted" in the soil through death we should not be surprised if our resurrection body is remarkably better than our old one. Yet, Paul continues, the new body will still be similar to the old one. He said that our new bodies would be just like Christ's resurrection body (verse 49). The Apostle John wrote much the same thing in I John 3:2: "Dear friends, now we are children of God, and what we will be has not yet been made known. But we know that when He appears, we shall be like Him, for we shall see Him as He is."

Therefore, in order to learn some information about our resurrection body, we can look to Jesus as our model. What was His resurrection body like? From what we can piece together of Christ's resurrection appearances, we can surmise that our own resurrection bodies will be awesome! We will be different in appearance but we will bear enough of our present likeness to be recognizable. We read where the disciples were not able to recognize Jesus at first (the disciples on the road to Emmaus). Furthermore, when Mary first saw His resurrected form, she mistakenly thought Jesus was a gardener. At the same time, Jesus could be recognized. His appearance, though somewhat different, was still recognizable. He even bore the scars of His crucifixion.

He had a body that could interact with the physical nature of this material world. He could be touched as a solid object. His touch could be felt. He cooked and ate with people. He even had breath that could be blown upon others. Yet, He was clearly not limited to this world's physical laws concerning time and space. He could appear and disappear at will. When He ascended from the Mount of Olives, He seemed to float or fly into the heaven above.

There was also a glorious aspect to Christ's resurrection body. When John saw the vision of Jesus that he described in chapter one of the Book of Revelation, His appearance was dazzling and awesome. Likewise, when Jesus was transfigured before His disciples at the Mount of Transfiguration, His clothes and appearance radiated with the glory of God. We, too, will have a glorious nature. The Book of Daniel reveals to us that the resurrected saints will "shine brightly like the brightness of the expanse of heaven" (Daniel 12:3).

But there will be much more to eternal life than only our resurrection bodies. We will no longer be tempted or be prone to Sin and its effects. "He will dwell among them, and they shall be His people, and God Himself will be among them, and He will wipe away every tear from their eyes; and there will no longer be any death; there will no longer be any mourning, or crying, or pain; the first things have passed away" (Revelation 21: 3,4; NASB).

After the resurrection, we will all stand before the Judgment Seat of Christ in order to be rewarded (and chastised) for the deeds we have done in this life: "For we must all appear before the judgment seat of Christ, so that each one may be recompensed for his deeds in the body, according to what he has done, whether good or bad" (2 Corinthians 5:10; NASB).

Just as we don't fully know all of what eternal life will be like, we certainly cannot comprehend what it will be like to be rewarded for our good deeds of service or chastised for our sinful behavior. In one of His parables, Jesus hinted that the reward for faithful service will be greater standing and responsibility in the life to come: "'Well done, my good servant!' his master replied. 'Because you have been trustworthy in a very small matter, take charge of ten cities.'" (Luke 19:17). Other passages mention the giving of crowns as rewards (i.e., "the crown of life" (James 1:12); "the crown of righteousness" (2 Timothy 4:8); "the crown of glory" (1 Peter 5:4), etc.). A crown can be a symbol or mark of authority. Whether we actually wear them is immaterial (how can someone wear many crowns?) We will have some rulership authority during the Millennium

Kingdom (a topic I will discuss in the next chapter). We also know from the Scriptures that the saints will judge the angels (1 Corinthians 6:3). So, at least part of our reward for faithfulness in this life will be our ultimate standing in heaven.

We must recognize that faithfulness does not mean the same thing as "success." We often equate God's blessing with numbers, money, or notoriety. But this is not how God will judge us. The missionary who might have died on his way to Africa is just as faithful to his calling as the evangelist who wins thousands of souls to Christ. The mother whose calling is to raise her children in the ways of the Lord is just as faithful as the pastor who trains disciples. The criteria for the reward is how we serve with the gifts and talents God gives us. Paul writes in 1 Corinthians 3:10-15:

> 10 By the grace God has given me, I laid a foundation as an expert builder, and someone else is building on it. But each one should be careful how he builds. 11 For no one can lay any foundation other than the one already laid, which is Jesus Christ. 12 If any man builds on this foundation using gold, silver, costly stones, wood, hay or straw, 13 his work will be shown for what it is, because the Day will bring it to light. It will be revealed with fire, and the fire will test the quality of each man's work. 14 If what he has built survives, he will receive his reward. 15 If it is burned up, he will suffer loss; he himself will be saved, but only as one escaping through the flames.

Therefore, what we do for the Lord in this life will have a direct bearing upon our standing in the next.[56] We may make it to heaven based upon our

---

[56] Many jokes have been made to illustrate this spiritual truth. For instance, A rich man died and went to heaven. He asked St. Peter if he could see the mansion that Jesus had promised. Together they walked through the celestial city on the streets of gold, passing by one palatial estate after another. The man asked Peter who were the new owners of each one. "Oh, that one belongs to the poor single mother from your town who raised her children to love and honor the Lord," responded Peter. "That one over there belongs to the baker, who donated his time and his bread to feed the poor," he continued. "Over there is the estate of your former pastor, the one who was forced out of the ministry because some of the influential members of the church would not pay him a salary he could live on," he continued. Eventually, the two of them arrived to the edge of town. The size and quality of the mansions had dropped considerably. While not yet shacks, they were modest in comparison. "Here live the 'televangelists' who squandered there golden opportunity to witness to the goodness of the Lord by raising their standards of living instead," Peter commented. Silently, the man nodded in agreement at the justice of God's reward for them. Finally, they arrived at the outskirts of the town. Peter waved his arm over a vacant lot and said, "Here you are!" The only things the man saw were

decision to repent and believe the gospel, but if our life fluctuates between faithfulness and selfishness, we may find that we will be in heaven without any attending rewards.

Both Jesus and Paul tell us that when we stand before the Judgment Seat of Christ we will be recompensed for our bad deeds as well as our good ones. Jesus said that, "That servant who knows his master's will and does not get ready or does not do what his master wants will be beaten with many blows. But the one who does not know and does things deserving punishment will be beaten with few blows. From everyone who has been given much, much will be demanded; and from the one who has been entrusted with much, much more will be asked" (Luke 12:47-48). Now, there is some debate over passages such as these as to whether the individual will even make it into heaven or not. Most such passages state that the person will be assigned to the place where there will be "weeping and wailing and gnashing of teeth" - a clear reference to the eternal pangs of hell's punishment. Nevertheless, the message is clear to us: be careful how we walk with the Lord. His grace is not to be treated with unthinking contempt!

In the glory of His presence we shall know as we have been fully known (1 Corinthians 13:12). We won't have to ask God any of the questions that so plague us now. We will simply know the answers. Indeed, they may seem so trivial in the light of His awesome glory that they will pale into insignificance!

Finally, the greatest of the rewards of heaven will be the very presence of the Lord Himself. It is a commentary against today's preaching that many people have a fear that eternity will be boring. They picture themselves playing harps on clouds, doing nothing but singing praises to God forever. This is tragic! Those who think that heaven will be a bore have just never experienced the fullness of God's plan for their lives here in this life!

The Resurrection's Promise for Us

What does the resurrection mean to us now? Though we cannot know all that God has for us in eternity, He has not left us without a clue about what it will be like. Jesus said that the Kingdom of God was among us. He showed us what it would be like when the Kingdom is fully realized on earth when He cast out demons, healed the sick, forgave sins, and raised the dead. Yet, He did not bring the Kingdom to earth in its complete fullness. We now live, as theologian Dr. George Eldon Ladd has succinctly put it, in the "presence of the future."

---

some piles of lumber, some old canvas tarpaulins and a few sacks of concrete. Thinking that perhaps his mansion was still in the design phase, the rich man inquired, "When will my house be finished?" "Oh, it is already complete;" Peter replied, "That's the best we could do with what you gave us to work with!"

185

We can get a taste of what that future will be like right now through the down payment of the Holy Spirit. Dr. Ladd's *A Theology of the New Testament* was a monumental work in the history of New Testament theology. In it he gave Evangelical and Pentecostal churches a much better theology than the predominant twentieth century theology of Dispensationalism. Ladd explained that Jesus brought the kingdom of God to earth through His incarnation. Jesus showed us the Kingdom's presence through His words and His works. He inaugurated the Kingdom among men through His death and resurrection. Now, we can have access to God through repentance and faith. As a down payment of our future inheritance, God sent His Holy Spirit to dwell inside us, His holy people! Through the power of the Holy Spirit we can preach His words and do His works, until He comes again (cf., 1 Corinthians 1:7; 13:8-10). However, until He does return, we still live in this present evil world and are still influenced by its powers. We now experience struggles both within and without. We can experience both the resurrection power of Christ when we manifest the powerful works of the Holy Spirit through our lives and ministries *and* we can experience the weakness of suffering as we go through life's trials. This is precisely what the Apostle Paul meant when he wrote, "I want to know Christ and the power of his resurrection and the fellowship of sharing in his sufferings, becoming like him in his death, and so, somehow, to attain to the resurrection from the dead" (Philippians 3:10-11). Therefore, no matter what happens to us in this life we will experience God's victory!

In other words, we can experience a taste of heaven right now. Paul wrote that the Holy Spirit is like a down payment of the powers of the age to come (Ephesians 1). When Jesus' Name is exalted in our midst through faith and worship, the Spirit of God can become present among us. At times, His presence is so tangible that He can be felt. Admittedly it is a subjective experience, but Christians down through the ages have all testified of what this is like. Sometimes He brings a feeling of love, peace, or comfort. Others experience a deeper faith, or knowledge of His reality. Sometimes He speaks, or acts through spiritual gifts such as prophecy, words of knowledge or wisdom, discernment of spirits, etc. His power can often be felt, as He works miracles or healing. Whatever the manifestation, it is like a little bit of the resurrection working its way into this age, and demonstrating to us what it will be like when Jesus comes back as King of kings and Lord of lords!

Those who have experienced the taste of the powers of the age to come (Hebrews 6:4,5) know that they will never be bored in heaven. It will be filled with pleasures of a different, yet better nature because we will be face to face with God! Best of all, we will be in His glorious presence, without stain or blemish and be able to gaze on His manifold glory without fear. We will be filled with life as it was meant to be, from the source of life Himself!

Christ's Chronology of the Resurrection and the Rapture

Now that we have a better idea of what the resurrection will be like for a believer, we need to address the mysterious issue of how it will take place when Christ returns. Jesus gave us the basic outline of events in the Olivet Discourse. In so doing, He included some interesting puzzle pieces that can easily be fit together with others written by Paul and John. In so doing we can arrive at a clear picture of that awesome event!

> 29 "Immediately after the distress [tribulation] of those days "'the sun will be darkened, and the moon will not give its light; the stars will fall from the sky, and the heavenly bodies will be shaken.'
> 30 "At that time the sign of the Son of Man will appear in the sky, and all the nations of the earth will mourn. They will see the Son of Man coming on the clouds of the sky, with power and great glory. 31 And he will send his angels with a loud trumpet call, and they will gather his elect from the four winds, from one end of the heavens to the other. (Matthew 24:29-31)

Let's look closely at the order of events Jesus gives us:

- After the tribulation of the saints, perpetrated by the Antichrist, the judgment of God will be poured out upon the earth.
- While the earth is still reeling under the effects of the judgment ("at that time"), Jesus will return. He will descend from above, through the atmosphere, and be visible to all nations.
- As He returns, three important facts are mentioned: (1) there will be a loud trumpet call; (2) angels will be sent to accomplish the task of (3) gathering His elect from the earth.

We see these same elements in two other New Testament passages.[57] The Apostle Paul refers to the same events at the Second Coming in 1 Corinthians 15 and 1 Thessalonians 4:13-18. In his treatise on the resurrection in 1 Corinthians 15, he deals with the issue of what must happen to those people who are still alive when Jesus resurrects the dead. What will be their lot? Will they remain in

---

[57] The Old Testament also contains the imagery of a trumpet blast and regathering of God's people. Isaiah prophesies, "In that day the Lord will thresh from the flowing Euphrates to the Wadi of Egypt, and you, O Israelites, will be gathered up one by one. And in that day a great trumpet will sound. Those who were perishing in Assyria and those who were exiled in Egypt will come and worship the Lord on the holy mountain in Jerusalem" (Isaiah 27:12-13).

their physical bodies? Will they have to die in order to be raised again? In answering these questions he introduces a new revelation to the church concerning what we call "the rapture."

> 50 I declare to you, brothers, that flesh and blood cannot inherit the kingdom of God, nor does the perishable inherit the imperishable. 51 Listen, I tell you a mystery: We will not all sleep, but we will all be changed—52 in a flash, in the twinkling of an eye, at the last trumpet. For the trumpet will sound, the dead will be raised imperishable, and we will be changed. 53 For the perishable must clothe itself with the imperishable, and the mortal with immortality. 54 When the perishable has been clothed with the imperishable, and the mortal with immortality, then the saying that is written will come true: "Death has been swallowed up in victory." (1 Corinthians 15:50-54)

In this remarkable revelation, Paul outlines what will happen when Jesus returns. Here, he reveals additional information about the resurrection. This information has been hidden in the past, but is now being revealed by the Holy Spirit to the church.

Paul asserts in I Corinthians 15:50 that the natural body will not be able to live in the supernatural eternal existence. It will have to be transformed at the return of Christ.

But there will need to be a special work of God for those people who have not yet died when Christ returns. Not everyone will die ("sleep" is just a Jewish euphemism for "die" - just as our culture has polite ways to express this tragic end of life, such as, "He passed away."). Instead, those who are still alive when the resurrection occurs will also be transformed into their new eternal bodies.

This transformation will be sudden. Paul uses the expression denoting the smallest unit of time a Jew could use - the time it took to see a reflection of sunlight in a person's iris. If he were speaking modern English he would probably use the term, "nanosecond."

Now, note what events will take place all at the same time. The transformation of the living (commonly called "the Rapture") will occur just after the resurrection. This transformation of the living will take place when that same trumpet that Jesus referred to will sound. Paul emphasizes that it will occur at the sounding of the *last* trumpet.[58]

In the First Thessalonian passage, Paul addresses the concern some early Christians had over the loss of their loved ones. What will Jesus do for the dead when He returns? How will we be reunited with those who have already died?

---

[58] See the appendix, "Times, Dates, and other Conjecture" for some interesting speculation regarding trumpets and Jewish holy days.

Once again, we see that Paul brings up the subject of the rapture. And again, we read about the same events taking place when the rapture occurs.

> 18 Brothers, we do not want you to be ignorant about those who fall asleep, or to grieve like the rest of men, who have no hope. 14 We believe that Jesus died and rose again and so we believe that God will bring with Jesus those who have fallen asleep in him. 15 According to the Lord's own word, we tell you that we who are still alive, who are left till the coming of the Lord, will certainly not precede those who have fallen asleep. 16 For the Lord himself will come down from heaven, with a loud command, with the voice of the archangel and with the trumpet call of God, and the dead in Christ will rise first. 17 After that, we who are still alive and are left will be caught up together with them in the clouds to meet the Lord in the air. And so we will be with the Lord forever. 18 Therefore encourage each other with these words. (1 Thessalonians 4:13-18)

Paul says that what he is telling the Thessalonians is directly from the Lord, Himself (referring to Christ's own words from the Olivet Discourse). Here we see a clear outline of the same chronology of Jesus:

- The Lord descends from heaven.
- There is a loud shout, or command (given by the voice of an archangel).
- A trumpet call sounds
- The dead are resurrected.
- After the resurrection, those disciples who are still alive and remain on earth will be "caught up with them (the resurrected dead) to meet the Lord in the air."[59]

It is clear from these three passages that the Bible is talking about the same event. The only difference is that Paul gives additional information about what will happen to those saints who have not yet died and, therefore, do not need to be raised from the dead!

Does the chronology of Christ and Paul match that of John's in the Book of Revelation? Yes, it does. We see a last trumpet sounding just prior to the return of Christ in Revelation 11:15-18. At the blowing of that seventh and final trumpet, loud voices announce that the "kingdom of this world has become the kingdom of our Lord and of His Christ, and He will reign for ever and ever" (Revelation 11:15). At the same time, the elders praise God, saying, "…the time

---

[59] We get our term "the rapture" from this passage. The words "caught up" are translated "rapturous" in Latin.

has come for *judging the dead*, and for *rewarding Your servants* the prophets and Your saints and those who reverence Your name, both small and great - and for destroying those who destroy the earth" (Revelation 11:18). As we showed in the last chapter, this is nothing other than the physical return of Christ to the earth. Therefore, the imagery both Jesus and Paul use of a loud, last trumpet at the Second Coming fits perfectly with the record of the Book of Revelation.

The conclusion is obvious. Whenever the Bible speaks about the visible return of Jesus Christ the same events are evident: the Lord descends, there is a loud trumpet call, the angels are mentioned as having a part, the resurrection occurs, and the rapture takes place.

Dispensationalists object to this chronology, saying that if the rapture occurs at the end of the Tribulation there will not be enough time for Christ to judge the church and issue His rewards. Furthermore, the Bible speaks about "the Marriage Supper of the Lamb." They place this feast of celebration during the time when the saints are in heaven prior to their triumphant return with Christ.

The Second Coming is described in greatest detail in the nineteenth chapter of the Book of Revelation. Here we see a great multitude in heaven. We are not sure from the context just who constitutes this assembly - it may be the angelic host of heaven, or it may be the resurrected and raptured church. The latter is unlikely, however, because the multitude is shouting in praise *about* the church in verse seven: "Let us rejoice and be glad and give Him glory! For the wedding of the Lamb has come, and His bride has made herself ready" - not "*we* have made *ourselves* ready." Nevertheless, we are told that the saints will be given fine, bright, and clean linen garments, which stand for their righteous deeds they have accomplished (verse eight). Clothed in righteousness, they will be allowed to attend the wedding feast of the Lamb (verse nine). These last two facts (the fine linen garments and the wedding feast) are references to Jesus' parable in Matthew 22:1-14 where a king prepared a lavish wedding banquet for his son, but the guests who ignored the invitation or who did not dress appropriately for the occasion were judged.

From the context of Revelation 19 we cannot be sure *when* the Wedding Feast of the Lamb will occur in relation to the Second Coming. Dispensationalists assume that it, as well as the Judgment Seat of Christ, will occur after the secret, pretribulation rapture. They feel that there must be a period of time after the saints are in heaven in order for there to be enough time for both these events to take place. The saints will be judged, and will be rewarded with their fine linen garments. Then there will be the great and glorious Wedding Feast with Jesus. After the meal, they will mount their chargers and follow Christ into the Last Battle.

However, this order of events is not clearly stated in Revelation 19. The Judgment Seat of Christ is not mentioned. It is only an assumption based upon the flimsy evidence of the giving of the linen garments. Nothing is said, either, about the timing of the Wedding Feast in relation to the return of Christ. The blessing of the invitation is given before the actual return of the King of kings, but John's Revelation does not state whether it will be actually enjoyed before Jesus' return. It may occur afterwards.

As for the reasoning that there has to be some time between the resurrection and rapture and the return of Christ in order to accomplish both the Judgement Seat of Christ and the Wedding Feast, I must reassert: once we are resurrected or raptured we will be changed into our new bodies. *For us, time will be no more!* We will be like Christ, where "a day is like a thousand years and a thousand years is like a day!" In that moment - that twinkling of an eye - we could easily experience the equivalence of a thousand years with Jesus before we have to dress up in our new robes of linen and become part of the army of saints who return triumphantly with Christ at the final battle of Armageddon. So, whether the Judgment Seat of Christ and the Wedding Banquet of the Lamb occur before or after the actual physical return of Christ is immaterial to us. All we really know is that they will happen. But their occurrence does not affect Christ's clear chronology of His return in one way or another!

The Pretribulation Rapture

This section is devoted to a short explanation of the background and beliefs of the doctrine of the pretribulation rapture. It is written with the recognition that those who hold to that position are godly, spiritual, and intelligent people. Differences of interpretation on such non-essential matters (as I mentioned in the Introduction) should not be the basis for separation of fellowship.

My intent is to briefly summarize what the pretribulation rapture position is, discuss why it has such popularity, analyze its strengths, and give those arguments as are necessary to show the improbability of its occurrence. My desire is not to go into great detail (other books do that adequately), but to positively assert an alternative, Biblical viewpoint without being critical or condescending.

Although there may be differences of opinion among Dispensationalist teachers on minor points, the following is a brief synopsis of the pretribulation rapture position:

If one is able to "rightly divide the Word of Truth" (as Dispensationalists tell us to do), he will discover that God has a plan of salvation for the Gentiles and a separate plan for the Jews. This plan is outlined in Daniel's seventy "sevens:" the Messiah (Jesus) will come exactly 483 years after the decree to rebuild Jerusalem is issued. He will be rejected by the Jews. Therefore, God's salvation will be offered to the Gentiles while they, the Jews, will be judged by God. The seventieth "seven" will not be fulfilled until the Gospel has been preached into all the world.

At that time, God will restore the Jews to their land. The world political situation will grow more and more intense, with wars, famines, earthquakes, and pestilences adding to the world's insecurities. The world will be longing for a single, powerful man to lead them into peace. The world situation will be ready for the final chapter of human history: the seven-year Great Tribulation.

However, because God has promised that the church was not appointed to suffer the wrath of God, but for obtaining salvation through Jesus Christ (1 Thessalonians 5:9), Jesus will come back suddenly and quietly, like "a thief in the night" to rapture the faithful at the beginning of this seven-year tribulation period. The Holy Spirit will depart with the church, allowing the Antichrist to come upon the world scene.

At that time God will begin to work among the Jews again. He will seal 144,000 young Jewish men as powerful evangelists. They will go throughout the world, warning both Jews and Gentiles alike of the coming judgment. They will win multitudes to Christ, including their own Jewish countrymen.

However, the rest of the world will receive the Antichrist as their savior. He will broker a major peace treaty between Israel and the Arabs. The Jewish temple will be rebuilt, probably as part of the peace treaty. At the same time, God will begin to visit the world with His judgments, expressed successively through the seals, trumpets and, finally, the bowls of God's wrath.

Mid-way through the seven years, the Antichrist will set himself up in the rebuilt temple as a god and savior, demanding to be worshipped. This act will break the treaty, and the Jews (along with their new Gentile converts) will be persecuted world-wide by the Antichrist.

Just when things can't get any worse, the entire world will invade the Holy Land. But at that moment, when Jerusalem is falling, Jesus will come back. Having come for His saints seven years before, He will come with them to vanquish the armies of the Beast. In the intervening seven years, the saints will enjoy the Marriage Supper of the Lamb and receive their eternal rewards at the Judgment Seat of Christ. When Jesus comes back this time, it will not be secret. Every eye will see Him, and the Jews will receive Him as their Lord and Savior!

The History of the Pretribulation Rapture

As explained in the Introduction, the dominant eschatological positions of believers have changed over the years. In the early church it was assumed that the rapture would occur just as Jesus and Paul clearly stated - after the Great Tribulation Jesus will return in the clouds with great glory, a loud trumpet, and the saints will all be resurrected to meet the Lord in the air. Those Christians who are still alive at this time would be raptured, or "caught up," to meet the Lord as well. This was the belief of the early church (called "Historic Premillenialism"), as the following writings from the early church fathers show:

Justin Martyr:

"The man of apostasy [the antichrist]…shall venture to do unlawful deeds on the earth against us the Christians…" (*Trypho* cx).

Irenaeus:

"And they [the ten kings] shall…give their kingdom to the beast, and put the church to flight" (*Against Heresies* V, 26,1).
"But he [John] indicates the number of the name [Antichrist, 666] now, that when this man comes we may avoid him, being aware of who he is" (*Against Heresies*, V, 30,4).

The Shepherd (Pastor) of Hermas:

"Happy are ye who endure the great tribulation that is coming on…"

The Teaching of the Twelve Apostles:

Matthew 24:31 (which concerns the gathering of the elect at the posttribulational coming of Christ) is quoted twice in *The Teaching of the Twelve Apostles*. What is notable is the writer's substitution of the word "church" for "elect" (chapters 9, 10).

"Watch for your life's sake. Let not your lamps be quenched, nor your loins unloosed; but be ye ready, for ye know not the hour in which our Lord cometh." [Here, some pretribulationist authors end the quote in an attempt to make the passage seem to teach the early church's belief in a pretribulational imminent return of Christ.] "…for the whole time of your faith will not profit you, if ye be not made perfect in the last time…then shall appear the world-deceiver as Son of God, and shall do signs and wonders…Then shall the creation of men come into the fire of trial, and many shall be made to stumble and perish, but they that endure in their faith shall be saved from under the curse itself" (chapter xvi).

Tertullian:

Tertullian identifies the rapture mentioned in 1 Thessalonians 4 with Christ's coming to earth to destroy the Antichrist and to establish His kingdom. Likewise, he connects the resurrection of the "church" with that coming (*Against Marcion* iii,25; *On the Resurrection of the Flesh* xxiv).

"...the beast Antichrist with his false prophet may wage war on the church of God...Since, then, the Scriptures both indicate the stages of the last times, and concentrate the harvest of the Christian hope in the very end of the world..." (*On the Resurrection* .xxv).

Although Historic Premillennialism was the belief of the early church, by the time of Augustine it had shifted to Amillennialism. Prophetic passages were interpreted to be symbolic, rather than literal. Even the Protestants generally believed that the Book of Revelation was to be interpreted as historical symbolism. For instance, they interpreted the Papacy as representing the Antichrist, or the Great Harlot. Few, if any, Protestant theologians viewed Revelation as literally predicting the future.

However, a movement arose at the beginning of the nineteenth century that brought the future element of prophecy back to where it should have been all along. Prophetic conferences began to spring up, both in England and America. After centuries of neglect, people flocked to hear the truth about Biblical prophecy. Of course, unbalanced and ignorant teachings also took place. Date-setters, such as William Miller and the Millerites (from which the Seventh-day Adventists later arose) predicted the immanent end of the world. Joseph Smith's Church of Jesus Christ of Latter-Day Saints was birthed during this period, as well.

The two major sources for the idea about a pretribulation rapture seem to come from Edward Irving, who led a movement in the early 1830's where supernatural charismatic gifts began to be manifested, and J. N. Darby, the leader of the Plymouth Brethren Church and the genius behind the spread of Dispensationalism. Both attended meetings where the pretribulation rapture was discussed. It is even rumored that one of Irving's disciples may have delivered a "tongue and interpretation" that introduced the original concept. Edward Irving died in 1834, along with his movement. It was Darby who advanced and promoted Dispensationalism, which included the pretribulation position. Darby visited America six times between 1859 and 1874. His teaching about prophecy was seen as returning the doctrine of the Second Coming to its rightful position. Through his teaching, the living and vital expectation of the return of Jesus brought hope and vibrancy to the church, as it was originally meant to!

But why did the evangelical church accept *all* of his interpretation of Scripture? Why did so few theologians attempt to contradict the new understanding of the secret and separate rapture of the church? The reason is because no one else was promoting any other teaching on the subject! Amillennialists were not enthusiastic about the subject, and Historic

Premillennialism had all but been forgotten. Only those people who believed in pretribulation Premillennialism were teaching about futuristic prophecy. And, when their prophecies concerning Israel began to come to pass in the twentieth century, history seemed to be validating their whole theological system.

Another factor played an important role in the overall acceptance of the pretribulation rapture. During the late nineteenth century, the historic mainline denominations began to be infected with a growing disbelief in the inerrency of Scripture. Liberalism began to replace evangelical fervor. In response to this apostasy, evangelicals and the new Pentecostal groups responded by accepting Dispensationalism's five-fold test of orthodoxy, known as "Fundamentalism" (the verbal inerrancy of Scripture, the deity and virgin birth of Christ, the substitutionary atonement, the physical resurrection of Christ, and His bodily return to earth). Conservative Christians across denominational lines were greatly influenced by the popularity of fundamentalist teaching in the Dispensational Scofield Reference Bible, which related each part of Scripture to a timetable of God's various "dispensations" of history. Because Dispensationalism became identified with conservative Christianity, any pastor or scholar who questioned Dispensational teaching on the Second Coming was often rejected as a liberal or a heretic.

Unfortunately, this is still the situation today. Those who honestly cannot find the secret pretribulation rapture in the Scripture are unfairly attacked because they "do not believe the Scriptures." Many Evangelical and Pentecostal churches make the pretribulation rapture position an absolute requirement for orthodoxy. Those who question it are not allowed to be ministers. Yet, as this book shows, it is possible to believe the fundamentals of Christianity and yet have a different understanding of how our Lord will fulfill the Scriptures when He returns!

The Appeal of a Pretribulation Rapture

Another reason for the overwhelming support the pretribulation rapture has in churches today is in its emotional appeal. This appeal works powerfully in people's lives on several levels.

First, we *do* live in an increasingly insecure era. We feel lost and powerless in the face of social, cultural, and political changes. We sense danger from within and without. If environmental pollution doesn't kill us, some terrorist with a biological weapon will. Marriage and family have disintegrated as social support systems. Neighborhoods are full of strangers who move every three or four years. The world *is* going to pot. Who wouldn't want to be rescued from all of this? The doctrine of a pretribulation rapture certainly helps us comfort our fears. It gives us hope that we will be able to escape the natural results of our world's sins. We can be saved from death and destruction! Who wouldn't want Jesus to save us from all this?

Second, because Jesus can return secretly at any time now, we must remain ready. Jesus commanded us to be watchful for the signs of His return. Since we have been seeing those signs take place, we should always be ready to meet Him. This readiness includes working for the Kingdom of God's advance. The doctrine of the immanence of His return *does* encourage the saints to work in His kingdom today. It *does* serve to help people to do things for God. It *does* motivate people to give more money for the spread of the Gospel. And so we should!

Third, because we have been seeing prophecy fulfilled right before our eyes, we can point to these fulfillments as proof of the truthfulness of God's word. People are saved because they are convinced that God is real, and that Jesus is coming back soon. The fact that those who do not respond to God's offer of salvation will be "left behind" gives unbelievers added incentive to making that final decision! The Bible does say that "now is the acceptable time of salvation." We do need to press people for a decision.

However, we do not need to preach a pretribulation rapture to get the same results. And no honest preacher would want to teach an erroneous doctrine just to get people to do something. The end never justifies the means. If people need to be motivated to serve the Lord because they might miss the rapture, then their focus is still on themselves rather than love for God. If people can only be comforted with the hope of escaping the tribulations of this world, then they have not really received the spiritual comfort of the one who said, "In this world you will have tribulations, but be of good courage for I have overcome the world" (John 16:33). If someone will only "accept the Lord" because they fear being left behind, then they are not truly turning to Jesus in honest repentance. The doctrine of the pretribulation rapture is not necessary to motivate people. The words of Jesus to His disciples will do that equally well, if not better.

The Biblical Support for a Pretribulation Rapture

The concept of the pretribulation rapture is not clearly stated in the Bible. It is developed by way of inference, not direct statements. What does "inference" mean? It means that the doctrine is one that is arrived at indirectly through concepts inferred by different verses. This is not an invalid method of interpreting the Bible. For instance, the doctrine of the Trinity is a truth inferred by what the Bible says about the relationship between the Father, the Son, and the Holy Spirit. No one verse clearly sets forth the doctrine of the Trinity, but it is inferred by many different verses. So, just because the doctrine of the pretribulation rapture comes from inference does not mean we can dismiss it out of hand.

So even though the direct statements of Christ seem to indicate a post-tribulation rapture, Dispensationalists do claim some Biblical support. Probably the most important Scripture supporting the pretribulation rapture is found in 1 Thessalonians 5:9: "For God did not appoint us to suffer wrath but to receive salvation through our Lord Jesus Christ."

If this verse is referring to the wrath of God that will be unleashed upon the world during the Great Tribulation, then there is a serious problem for the post-tribulation position. This verse seems to be promising believers exemption from that wrath. It is on the basis of this verse that those nineteenth century prophecy scholars went on their search for another rapture.

They believed that they found it by implication in those verses which state that Jesus would come back "like a thief in the night" (1 Thessalonians 5:2). His coming, they surmise, would be a complete surprise to the world and believers alike. This thought is further supported by verses which imply that believers must be always ready, because He will come back "at a time when you think not" (Matthew 24:44). Furthermore, we will not know the "day or the hour" of his return (Matthew 24:36). Since this is the case, Jesus cannot come back at the end of the tribulation, because we would be able to calculate his arrival based upon the signing of the covenant between the Antichrist and Israel at the beginning of the seven years prophesied by Daniel. Referring to the tribulation, Jesus said, "Be always on the watch, and pray that you may be able to escape all that is about to happen, and that you may be able to stand before the Son of Man" (Luke 21:36). Finally, if the seven churches in the Book of Revelation represent various stages of church history, then Jesus seems to have promised one of the churches some kind of deliverance: "Since you have kept my command to endure patiently, I will also keep you from the hour of trial that is going to come upon the whole world to test those who live on the earth" (Revelation 3:10). Since the word "church" is not found throughout the rest of the Book of Revelation, the church must have been raptured prior to the judgments of the seals, trumpets, and bowls.

These are impressive, logical, and Scriptural arguments - if those Scriptures can *only* be interpreted in that manner. And that is the problem with using inferential arguments. The interpretation hinges upon looking at the Scriptures from only one perspective. And if there are contradictory passages, they must be made to fit into that system, even if it is clear that they don't.

For instance, what do Dispensationalists do with the clear chronology that Jesus gave: "But immediately after the tribulation…and then the sign of the Son of Man will appear in the sky…and they will see the Son of Man coming on the clouds of the sky with power and great glory. And He will send forth His angels with a great trumpet and they will gather together His elect…" (Matthew 24:29,30, 31)? Here Jesus is clearly referring to His Second Coming where He will rapture those elect who are still alive "after the tribulation!"

197

Here's how Dispensationalists fit this passage into their framework. They say that we must stand back and see exactly who it is that Jesus is talking to here. Who are the "elect?" Although other passages in the New Testament say that all Christians (Jewish and Gentile believers alike) are the "elect," (c.f., Romans 8:33: "Who will bring a charge against God's elect? God is the one who justifies…"). Dispensationalists say that Jesus was referring only to Jewish people who are alive during the Great Tribulation. Therefore, this passage only refers to what will happen to Jewish believers who have missed the rapture. He was not referring to Gentile believers at all.

What is the rationale behind this interpretation? Dispensationalists say that we must be able to "rightly divide the word of truth." In other words, we need to be able to decide what passages are referring to God's plan for the Jews, and what passages are meant for the Gentiles. Yet, this approach is applied in an arbitrary way, using circular reasoning.[60] For instance, since the last seven years of human history will be the time when God is working again with the Jews, the "elect" can only be those Jews who get saved at that time. Why *must* the "elect" only be Jews? Using circular reasoning, they say that since God is finished with the Gentiles, the church has to be raptured in order to protect them from the wrath of God! However, there is nothing in Jesus' words themselves that would hint that He was only referring to Jewish believers. That interpretation must be read into the text.

The pretribulation rapture is a sincerely held belief that is taught by intelligent and godly people. Nevertheless, there are some serious errors in the Dispensationalist system of thought. Though the inferences can be made, they cannot be consistently demonstrated when all the prophetic puzzle pieces are examined.

The Problems for a Pretribulation Rapture

The Question of God's Wrath

The primary basis for the pretribulation position is found in the 1 Thessalonians passage quoted above. It is true that "God did not appoint us to suffer wrath but to receive salvation through our Lord Jesus Christ." The proper interpretation of the passage hinges upon just what Paul meant when he used the word "wrath." Was he referring to the wrath of God during the Tribulation period? Or was this wrath the judgment of God upon people by sending them to

---

[60] Using the same technique, Dispensationalists interpret the "Sermon on the Mount" as referring to God's laws for the Kingdom of Heaven in the future, and not having application to us today!

eternal punishment in Hell (as he means when he uses the term in Romans 2:5-1)?[61]

It is most likely that Paul was only referring to the eternal nature of God's wrath. In the verse itself, Paul contrasts the Christian's exemption from wrath with his eternal salvation through Jesus Christ. The next verse emphasizes the spiritual and eternal nature of this salvation: "He died for us so that, whether we are awake or asleep, we may live together with Him" (1 Thessalonians 5:10). No, Paul is not referring to the temporary, earthly wrath just a few people (comparatively speaking over the whole period of human history) will experience at the end of the Great Tribulation. He is referring to the eternal wrath that will be visited upon all unregenerate mankind in Hell! These two verses conclude his thoughts upon the comfort we can have because we know Christ, whether we are dead or alive. Christians in any age of mankind's history can know that we are eternally saved from the wrath of God!

I do not believe, as most post-tribulationists do, that this verse promises Christians supernatural protection from *all* the effects of the seals, trumpets, and bowls. Although God does promise a measure of protection from the demonically inflicted sores, it is doubtful that it could be extended to the world-wide disasters of the end. A tidal wave or an earthquake will kill Christians just as readily as unbelievers. For Christians, however, death from these kinds of causes will be no different than if they had been killed by any other natural disaster during mankind's long history. They will immediately be ushered into the presence of the Lord. And that is not a bad thing, as Paul writes in Philippians 1:21-23: "For to me, to live is Christ and to die is gain. If I am to go on living in the body, this will mean fruitful labor for me. Yet what shall I choose? I do not know! I am torn between the two: I desire to depart and be with Christ, which is better by far..." So, the outcome will be different for a Christian killed by the disasters. The believer will go be with the Lord forever, while the unbeliever will discover that his punishment of eternal wrath has only just begun.

There are two other logical problems with the concept that God will remove believers prior to the outpouring of the judgments. First, if the Gentile believers all get raptured prior to the outpouring of God's wrath, what about the Jewish

---

[61] We have already demonstrated that the judgments of God's wrath will not be unleashed until the very end of the tribulation. Hence, people like Marv Rosenthal have postulated a "pre-wrath rapture" theory. (Similar to mid-tribulation rapture, but it is located at the very end of the seven years.) This theory admits that the Church will go through the tribulation's persecution, but it will be raptured just prior to the outpouring of God's wrath through the seals, trumpets, and bowls. In rapid order, God's judgments will be soon followed by the triumphant return of Christ. This certainly is a better theory, but it still presents one problem - what about those who accept the Lord after the rapture and before the second coming - will there be another resurrection and rapture at the very end?

Messianic believers who come to Christ after the rapture? Why doesn't this promise apply to them? Why must they endure the horrors of the wrath of God? Why won't God's promise apply to them as well? Secondly, what about the thousands of Jewish Messianic Christians who believe right now? Will they get raptured with all the Gentile believers, or will they have to stay to face the tribulation just because they are Jewish?

Questions We Have Already Addressed

My purpose for this section is not to give an in-depth analysis of each argument, pro or con. I have already torn down most of the support for the pretribulation position in the course of this book. Rather, I will review only the major arguments for the pretribulation position.

We have seen, for instance, that a "secret" coming of Christ is nowhere to be found in Scripture. While the return of Christ will come as a surprise for most people, it will not be so for Christians. He will not be coming "like a thief in the night" for those who are spiritually awake! "But you, brothers, are not in darkness so that this day should surprise you like a thief" (1 Thessalonians 5:4). Furthermore, the coming of the Lord will not be secret. When John saw Jesus return during the Battle of Armageddon, he reported that Jesus will say, "Behold, I come like a thief! Blessed is he who stays awake and keeps his clothes with him..." (Revelation 16:15). The *same* metaphor that pretribluationists use to describe a "secret" coming is used by Jesus to describe His *visible* coming!

While we are to stay awake and watch for the signs of Christ's return, it will not come as a complete surprise. We are told to watch and be ready. Jesus gave us signs to look for. Their purpose was to give us encouragement - especially when things get bleak. "When these things begin to take place, stand up and lift up your heads, because your redemption is drawing near" (Luke 21:28). What things was He referring to? In the context, He had just mentioned the final signs in the sun, moon, and stars, causing distress at the very end of the age. We will not know the exact day or the hour, but will know when the time of the end is approaching.

Another pretribulation Scripture I have already dealt with is found in Revelation 3:10: "Since you have kept my command to endure patiently, I will also keep you from the hour of trial that is going to come upon the whole world to test those who live on the earth." It might appear that Jesus is promising this church some sort of exemption from the coming judgment.[62] But is this the only way to interpret this verse?

---

[62] Since this is the only church that was given this promise, some interpreters have gone a step further and suggest that only faithful, loving Christians will be raptured at the secret coming. Those who are carnal - who are sinning or backsliding - will miss the rapture.

As we have seen, the pretribulation position requires us to interpret the second and third chapters of Revelation from the historical perspective - that is, the seven churches represent seven successive ages of church history. Then from chapter four onward, the book must be seen from the light of future prophecy that will be fulfilled during the last seven years of this present age. This interpretation is rather arbitrary, as is the assigning of historical churches to the seven churches of Revelation. Rather, we have seen that the characteristics of the seven churches of Revelation can be found in every age of church history. The seven churches more properly represent Jesus' message to the whole church at any time in history, from the first century to the last days. It stands to reason then, that a church able to walk in the Spirit as the Philadelphian one does will be able to both discern the signs of the times and hear God's protective directions. These abilities, therefore, will afford them greater protection and deliverance when times get tough.

Furthermore, the Greek words used in this passage do not necessarily guarantee exemption "*from* the hour of trial" (*teresso ek*). Jesus used the same words in His High Priestly prayer in John 17:15: "My prayer is not that you take them out of the world but that you protect them *from* the evil one" (*tereses ek*). Here, Jesus specifically denies the possibility of being taken out of the world in order to protect the saints from Satan's attacks. Instead, He will leave us in the world to demonstrate His ability to guide us through them!

Finally, one of the major cornerstones for the pretribulation position comes directly from their Dispensational approach to "rightly dividing the Scriptures." What they mean by this statement is that we need to see that some Scriptures apply only to some peoples, times, and situations, while others only apply to us now as the recipients of God's age of grace. God has a special plan for the Jews, and a different plan for the Gentiles. The Jews were saved by the Law in the Old Dispensation; the Gentiles are saved by Grace in the new one inaugurated by Christ. Daniel prophesied that the Jews had 490 years where God was going to deal specifically with them. The first 483 years were fulfilled up until they rejected Jesus and crucified Him. The last seven years will be the Tribulation period where God once again will deal exclusively with the Jews. In the interim period, known as the Time of the Gentiles, God will save people by His grace through Jesus Christ. Once every Gentile has had the opportunity to hear the Good News, then the Time of the Gentiles will be over, the church will be raptured, and the Seventieth Seven will commence, where the Jews will once again be offered salvation.

This is called the "partial rapture" theory. The Tribulation will be something like a purgatory experience for these "Christians." They will have to endure and will be purified through it. Though unintentional, this theory can breed a kind of works righteousness in its adherents.

Because of this approach to the Scriptures, Dispensationalists are able to categorically state that "the elect" Jesus was referring to in Matthew 24 was Israel, not the church. The rapture He refers to that takes place "after the Great Tribulation" will be for the Jews. The Gentiles will have already been raptured in His secret coming.

However, we have seen in Chapter 3 that God's plan of salvation for both Jews and Gentiles has always been by grace through faith. From Adam to the last person to be saved, everyone has to come through the same door: turning from going their own way and believing in God's way. Furthermore, to say that the Time of the Jews ended with the crucifixion denies the facts of the first century. For the first few decades of the church's life, the majority of Christians were Jewish believers! Just as there was an overlap between the beginning of the Time of the Gentiles and the end of the Time of the Jews, so there will be an overlap of the two times at the very end of the Age!

The Two Raptures

One of the problems of the pretribulation position is its necessity of having two raptures and two resurrections. According to the pretribulation system, Jews and Gentiles will get saved during the Great Tribulation. Even though the church is no longer around to give a witness, and the Holy Spirit has been taken away, these Jews and Gentiles will come to Christ and will have to endure the persecution of the Antichrist. Many will be arrested and martyred. What will happen to these people when Jesus comes back in the clouds with great glory? He will have to resurrect the martyred saints and rapture those believers who have escaped the tribulation. There is no other way around it, for "flesh and blood cannot inherit the Kingdom of God" (1 Corinthians 15:50). Yet, the Scripture clearly contradicts the pretribulation scenario at this point. The Bible talks about two resurrections to be sure. But the first one occurs prior to the Millennium and includes only the righteous, while the second one occurs after the Millennium and it includes all the unrighteous. In order to answer this discrepancy, Pretribulationists must conclude that the first resurrection has to occur in two stages. Their puzzle pieces do not fit without having to be bent!

The Book of Revelation clearly denies this possibility. John reports what will occur after Jesus comes back in the clouds:

> 4 I saw thrones on which were seated those who had been given authority to judge. And I saw the souls of those who had been beheaded because of their testimony for Jesus and because of the word of God. They had not worshiped the beast or his image and had not received his mark on their foreheads or their hands. They came to life and reigned with Christ a thousand years. 5 (The rest of the dead did not come to life

until the thousand years were ended.) This is the first resurrection. 6 Blessed and holy are those who have part in the first resurrection. The second death has no power over them, but they will be priests of God and of Christ and will reign with him for a thousand years. (Revelation 20:4-6)

We are introduced to two groups of people in this passage, both of whom had just come to life to reign with Christ for a thousand years (those who had been martyred during the tribulation, and—by implication—all the rest of believers who had just been resurrected). Both groups are called blessed and holy. Both groups will be priests with God and will reign with Christ for a thousand years. The only difference is that one group had been martyred during the tribulation, while the other group were simply those who had "died in Christ." And both groups were resurrected at the same time! There is no hint of a time interval, or a two-stage process.

We are now ready to proceed to the last part of our prophetic picture: what will take place after Jesus comes back to earth.

Chapter Ten

To the Millennium and Beyond

What is the Millennium? The term comes from the Latin for "thousand years." It refers to Christ's thousand-year reign on earth after His triumphant return, as revealed in Revelation 20:1-9. The Millennium has been the subject of many debates throughout church history (see the Introduction for a more in depth analysis of the issues surrounding "Millennialism"). Will the Millennium literally be a period of one thousand years, or is it to be symbolically interpreted as the period of time between the Cross and the Second Coming? What else does the Bible say, if anything, about this period of peace on earth? Though the picture is not very detailed, the Bible does give us enough information to put together a portion of this part of the prophetic puzzle. Unfortunately, we are not told too much about it. Many of our questions are left unanswered. It is like looking at a distant solar system through our best telescope. We may be able to see one or two planets circling that star, but we can be certain that we are not seeing everything that is there!

The Necessity for a Literal Millennium Rule of Christ

Why is there such debate over this subject? The Millennium is only mentioned in one passage of the Book of Revelation. Because Revelation is prone to so many interpretive approaches, people look at this concept from widely differing viewpoints. Since the time of Augustine, most theologians have interpreted Revelation as a symbolic account of either the Church Age in its entirety, or as John's veiled picture of the church's struggle against the powers of the Roman Empire. As a result of this tradition, some two-thirds of Christians could be classified as Amillennialists today, including the Roman Catholics, the Lutherans, and the Reformed denominations.

Amillennialists insist that Christ has fulfilled the promises made to Abraham, David, and the nation of Israel during this age, which they say is the Millennium. The "thousand years" are symbolic of the entire Church Age, how ever long it will actually be. How, then, do Amillilennialists (and Postmillennialists, for that matter) deal with the regathering of the Jews back into their homeland? What do they say about the formation of the modern nation of Israel? Don't these miraculous events prove to them that their symbolic approach is invalid? No, because they explain that Israel's existence today is nothing more than an historic fluke! It has no bearing upon prophecy. Why not? They insist that since the Jews rejected their Messiah, the promises God gave them have been given to the True Israel, the church.

This argument is reminiscent of the Pharisees' inability to recognize Jesus as their Messiah. They certainly knew all the prophecies of Christ. But because they had a narrow interpretation of what the Messiah would do for them, they refused to accept Jesus. They wanted the Davidic conqueror - a deliverer for their nation. They could not and would not accept Christ's miracles or teachings as evidence that He was their savior.

The difference between the Pharisees' attitudes and those of the "A-" and "Post-" millennial positions is that they have no effect upon a Christian's salvation. The Pharisees missed their opportunity to accept their Christ because they refused to believe in who Jesus was. Those who hold differing positions on how Christ will return will not miss His salvation, even if He comes back in a way that will surprise them!

Although one's viewpoint on the Millennium has no bearing upon salvation, it is important to us nevertheless. Why *must* there be a Millennium? Why *must* God bring it to pass? Because the glory and honor of the Lord's word is at stake. There are many passages in both the Old and New Testaments that promise a period of peace on earth, under the benevolent rulership of the Messiah. "For the earth will be full of the knowledge of the Lord as the waters cover the sea" (Isaiah 11:9, NASB).

God is going to bring in the Millennium in order to show the world that He can and will fulfill everything He has promised. He declared through Isaiah:

> Remember this, and be assured; recall it to mind, you transgressors. 9 Remember the former things long past, for I am God, and there is no other; I am God, and there is no one like Me, 10 declaring the end from the beginning and from ancient times things which have not been done, saying, 'My purpose will be established, and I will accomplish all My good pleasure'; 11 calling a bird of prey from the east, the man of My purpose from a far country. Truly I have spoken; truly I will bring it to pass. I have planned it, surely I will do it. 12 Listen to Me, you stubborn-minded, who are far from righteousness. 13 I bring near My righteousness, it is not far off; and My salvation will not delay. and I will grant salvation in Zion, and My glory for Israel (Isaiah 46:8-13 NASB).

Note that God will accomplish His purposes, in spite of the sin and rebellion of mankind. He promised, therefore, He will act. In another place, Isaiah prophesies, "For My own sake, for My own sake, I will act; for how can My name be profaned? And My glory I will not give to another" (Isaiah 48:11, NASB). God will act to fulfill His promises not because anyone deserves His favor, but for the glory of His Name! He refuses to allow people to think that He can't or won't fulfill His Word!

Though theologians have re-interpreted God's promises to apply symbolically to the church, those promises have not been fulfilled in a literal sense. Until they are, mankind can say that God does not keep His promises or that He is unable to fulfill them. God does not need us to resort to re-interpreting or "spiritualizing" His own word. For instance, concerning Israel, He declared that "the gifts and calling of God are irrevocable" (Romans 10:29). We have seen that God has begun to bring the Jewish people back to Himself. More and more Jews are becoming Messianic believers. He has also regathered the Jews back into their land. Today, Jerusalem is the "cup that causes reeling to all the peoples around" (Zechariah 12:2). Someday soon Jesus will return to the Mount of Olives and they will "look upon Him whom they have pierced" (Zechariah 12:10). Since God has done this much to fulfill prophecy literally, perhaps He intends to glorify His Name by fulfilling those Scriptures promising that there really will be "peace on earth!"

The Millennium in Scripture

Although the thousand-year reign of the Millennium is only spoken about once in Scripture, it is built upon a concept that occurs several times throughout the Bible. From these passages we can piece together various parts of the puzzle in order to get a good idea of what the Millennial reign of Christ will be like.

God promised King David that he would have a son who would reign forever. Solomon's kingdom became a prophetic type for the fulfillment of that promise. His kingdom was characterized by wise rulership, prosperity, power, and peace. Jesus, the son of David, came the first time to bring the Kingdom reign to mankind, allowing us to willingly become His subjects through repentance and faith. When He comes again, He will institute His Kingdom's realm over all the earth, as Isaiah prophecies:

> 6 For a child will be born to us, a son will be given to us; and the government will rest on His shoulders; and His name will be called Wonderful Counselor, Mighty God, Eternal Father, Prince of Peace. 7 There will be no end to the increase of His government or of peace, and the throne of David and over his kingdom, to establish it and to uphold it with justice and righteousness from then on and forevermore. The zeal of the Lord of hosts will accomplish this (Isaiah 9:6-7, NASB).

God wants to bring peace and tranquility to mankind. He will do this through Jesus, the Son of David, the Prince of Peace, who is the Mighty God! He is the fulfillment of God's promise to David for a son who will rule forever! Note the emphasis upon God's motive for fulfilling this promise: God is zealously protecting the honor of His own character!

When He begins His reign, the promise of Isaiah 11:1-10 will be realized:

1 Then a shoot will spring from the stem of Jesse, and a branch from his roots will bear fruit. 2 And the Spirit of the Lord will rest on Him, the spirit of wisdom and understanding, The spirit of counsel and strength, the spirit of knowledge and the fear of the Lord. 3 And He will delight in the fear of the Lord, and He will not judge by what His eyes see, nor make a decision by what His ears hear; 4 but with righteousness He will judge the poor, and decide with fairness for the afflicted of the earth; and He will strike the earth with the rod of His mouth, and with the breath of His lips He will slay the wicked.

5 Also righteousness will be the belt about His loins, and faithfulness the belt about His waist. 6 and the wolf will dwell with the lamb, and the leopard will lie down with the kid, and the calf and the young lion and the fatling together; and a little boy will lead them. 7 Also the cow and the bear will graze; their young will lie down together; and the lion will eat straw like the ox. 8 And the nursing child will play by the hole of the cobra, and the weaned child will put his hand on the viper's den. 9 They will not hurt or destroy in all My holy mountain, for the earth will be full of the knowledge of the Lord as the waters cover the sea.

10 Then it will come about in that day that the nations will resort to the root of Jesse, who will stand as a signal for the peoples; and His resting place will be glorious. (Isaiah 11:1-10, NASB).

Part of this passage was fulfilled in Christ's first coming. Jesus did possess the Spirit of the Lord for wisdom, understanding, power, and strength. However, He did not bring about the judgment, nor did He institute complete righteousness on earth. Both the disciples and the Pharisees thought the Messiah would bring about the fullness of the Davidic Kingdom. Their expectations caused them to misunderstand Jesus at best, and reject Him at worst. Yet, Jesus will come again. When He does, the rest of this passage will be completely fulfilled. He will strike the world in judgment and will slay the wicked. (Revelation 19:15 uses a similar metaphor: "from His mouth comes a sharp sword, so that with it He may strike down the nations, and He will rule them with a rod of iron; and He treads the wine press of the fierce wrath of God, the Almighty").

Christ's return will change everything on earth. Verses five through nine indicate that even the animal kingdom will be physically changed. No longer will there be violence and bloodshed, but all living creatures will live in harmony with one another and their environments. It is possible, however, that these verses may not apply until the complete re-creation of the heavens and earth takes place, as revealed to us in Revelation 20. Nevertheless, Christ alone will be

King of all the nations in that day (verse 10). The whole earth will experience the knowledge and blessing of the Lord. Peace and harmony will prevail.

Similarly, Isaiah foresaw the same scene in this prophecy:

> 2 Now it will come about that in the last days, the mountain of the house of the Lord will be established as the chief of the mountains, and will be raised above the hills; and all the nations will stream to it. 3 And many peoples will come and say, "Come, let us go up to the mountain of the Lord, to the house of the God of Jacob; that He may teach us concerning His ways, and that we may walk in His paths." For the law will go forth from Zion, and the word of the Lord from Jerusalem. 4 And He will judge between the nations, and will render decisions for many peoples; and they will hammer their swords into plowshares, and their spears into pruning hooks. Nation will not lift up sword against nation, and never again will they learn war (Isaiah 2:2-4; NASB).

In this passage, we learn that Christ will rule from Jerusalem. All the nations will come to learn from Him. And, as it says in the oft-quoted verse, they will "...hammer their swords into plowshares, and their spears into pruning hooks. Nation will not lift up sword against nation, and never again will they learn war." People are fearful of what it would be like to be ruled by a "theocracy." Granted, earthly "theocracies" have always used religion to control and oppress their people. Sinful men can never run a theocratic form of government simply because they are sinful. Eventually they must resort to force to impose their own will upon others, all in the name of God.[63] However, Christ's rule will be a loving, beneficial theocracy. Yes, He will be the absolute ruler - but who could ask for a better one!

The Coming of the Millennial Kingdom

The Book of Revelation describes how Jesus will return at the height of the last battle (see Revelation 16:13-16; 19:11-19). This same battle is prophetically described in the Zechariah 12 - 14. Zechariah gives us great detail about what will happen after the Lord comes back:

---

[63] That is why our founding fathers did not form a theocracy, but a republic with a separation of powers within the government. They knew that Sin resulted in one man or one group's quest for absolute rule. Therefore they separated the powers of the federal and state governments, as well as instituted the system of checks and balances between the executive, legislative, and judicial branches of government. It is a system designed with the Sinful nature in mind!

9 And the Lord will be king over all the earth; in that day the Lord will be the only one, and His name the only one.

11 And people will live in it, and there will be no more curse, for Jerusalem will dwell in security. 12 Now this will be the plague with which the Lord will strike all the peoples who have gone to war against Jerusalem; their flesh will rot while they stand on their feet, and their eyes will rot in their sockets, and their tongue will rot in their mouth. 13 And it will come about in that day that a great panic from the Lord will fall on them; and they will seize one another's hand, and the hand of one will be lifted against the hand of another. 14 And Judah also will fight at Jerusalem; and the wealth of all the surrounding nations will be gathered, gold and silver and garments in great abundance. 15 So also like this plague will be the plague on the horse, the mule, the camel, the donkey and all the cattle that will be in those camps.

16 Then it will come about that any who are left of all the nations that went against Jerusalem will go up from year to year to worship the King, the Lord of hosts, and to celebrate the Feast of Booths. 17 And it will be that whichever of the families of the earth does not go up to Jerusalem to worship the King, the Lord of hosts, there will be no rain on them. 18 And if the family of Egypt does not go up or enter, then no rain will fall on them; it will be the plague with which the Lord smites the nations who do not go up to celebrate the Feast of Booths. 19 This will be the punishment of Egypt, and the punishment of all the nations who do not go up to celebrate the Feast of Booths (Zechariah 14:9, 11-19, NASB).

The language here is clearly not metaphorical. Instead, in graphic detail we read that the people who oppose Jesus at His return will experience great physical suffering and emotional terror. However, mortal men will still be alive after Jesus comes back to the earth! He will be King of kings (Revelation 19:16) over all the nations and Jerusalem will become the center of the world's attention, receiving riches and honor from all people. If these people do not worship their benevolent and wise King, He will enforce His rule by directly influencing their weather patterns!

Another passage in Isaiah tells us much the same thing:

9 Behold, the day of the Lord is coming, cruel, with fury and burning anger, to make the land a desolation; and He will exterminate its sinners from it. 10 For the stars of heaven and their constellations will not flash forth their light; the sun will be dark when it rises, and the moon will not shed its light. 11 Thus I will punish the world for its evil, and the wicked for their iniquity; I will also put an end to the arrogance of the

proud, and abase the haughtiness of the ruthless. 12 I will make mortal man scarcer than pure gold, and mankind than the gold of Ophir (Isaiah 13:9-12; NASB).

Here, also, we see that there will be a few people who survive the day of God's wrath. They will live and propagate during the Millennium.

What will life be like for mortal man during the Millennium? And what will resurrected believers do during that time?

Life in the Millennial Kingdom

Once again, Isaiah gives us some more insight. In the following passage, God tells us that He will bring about a new order upon the earth:

> 17 "For behold, I create new heavens and a new earth; and the former things shall not be remembered or come to mind. 18 But be glad and rejoice forever in what I create; for behold, I create Jerusalem for rejoicing, and her people for gladness. 19 I will also rejoice in Jerusalem, and be glad in My people; and there will no longer be heard in her the voice of weeping and the sound of crying.
>
> 20 "No longer will there be in it an infant who lives but a few days, or an old man who does not live out his days; for the youth will die at the age of one hundred and the one who does not reach the age of one hundred shall be thought accursed. 21 And they shall build houses and inhabit them; they shall also plant vineyards and eat their fruit. 22 They shall not build, and another inhabit, they shall not plant, and another eat; for as the lifetime of a tree, so shall be the days of My people, and My chosen ones shall wear out the work of their hands. 23 They shall not labor in vain, or bear children for calamity; for they are the offspring of those blessed by the Lord, and their descendants with them. 24 It will also come to pass that before they call, I will answer; and while they are still speaking, I will hear.
>
> 25 The wolf and the lamb shall graze together, and the lion shall eat straw like the ox; and dust shall be the serpent's food. They shall do no evil or harm in all My holy mountain," says the Lord (Isaiah 65:17-25; NASB).

Before we examine what the text says about life in the age to come, we must first determine where the events described in this passage fit into the prophetic puzzle. While Isaiah seems to be describing life in the Millennial Kingdom, the apostle John places the creation of a "new heavens and new earth" *after* the Millennium and the Second Resurrection (Revelation 21). But in Isaiah's passage, people are still facing death, while in the Book of Revelation, "there will no longer be any death" (Revelation 20:4). How can we reconcile this conflict? It appears that Isaiah's description is what I have termed a "telescopic" prophecy. It looks far into the future and blends together the entire Millennium with that time which John says will take place after the Millennium. Isaiah, therefore, labels the entire period after the climax of this age as part of the creation of the new heavens and new earth.

Isaiah's picture of the Millennium shows us that the Lord's reign will be benevolent and wise. There will be peace, prosperity, and rejoicing throughout the world. Every living thing on earth will benefit from the Lord's rule, from humans to animals. Though there will only be a few mortal humans left alive at the beginning of this time, they will not only multiply but they will enjoy long and abundant life. If we think that the medical and scientific advances of the last one hundred years have been awesome, wait until our Lord reveals to us the wisdom and knowledge of God! It will truly be a utopian society!

Furthermore, a new temple will be built during the Millennium. Zechariah 14 tells us that the nations will come yearly to bring their sacrifices to the Lord in Jerusalem. Ezekiel 40 through 48 describes a perfect temple built in the renewed Israel. Both passages tell us that "the Lord is there" (Ezekiel 48:35).

Unfortunately, even this utopia must end. The Book of Revelation gives us the most detail about what will take place during the Millennial Kingdom:

> 1 And I saw an angel coming down from heaven, having the key of the abyss and a great chain in his hand. 2 And he laid hold of the dragon, the serpent of old, who is the devil and Satan, and bound him for a thousand years, 3 and threw him into the abyss, and shut it and sealed it over him, so that he should not deceive the nations any longer, until the thousand years were completed; after these things he must be released for a short time.
>
> 4 And I saw thrones, and they sat upon them, and judgment was given to them. And I saw the souls of those who had been beheaded because of the testimony of Jesus and because of the word of God, and those who had not worshiped the beast or his image, and had not received the mark upon their forehead and upon their hand; and they came to life and reigned with Christ for a thousand years. 5 The rest of the dead did not come to life until the thousand years were completed. This is the first resurrection. 6 Blessed and holy is the one who has a part in the first resurrection; over these the second death has no power, but they will be priests of God and of Christ and will reign with Him for a thousand years.
>
> 7 And when the thousand years are completed, Satan will be released from his prison, 8 and will come out to deceive the nations which are in

the four corners of the earth, Gog and Magog, to gather them together for the war; the number of them is like the sand of the seashore. 9 And they came up on the broad plain of the earth and surrounded the camp of the saints and the beloved city, and fire came down from heaven and devoured them. 10 And the devil who deceived them was thrown into the lake of fire and brimstone, where the beast and the false prophet are also; and they will be tormented day and night forever and ever (Revelation 20:1-10; NASB).

The devil will be spiritually bound in a place called the Abyss. We do not know how this will be accomplished but we do know that he will not be allowed to influence life on this planet any longer.

We also discover that the saints will rule and reign with Christ for the thousand years. Apparently, Jesus was speaking literally when He said that one of the rewards for being faithful in service was to be given authority over many cities: "And he said to him, 'Well done, good slave, because you have been faithful in a very little thing, be in authority over ten cities'" (Luke 19:17; NASB). During this reign, the earth will be restored and healed. The planet will enjoy unbroken peace, prosperity, and growth. Imagine what society will be like at the end of the thousand years!

Nevertheless, at the end of this time Satan will be allowed to roam free again. Why? We really do not know. One reason could be to show the human race that all people are inherently rebellious. Even with the wisest and most beneficial rulership, resulting in the greatest peace and prosperity of all time, they will still want to rule their own lives. It will demonstrate for all time that sinful mankind is without excuse. Even when God takes perfect care of us we still want to be gods unto ourselves!

We are told that all the nations, led by the nations Gog and Magog, will rebel against Christ and the saints (verse eight). The Lord Himself will quickly dispatch their insurrection. Satan will then be cast into the "lake of fire" where he will suffer torment forever and ever.

But there is a problem with this passage. Gog and Magog are also mentioned in Ezekiel 38-39 as the leaders of a confederacy of nations that will attack Israel in the last days. The difficulty arises in trying to reconcile the two passages. In Revelation, Gog and Magog are clearly the nations leading the final human rebellion at the end of the Millennium. But in Ezekiel, it appears that their attack against Israel takes place before the Millennium: "After many days you will be summoned; in the latter years you will come into the land that is restored from the sword, whose inhabitants have been gathered from many nations to the mountains of Israel which had been a continual waste; but its people were brought out from the nations, and they are living securely, all of them" (Ezekiel 38:8, NASB). The puzzle pieces do not seem to fit together snugly!

Premillennialists have usually assigned the fulfillment of Ezekiel's prophecy to the beginning of the Daniel's seventieth seven - the last seven years of this age when God is going to deal with His people, the Jews. There are two reasons for this interpretation. First, Ezekiel says that after Magog's armies are destroyed, it will take seven years to decontaminate and clean up the land: "Then those who inhabit the cities of Israel will go out, and make fires with the weapons and burn them, both shields and bucklers, bows and arrows, war clubs and spears and for seven years they will make fires of them" (Ezekiel 39:9, NASB). Dispensationalists link these seven years with the seven years of the Tribulation.

The second reason Ezekiel's prophecy seems to fit in the time period before the Millennium is that the allies of Gog and Magog are the same nations that make up the Islamic enemies of Israel today. Ezekiel writes,

> 'Thus says the Lord God, Behold, I am against you, O Gog, prince of Rosh, Meshech, and Tubal. 4 And I will turn you about, and put hooks into your jaws, and I will bring you out, and all your army, horses and horsemen, all of them splendidly attired, a great company with buckler and shield, all of them wielding swords; 5 Persia, Ethiopia, and Put with them, all of them with shield and helmet; 6 Gomer with all its troops; Beth-togarmah from the remote parts of the north with all its troops—many peoples with you" (Ezekiel 38:3-6; NASB).

Where are these countries today? In his book, *The Late Great Planet Earth*, Hal Lindsey identifies these nations for us, using the "Table of Nations" found in Genesis 10, the fifth century BC Greek historian Herodotus, the ancient Jewish historian Josephus, and Pliny, the Roman writer and philosopher. Gog, Magog, Rosh, Meshech and Tubal all were peoples who settled in what is now Russia and some of the southern republics of the former Soviet Empire. He traces how these people's ancient names are still found in modern place names as Russia (Rosh), Moscow (Meshech), and Tublinsk (Tubal). We easily identify Persia as the ancient name for the Islamic state of Iran. He traces Ethiopia to the ancient nation of Cush, located in the upper Nile area that we know today as Sudan and parts of modern Ethiopia. Put is found today in the northern African region of Libya. All of these allies are sworn enemies of the nation of Israel today.[64]

Until the Soviet Union broke up, it was quite easy to place Ezekiel's prophecy into the Dispensational timetable. (Even President Ronald Reagan was familiar with this prophecy.) Now we cannot be so sure. It is still possible that Russia, her former Muslim republics in the south, and these other Islamic allies will mount an attack against Israel at some point before the return of Christ. But

---

[64] Lindsey, Hal, *The Late Great Planet Earth*, Grand Rapids: Zondervan Publishing, 1970, pp. 63-71.

even if that battle takes place (as Dispensationalists predict), we are still faced with the Biblical difficulty of the reference to Gog and Magog rising up against God's people at the end of the Millennium. How can these two passages be reconciled?

Once again, our understanding about the different Jewish styles of prophecy helps us. What we have here is probably an example of a eschatological dualism. Ezekiel was looking forward into the future and saw what appears to us as one event - the war of Gog and Magog against Israel. It appears that Ezekiel 38-39 will have its fulfillment at the end of this age, but it will also have a second fulfillment at the end of the Millennium. We don't know what parts of the prophecy will come to pass in the initial fulfillment and what parts will take place at the end of the Millennium. But the fact that this prophecy will have a complete fulfillment is underscored by the words of the prophecy itself: "'This is what the Sovereign LORD says: Are you not the one I spoke of in former days by my servants the prophets of Israel? At that time they prophesied for years that I would bring you against them" (Ezekiel 38:17, NIV).

The Bible is clear about one thing: after the insurrection at the end of the Millennium: the old way of life on earth will pass away and a new order will come.

The Second Resurrection and the Judgment of Hell

The Millennium ends with the great and final Judgment of God. All of those who have opposed God throughout mankind's history will have to stand before the Lord:

> 10 And the devil, who deceived them, was thrown into the lake of burning sulfur, where the beast and the false prophet had been thrown. They will be tormented day and night for ever and ever.
> 11 Then I saw a great white throne and him who was seated on it. Earth and sky fled from his presence, and there was no place for them.
> 12 And I saw the dead, great and small, standing before the throne, and books were opened. Another book was opened, which is the book of life. The dead were judged according to what they had done as recorded in the books. 13 The sea gave up the dead that were in it, and death and Hades gave up the dead that were in them, and each person was judged according to what he had done. 14 Then death and Hades were thrown into the lake of fire. The lake of fire is the second death. 15 If anyone's name was not found written in the book of life, he was thrown into the lake of fire (Revelation 20:10-15; NASB).

Just as we do not have a complete picture of exactly what the Millennium or Heaven will be like, we do not know much about the punishment of the wicked in Hell. But we do understand enough to know that it will not be pleasant place to spend eternity! In this passage we discover that the devil will be cast into a place called "the lake of burning sulfur." After that, there will be a general resurrection of all the dead. A second resurrection has to occur at the end of the Millennium. Not only will all those who have died since the creation of the world come to life in order to be judged, but there will be many mortal humans (I'm sure) who will find salvation during the Millennium. We do not know exactly what the vehicle for their salvation will be, but we can assume that it will involve some form of repentance and belief!

All those whose names are not found in the Book of Life will also be cast into the lake of fire. The Bible is clear on this. They will not be resurrected only to be annihilated into non-existence. No, humans are created with eternal spirits. We have to have some place to dwell for eternity. Those places will either be with God, enjoying the blessings of relationship with Him, or away from God, reaping the consequences of being cut off from Him. God is very magnanimous about this. If a person has chosen to live without God in this life, he will get to keep that choice for all of eternity!

What will Hell be like? The Bible has revealed to us only what is necessary for us to know. In ancient Hebrew understanding, all the dead went to a place called "Sheol" (known as *Hades* in Greek). This was a kind of waiting place where their spirits (literally, *rapha,* or "shades") were kept until the resurrection and judgment: "Your dead will live; their corpses will rise. You who lie in the dust, awake and shout for joy, for your dew is as the dew of the dawn, and the earth will give birth to the departed spirits" (Isaiah 26:19, NASB).

According to Jesus' parable about the rich man and Lazarus, Sheol was divided between the righteous and the unrighteous. A great gulf separated the two groups. The righteous enjoyed a place of blessing (in the "bosom of Abraham") while the wicked had already begun their eternal torment (c.f. Luke 16:19-31).

When the church creeds speak of Jesus "descending into hell" they are referring to this waiting place of the dead, known by its Old Testament word, Sheol. Paul tells us in Ephesians 4:8-9 that Jesus freed those righteous souls who were waiting in Sheol, and took them into His presence: "Therefore it says, 'When He ascended on high, he led captive a host of captives, and He gave gifts to men.' Now this expression, 'He ascended,' what does it mean except that He also had descended into the lower parts of the earth?"

All believers who die now go to be "at home with the Lord" (cf. 2 Corinthians 5:8) in a place often called "Paradise" (2 Corinthians 12:4). We see a glimpse of this place of the righteous dead in the Book of Revelation: "I saw underneath the altar the souls of those who had been slain because of the word of

God, and because of the testimony which they had maintained; and they cried out with a loud voice, saying, 'How long, O Lord, holy and true, will you refrain from judging and avenging our blood on those who dwell on the earth?'" (Revelation 6:9,10, NASB).

However, all the unrighteous who die in this age continue to go to Sheol. Although we can be sure that it is a place of torment, it is *not* Hell itself.[65] The Bible says that the devil and the unrighteous will not be cast into Hell until the Final Judgment, spoken about in Revelation 20:11-14.

What is Hell like? The Bible describes it in horrible terms. The Greek word that is used for this place of God's eternal wrath (*gehenna*) is very picturesque. It refers to the perpetual fires that burned the garbage outside the city of Jerusalem in the Valley of Hinnom. Jesus often used the metaphor "where their worm does not die, and the fire is not quenched" (Mark 9:48) when He spoke about Hell.

The Bible uses other terms to warn mankind about Hell. In addition to being called the "lake of fire", it is known as a place of "darkness" (Matthew 22:13; 2 Peter 2:17; Jude 13), "eternal fire prepared for the devil and his angels" (Matthew 25:41), "torment with fire and brimstone" (Revelation 14:10), and "eternal destruction" (2 Thessalonians 1:9). The Bible uses the strongest human images of torture, pain, and anguish to warn people of the finality and severity of the wrath of God.

We cringe at the thought of a person having to spend eternity in Hell. We try to ignore it, or hope that God will somehow change His mind after a few thousand years. Others believe that God will simply annihilate the souls of those who have refused His rulership in their lives. Yet the Bible is clear: Hell is real, it is punishment, and it is eternal. Jesus knew about the reality of Hell and He warned us of it by speaking more about it than did any other person in the Bible.

But why must people go to Hell? Why must Hell be so harsh?

We must first understand this fact: God created us for His glory. "Bring my sons from afar and my daughters from the end of the earth, everyone who is called by my name, *whom I created for my glory*" (Isaiah 43:6-7). He created us "in His image" so that we would reflect His glory in the world. Why God would want to give us a share in shining with His glory is a mysterious act of His love. We cannot fathom it.

Therefore it is the duty and calling of every person on earth to live for the glory of God. "So, whether you eat or drink or whatever you do, do all to the glory of God" (I Corinthians 10:31). Our duty comes from God's design for us. We were created for His glory; therefore, we should live to glorify Him.

---

[65]In his book, *The Great Divorce*, C.S. Lewis likens this waiting place as a large, gray, dreary city where the inhabitants are still afflicted with their sins while they await the dreaded coming judgment.

What does it mean to glorify God? Giving glory is the natural human response to experiencing grandeur or beauty: we praise it, we extol it, and we share the joy of the experience with others. So to give glory to God means to acknowledge God for who He is, to value Him above all things, and to make Him known to others. It implies heartfelt gratitude: "He who brings thanksgiving as his sacrifice glorifies me" (Psalm 50:23). It also implies trust: Abraham "grew strong in his faith, giving glory to God" (Romans 4:20).

All mankind has experienced to varying degrees the glory of God's nature: "The heavens declare the glory of God; the skies proclaim the work of His hands" (Psalm 19:1). "Ever since the creation of the world His invisible nature, namely, His eternal power and deity, has been clearly perceived in the things that have been made. So they are without excuse; for although they knew God they did not glorify Him as God (Romans 1:20-21).

But all of us have failed to glorify God as we ought: "All have sinned and fallen short of the glory of God" (Romans 3:23).

What does it mean to fall short of the glory of God? The best explanation of Romans 3:23 is found in Romans 1:23. It says that those who did not glorify or thank God "became fools, and exchanged the glory of the immortal God for images." This is the way we "fall short" of the glory of God: We exchange it for something of lesser value. Our unbelief causes us to want to seek after things of infinitely lesser value rather than the infinitely valuable One.

We have all sinned. "None is righteous, no, not one" (Romans 3:10). None of us has trusted God as we should. None of us has obeyed Him according to His wisdom and righteousness. We have exchanged and dishonored His glory again and again. In all this we have held the glory of the Lord in contempt. For instance, when David committed adultery with Bathsheba and had her husband killed, what did God say to him? He said, "You have despised *Me*...You have utterly scorned the Lord" (2 Sam. 12:10,14). Ultimately, his sin dishonored God.

Because we have all sinned, all of us are subject to eternal condemnation by God. "They shall suffer the punishment of eternal destruction and exclusion from the presence of the Lord and from the glory of His might" (II Thessalonians 1:9).

Having held the glory of God in contempt through unbelief and disobedience, we will be sentenced to be excluded from the enjoyment of that glory forever in the eternal torment of Hell. Hell is not remedial. Jesus said, "Depart from me, you cursed, into the eternal fire prepared for the devil and his angels...And they will go away into eternal punishment, but the righteous into eternal life" (Matthew 25:41,46). The "punishment" is eternal in the same way that "life" is eternal. John sums up the terrible reality of the eternal Hell in Revelation 14:11, "And the smoke of their torment goes up forever and ever: and they have no rest, day or night."

Hell is also just. Some people have objected that an everlasting punishment is out of proportion to the seriousness of the sin committed. But this is not true, because *the seriousness of our sin is infinite.* The great American theologian Jonathan Edwards explains:

"The crime of one being despising and casting contempt on another, is proportionally more or less heinous, as he was under greater or less obligations to obey him. And therefore if there be any being that we are under infinite obligations to love, and honor, and obey, the contrary towards him must be infinitely faulty.

Our obligation to love, honor, and obey any being is in proportion to his loveliness, honorableness, and authority...But God is a being infinitely lovely, because he hath infinite excellency and beauty...

So sin against God, being a violation of infinite obligations, must be a crime infinitely heinous, and so deserving infinite punishment...The eternity of the punishment of ungodly men renders it infinite...and therefore renders no more than proportionable to the heinousness of what they are guilty of. (From "The Justice of God in the Damnation of Sinners," The *Works of Jonathan Edwards*, vol. 1.)

Thanks be to God for His gift of mercy through Jesus Christ!

The New Heavens and the New Earth

We are now at the end of our puzzle. Only a few pieces are left. Unfortunately, they become very blurred and out of focus, because we are looking at an event that is at the edge of God's revelation to us. The words God uses to describe the New Heavens and the New Earth are nearly beyond our comprehension. Chapters 21 and 22 of the Book of Revelation reveal the mystery of our future:

> Revelation 21:1 Then I saw a new heaven and a new earth, for the first heaven and the first earth had passed away, and there was no longer any sea. 2 I saw the Holy City, the new Jerusalem, coming down out of heaven from God, prepared as a bride beautifully dressed for her husband. 3 And I heard a loud voice from the throne saying, "Now the dwelling of God is with men, and he will live with them. They will be his people, and God himself will be with them and be their God. 4 He will wipe every tear from their eyes. There will be no more death or mourning or crying or pain, for the old order of things has passed away."
>
> 5 He who was seated on the throne said, "I am making everything new!" Then he said, "Write this down, for these words are trustworthy and true."

6 He said to me: "It is done. I am the Alpha and the Omega, the Beginning and the End. To him who is thirsty I will give to drink without cost from the spring of the water of life. 7 He who overcomes will inherit all this, and I will be his God and he will be my son. 8 But the cowardly, the unbelieving, the vile, the murderers, the sexually immoral, those who practice magic arts, the idolaters and all liars—their place will be in the fiery lake of burning sulfur. This is the second death."

9 One of the seven angels who had the seven bowls full of the seven last plagues came and said to me, "Come, I will show you the bride, the wife of the Lamb." 10 And he carried me away in the Spirit to a mountain great and high, and showed me the Holy City, Jerusalem, coming down out of heaven from God. 11 It shone with the glory of God, and its brilliance was like that of a very precious jewel, like a jasper, clear as crystal. 12 It had a great, high wall with twelve gates, and with twelve angels at the gates. On the gates were written the names of the twelve tribes of Israel. 13 There were three gates on the east, three on the north, three on the south and three on the west. 14 The wall of the city had twelve foundations, and on them were the names of the twelve apostles of the Lamb.

15 The angel who talked with me had a measuring rod of gold to measure the city, its gates and its walls. 16 The city was laid out like a square, as long as it was wide. He measured the city with the rod and found it to be 12,000 stadia in length, and as wide and high as it is long. 17 He measured its wall and it was 144 cubits thick, by man's measurement, which the angel was using. 18 The wall was made of jasper, and the city of pure gold, as pure as glass. 19 The foundations of the city walls were decorated with every kind of precious stone. The first foundation was jasper, the second sapphire, the third chalcedony, the fourth emerald, 20 the fifth sardonyx, the sixth carnelian, the seventh chrysolite, the eighth beryl, the ninth topaz, the tenth chrysoprase, the eleventh jacinth, and the twelfth amethyst. 21 The twelve gates were twelve pearls, each gate made of a single pearl. The great street of the city was of pure gold, like transparent glass.

22 I did not see a temple in the city, because the Lord God Almighty and the Lamb are its temple. 23 The city does not need the sun or the moon to shine on it, for the glory of God gives it light, and the Lamb is its lamp. 24 The nations will walk by its light, and the kings of the earth will bring their splendor into it. 25 On no day will its gates ever be shut, for there will be no night there. 26 The glory and honor of the nations will be brought into it. 27 Nothing impure will ever enter it, nor will anyone who does what is shameful or deceitful, but only those whose names are written in the Lamb's book of life.

Revelation 22:1 Then the angel showed me the river of the water of life, as clear as crystal, flowing from the throne of God and of the Lamb 2 down the middle of the great street of the city. On each side of the river stood the tree of life, bearing twelve crops of fruit, yielding its fruit every month. And the leaves of the tree are for the healing of the nations. 3 No longer will there be any curse. The throne of God and of the Lamb will be in the city, and his servants will serve him. 4 They will see his face, and his name will be on their foreheads. 5 There will be no more night. They will not need the light of a lamp or the light of the sun, for the Lord God will give them light. And they will reign for ever and ever (Revelation 21: 1-27; 22: 1-5; NASB).

Eternity is a long time. As finite humans we cannot even fathom it. Oh, we can imagine a billion years but it is impossible for us to grasp the concept of timelessness. Nor can we even begin to comprehend the glories and wonder of what life in God's eternal presence would be like. Yet, here in these chapters we are given just a glimpse. Out of necessity, the words John uses are highly symbolic. The full meaning of the descriptions goes beyond our human capacity to understand. For instance, John describes the New Jerusalem in terms of golden streets and gates of precious gems and minerals. What John is saying is that those things we value so highly in this earthly kingdom will be of common usage in the new order. That is not to say that there might not be streets of gold and gates of pearls. They may be made out of these things or something even more wonderful that look like them. (Why? Because the golden streets will be transparent, like glass.)

John tells us that the old order will pass away and a new heaven and a new earth will be created. Questions immediately come to us faster than there are answers. Does this mean that God will not only do away with earth (an act that might have justification, given what has transpired here) but that He will also create a new heaven? Is this the heaven where He dwells, or does He mean the heavens, or universe, above. The latter is more likely, though we cannot be sure. C.S. Lewis does a wonderful job painting a word picture of the creation of the new heavens and the new earth in the last volume of the Narnia Chronicles series entitled, *The Last Battle*. The redeemed of Narnia watch from the doorway of time as their beloved land passes away before them. Although they realize that from Narnia's viewpoint time is passing at its normal speed, they are seeing it transpire in mere moments. They watch as Narnia's sun dies out, as well as all the stars in the sky. Finally, the Christ-figure Aslan closes the door on the old and they all turn around and find themselves in the perfect Narnia - a better and somehow more real one! Likewise, we, too, will be present to witness the glory of God's creative power!

What will the new creation be like? The first thing we are told about it is that there will no longer be any sea (Revelation 21:1). This one verse has caused a lot of consternation for surfers and ocean lovers. Having grown up in Southern California, I have done my share of surfing. I have heard the groans of anguish among my surfing buddies who have read this verse. For them, what is heaven without the perfect wave? Some may think this is a little childish, but it does bring to light some attitudes many people have. We do question whether heaven will be all that wonderful. We may even think that someday in the far, far distant future that God will decide that He's had enough of us and He will just start over with another "game." These kinds of thoughts are just symptoms of our unbelief in the character of God (which is Sin). What God has for us will be good, and good forever.

But the point of this verse has nothing to do with the existence of an ocean at all. We must look to Biblical images or metaphors in order to get the meaning of this verse. Earlier in the Book of Revelation we see scenes of the heavenly throne room where there a "sea of glass, like crystal" (Revelation 4:6) and a "sea of glass, mixed with fire" (15:2). What is the significance of this "sea?"

The Jews believed that an impassable "sea" separated God's throne room from the rest of creation. We first discover this concept in the Book of Genesis at the second day of creation. God separated the waters on the earth below from the waters of heaven by a great "expanse," often-translated "the heavens." The Psalms often refer to these "waters" of heaven (Psalm 148:4 - "Praise Him highest heavens and the waters that are above the heavens!;" Psalm 104:3 - "He lays the beams of His upper chambers in the waters…"). The sea before the throne of God was symbolized in Solomon's temple by the construction of the "bronze sea" located between the Holy of Holies and the outer court (see 1 Kings 7:23-26 and 2 Chronicles 4:1-8). Extra-biblical writings of the intertestimental period also contain references to this separating sea. In 2 Enoch 3:1-3, Enoch is taken up by the angels into the first heaven and is shown "a great sea, greater than the earthly sea." In the Testament of Levi 2:7, this sea is located between the first and the second heaven. The concept here is that there is a barrier between the realm of the creation (the first heaven) and God. In 1 Enoch, this sea is described as being made of crystal and surrounded by tongues of fire. Hence, when John writes about the sea before the throne of God, he is referring to the barrier between God and man.

This interpretation fits the context of Revelation 21 best. Over and over we are told that God and man will have no more barriers between them. A voice cries out, "Now the dwelling of God is with men, and He will live with them" (verse 3). There will no longer be any need for a temple as there was during the Millennium (verse 22). God will be able to dwell with man. He will be their light and their glory (verse 23). The water of life, flowing directly and unhindered from the throne of God, will nourish and sustain redeemed mankind

(Revelation 22:1). God and man will be united again, just as they were in the Garden of Eden.

However, we will not return to the garden. We will live in the city of peace, the perfect Jerusalem. In mysterious and majestic imagery, John describes our new dwelling place. When John gives us a description of its shape and size he uses numbers that symbolize perfection. It is doubtful, therefore, that we can expect to live in a cube-shaped space ship (like the Borgs of the *Star Trek* series). Instead, the numbers (twelve times twelve times ten to the third power) all speak of the perfections of God and man). The passage is symbolically describing a place of perfect safety, perfect peace, perfect life, and perfect fellowship between God and man.

God Himself will dwell with us. The tree of life from the Garden of Eden will be there. All sin and rebellion will be gone; death will be no more. Nothing will hinder us from direct fellowship with God. In this life, we see and experience God through the clouded lens of Sin and death. Though we know Him and can have fellowship with Him through the blood of Jesus and the gift of the Holy Spirit, that fellowship is often obscured or imperfect. We joyously taste and see that the Lord is good. And we are thankful for those times of sweet intimacy with our Lord through the down payment of the Holy Spirit's presence. Nevertheless, in this life we still "see through a glass darkly" (1 Corinthians 13:12). But someday we shall see Him "face to face." If you know Him now, you already know "what a day of rejoicing that will be!"

Chapter Eleven

Our Blessed Hope

We have come to the end of our study. We have learned that Jesus Christ is coming back soon. How soon, we still don't know. But the two primary signs are being fulfilled: Jerusalem is the capital city of the modern Jewish nation, and the gospel is being preached in those few remaining nations that have never heard the good news. What does this mean for us? Jesus said that we should always be ready for His return. But the knowledge that the signs are being fulfilled before our eyes gives us an added sense of anticipation. But along with this expectancy comes the sober realization that the Antichrist and the Great Tribulation may be near.

We have discovered that Christians will not completely escape the Great Tribulation. Though the prospect of His return is sweet, the process will be bitter. Darkness will come when no man can work. The tribulation is not something to look forward to in the natural sense. Yet we do have hope. Jesus said that "when you see these things take place, lift up your heads for your redemption is drawing near" (Luke 21:28). He warned us to be strong and of good courage, for he who endures to the end will be saved. It will be a time when we will "...wait for the blessed hope—the glorious appearing of our great God and Savior, Jesus Christ..." (Titus 2:13).

What is hope? Why is it so important for us?

Hope means waiting with anticipation for something good to happen in the future. While faith is something we exercise or act upon, hope is that spiritual state in which we rest when there is nothing else we can do. Faith is active. It unlocks mysteries, removes mountains, and brings assurance of God's will. But hope is passive. It looks forward with expectation to what God will do. But it is no less powerful. In fact, faith without hope becomes frustrating because God's mysteries, power, and assurance do not come to us in a speedy manner! If we never have to wait in hope for God to reveal His timing and will, faith becomes little more than a magician's wand to be used whenever we want something for ourselves.

Our hope in God and His salvation helps us through the pain and struggles of life in this age. In this final chapter I would like to offer six reasons why hope - our blessed hope - gives us strength to live for Christ through any situation or circumstance.

First, hope dispels our fear of death. Though death is inevitable, we try to ignore it as long as possible. We live in denial with false bravado. Yet we all must face it at some time: in the quietness of the night, in the grim announcement of the doctor's verdict, or the unexpected terror of an accident. But for the one who has believed in the Lord Jesus Christ, death holds no such terror. For us it is just a passing from one stage of life to the next. We may not look forward to whatever means of death we may face, but we know that the final outcome will be worth whatever pain we have to suffer. Paul's words to the Thessalonians are often repeated at the funerals of those who have died in the Lord:

> 13 Brothers, we do not want you to be ignorant about those who fall asleep, or to grieve like the rest of men, who have no hope.
> 14 We believe that Jesus died and rose again and so we believe that God will bring with Jesus those who have fallen asleep in him. 15 According to the Lord's own word, we tell you that we who are still alive, who are left till the coming of the Lord, will certainly not precede those who have fallen asleep. 16 For the Lord himself will come down from heaven, with a loud command, with the voice of the archangel and with the trumpet call of God, and the dead in Christ will rise first. 17 After that, we who are still alive and are left will be caught up together with them in the clouds to meet the Lord in the air. And so we will be with the Lord forever.
> 18 Therefore encourage each other with these words (1 Thessalonians 4:13-18).

Christians do not face the same kind of grief that the rest of the world must endure. Yes, we will miss our loved ones. We will have to wait to see them again, often for many lonely years. But we do have hope! We will see them again. We look forward in hope to the return of Jesus Christ when the dead in Christ will all live again!

Some see the Blessed Hope as referring only to the rapture of those Christians who are alive in the last days. But the emphasis in Titus 2:13 is not upon those who will be raptured (as wonderful as that will be for them) but for those who have already died in Christ. The encouragement of hope is that we will *all* live with the Lord forever!

Other passages give us added reasons for rejoicing in hope. Our place in God's kingdoms will be awesomely wonderful! Jesus Himself tells us to: "…not let your hearts be troubled. Trust in God; trust also in me. In my Father's house are many rooms; if it were not so, I would have told you. I am going there to prepare a place for you. And if I go and prepare a place for you, I will come back and take you to be with me that you also may be where I am" (John 14:1-3). Again, the return of Jesus gives us reason for peace. Jesus will come back to be with us in a place that He has specially prepared for our benefit.

Because of hope, a Christian can rest in such a state of assurance that he can say, like Paul, "for me to live is Christ, to die is gain" (Philippians 1:21) and,

"We are confident, I say, and would prefer to be away from the body and at home with the Lord" (2 Corinthians 5:8).

Second, hope gives us the courage to face whatever tragedies of life that may afflict us. Sin and death work their way throughout all of life, touching us with their pain. In this world our bodies suffer from illness, accident and age. Good diet, exercise, and modern medicine may help us live a few years longer, but no one is immune from senseless tragedy. How can we continue to live if we are struck with some debilitating illness or the horrible mutilation from an accident? What sense can we make out of someone's premature death or a child's retardation from a birth defect? The Apostle Paul reminds us that as long as we are living in "this earthly tent" we will groan, "longing to be clothed with our dwelling from heaven" (cf. 2 Corinthians 5:1-10). Someday one of us could lose a limb in an accident, another could become paralyzed by a stroke, or another might suffer terribly from cancer. Only hope in the resurrection life can help us cope. We can look forward in hope to the day when Jesus will resurrect these tired, imperfect bodies. No, we do not minimize the pain of suffering. But hope becomes the strength that can lead a person through it! Paul writes, "Though outwardly we are wasting away, yet inwardly we are being renewed day by day. For our light and momentary troubles are achieving for us an eternal glory that far outweighs them all. So we fix our eyes not on what is seen, but on what is unseen. For what is seen is temporary, but what is unseen is eternal" (2 Corinthians 4:16-17). Though our outer man may decay, our inner man will live forever in the presence and glory of God!

Third, hope in the return of Christ helps us make the kinds of moral decisions that will last for eternity. We know that all of us will appear before the judgment seat of Christ where we will be asked to give an account of how we lived our lives of faith. In the same section of Second Corinthians, Paul gives us another reason why our hope in the return of Christ is so important: "We live by faith, not by sight. We are confident, I say, and would prefer to be away from the body and at home with the Lord. So we make it our goal to please him, whether we are at home in the body or away from it. For we must all appear before the judgment seat of Christ, that each one may receive what is due him for the things done while in the body, whether good or bad" (2 Corinthians 5:7-10).

In other words, what we do here in this life will have an affect upon our eternal destiny. Not only is our salvation dependent upon accepting the Lordship of Christ, but our position in the heavenly kingdom will be measured by how we respond in faithful obedience to His will. For many Christians, this heavenly judgment is so distant, or so ignored, that we live as if it will never happen. If one does not learn the fear of the Lord in this life, he will certainly experience it at that moment! Yet if our hope is fixed upon the reward of faithfulness, as this passage suggests, then our goal will always be to please God at all times. "So whether you eat or drink or whatever you do, do it all for the glory of God" (1 Corinthians 10:31).

By placing our hope in Christ, instead of upon the pleasures and pursuits of this sinful world, an amazing transformation occurs in our lives. No longer are our moral choices and personal decisions made from our selfish perspectives, but they are made from the viewpoint of our eternal perspective. We now ask ourselves, "How will this action or these words affect the destiny of myself and those around me?" In the passage where he refers to "our blessed hope," Paul gives us the reason for that hope: "For the grace of God that brings salvation has appeared to all men. It teaches us to say 'No' to ungodliness and worldly passions, and to live self-controlled, upright and godly lives in this present age, while we wait for the blessed hope—the glorious appearing of our great God and Savior, Jesus Christ, who gave himself for us to redeem us from all wickedness and to purify for himself a people that are his very own, eager to do what is good" (Titus 2:11-14). John echoes this transforming power of hope in his first letter: "Dear friends, now we are children of God, and what we will be has not yet been made known. But we know that when he appears, we shall be like him, for we shall see him as he is. Everyone who has this hope in him purifies himself, just as he is pure" (1 John 3:2-3).

Fourth, our hope in the return of Christ puts an urgency into our efforts to transform the lives of others through evangelism. Because we know the judgment is coming, and that an awful hell awaits those who refuse Christ, love prompts us to seek the conversion of others - even if they don't seem to want it! Paul writes, "Therefore, knowing the fear of the Lord, we persuade men..." (2 Corinthians 5:10, NASB). People will all die. We must warn them that they will not have a second chance: "Just as man is destined to die once, and after that to face judgment, so Christ was sacrificed once to take away the sins of many people; and he will appear a second time, not to bear sin, but to bring salvation to those who are waiting for him" (Hebrews 9:27-28).

Christ commissioned us to go into all the world to preach the Gospel. We are the visible expression of His body to the world today. We see the world through His eyes of compassion. We minister to the needs of the world through His hands of healing. We go to the farthest places with our feet shod with the preparation of the Gospel of peace. We express His love through His heart of compassion through us. If we don't go, He won't come back. His word even tells us that the only thing that we can do to hasten His return is to spread the good news to all nations (cf. 2 Peter 3:12).

Fifth, our hope in the judgment of Christ helps us to forgive those who have offended us. It urges us to seek their salvation instead. Forgiveness is releasing people from the debt they owe us. Justice will be meted out at the return of Christ. Therefore, like Stephen as he was being stoned, we can look upon the risen Lord who will come back to judge the living and the dead and say, "Forgive them!" In doing so, we release them from God's judgment and offer them the opportunity to receive the grace of God themselves. What would have happened if Stephen had not forgiven Paul?

But if people refuse to turn and receive forgiveness, they will not be able to enjoy any relationship with God, or with us. Not every offense will be forgiven, but when Christ returns, he will make right all the injustices of the world. Paul reminds us of this fact in Romans 12:19-21: "Do not take revenge, my friends, but leave room for God's wrath, for it is written: 'It is mine to avenge; I will repay,' says the Lord. On the contrary: 'If your enemy is hungry, feed him; if he is thirsty, give him something to drink. In doing this, you will heap burning coals on his head.' Do not be overcome by evil, but overcome evil with good."

Finally, hope in Christ's return helps us deny ourselves in order to minister to others. What God has promised us is so great, that it is worth whatever price we are asked to pay in order to serve Him. Jesus, who ought to know about life in heaven, put it like this: "The kingdom of heaven is like treasure hidden in a field. When a man found it, he hid it again, and then in his joy went and sold all he had and bought that field. Again, the kingdom of heaven is like a merchant looking for fine pearls. When he found one of great value, he went away and sold everything he had and bought it" (Matthew 13:44-46).

Therefore, our hearts are no to be longer focused upon this world. Like Abraham, we look forward to the fulfillment of God's promises: "By faith Abraham, when called to go to a place he would later receive as his inheritance, obeyed and went, even though he did not know where he was going. By faith he made his home in the promised land like a stranger in a foreign country; he lived in tents, as did Isaac and Jacob, who were heirs with him of the same promise. For he was looking forward to the city with foundations, whose architect and builder is God. It will pass away with a roar. It's all going to burn. Instead, we place our hope in an eternal world, one that will never wear out" (Hebrews 11:8-9).

If there is no resurrection; if Christ will never return to put an end to Sin and death, then there is nothing to look forward to in this life. Everything would be meaningless. The best philosophy of life would have to be that of the beer commercial: "You only go round once in life so you've got to grab all the gusto you can!" This sentiment was understood even in the ancient world, as Paul tells us in 1 Corinthians 15:30-32: "And as for us, why do we endanger ourselves every hour? I die every day—I mean that, brothers—just as surely as I glory over you in Christ Jesus our Lord. If I fought wild beasts in Ephesus for merely human reasons, what have I gained? If the dead are not raised, "Let us eat and drink, for tomorrow we die.'"

But there is a reward awaiting us at the resurrection and return of Jesus Christ. We will be able to receive the prize for our faithful service in Christ. Sometimes that hope of reward is all we have to hold onto. God will recognize our sacrifices someday, when it counts the most, as Peter tells us that we serve, either as leaders or workers, because we will be rewarded with the glory of Christ when He comes back:

"Be shepherds of God's flock that is under your care, serving as overseers— not because you must, but because you are willing, as God wants you to be; not greedy for money, but eager to serve; not lording it over those entrusted to you, but being examples to the flock. And when the Chief Shepherd appears, you will receive the crown of glory that will never fade away. Young men, in the same way be submissive to those who are older. All of you, clothe yourselves with humility toward one another, because, 'God opposes the proud but gives grace to the humble'" (1 Peter 5:2-5).

The imminence of the return of Jesus Christ has been used to scare people into salvation. It has been used to motivate and prepare people for greater service for the Kingdom of God. It has helped fuel the modern missionary movement to the unreached and hidden people groups of the world. But perhaps the greatest ministry that can flow out of teaching about Christ's soon return is in this area of hope.

May these words of hope's power encourage us to live beyond the here and now. May these concepts broaden our lives to include those around us who do not yet know the salvation and life in Jesus that they can enjoy. But the Apostle Paul tells us in 1 Corinthians 13 that there is an even greater blessing of the Second Coming:

> 8 Love never fails. But where there are prophecies, they will cease; where there are tongues, they will be stilled; where there is knowledge, it will pass away. 9 For we know in part and we prophesy in part, 10 but when perfection comes, the imperfect disappears.
>
> 11 When I was a child, I talked like a child, I thought like a child, I reasoned like a child. When I became a man, I put childish ways behind me. 12 Now we see but a poor reflection as in a mirror; then we shall see face to face. Now I know in part; then I shall know fully, even as I am fully known.
>
> 13 And now these three remain: faith, hope and love. But the greatest of these is love.

"Faith, hope, and love - but the greatest of these is love." Why is love the greatest in comparison? When Jesus returns we will no longer need to see Him through the eyes of faith. Instead, we will all know Him. Though we have been saved by faith and we now live through faith in the Son of God, faith will no longer be necessary when Jesus returns. Hope will no longer be necessary, either. We will have received all that we have ever hoped for. Only one of these dear precious qualities will last into eternity. And that is what makes love the greatest of Christian virtues, because we will live in love forever!

Jesus Christ is coming back soon. The signs are out; the world is being made ready. Behold, the Judge is standing at the door. Come quickly, Lord!

Appendices

Prophetic
Scriptures

Appendix I

Prophetic Scriptures

Please note: not every prophetic passage is listed in this appendix. The Book of Daniel and the Book of Revelation are not included, as they would have to be printed in their entirety. The pertinent passages from these books are already quoted in the text of *The Door of Judgment.* Unless otherwise noted, all Scriptures are taken from the New International Version.

Introduction

Jesus is Coming Back:

Acts 1:4-12 On one occasion, while he was eating with them, he gave them this command: "Do not leave Jerusalem, but wait for the gift my Father promised, which you have heard me speak about. 5 For John baptized with water, but in a few days you will be baptized with the Holy Spirit."

6 So when they met together, they asked him, "Lord, are you at this time going to restore the kingdom to Israel?"

7 He said to them: "It is not for you to know the times or dates the Father has set by his own authority. 8 But you will receive power when the Holy Spirit comes on you; and you will be my witnesses in Jerusalem, and in all Judea and Samaria, and to the ends of the earth."

9 After he said this, he was taken up before their very eyes, and a cloud hid him from their sight.

10 They were looking intently up into the sky as he was going, when suddenly two men dressed in white stood beside them. 11 "Men of Galilee," they said, "why do you stand here looking into the sky? This same Jesus, who has been taken from you into heaven, will come back in the same way you have seen him go into heaven."

12 Then they returned to Jerusalem from the hill called the Mount of Olives, a Sabbath day's walk from the city.

2 Peter 3:3-12 First of all, you must understand that in the last days scoffers will come, scoffing and following their own evil desires. 4 They will say, "Where is this 'coming' he promised? Ever since our fathers died, everything goes on as it has since the beginning of creation." 7 By the same word the present heavens and earth are reserved for fire, being kept for the day of judgment and destruction of ungodly men.

8 But do not forget this one thing, dear friends: With the Lord a day is like a thousand years, and a thousand years are like a day. 9 The Lord is not slow in keeping his promise, as some understand slowness. He is patient with you, not wanting anyone to perish, but everyone to come to repentance.

10 But the day of the Lord will come like a thief. The heavens will disappear with a roar; the elements will be destroyed by fire, and the earth and everything in it will be laid bare.

11 Since everything will be destroyed in this way, what kind of people ought you to be? You ought to live holy and godly lives 12 as you look forward to the day of God and speed its coming. That day will bring about the destruction of the heavens by fire, and the elements will melt in the heat.

We will know when the return of Christ is near.

Matthew 16:1-4 The Pharisees and Sadducees came to Jesus and tested him by asking him to show them a sign from heaven.

2 He replied, "When evening comes, you say, 'It will be fair weather, for the sky is red,' 3 and in the morning, 'Today it will be stormy, for the sky is red and overcast.' You know how to interpret the appearance of the sky, but you cannot interpret the signs of the times. 4 A wicked and adulterous generation looks for a miraculous sign, but none will be given it except the sign of Jonah." Jesus then left them and went away.

Matthew 24:1-51 1 Jesus left the temple and was walking away when his disciples came up to him to call his attention to its buildings. 2 "Do you see all these things?" he asked. "I tell you the truth, not one stone here will be left on another; every one will be thrown down.

3 As Jesus was sitting on the Mount of Olives, the disciples came to him privately. "Tell us," they said, "when will this happen, and <u>what will be the sign of your coming and of the end of the age?</u>"

4 Jesus answered: "Watch out that no one deceives you. 5 For many will come in my name, claiming, 'I am the Christ,' and will deceive many. 6 You will hear of wars and rumors of wars, but see to it that you are not alarmed. Such things must happen, but the end is still to come. 7 Nation will rise against nation, and kingdom against kingdom. There will be famines and earthquakes in various places. 8 All these are the beginning of birth pains.

Matthew 24:32-51 "Now learn this lesson from the fig tree: As soon as its twigs get tender and its leaves come out, you know that summer is near. 33 <u>Even so, when you see all these things, you know that it is near, right at the door</u>. 34 I tell you the truth, this generation will certainly not pass away until all these things have happened. 35 Heaven and earth will pass away, but my words will never pass away.

36 "No one knows about that day or hour, not even the angels in heaven, nor the Son, but only the Father. 37 As it was in the days of Noah, so it will be at the coming of the Son of Man. 38 For in the days before the flood, people were eating and drinking, marrying and giving in marriage, up to the day Noah entered the ark; 39 and they knew nothing about what would happen until the flood came and took them all away. That is how it will be at the coming of the Son of Man. 40 Two men will be in the field; one will be taken and the other left. 41 Two women will be grinding with a hand mill; one will be taken and the other left.

42 "Therefore keep watch, because you do not know on what day your Lord will come. 43 But understand this: If the owner of the house had known at what time of night the thief was coming, he would have kept watch and would not have let his house be broken into. 44 So you also must be ready, because the Son of Man will come at an hour when you do not expect him.

Matt. 24:45 "Who then is the faithful and wise servant, whom the master has put in charge of the servants in his household to give them their food at the proper time? 46 It will be good for that servant whose master finds him doing so when he returns. 47 I tell you the truth, he will put him in charge of all his possessions. 48 But suppose that servant is wicked and says to himself, 'My master is staying away a long time,' 49 and he then begins to beat his fellow servants and to eat and drink with drunkards. 50 The master of that servant will come on a day when he does not expect him and at an hour he is not aware of. 51 He will cut him to pieces and assign him a place with the hypocrites, where there will be weeping and gnashing of teeth.

Luke 21:8-9, 25-28, 34-36 8 He replied: "Watch out that you are not deceived. For many will come in my name, claiming, 'I am he,' and, 'The time is near.' Do not follow them. 9 When you hear of wars and revolutions, do not be frightened. These things must happen first, but the end will not come right away."

10 Then he said to them: "Nation will rise against nation, and kingdom against kingdom. 11 There will be great earthquakes, famines

and pestilences in various places, and fearful events and great signs from heaven. "There will be signs in the sun, moon and stars. On the earth, nations will be in anguish and perplexity at the roaring and tossing of the sea. 26 Men will faint from terror, apprehensive of what is coming on the world, for the heavenly bodies will be shaken. 27 At that time they will see the Son of Man coming in a cloud with power and great glory. 28 When these things begin to take place, stand up and lift up your heads, because your redemption is drawing near."

34 "Be careful, or your hearts will be weighed down with dissipation, drunkenness and the anxieties of life, and that day will close on you unexpectedly like a trap. 35 For it will come upon all those who live on the face of the whole earth. 36 Be always on the watch, and pray that you may be able to escape all that is about to happen, and that you may be able to stand before the Son of Man."

Luke 21:20-24 "When you see Jerusalem surrounded by armies, you will know that its desolation is near. 21 Then let those who are in Judea flee to the mountains, let those in the city get out, and let those in the country not enter the city. 22 For this is the time of punishment in fulfillment of all that has been written. 23 How dreadful it will be in those days for pregnant women and nursing mothers! There will be great distress in the land and wrath against this people. 24 They will fall by the sword and will be taken as prisoners to all the nations. Jerusalem will be trampled on by the Gentiles until the times of the Gentiles are fulfilled."

1 Thessalonians 5:1-11 Now, brothers, about times and dates we do not need to write to you, 2 for you know very well that the day of the Lord will come like a thief in the night. 3 While people are saying, "Peace and safety," destruction will come on them suddenly, as labor pains on a pregnant woman, and they will not escape.

4 But *you, brothers,* are not in darkness so that this day should surprise you like a thief. 5 You are all sons of the light and sons of the day. We do not belong to the night or to the darkness. 6 So then, let us not be like others, who are asleep, but let us be alert and self-controlled. 7 For those who sleep, sleep at night, and those who get drunk, get drunk at night. 8 But since we belong to the day, let us be self-controlled, putting on faith and love as a breastplate, and the hope of salvation as a helmet.

9 For God did not appoint us to suffer wrath but to receive salvation through our Lord Jesus Christ. 10 He died for us so that, whether we are awake or asleep, we may live together with him. 11 Therefore

encourage one another and build each other up, just as in fact you are doing.

1. The Problem of Mankind

Sin

Genesis 3:4-8 "You will not surely die," the serpent said to the woman. 5 "For God knows that when you eat of it your eyes will be opened, and you will be like God, knowing good and evil."
6 When the woman saw that the fruit of the tree was good for food and pleasing to the eye, and also desirable for gaining wisdom, she took some and ate it. She also gave some to her husband, who was with her, and he ate it. 7 Then the eyes of both of them were opened, and they realized they were naked; so they sewed fig leaves together and made coverings for themselves. 8 Then the man and his wife heard the sound of the LORD God as he was walking in the garden in the cool of the day, and they hid from the LORD God among the trees of the garden.

Judges. 21:25 In those days Israel had no king; everyone did as he saw fit. (or, "everyone did what was right in his own eyes" NASB)

Jeremiah 18:12 But they will reply, 'It's no use. We will continue with our own plans; each of us will follow the stubbornness of his evil heart.'"

Isaiah 53: 6 All we like sheep have gone astray, each of us has turned to his own way...

Hebrews 3:12 "See to it, brothers, that none of you has a sinful, unbelieving heart that turns away from the living God"

James 4:1-7 What causes fights and quarrels among you? Don't they come from your desires that battle within you? 2 You want something but don't get it. You kill and covet, but you cannot have what you want. You quarrel and fight. You do not have, because you do not ask God. 3 When you ask, you do not receive, because you ask with wrong motives, that you may spend what you get on your pleasures.
4 You adulterous people, don't you know that friendship with the world is hatred toward God? Anyone who chooses to be a friend of the world becomes an enemy of God. 5 Or do you think Scripture says

without reason that the spirit he caused to live in us envies intensely? 6 But he gives us more grace. That is why Scripture says: "God opposes the proud but gives grace to the humble." 7 Submit yourselves, then, to God. Resist the devil, and he will flee from you.

Salvation from Sin:

Matthew 16:24-28 Then Jesus said to his disciples, "If anyone would come after me, he must deny himself and take up his cross and follow me. 25 For whoever wants to save his life will lose it, but whoever loses his life for me will find it. 26 What good will it be for a man if he gains the whole world, yet forfeits his soul? Or what can a man give in exchange for his soul? 27 For the Son of Man is going to come in his Father's glory with his angels, and then he will reward each person according to what he has done. 28 I tell you the truth, some who are standing here will not taste death before they see the Son of Man coming in his kingdom."

2.   How to Interpret Biblical Prophecy

The following are some examples of various Jewish styles of prophecy. These Scriptures are meant as examples, not inclusive lists.

Prophetic Pictures

Isaiah 8:18-22 Here am I, and the children the LORD has given me. We are signs and symbols in Israel from the LORD Almighty, who dwells on Mount Zion.
19   When men tell you to consult mediums and spiritists, who whisper and mutter, should not a people inquire of their God? Why consult the dead on behalf of the living?
20   To the law and to the testimony! If they do not speak according to this word, they have no light of dawn.
21   Distressed and hungry, they will roam through the land; when they are famished, they will become enraged and, looking upward, will curse their king and their God. 22   Then they will look toward the earth and see only distress and darkness and fearful gloom, and they will be thrust into utter darkness.

Ezekiel 4:1-13 "Now, son of man, take a clay tablet, put it in front of you and draw the city of Jerusalem on it. 2 Then lay siege to it: Erect siege works against it, build a ramp up to it, set up camps against it and put battering rams around it. 3 Then take an iron pan, place it as an iron wall between you and the city and turn your face toward it. It will be under siege, and you shall besiege it. This will be a sign to the house of Israel.

4 "Then lie on your left side and put the sin of the house of Israel upon yourself. You are to bear their sin for the number of days you lie on your side. 5 I have assigned you the same number of days as the years of their sin. So for 390 days you will bear the sin of the house of Israel.

6 "After you have finished this, lie down again, this time on your right side, and bear the sin of the house of Judah. I have assigned you 40 days, a day for each year. 7 Turn your face toward the siege of Jerusalem and with bared arm prophesy against her. 8 I will tie you up with ropes so that you cannot turn from one side to the other until you have finished the days of your siege.

9 "Take wheat and barley, beans and lentils, millet and spelt; put them in a storage jar and use them to make bread for yourself. You are to eat it during the 390 days you lie on your side. 10 Weigh out twenty shekels of food to eat each day and eat it at set times. 11 Also measure out a sixth of a hin of water and drink it at set times. 12 Eat the food as you would a barley cake; bake it in the sight of the people, using human excrement for fuel." 13 The LORD said, "In this way the people of Israel will eat defiled food among the nations where I will drive them." (a prophetic picture where the number of days equals the number of years)

Matthew 16:28-17:13 I tell you the truth, some who are standing here will not taste death before they see the Son of Man coming in his kingdom."

1 After six days Jesus took with him Peter, James and John the brother of James, and led them up a high mountain by themselves. 2 There he was transfigured before them. His face shone like the sun, and his clothes became as white as the light. 3 Just then there appeared before them Moses and Elijah, talking with Jesus.

4 Peter said to Jesus, "Lord, it is good for us to be here. If you wish, I will put up three shelters—one for you, one for Moses and one for Elijah."

5 While he was still speaking, a bright cloud enveloped them, and a voice from the cloud said, "This is my Son, whom I love; with him I am well pleased. Listen to him!"

6 When the disciples heard this, they fell facedown to the ground, terrified. 7 But Jesus came and touched them. "Get up," he said. "Don't be afraid." 8 When they looked up, they saw no one except Jesus.

9 As they were coming down the mountain, Jesus instructed them, "Don't tell anyone what you have seen, until the Son of Man has been raised from the dead."

10 The disciples asked him, "Why then do the teachers of the law say that Elijah must come first?"

11 Jesus replied, "To be sure, Elijah comes and will restore all things. 12 But I tell you, Elijah has already come, and they did not recognize him, but have done to him everything they wished. In the same way the Son of Man is going to suffer at their hands." 13 Then the disciples understood that he was talking to them about John the Baptist.

Eschatological Dualism, or the Dual Fulfillment of Prophecy

Zephaniah 1:1-18 The word of the LORD that came to Zephaniah son of Cushi, the son of Gedaliah, the son of Amariah, the son of Hezekiah, during the reign of Josiah son of Amon king of Judah:
2 "I will sweep away everything from the face of the earth," declares the LORD.
3 "I will sweep away both men and animals; I will sweep away the birds of the air and the fish of the sea. The wicked will have only heaps of rubble when I cut off man from the face of the earth," declares the LORD.
4 "I will stretch out my hand against Judah and against all who live in Jerusalem. I will cut off from this place every remnant of Baal, the names of the pagan and the idolatrous priests—5 those who bow down on the roofs to worship the starry host, those who bow down and swear by the LORD and who also swear by Molech, 6 those who turn back from following the LORD and neither seek the LORD nor inquire of him. 7 Be silent before the Sovereign LORD, for the day of the LORD is near. The LORD has prepared a sacrifice; he has consecrated those he has invited. 8 On the day of the LORD's sacrifice I will punish the princes and the king's sons and all those clad in foreign clothes. 9 On that day I will punish all who avoid stepping on the threshold, who fill the temple of their gods with violence and deceit. 10 "On that day," declares the LORD, "a cry will go up from the Fish Gate, wailing from the New Quarter, and a loud crash from the hills. 11 Wail, you who live in the market district; all your merchants will be wiped out, all who trade with silver will be ruined. 12 At that time I will search Jerusalem with lamps and punish those who are complacent, who are like wine left on its

dregs, who think, 'The LORD will do nothing, either good or bad.' 13 Their wealth will be plundered, their houses demolished. They will build houses but not live in them; they will plant vineyards but not drink the wine.

14 "The great day of the LORD is near—near and coming quickly. Listen! The cry on the day of the LORD will be bitter, the shouting of the warrior there. 15 That day will be a day of wrath, a day of distress and anguish, a day of trouble and ruin, a day of darkness and gloom, a day of clouds and blackness, 16 a day of trumpet and battle cry against the fortified cities and against the corner towers. 17 I will bring distress on the people and they will walk like blind men, because they have sinned against the LORD. Their blood will be poured out like dust and their entrails like filth. 18 Neither their silver nor their gold will be able to save them on the day of the LORD's wrath. In the fire of his jealousy the whole world will be consumed, for he will make a sudden end of all who live in the earth."

Telescopic Prophecy

Ezekiel 26:1-14 In the eleventh year, on the first day of the month, the word of the LORD came to me: 2 "Son of man, because Tyre has said of Jerusalem, 'Aha! The gate to the nations is broken, and its doors have swung open to me; now that she lies in ruins I will prosper,' 3 therefore this is what the Sovereign LORD says: I am against you, O Tyre, and I will bring many nations against you, like the sea casting up its waves. 4 They will destroy the walls of Tyre and pull down her towers; I will scrape away her rubble and make her a bare rock. 5 Out in the sea she will become a place to spread fishnets, for I have spoken, declares the Sovereign LORD. She will become plunder for the nations, 6 and her settlements on the mainland will be ravaged by the sword. Then they will know that I am the LORD.

7 "For this is what the Sovereign LORD says: From the north I am going to bring against Tyre Nebuchadnezzar king of Babylon, king of kings, with horses and chariots, with horsemen and a great army. 8 He will ravage your settlements on the mainland with the sword; he will set up siege works against you, build a ramp up to your walls and raise his shields against you. 9 He will direct the blows of his battering rams against your walls and demolish your towers with his weapons. 10 His horses will be so many that they will cover you with dust. Your walls will tremble at the noise of the war horses, wagons and chariots when he enters your gates as men enter a city whose walls have been broken through. 11 The hoofs of his horses will trample all your streets; he will

kill your people with the sword, and your strong pillars will fall to the ground. 12 They will plunder your wealth and loot your merchandise; they will break down your walls and demolish your fine houses and throw your stones, timber and rubble into the sea. 13 I will put an end to your noisy songs, and the music of your harps will be heard no more. 14 I will make you a bare rock, and you will become a place to spread fishnets. You will never be rebuilt, for I the LORD have spoken, declares the Sovereign LORD.

Isaiah 9:1-7 Nevertheless, there will be no more gloom for those who were in distress. In the past he humbled the land of Zebulun and the land of Naphtali, but in the future he will honor Galilee of the Gentiles, by the way of the sea, along the Jordan—
2 The people walking in darkness have seen a great light; on those living in the land of the shadow of death a light has dawned. 3 You have enlarged the nation and increased their joy; they rejoice before you as people rejoice at the harvest, as men rejoice when dividing the plunder. 4 For as in the day of Midian's defeat, you have shattered the yoke that burdens them, the bar across their shoulders, the rod of their oppressor. 5 Every warrior's boot used in battle and every garment rolled in blood will be destined for burning, will be fuel for the fire.
Isa. 9:6 For to us a child is born, to us a son is given, and the government will be on his shoulders. And he will be called Wonderful Counselor, Mighty God, Everlasting Father, Prince of Peace. 7 <u>Of the increase of his government and peace there will be no end. He will reign on David's throne and over his kingdom, establishing and upholding it with justice and righteousness from that time on and forever</u>. The zeal of the LORD Almighty will accomplish this.

Isaiah 11:1-9 A shoot will come up from the stump of Jesse; from his roots a Branch will bear fruit. 2 The Spirit of the LORD will rest on him—the Spirit of wisdom and of understanding, the Spirit of counsel and of power, the Spirit of knowledge and of the fear of the LORD—3 and he will delight in the fear of the LORD. He will not judge by what he sees with his eyes, or decide by what he hears with his ears; 4 but with righteousness he will judge the needy, with justice he will give decisions for the poor of the earth. He will strike the earth with the rod of his mouth; with the breath of his lips he will slay the wicked. 5 Righteousness will be his belt and faithfulness the sash around his waist.
6 The wolf will live with the lamb, the leopard will lie down with the goat, the calf and the lion and the yearling together; and a little child will lead them. 7 The cow will feed with the bear, their young will lie

down together, and the lion will eat straw like the ox. 8 The infant will play near the hole of the cobra, and the young child put his hand into the viper's nest. 9 They will neither harm nor destroy on all my holy mountain, for the earth will be full of the knowledge of the LORD as the waters cover the sea.

Isaiah 61:1-9 The Spirit of the Sovereign LORD is on me, because the LORD has anointed me to preach good news to the poor. He has sent me to bind up the brokenhearted, to proclaim freedom for the captives and release from darkness for the prisoners, 2 to proclaim the year of the LORD's favor and the day of vengeance of our God, to comfort all who mourn, 3 and provide for those who grieve in Zion—to bestow on them a crown of beauty instead of ashes, the oil of gladness instead of mourning, and a garment of praise instead of a spirit of despair. They will be called oaks of righteousness, a planting of the LORD for the display of his splendor.

4 They will rebuild the ancient ruins and restore the places long devastated; they will renew the ruined cities that have been devastated for generations. 5 Aliens will shepherd your flocks; foreigners will work your fields and vineyards. 6 And you will be called priests of the LORD, you will be named ministers of our God. You will feed on the wealth of nations, and in their riches you will boast. 7 Instead of their shame my people will receive a double portion, and instead of disgrace they will rejoice in their inheritance; and so they will inherit a double portion in their land, and everlasting joy will be theirs.

8 "For I, the LORD, love justice; I hate robbery and iniquity. In my faithfulness I will reward them and make an everlasting covenant with them. 9 Their descendants will be known among the nations and their offspring among the peoples. All who see them will acknowledge that they are a people the LORD has blessed."

Micah 5:2-15 "But you, Bethlehem Ephrathah, though you are small among the clans of Judah, out of you will come for me one who will be ruler over Israel, whose origins are from of old, from ancient times."

3 Therefore Israel will be abandoned until the time when she who is in labor gives birth and the rest of his brothers return to join the Israelites.

4 He will stand and shepherd his flock in the strength of the LORD, in the majesty of the name of the LORD his God. And they will live securely, for then his greatness will reach to the ends of the earth. 5 And he will be their peace.

When the Assyrian invades our land and marches through our fortresses, we will raise against him seven shepherds, even eight leaders of men.

7 The remnant of Jacob will be in the midst of many peoples like dew from the LORD, like showers on the grass, which do not wait for man or linger for mankind. 8 The remnant of Jacob will be among the nations, in the midst of many peoples, like a lion among the beasts of the forest, like a young lion among flocks of sheep, which mauls and mangles as it goes, and no one can rescue. 9 Your hand will be lifted up in triumph over your enemies, and all your foes will be destroyed.

10 "In that day," declares the LORD, "I will destroy your horses from among you and demolish your chariots. 11 I will destroy the cities of your land and tear down all your strongholds. 12 I will destroy your witchcraft and you will no longer cast spells. 13 I will destroy your carved images and your sacred stones from among you; you will no longer bow down to the work of your hands. 14 I will uproot from among you your Asherah poles and demolish your cities. 15 I will take vengeance in anger and wrath upon the nations that have not obeyed me."

3. God's Plan for the Ages

The Promise and Calling for the Jews

God's Call of Abraham: the Father of the Faith

Genesis 12:1-7 The LORD had said to Abram, "Leave your country, your people and your father's household and go to the land I will show you. 2 "I will make you into a great nation and I will bless you; I will make your name great, and you will be a blessing. 3 I will bless those who bless you, and whoever curses you I will curse; and all peoples on earth will be blessed through you."

4 So Abram left, as the LORD had told him; and Lot went with him. Abram was seventy-five years old when he set out from Haran. 5 He took his wife Sarai, his nephew Lot, all the possessions they had accumulated and the people they had acquired in Haran, and they set out for the land of Canaan, and they arrived there. 6 Abram traveled through the land as far as the site of the great tree of Moreh at Shechem. At that time the Canaanites were in the land.

7 The LORD appeared to Abram and said, "<u>To your offspring I will
give this land</u>." So he built an altar there to the LORD, who had
appeared to him.

Genesis 15:1-6 After this, the word of the LORD came to Abram in
a vision: "Do not be afraid, Abram. I am your shield, your very great
reward."

2 But Abram said, "O Sovereign LORD, what can you give me
since I remain childless and the one who will inherit my estate is Eliezer
of Damascus?" 3 And Abram said, "You have given me no children; so
a servant in my household will be my heir."

4 Then the word of the LORD came to him: "This man will not be
your heir, but a son coming from your own body will be your heir." 5
He took him outside and said, "Look up at the heavens and count the
stars—if indeed you can count them." Then he said to him, "So shall
your offspring be."

6 <u>Abram believed the LORD, and he credited it to him as
righteousness.</u>

Genesis 15:13-20 Then the LORD said to him, "Know for certain
that your descendants will be strangers in a country not their own, and
they will be enslaved and mistreated four hundred years. 14 But I will
punish the nation they serve as slaves, and afterward they will come out
with great possessions. 15 You, however, will go to your fathers in
peace and be buried at a good old age. 16 In the fourth generation your
descendants will come back here, for the sin of the Amorites has not yet
reached its full measure."

17 When the sun had set and darkness had fallen, a smoking firepot
with a blazing torch appeared and passed between the pieces. 18 On
that day the LORD made a covenant with Abram and said, "To your
descendants I give this land, from the river of Egypt to the great river,
the Euphrates—19 the land of the Kenites, Kenizzites, Kadmonites, 20
Hittites, Perizzites, Rephaites, 21 Amorites, Canaanites, Girgashites and
Jebusites."

The Jew's Calling to be a Light to the Nations

Deuteronomy 4:5-9 See, I have taught you decrees and laws as the
LORD my God commanded me, so that you may follow them in the land
you are entering to take possession of it. 6 Observe them carefully, for
<u>this will show your wisdom and understanding to the nations, who will
hear about all these decrees and say, "Surely this great nation is a wise</u>

and understanding people." 7 What other nation is so great as to have their gods near them the way the LORD our God is near us whenever we pray to him? 8 And what other nation is so great as to have such righteous decrees and laws as this body of laws I am setting before you today? 9 Only be careful, and watch yourselves closely so that you do not forget the things your eyes have seen or let them slip from your heart as long as you live. Teach them to your children and to their children after them.

Deuteronomy 26:16-19 The LORD your God commands you this day to follow these decrees and laws; carefully observe them with all your heart and with all your soul. 17 You have declared this day that the LORD is your God and that you will walk in his ways, that you will keep his decrees, commands and laws, and that you will obey him. 18 And the LORD has declared this day that you are his people, his treasured possession as he promised, and that you are to keep all his commands. 19 He has declared that he will set you in praise, fame and honor high above all the nations he has made and that you will be a people holy to the LORD your God, as he promised.

1 Kings 10:1-13 When the queen of Sheba heard about the fame of Solomon and his relation to the name of the LORD, she came to test him with hard questions. 2 Arriving at Jerusalem with a very great caravan—with camels carrying spices, large quantities of gold, and precious stones—she came to Solomon and talked with him about all that she had on her mind. 3 Solomon answered all her questions; nothing was too hard for the king to explain to her. 4 When the queen of Sheba saw all the wisdom of Solomon and the palace he had built, 5 the food on his table, the seating of his officials, the attending servants in their robes, his cupbearers, and the burnt offerings he made at the temple of the LORD, she was overwhelmed.

10:6 She said to the king, "The report I heard in my own country about your achievements and your wisdom is true. 7 But I did not believe these things until I came and saw with my own eyes. Indeed, not even half was told me; in wisdom and wealth you have far exceeded the report I heard. 8 How happy your men must be! How happy your officials, who continually stand before you and hear your wisdom! 9 Praise be to the LORD your God, who has delighted in you and placed you on the throne of Israel. Because of the LORD's eternal love for Israel, he has made you king, to maintain justice and righteousness."

10 And she gave the king 120 talents of gold, large quantities of spices, and precious stones. Never again were so many spices brought in as those the queen of Sheba gave to King Solomon.

11 (Hiram's ships brought gold from Ophir; and from there they brought great cargoes of almugwood and precious stones. 12 The king used the almugwood to make supports for the temple of the LORD and for the royal palace, and to make harps and lyres for the musicians. So much almugwood has never been imported or seen since that day.)

13 King Solomon gave the queen of Sheba all she desired and asked for, besides what he had given her out of his royal bounty. Then she left and returned with her retinue to her own country.

2 Chronicles 6:24-33 "When your people Israel have been defeated by an enemy because they have sinned against you and when they turn back and confess your name, praying and making supplication before you in this temple, 25 then hear from heaven and forgive the sin of your people Israel and bring them back to the land you gave to them and their fathers.

26 "When the heavens are shut up and there is no rain because your people have sinned against you, and when they pray toward this place and confess your name and turn from their sin because you have afflicted them, 27 then hear from heaven and forgive the sin of your servants, your people Israel. Teach them the right way to live, and send rain on the land you gave your people for an inheritance.

28 "When famine or plague comes to the land, or blight or mildew, locusts or grasshoppers, or when enemies besiege them in any of their cities, whatever disaster or disease may come, 29 and when a prayer or plea is made by any of your people Israel—each one aware of his afflictions and pains, and spreading out his hands toward this temple— 30 then hear from heaven, your dwelling place. Forgive, and deal with each man according to all he does, since you know his heart (for you alone know the hearts of men), 31 so that they will fear you and walk in your ways all the time they live in the land you gave our fathers.

32 "As for the foreigner who does not belong to your people Israel but has come from a distant land because of your great name and your mighty hand and your outstretched arm—when he comes and prays toward this temple, 33 then hear from heaven, your dwelling place, and do whatever the foreigner asks of you, so that all the peoples of the earth may know your name and fear you, as do your own people Israel, and may know that this house I have built bears your Name.

God's Blessing for the Jews for their Obedience

Deuteronomy 28:1-10 If you fully obey the LORD your God and carefully follow all his commands I give you today, the LORD your God will set you high above all the nations on earth. 2 All these blessings will come upon you and accompany you if you obey the LORD your God:

3 You will be blessed in the city and blessed in the country.

4 The fruit of your womb will be blessed, and the crops of your land and the young of your livestock—the calves of your herds and the lambs of your flocks.

5 Your basket and your kneading trough will be blessed.

6 You will be blessed when you come in and blessed when you go out.

7 The LORD will grant that the enemies who rise up against you will be defeated before you. They will come at you from one direction but flee from you in seven.

8 The LORD will send a blessing on your barns and on everything you put your hand to. The LORD your God will bless you in the land he is giving you.

9 The LORD will establish you as his holy people, as he promised you on oath, if you keep the commands of the LORD your God and walk in his ways. 10 <u>Then all the peoples on earth will see that you are called by the name of the LORD, and they will fear you</u>.

God's Chastisement for the Jews for their Disobedience

Deuteronomy 29:18-28 Make sure there is no man or woman, clan or tribe among you today whose heart turns away from the LORD our God to go and worship the gods of those nations; make sure there is no root among you that produces such bitter poison. 19 When such a person hears the words of this oath, he invokes a blessing on himself and therefore thinks, "I will be safe, even though I persist in going my own way." This will bring disaster on the watered land as well as the dry. 20 The LORD will never be willing to forgive him; his wrath and zeal will burn against that man. All the curses written in this book will fall upon him, and the LORD will blot out his name from under heaven. 21 The LORD will single him out from all the tribes of Israel for disaster, according to all the curses of the covenant written in this Book of the Law.

22 Your children who follow you in later generations and foreigners who come from distant lands will see the calamities that have fallen on

the land and the diseases with which the LORD has afflicted it. 23 The whole land will be a burning waste of salt and sulfur—nothing planted, nothing sprouting, no vegetation growing on it. It will be like the destruction of Sodom and Gomorrah, Admah and Zeboiim, which the LORD overthrew in fierce anger. 24 All the nations will ask: "Why has the LORD done this to this land? Why this fierce, burning anger?"

25 And the answer will be: "It is because this people abandoned the covenant of the LORD, the God of their fathers, the covenant he made with them when he brought them out of Egypt. 26 They went off and worshiped other gods and bowed down to them, gods they did not know, gods he had not given them. 27 Therefore the LORD's anger burned against this land, so that he brought on it all the curses written in this book. 28 <u>In furious anger and in great wrath the LORD uprooted them from their land and thrust them into another land</u>, as it is now."

God's Timetable for the Jews

Daniel 9:21-27 while I was still in prayer, Gabriel, the man I had seen in the earlier vision, came to me in swift flight about the time of the evening sacrifice. 22 He instructed me and said to me, "Daniel, I have now come to give you insight and understanding. 23 As soon as you began to pray, an answer was given, which I have come to tell you, for you are highly esteemed. Therefore, consider the message and understand the vision:

24 "Seventy 'sevens' are decreed for your people and your holy city to finish transgression, to put an end to sin, to atone for wickedness, to bring in everlasting righteousness, to seal up vision and prophecy and to anoint the most holy.

25 "Know and understand this: From the issuing of the decree to restore and rebuild Jerusalem until the Anointed One [greek, "Christ"], the ruler, comes, there will be seven 'sevens,' and sixty-two 'sevens.' It will be rebuilt with streets and a trench, but in times of trouble. 26 After the sixty-two 'sevens,' the Anointed One will be cut off and will have nothing. The people of the ruler who will come will destroy the city and the sanctuary. The end will come like a flood: War will continue until the end, and desolations have been decreed. 27 <u>He will confirm a covenant with many for one 'seven.' In the middle of the 'seven' he will put an end to sacrifice and offering. And on a wing [of the temple] he will set up an abomination that causes desolation, until the end that is decreed is poured out on him.</u>"

Israel's Rejection of the Messiah and their Judgment

Luke 19:30-44 "Go to the village ahead of you, and as you enter it, you will find a colt tied there, which no one has ever ridden. Untie it and bring it here. 31 If anyone asks you, 'Why are you untying it?' tell him, 'The Lord needs it.'"

32 Those who were sent ahead went and found it just as he had told them. 33 As they were untying the colt, its owners asked them, "Why are you untying the colt?"

34 They replied, "The Lord needs it."

35 They brought it to Jesus, threw their cloaks on the colt and put Jesus on it. 36 As he went along, people spread their cloaks on the road.

37 When he came near the place where the road goes down the Mount of Olives, the whole crowd of disciples began joyfully to praise God in loud voices for all the miracles they had seen:

38 "Blessed is the king who comes in the name of the Lord!" "Peace in heaven and glory in the highest!"

39 Some of the Pharisees in the crowd said to Jesus, "Teacher, rebuke your disciples!"

40 "I tell you," he replied, "<u>if they keep quiet, the stones will cry out</u>."

41 As he approached Jerusalem and saw the city, he wept over it 42 and said, "If you, even you, had only known on this day what would bring you peace—but now it is hidden from your eyes. 43 The days will come upon you when your enemies will build an embankment against you and encircle you and hem you in on every side. 44 They will dash you to the ground, you and the children within your walls. They will not leave one stone on another, <u>because you did not recognize the time of God's coming to you</u>."

Luke 21:20-24 "When you see Jerusalem surrounded by armies, you will know that its desolation is near. 21 Then let those who are in Judea flee to the mountains, let those in the city get out, and let those in the country not enter the city. 22 <u>For this is the time of punishment in fulfillment of all that has been written.</u> 23 How dreadful it will be in those days for pregnant women and nursing mothers! There will be great distress in the land and wrath against this people. 24 They will fall by the sword and will be taken as prisoners to all the nations. Jerusalem will be trampled on by the Gentiles <u>until the times of the Gentiles are fulfilled</u>."

Matthew 23:37-39 "O Jerusalem, Jerusalem, you who kill the prophets and stone those sent to you, how often I have longed to gather your children together, as a hen gathers her chicks under her wings, but you were not willing. 38 Look, your house is left to you desolate. 39 For I tell you, <u>you will not see me again until you say, 'Blessed is he who comes in the name of the Lord.'</u>"

Deuteronomy 28:62-68 You who were as numerous as the stars in the sky will be left but few in number, because you did not obey the LORD your God. 63 Just as it pleased the LORD to make you prosper and increase in number, so it will please him to ruin and destroy you. You will be uprooted from the land you are entering to possess.

64 Then the LORD will scatter you among all nations, from one end of the earth to the other. There you will worship other gods—gods of wood and stone, which neither you nor your fathers have known. 65 Among those nations you will find no repose, no resting place for the sole of your foot. There the LORD will give you an anxious mind, eyes weary with longing, and a despairing heart. 66 You will live in constant suspense, filled with dread both night and day, never sure of your life. 67 In the morning you will say, "If only it were evening!" and in the evening, "If only it were morning!"—because of the terror that will fill your hearts and the sights that your eyes will see.

The LORD will send you back in ships to Egypt on a journey I said you should never make again.

There you will offer yourselves for sale to your enemies as male and female slaves, but no one will buy you.

(Jesus referred to this prophecy in one of His parables against the Jewish leaders rejection of His calling.)

Isaiah 5:1-30 I will sing for the one I love a song about his vineyard: My loved one had a vineyard on a fertile hillside. 2 He dug it up and cleared it of stones and planted it with the choicest vines. He built a watchtower in it and cut out a winepress as well. Then he looked for a crop of good grapes, but it yielded only bad fruit.

3 "Now you dwellers in Jerusalem and men of Judah, judge between me and my vineyard. 4 What more could have been done for my vineyard than I have done for it? When I looked for good grapes, why did it yield only bad? 5 Now I will tell you what I am going to do to my vineyard: I will take away its hedge, and it will be destroyed; I will break down its wall, and it will be trampled. 6 I will make it a wasteland,

neither pruned nor cultivated, and briers and thorns will grow there. I will command the clouds not to rain on it."

7 The vineyard of the LORD Almighty is the house of Israel, and the men of Judah are the garden of his delight. And he looked for justice, but saw bloodshed; for righteousness, but heard cries of distress.

8 Woe to you who add house to house and join field to field till no space is left and you live alone in the land.

9 The LORD Almighty has declared in my hearing: "Surely the great houses will become desolate, the fine mansions left without occupants. 10 A ten-acre vineyard will produce only a bath of wine, a homer of seed only an ephah of grain."

11 Woe to those who rise early in the morning to run after their drinks, who stay up late at night till they are inflamed with wine. 12 They have harps and lyres at their banquets, tambourines and flutes and wine, but they have no regard for the deeds of the LORD, no respect for the work of his hands.

13 Therefore my people will go into exile for lack of understanding; their men of rank will die of hunger and their masses will be parched with thirst.

14 Therefore the grave enlarges its appetite and opens its mouth without limit; into it will descend their nobles and masses with all their brawlers and revelers.

15 So man will be brought low and mankind humbled, the eyes of the arrogant humbled. 16 But the LORD Almighty will be exalted by his justice, and the holy God will show himself holy by his righteousness.

17 Then sheep will graze as in their own pasture; lambs will feed among the ruins of the rich.

18 Woe to those who draw sin along with cords of deceit, and wickedness as with cart ropes, 19 to those who say, "Let God hurry, let him hasten his work so we may see it. Let it approach, let the plan of the Holy One of Israel come, so we may know it."

20 Woe to those who call evil good and good evil, who put darkness for light and light for darkness, who put bitter for sweet and sweet for bitter.

21 Woe to those who are wise in their own eyes and clever in their own sight.

22 Woe to those who are heroes at drinking wine and champions at mixing drinks, 23 who acquit the guilty for a bribe, but deny justice to the innocent.

24 Therefore, as tongues of fire lick up straw and as dry grass sinks down in the flames, so their roots will decay and their flowers blow

away like dust; for they have rejected the law of the LORD Almighty and spurned the word of the Holy One of Israel.

25 Therefore the LORD's anger burns against his people; his hand is raised and he strikes them down. The mountains shake, and the dead bodies are like refuse in the streets. Yet for all this, his anger is not turned away, his hand is still upraised. 26 He lifts up a banner for the distant nations, he whistles for those at the ends of the earth. Here they come, swiftly and speedily! 27 Not one of them grows tired or stumbles, not one slumbers or sleeps; not a belt is loosened at the waist, not a sandal thong is broken. 28 Their arrows are sharp, all their bows are strung; their horses' hoofs seem like flint, their chariot wheels like a whirlwind. 29 Their roar is like that of the lion, they roar like young lions; they growl as they seize their prey and carry it off with no one to rescue.

30 In that day they will roar over it like the roaring of the sea. And if one looks at the land, he will see darkness and distress; even the light will be darkened by the clouds.

The Mystery of Israel and the Time of the Gentiles

Romans 9-12 1 I speak the truth in Christ—I am not lying, my conscience confirms it in the Holy Spirit—2 I have great sorrow and unceasing anguish in my heart. 3 For I could wish that I myself were cursed and cut off from Christ for the sake of my brothers, those of my own race, 4 the people of Israel. Theirs is the adoption as sons; theirs the divine glory, the covenants, the receiving of the law, the temple worship and the promises. 5 Theirs are the patriarchs, and from them is traced the human ancestry of Christ, who is God over all, forever praised! Amen.

6 It is not as though God's word had failed. For not all who are descended from Israel are Israel. 7 Nor because they are his descendants are they all Abraham's children. On the contrary, "It is through Isaac that your offspring will be reckoned." 8 In other words, it is not the natural children who are God's children, but it is the children of the promise who are regarded as Abraham's offspring. 9 For this was how the promise was stated: "At the appointed time I will return, and Sarah will have a son."

10 Not only that, but Rebekah's children had one and the same father, our father Isaac. 11 Yet, before the twins were born or had done anything good or bad—in order that God's purpose in election might stand: 12 not by works but by him who calls—she was told, "The older

will serve the younger." 13 Just as it is written: "Jacob I loved, but Esau I hated."

14 What then shall we say? Is God unjust? Not at all! 15 For he says to Moses, "I will have mercy on whom I have mercy, and I will have compassion on whom I have compassion."

16 It does not, therefore, depend on man's desire or effort, but on God's mercy. 17 For the Scripture says to Pharaoh: "I raised you up for this very purpose, that I might display my power in you and that my name might be proclaimed in all the earth." 18 Therefore God has mercy on whom he wants to have mercy, and he hardens whom he wants to harden.

19 One of you will say to me: "Then why does God still blame us? For who resists his will?" 20 But who are you, O man, to talk back to God? "Shall what is formed say to him who formed it, 'Why did you make me like this?'" 21 Does not the potter have the right to make out of the same lump of clay some pottery for noble purposes and some for common use?

22 What if God, choosing to show his wrath and make his power known, bore with great patience the objects of his wrath—prepared for destruction? 23 What if he did this to make the riches of his glory known to the objects of his mercy, whom he prepared in advance for glory—24 even us, whom he also called, not only from the Jews but also from the Gentiles? 25 As he says in Hosea: "I will call them 'my people' who are not my people; and I will call her 'my loved one' who is not my loved one,"

26 and, "It will happen that in the very place where it was said to them, 'You are not my people,' they will be called 'sons of the living God.'"

27 Isaiah cries out concerning Israel: "Though the number of the Israelites be like the sand by the sea, only the remnant will be saved. 28 For the Lord will carry out his sentence on earth with speed and finality."

29 It is just as Isaiah said previously: "Unless the Lord Almighty had left us descendants, we would have become like Sodom, we would have been like Gomorrah."

30 What then shall we say? That the Gentiles, who did not pursue righteousness, have obtained it, a righteousness that is by faith; 31 but Israel, who pursued a law of righteousness, has not attained it. 32 Why not? Because they pursued it not by faith but as if it were by works. They stumbled over the "stumbling stone." 33 As it is written: "See, I lay in Zion a stone that causes men to stumble and a rock that makes them fall, and the one who trusts in him will never be put to shame."

Rom. 10:1 Brothers, my heart's desire and prayer to God for the Israelites is that they may be saved. 2 For I can testify about them that they are zealous for God, but their zeal is not based on knowledge. 3 Since they did not know the righteousness that comes from God and sought to establish their own, they did not submit to God's righteousness. 4 Christ is the end of the law so that there may be righteousness for everyone who believes.

5 Moses describes in this way the righteousness that is by the law: "The man who does these things will live by them." 6 But the righteousness that is by faith says: "Do not say in your heart, 'Who will ascend into heaven?'" (that is, to bring Christ down) 7 "or 'Who will descend into the deep?'" (that is, to bring Christ up from the dead). 8 But what does it say? "The word is near you; it is in your mouth and in your heart," that is, the word of faith we are proclaiming: 9 That if you confess with your mouth, "Jesus is Lord," and believe in your heart that God raised him from the dead, you will be saved. 10 For it is with your heart that you believe and are justified, and it is with your mouth that you confess and are saved. 11 As the Scripture says, "Anyone who trusts in him will never be put to shame." 12 For there is no difference between Jew and Gentile—the same Lord is Lord of all and richly blesses all who call on him, 13 for, "Everyone who calls on the name of the Lord will be saved."

14 How, then, can they call on the one they have not believed in? And how can they believe in the one of whom they have not heard? And how can they hear without someone preaching to them? 15 And how can they preach unless they are sent? As it is written, "How beautiful are the feet of those who bring good news!"

16 But not all the Israelites accepted the good news. For Isaiah says, "Lord, who has believed our message?" 17 Consequently, faith comes from hearing the message, and the message is heard through the word of Christ. 18 But I ask: Did they not hear? Of course they did: "Their voice has gone out into all the earth, their words to the ends of the world."

19 Again I ask: Did Israel not understand? First, Moses says, "I will make you envious by those who are not a nation; I will make you angry by a nation that has no understanding."

20 And Isaiah boldly says, "I was found by those who did not seek me; I revealed myself to those who did not ask for me."

21 But concerning Israel he says, "All day long I have held out my hands to a disobedient and obstinate people."

Rom. 11:1 I ask then: Did God reject his people? By no means! I am an Israelite myself, a descendant of Abraham, from the tribe of Benjamin. 2 God did not reject his people, whom he foreknew. Don't you know what the Scripture says in the passage about Elijah—how he appealed to God against Israel: 3 "Lord, they have killed your prophets and torn down your altars; I am the only one left, and they are trying to kill me"? 4 And what was God's answer to him? "I have reserved for myself seven thousand who have not bowed the knee to Baal." 5 So too, at the present time there is a remnant chosen by grace. 6 And if by grace, then it is no longer by works; if it were, grace would no longer be grace.

7 What then? What Israel sought so earnestly it did not obtain, but the elect did. The others were hardened, 8 as it is written: "God gave them a spirit of stupor, eyes so that they could not see and ears so that they could not hear, to this very day."

9 And David says: "May their table become a snare and a trap, a stumbling block and a retribution for them. 10 May their eyes be darkened so they cannot see, and their backs be bent forever."

11 Again I ask: Did they stumble so as to fall beyond recovery? Not at all! Rather, because of their transgression, salvation has come to the Gentiles to make Israel envious. 12 But if their transgression means riches for the world, and their loss means riches for the Gentiles, how much greater riches will their fullness bring!

13 I am talking to you Gentiles. Inasmuch as I am the apostle to the Gentiles, I make much of my ministry 14 in the hope that I may somehow arouse my own people to envy and save some of them. 15 For if their rejection is the reconciliation of the world, what will their acceptance be but life from the dead? 16 If the part of the dough offered as firstfruits is holy, then the whole batch is holy; if the root is holy, so are the branches.

17 If some of the branches have been broken off, and you, though a wild olive shoot, have been grafted in among the others and now share in the nourishing sap from the olive root, 18 do not boast over those branches. If you do, consider this: You do not support the root, but the root supports you. 19 You will say then, "Branches were broken off so that I could be grafted in." 20 Granted. But they were broken off because of unbelief, and you stand by faith. Do not be arrogant, but be afraid. 21 For if God did not spare the natural branches, he will not spare you either.

22 Consider therefore the kindness and sternness of God: sternness to those who fell, but kindness to you, provided that you continue in his kindness. Otherwise, you also will be cut off. 23 And if they do not

persist in unbelief, they will be grafted in, for God is able to graft them in again. 24 After all, if you were cut out of an olive tree that is wild by nature, and contrary to nature were grafted into a cultivated olive tree, how much more readily will these, the natural branches, be grafted into their own olive tree!

25 I do not want you to be ignorant of this mystery, brothers, so that you may not be conceited: Israel has experienced a hardening in part until the full number of the Gentiles has come in. 26 And so all Israel will be saved, as it is written: "The deliverer will come from Zion; he will turn godlessness away from Jacob. 27 And this is my covenant with them when I take away their sins."

28 As far as the gospel is concerned, they are enemies on your account; but as far as election is concerned, they are loved on account of the patriarchs, 29 for God's gifts and his call are irrevocable. 30 Just as you who were at one time disobedient to God have now received mercy as a result of their disobedience, 31 so they too have now become disobedient in order that they too may now receive mercy as a result of God's mercy to you. 32 For God has bound all men over to disobedience so that he may have mercy on them all.

33 Oh, the depth of the riches of the wisdom and knowledge of God! How unsearchable his judgments, and his paths beyond tracing out! 34 "Who has known the mind of the Lord? Or who has been his counselor?" 35 "Who has ever given to God, that God should repay him?" 36 For from him and through him and to him are all things. To him be the glory forever! Amen.

The Regathering and Restoration of the Jews

Ps. 115:1-3 Not to us, O LORD, not to us but to your name be the glory, because of your love and faithfulness.

2 Why do the nations say, "Where is their God?"

3 Our God is in heaven; he does whatever pleases him.

Isaiah 14:1-24 The LORD will have compassion on Jacob; once again he will choose Israel and will settle them in their own land. Aliens will join them and unite with the house of Jacob. 2 Nations will take them and bring them to their own place. And the house of Israel will possess the nations as menservants and maidservants in the LORD's land. They will make captives of their captors and rule over their oppressors.

3 On the day the LORD gives you relief from suffering and turmoil and cruel bondage, 4 you will take up this taunt against the king of

Babylon: How the oppressor has come to an end! How his fury has ended!

5 The LORD has broken the rod of the wicked, the scepter of the rulers, 6 which in anger struck down peoples with unceasing blows, and in fury subdued nations with relentless aggression.

7 All the lands are at rest and at peace; they break into singing. 8 Even the pine trees and the cedars of Lebanon exult over you and say, "Now that you have been laid low, no woodsman comes to cut us down."

9 The grave below is all astir to meet you at your coming; it rouses the spirits of the departed to greet you—all those who were leaders in the world; it makes them rise from their thrones—all those who were kings over the nations. 10 They will all respond, they will say to you, "You also have become weak, as we are; you have become like us."

11 All your pomp has been brought down to the grave, along with the noise of your harps; maggots are spread out beneath you and worms cover you.

12 How you have fallen from heaven, O morning star, son of the dawn! You have been cast down to the earth, you who once laid low the nations! 13 You said in your heart, "I will ascend to heaven; I will raise my throne above the stars of God; I will sit enthroned on the mount of assembly, on the utmost heights of the sacred mountain. 14 I will ascend above the tops of the clouds; I will make myself like the Most High."

15 But you are brought down to the grave, to the depths of the pit. 16 Those who see you stare at you, they ponder your fate: "Is this the man who shook the earth and made kingdoms tremble, 17 the man who made the world a desert, who overthrew its cities and would not let his captives go home?"

18 All the kings of the nations lie in state, each in his own tomb. 19 But you are cast out of your tomb like a rejected branch; you are covered with the slain, with those pierced by the sword, those who descend to the stones of the pit. Like a corpse trampled underfoot, 20 you will not join them in burial, for you have destroyed your land and killed your people. The offspring of the wicked will never be mentioned again. 21 Prepare a place to slaughter his sons for the sins of their forefathers; they are not to rise to inherit the land and cover the earth with their cities.

22 "I will rise up against them," declares the LORD Almighty. "I will cut off from Babylon her name and survivors, her offspring and descendants," declares the LORD. 23 "I will turn her into a place for owls and into swampland; I will sweep her with the broom of destruction," declares the LORD Almighty. 24 The LORD Almighty

has sworn, "Surely, as I have planned, so it will be, and as I have purposed, so it will stand.

Isaiah 26:17-21   As a woman with child and about to give birth writhes and cries out in her pain, so were we in your presence, O LORD. 18 We were with child, we writhed in pain, but we gave birth to wind. We have not brought salvation to the earth; we have not given birth to people of the world.

19 But your dead will live; their bodies will rise. You who dwell in the dust, wake up and shout for joy. Your dew is like the dew of the morning; the earth will give birth to her dead. 20 Go, my people, enter your rooms and shut the doors behind you; hide yourselves for a little while until his wrath has passed by.

21 See, the LORD is coming out of his dwelling to punish the people of the earth for their sins. The earth will disclose the blood shed upon her; she will conceal her slain no longer.

Isaiah 33:17-24   Your eyes will see the king in his beauty and view a land that stretches afar. 18 In your thoughts you will ponder the former terror: "Where is that chief officer? Where is the one who took the revenue? Where is the officer in charge of the towers?" 19 You will see those arrogant people no more, those people of an obscure speech, with their strange, incomprehensible tongue.

20 Look upon Zion, the city of our festivals; your eyes will see Jerusalem, a peaceful abode, a tent that will not be moved; its stakes will never be pulled up, nor any of its ropes broken. 21 There the LORD will be our Mighty One. It will be like a place of broad rivers and streams. No galley with oars will ride them, no mighty ship will sail them. 22 For the LORD is our judge, the LORD is our lawgiver, the LORD is our king; it is he who will save us.

23 Your rigging hangs loose: The mast is not held secure, the sail is not spread. Then an abundance of spoils will be divided and even the lame will carry off plunder. 24 No one living in Zion will say, "I am ill"; and the sins of those who dwell there will be forgiven.

Isaiah 35:1-10   The desert and the parched land will be glad; the wilderness will rejoice and blossom. Like the crocus, 2 it will burst into bloom; it will rejoice greatly and shout for joy. The glory of Lebanon will be given to it, the splendor of Carmel and Sharon; they will see the glory of the LORD, the splendor of our God.

3 Strengthen the feeble hands, steady the knees that give way; 4 say to those with fearful hearts, "Be strong, do not fear; your God will come,

he will come with vengeance; with divine retribution he will come to save you."

5 Then will the eyes of the blind be opened and the ears of the deaf unstopped. 6 Then will the lame leap like a deer, and the mute tongue shout for joy. Water will gush forth in the wilderness and streams in the desert. 7 The burning sand will become a pool, the thirsty ground bubbling springs. In the haunts where jackals once lay, grass and reeds and papyrus will grow.

8 And a highway will be there; it will be called the Way of Holiness. The unclean will not journey on it; it will be for those who walk in that Way; wicked fools will not go about on it. 9 No lion will be there, nor will any ferocious beast get up on it; they will not be found there. But only the redeemed will walk there, 10 and the ransomed of the LORD will return. They will enter Zion with singing; everlasting joy will crown their heads. Gladness and joy will overtake them, and sorrow and sighing will flee away.

Isaiah 42:18-25 "Hear, you deaf; look, you blind, and see! 19 Who is blind but my servant, and deaf like the messenger I send? Who is blind like the one committed to me, blind like the servant of the LORD? 20 You have seen many things, but have paid no attention; your ears are open, but you hear nothing." 21 It pleased the LORD for the sake of his righteousness to make his law great and glorious. 22 But this is a people plundered and looted, all of them trapped in pits or hidden away in prisons. They have become plunder, with no one to rescue them; they have been made loot, with no one to say, "Send them back."

23 Which of you will listen to this or pay close attention in time to come? 24 Who handed Jacob over to become loot, and Israel to the plunderers? Was it not the LORD, against whom we have sinned? For they would not follow his ways; they did not obey his law. 25 So he poured out on them his burning anger, the violence of war. It enveloped them in flames, yet they did not understand; it consumed them, but they did not take it to heart.

Isaiah 44:1-5 "But now listen, O Jacob, my servant, Israel, whom I have chosen. 2 This is what the LORD says—he who made you, who formed you in the womb, and who will help you: Do not be afraid, O Jacob, my servant, Jeshurun, whom I have chosen. 3 For I will pour water on the thirsty land, and streams on the dry ground; I will pour out my Spirit on your offspring, and my blessing on your descendants. 4 They will spring up like grass in a meadow, like poplar trees by flowing streams. 5 One will say, 'I belong to the LORD'; another will call himself by the name of Jacob; still another will write on his hand, 'The LORD's,' and will take the name Israel.

Isaiah 44:21   "Remember these things, O Jacob, for you are my servant, O Israel. I have made you, you are my servant; O Israel, I will not forget you.

Isaiah 45:17   But Israel will be saved by the LORD with an everlasting salvation; you will never be put to shame or disgraced, to ages everlasting.

Isaiah 48:1-11   "Listen to this, O house of Jacob, you who are called by the name of Israel and come from the line of Judah, you who take oaths in the name of the LORD and invoke the God of Israel—but not in truth or righteousness—2   you who call yourselves citizens of the holy city and rely on the God of Israel—the LORD Almighty is his name: 3   I foretold the former things long ago, my mouth announced them and I made them known; then suddenly I acted, and they came to pass. 4   For I knew how stubborn you were; the sinews of your neck were iron, your forehead was bronze.   5   Therefore I told you these things long ago; before they happened I announced them to you so that you could not say, 'My idols did them; my wooden image and metal god ordained them.' 6   You have heard these things; look at them all. Will you not admit them? "From now on I will tell you of new things, of hidden things unknown to you.

7   They are created now, and not long ago; you have not heard of them before today. So you cannot say, 'Yes, I knew of them.' 8   You have neither heard nor understood; from of old your ear has not been open. Well do I know how treacherous you are; you were called a rebel from birth. 9   For my own name's sake I delay my wrath; for the sake of my praise I hold it back from you, so as not to cut you off. 10   See, I have refined you, though not as silver; I have tested you in the furnace of affliction.

11   For my own sake, for my own sake, I do this. How can I let myself be defamed? I will not yield my glory to another.

Isaiah 49:1-23   Listen to me, you islands; hear this, you distant nations: Before I was born the LORD called me; from my birth he has made mention of my name. 2   He made my mouth like a sharpened sword, in the shadow of his hand he hid me; he made me into a polished arrow and concealed me in his quiver. 3   He said to me, "You are my servant, Israel, in whom I will display my splendor." 4   But I said, "I have labored to no purpose; I have spent my strength in vain and for nothing. Yet what is due me is in the LORD's hand, and my reward is with my God."

5 And now the LORD says—he who formed me in the womb to be his servant to bring Jacob back to him and gather Israel to himself, for I am honored in the eyes of the LORD and my God has been my strength—6 he says: "It is too small a thing for you to be my servant to restore the tribes of Jacob and bring back those of Israel I have kept. I will also make you a light for the Gentiles, that you may bring my salvation to the ends of the earth."

7 This is what the LORD says—the Redeemer and Holy One of Israel—to him who was despised and abhorred by the nation, to the servant of rulers: "Kings will see you and rise up, princes will see and bow down, because of the LORD, who is faithful, the Holy One of Israel, who has chosen you."

8 This is what the LORD says: "In the time of my favor I will answer you, and in the day of salvation I will help you; I will keep you and will make you to be a covenant for the people, to restore the land and to reassign its desolate inheritances, 9 to say to the captives, 'Come out,' and to those in darkness, 'Be free!'" "They will feed beside the roads and find pasture on every barren hill. 10 They will neither hunger nor thirst, nor will the desert heat or the sun beat upon them. He who has compassion on them will guide them and lead them beside springs of water. 11 I will turn all my mountains into roads, and my highways will be raised up. 12 See, they will come from afar—some from the north, some from the west, some from the region of Aswan."

13 Shout for joy, O heavens; rejoice, O earth; burst into song, O mountains! For the LORD comforts his people and will have compassion on his afflicted ones.

14 But Zion said, "The LORD has forsaken me, the Lord has forgotten me."

15 "Can a mother forget the baby at her breast and have no compassion on the child she has borne? Though she may forget, I will not forget you! 16 See, I have engraved you on the palms of my hands; your walls are ever before me. 17 Your sons hasten back, and those who laid you waste depart from you. 18 Lift up your eyes and look around; all your sons gather and come to you. As surely as I live," declares the LORD, "you will wear them all as ornaments; you will put them on, like a bride.

19 "Though you were ruined and made desolate and your land laid waste, now you will be too small for your people, and those who devoured you will be far away. 20 The children born during your

bereavement will yet say in your hearing, 'This place is too small for us; give us more space to live in.' 21 Then you will say in your heart, 'Who bore me these? I was bereaved and barren; I was exiled and rejected. Who brought these up? I was left all alone, but these—where have they come from?'"

22 This is what the Sovereign LORD says: "See, <u>I will beckon to the Gentiles, I will lift up my banner to the peoples; they will bring your sons in their arms and carry your daughters on their shoulders</u>. 23 Kings will be your foster fathers, and their queens your nursing mothers. They will bow down before you with their faces to the ground; they will lick the dust at your feet. Then you will know that I am the LORD; those who hope in me will not be disappointed."

Isaiah 54:4-13 "Do not be afraid; you will not suffer shame. Do not fear disgrace; you will not be humiliated. You will forget the shame of your youth and remember no more the reproach of your widowhood. 5 For your Maker is your husband—the LORD Almighty is his name—the Holy One of Israel is your Redeemer; he is called the God of all the earth. 6 The LORD will call you back as if you were a wife deserted and distressed in spirit—a wife who married young, only to be rejected," says your God.

7 "For a brief moment I abandoned you, but with deep compassion I will bring you back. 8 In a surge of anger I hid my face from you for a moment, but with everlasting kindness I will have compassion on you," says the LORD your Redeemer.

9 "To me this is like the days of Noah, when I swore that the waters of Noah would never again cover the earth. So now I have sworn not to be angry with you, never to rebuke you again. 10 Though the mountains be shaken and the hills be removed, yet my unfailing love for you will not be shaken nor my covenant of peace be removed," says the LORD, who has compassion on you.

11 "O afflicted city, lashed by storms and not comforted, I will build you with stones of turquoise, your foundations with sapphires. 12 I will make your battlements of rubies, your gates of sparkling jewels, and all your walls of precious stones. 13 All your sons will be taught by the LORD, and great will be your children's peace.

Isaiah 60:1-22 "Arise, shine, for your light has come, and the glory of the LORD rises upon you. 2 See, darkness covers the earth and thick darkness is over the peoples, but the LORD rises upon you and his glory appears over you. 3 Nations will come to your light, and kings to the brightness of your dawn.

4 "Lift up your eyes and look about you: All assemble and come to you; your sons come from afar, and your daughters are carried on the arm. 5 Then you will look and be radiant, your heart will throb and swell with joy; the wealth on the seas will be brought to you, to you the riches of the nations will come. 6 Herds of camels will cover your land, young camels of Midian and Ephah. And all from Sheba will come, bearing gold and incense and proclaiming the praise of the LORD. 7 All Kedar's flocks will be gathered to you, the rams of Nebaioth will serve you; they will be accepted as offerings on my altar, and I will adorn my glorious temple.

8 "Who are these that fly along like clouds, like doves to their nests? 9 Surely the islands look to me; in the lead are the ships of Tarshish, bringing your sons from afar, with their silver and gold, to the honor of the LORD your God, the Holy One of Israel, for he has endowed you with splendor.

10 "Foreigners will rebuild your walls, and their kings will serve you. Though in anger I struck you, in favor I will show you compassion. 11 Your gates will always stand open, they will never be shut, day or night, so that men may bring you the wealth of the nations—their kings led in triumphal procession. 12 For the nation or kingdom that will not serve you will perish; it will be utterly ruined.

13 "The glory of Lebanon will come to you, the pine, the fir and the cypress together, to adorn the place of my sanctuary; and I will glorify the place of my feet. 14 The sons of your oppressors will come bowing before you; all who despise you will bow down at your feet and will call you the City of the LORD, Zion of the Holy One of Israel.

15 "Although you have been forsaken and hated, with no one traveling through, I will make you the everlasting pride and the joy of all generations. 16 You will drink the milk of nations and be nursed at royal breasts. Then you will know that I, the LORD, am your Savior, your Redeemer, the Mighty One of Jacob. 17 Instead of bronze I will bring you gold, and silver in place of iron. Instead of wood I will bring you bronze, and iron in place of stones. I will make peace your governor and righteousness your ruler. 18 No longer will violence be heard in your land, nor ruin or destruction within your borders, but you will call your walls Salvation and your gates Praise. 19 The sun will no more be your light by day, nor will the brightness of the moon shine on you, for the LORD will be your everlasting light, and your God will be your glory. 20 Your sun will never set again, and your moon will wane no more; the LORD will be your everlasting light, and your days of sorrow will end. 21 Then will all your people be righteous and they will possess the land forever. They are the shoot I have planted, the work of

my hands, for the display of my splendor. 22 The least of you will become a thousand, the smallest a mighty nation. I am the LORD; in its time I will do this swiftly."

Isaiah 61:1-9 The Spirit of the Sovereign LORD is on me, because the LORD has anointed me to preach good news to the poor. He has sent me to bind up the brokenhearted, to proclaim freedom for the captives and release from darkness for the prisoners, 2 to proclaim the year of the LORD's favor and the day of vengeance of our God, to comfort all who mourn, 3 and provide for those who grieve in Zion—to bestow on them a crown of beauty instead of ashes, the oil of gladness instead of mourning, and a garment of praise instead of a spirit of despair. They will be called oaks of righteousness, a planting of the LORD for the display of his splendor.
4   They will rebuild the ancient ruins and restore the places long devastated; they will renew the ruined cities that have been devastated for generations. 5   Aliens will shepherd your flocks; foreigners will work your fields and vineyards. 6 And you will be called priests of the LORD, you will be named ministers of our God. You will feed on the wealth of nations, and in their riches you will boast. 7 Instead of their shame my people will receive a double portion, and instead of disgrace they will rejoice in their inheritance; and so they will inherit a double portion in their land, and everlasting joy will be theirs.
8 "For I, the LORD, love justice; I hate robbery and iniquity. In my faithfulness I will reward them and make an everlasting covenant with them. 9 Their descendants will be known among the nations and their offspring among the peoples. All who see them will acknowledge that they are a people the LORD has blessed."

Isaiah 62:1-12   For Zion's sake I will not keep silent, for Jerusalem's sake I will not remain quiet, till her righteousness shines out like the dawn, her salvation like a blazing torch. 2 The nations will see your righteousness, and all kings your glory; you will be called by a new name that the mouth of the LORD will bestow. 3 You will be a crown of splendor in the LORD's hand, a royal diadem in the hand of your God. 4 No longer will they call you Deserted, or name your land Desolate. But you will be called Hephzibah, and your land Beulah; for the LORD will take delight in you, and your land will be married. 5 As a young man marries a maiden, so will your sons marry you; as a bridegroom rejoices over his bride, so will your God rejoice over you.
6 I have posted watchmen on your walls, O Jerusalem; they will never be silent day or night. You who call on the LORD, give yourselves

no rest, 7 and give him no rest till he establishes Jerusalem and makes her the praise of the earth.

8 The LORD has sworn by his right hand and by his mighty arm: "Never again will I give your grain as food for your enemies, and never again will foreigners drink the new wine for which you have toiled; 9 but those who harvest it will eat it and praise the LORD, and those who gather the grapes will drink it in the courts of my sanctuary."

10 Pass through, pass through the gates! Prepare the way for the people. Build up, build up the highway! Remove the stones. Raise a banner for the nations.

11 The LORD has made proclamation to the ends of the earth: "Say to the Daughter of Zion, 'See, your Savior comes! See, his reward is with him, and his recompense accompanies him.'" 12 They will be called the Holy People, the Redeemed of the LORD; and you will be called Sought After, the City No Longer Deserted.

Ezekiel 20:33-44 As surely as I live, declares the Sovereign LORD, I will rule over you with a mighty hand and an outstretched arm and with outpoured wrath. 34 I will bring you from the nations and gather you from the countries where you have been scattered—with a mighty hand and an outstretched arm and with outpoured wrath. 35 I will bring you into the desert of the nations and there, face to face, I will execute judgment upon you. 36 As I judged your fathers in the desert of the land of Egypt, so I will judge you, declares the Sovereign LORD. 37 I will take note of you as you pass under my rod, and I will bring you into the bond of the covenant. 38 I will purge you of those who revolt and rebel against me. Although I will bring them out of the land where they are living, yet they will not enter the land of Israel. Then you will know that I am the LORD.

39 "'As for you, O house of Israel, this is what the Sovereign LORD says: Go and serve your idols, every one of you! But afterward you will surely listen to me and no longer profane my holy name with your gifts and idols. 40 For on my holy mountain, the high mountain of Israel, declares the Sovereign LORD, there in the land the entire house of Israel will serve me, and there I will accept them. There I will require your offerings and your choice gifts, along with all your holy sacrifices. 41 I will accept you as fragrant incense when I bring you out from the nations and gather you from the countries where you have been scattered, and I will show myself holy among you in the sight of the nations. 42 Then you will know that I am the LORD, when I bring you into the land of Israel, the land I had sworn with uplifted hand to give to your fathers. 43 There you will remember your conduct and all the actions by which you

have defiled yourselves, and you will loathe yourselves for all the evil you have done. 44 <u>You will know that I am the LORD, when I deal with you for my name's sake and not according to your evil ways and your corrupt practices</u>, O house of Israel, declares the Sovereign LORD.'"

Ezekiel 34:1-31 The word of the LORD came to me: 2 "Son of man, prophesy against the shepherds of Israel; prophesy and say to them: 'This is what the Sovereign LORD says: Woe to the shepherds of Israel who only take care of themselves! Should not shepherds take care of the flock? 3 You eat the curds, clothe yourselves with the wool and slaughter the choice animals, but you do not take care of the flock. 4 You have not strengthened the weak or healed the sick or bound up the injured. You have not brought back the strays or searched for the lost. You have ruled them harshly and brutally. 5 So they were scattered because there was no shepherd, and when they were scattered they became food for all the wild animals. 6 My sheep wandered over all the mountains and on every high hill. They were scattered over the whole earth, and no one searched or looked for them.

7 "'Therefore, you shepherds, hear the word of the LORD: 8 As surely as I live, declares the Sovereign LORD, because my flock lacks a shepherd and so has been plundered and has become food for all the wild animals, and because my shepherds did not search for my flock but cared for themselves rather than for my flock, 9 therefore, O shepherds, hear the word of the LORD: 10 This is what the Sovereign LORD says: I am against the shepherds and will hold them accountable for my flock. I will remove them from tending the flock so that the shepherds can no longer feed themselves. I will rescue my flock from their mouths, and it will no longer be food for them.

11 "'For this is what the Sovereign LORD says: I myself will search for my sheep and look after them. 12 As a shepherd looks after his scattered flock when he is with them, so will I look after my sheep. I will rescue them from all the places where they were scattered on a day of clouds and darkness. 13 I will bring them out from the nations and gather them from the countries, and I will bring them into their own land. I will pasture them on the mountains of Israel, in the ravines and in all the settlements in the land. 14 I will tend them in a good pasture, and the mountain heights of Israel will be their grazing land. There they will lie down in good grazing land, and there they will feed in a rich pasture on the mountains of Israel. 15 I myself will tend my sheep and have them lie down, declares the Sovereign LORD. 16 I will search for the lost and bring back the strays. I will bind up the injured and strengthen

the weak, but the sleek and the strong I will destroy. I will shepherd the flock with justice.

17 "'As for you, my flock, this is what the Sovereign LORD says: I will judge between one sheep and another, and between rams and goats. 18 Is it not enough for you to feed on the good pasture? Must you also trample the rest of your pasture with your feet? Is it not enough for you to drink clear water? Must you also muddy the rest with your feet? 19 Must my flock feed on what you have trampled and drink what you have muddied with your feet?

20 "'Therefore this is what the Sovereign LORD says to them: See, I myself will judge between the fat sheep and the lean sheep. 21 Because you shove with flank and shoulder, butting all the weak sheep with your horns until you have driven them away, 22 I will save my flock, and they will no longer be plundered. I will judge between one sheep and another. 23 <u>I will place over them one shepherd, my servant David, and he will tend them; he will tend them and be their shepherd. 24 I the LORD will be their God, and my servant David will be prince among them. I the LORD have spoken.</u>

25 "'I will make a covenant of peace with them and rid the land of wild beasts so that they may live in the desert and sleep in the forests in safety. 26 I will bless them and the places surrounding my hill. I will send down showers in season; there will be showers of blessing. 27 The trees of the field will yield their fruit and the ground will yield its crops; the people will be secure in their land. They will know that I am the LORD, when I break the bars of their yoke and rescue them from the hands of those who enslaved them. 28 They will no longer be plundered by the nations, nor will wild animals devour them. They will live in safety, and no one will make them afraid. 29 I will provide for them a land renowned for its crops, and they will no longer be victims of famine in the land or bear the scorn of the nations. 30 Then they will know that I, the LORD their God, am with them and that they, the house of Israel, are my people, declares the Sovereign LORD. 31 You my sheep, the sheep of my pasture, are people, and I am your God, declares the Sovereign LORD.'"

Ezekiel 36:1-38 "Son of man, prophesy to the mountains of Israel and say, 'O mountains of Israel, hear the word of the LORD. 2 This is what the Sovereign LORD says: The enemy said of you, "Aha! The ancient heights have become our possession." 3 Therefore prophesy and say, 'This is what the Sovereign LORD says: Because they ravaged and hounded you from every side so that you became the possession of the rest of the nations and the object of people's malicious talk and slander, 4 therefore, O mountains of Israel, hear the word of the Sovereign LORD: This is what the Sovereign LORD says to the mountains and hills, to the ravines and valleys, to the desolate ruins and the deserted towns that have been plundered and ridiculed by the rest of the nations around you—5 this is what the Sovereign LORD says: In my burning zeal I have spoken against the rest of the nations, and against all Edom, for with glee and with malice in their hearts they made my land their own possession so that they might plunder its pastureland.' 6 Therefore prophesy concerning the land of Israel and say to the mountains and hills, to the ravines and valleys: 'This is what the Sovereign LORD says: I speak in my jealous wrath because you have suffered the scorn of the nations. 7 Therefore this is what the Sovereign LORD says: I swear with uplifted hand that the nations around you will also suffer scorn.

8 "'But you, O mountains of Israel, will produce branches and fruit for my people Israel, for they will soon come home. 9 I am concerned for you and will look on you with favor; you will be plowed and sown, 10 and I will multiply the number of people upon you, even the whole house of Israel. The towns will be inhabited and the ruins rebuilt. 11 I will increase the number of men and animals upon you, and they will be fruitful and become numerous. I will settle people on you as in the past and will make you prosper more than before. Then you will know that I am the LORD. 12 I will cause people, my people Israel, to walk upon you. They will possess you, and you will be their inheritance; you will never again deprive them of their children.

13 "'This is what the Sovereign LORD says: Because people say to you, "You devour men and deprive your nation of its children,"14 therefore you will no longer devour men or make your nation childless, declares the Sovereign LORD. 15 No longer will I make you hear the taunts of the nations, and no longer will you suffer the scorn of the peoples or cause your nation to fall, declares the Sovereign LORD.'"

16 Again the word of the LORD came to me: 17 "Son of man, when the people of Israel were living in their own land, they defiled it by their conduct and their actions. Their conduct was like a woman's monthly uncleanness in my sight. 18 So I poured out my wrath on them because they had shed blood in the land and because they had defiled it with their idols. 19 I dispersed them among the nations, and they were scattered through the countries; I judged them according to their conduct and their actions. 20 And wherever they went among the nations they profaned my holy name, for it was said of them, 'These are the LORD's people, and yet they had to leave his land.' 21 I had concern for my

holy name, which the house of Israel profaned among the nations where they had gone.

22 "Therefore say to the house of Israel, 'This is what the Sovereign LORD says: It is not for your sake, O house of Israel, that I am going to do these things, but for the sake of my holy name, which you have profaned among the nations where you have gone. 23 I will show the holiness of my great name, which has been profaned among the nations, the name you have profaned among them. Then the nations will know that I am the LORD, declares the Sovereign LORD, when I show myself holy through you before their eyes.

24 "'For I will take you out of the nations; I will gather you from all the countries and bring you back into your own land. 25 I will sprinkle clean water on you, and you will be clean; I will cleanse you from all your impurities and from all your idols. 26 I will give you a new heart and put a new spirit in you; I will remove from you your heart of stone and give you a heart of flesh. 27 And I will put my Spirit in you and move you to follow my decrees and be careful to keep my laws. 28 You will live in the land I gave your forefathers; you will be my people, and I will be your God. 29 I will save you from all your uncleanness. I will call for the grain and make it plentiful and will not bring famine upon you. 30 I will increase the fruit of the trees and the crops of the field, so that you will no longer suffer disgrace among the nations because of famine. 31 Then you will remember your evil ways and wicked deeds, and you will loathe yourselves for your sins and detestable practices. 32 I want you to know that I am not doing this for your sake, declares the Sovereign LORD. Be ashamed and disgraced for your conduct, O house of Israel!

33 "'This is what the Sovereign LORD says: On the day I cleanse you from all your sins, I will resettle your towns, and the ruins will be rebuilt. 34 The desolate land will be cultivated instead of lying desolate in the sight of all who pass through it. 35 They will say, "This land that was laid waste has become like the garden of Eden; the cities that were lying in ruins, desolate and destroyed, are now fortified and inhabited." 36 Then the nations around you that remain will know that I the LORD have rebuilt what was destroyed and have replanted what was desolate. I the LORD have spoken, and I will do it.'

37 "This is what the Sovereign LORD says: Once again I will yield to the plea of the house of Israel and do this for them: I will make their people as numerous as sheep, 38 as numerous as the flocks for offerings at Jerusalem during her appointed feasts. So will the ruined cities be filled with flocks of people. Then they will know that I am the LORD."

God's Plan for the Gentiles

Matthew 24:14 And this gospel of the kingdom will be preached in the whole world as a testimony to all nations, and then the end will come.

Genesis 49:10 The scepter will not depart from Judah, nor the ruler's staff from between his feet, until he comes to whom it belongs and the obedience of the nations is his.

Isaiah 49:5-6 And now the LORD says—he who formed me in the womb to be his servant to bring Jacob back to him and gather Israel to himself, for I am honored in the eyes of the LORD and my God has been my strength—6 he says: "It is too small a thing for you to be my servant to restore the tribes of Jacob and bring back those of Israel I have kept. I will also make you a light for the Gentiles, that you may bring my salvation to the ends of the earth."

Isaiah 51:4-6 "Listen to me, my people; hear me, my nation: The law will go out from me; my justice will become a light to the nations. 5 My righteousness draws near speedily, my salvation is on the way, and my arm will bring justice to the nations. The islands will look to me and wait in hope for my arm. 6 Lift up your eyes to the heavens, look at the earth beneath; the heavens will vanish like smoke, the earth will wear out like a garment and its inhabitants die like flies. But my salvation will last forever, my righteousness will never fail.

Isaiah 66:18 -24 "And I, because of their actions and their imaginations, am about to come and gather all nations and tongues, and they will come and see my glory.
19 "I will set a sign among them, and I will send some of those who survive to the nations—to Tarshish, to the Libyans and Lydians (famous as archers), to Tubal and Greece, and to the distant islands that have not heard of my fame or seen my glory. They will proclaim my glory among the nations. 20 And they will bring all your brothers, from all the nations, to my holy mountain in Jerusalem as an offering to the LORD— on horses, in chariots and wagons, and on mules and camels," says the LORD. "They will bring them, as the Israelites bring their grain offerings, to the temple of the LORD in ceremonially clean vessels. 21 And I will select some of them also to be priests and Levites," says the LORD.

22 "As the new heavens and the new earth that I make will endure before me," declares the LORD, "so will your name and descendants endure. 23 From one New Moon to another and from one Sabbath to another, all mankind will come and bow down before me," says the LORD. 24 "And they will go out and look upon the dead bodies of those who rebelled against me; their worm will not die, nor will their fire be quenched, and they will be loathsome to all mankind."

4.   The Picture of the Second Coming

Matthew 24:1-51 1 Jesus left the temple and was walking away when his diciples came up to him to call his attention to its buildings. 2 "Do you see all these things?" he asked. "I tell you the truth, not one stone here will be left on another; every one will be thrown down.

3 As Jesus was sitting on the Mount of Olives, the disciples came to him privately. "Tell us," they said, "when will this happen, and what will be the sign of your coming and of the end of the age.?"

4 Jesus answered: "Watch out that no one deceives you. 5 For many will come in my name, claiming, 'I am the Christ,' and will deceive many. 6 You will hear of wars and rumors of wars, but see to it that you are not alarmed. Such things must happen, but the end is still to come. 7 Nation will rise against nation, and kingdom against kingdom. There will be famines and earthquakes in various places. 8 <u>All these are the beginning of birth pains.</u>

9 "Then you will be handed over to be persecuted and put to death, and you will be hated by all nations because of me. 10 At that time many will turn away from the faith and will betray and hate each other, 11 and many false prophets will appear and deceive many people. 12 Because of the increase of wickedness, the love of most will grow cold, 13 but he who stands firm to the end will be saved.

14 And this gospel of the kingdom will be preached in the whole world as a testimony to all nations, and then the end will come.

15 "So when you see standing in the holy place 'the abomination that causes desolation,' spoken of through the prophet Daniel—let the reader understand—16 then let those who are in Judea flee to the mountains. 17 Let no one on the roof of his house go down to take anything out of the house. 18 Let no one in the field go back to get his cloak. 19 How dreadful it will be in those days for pregnant women and nursing mothers! 20 Pray that your flight will not take place in winter or on the Sabbath.

21 "For then there will be great distress, unequaled from the beginning of the world until now—and never to be equaled again. 22 If those days had not been cut short, no one would survive, but for the sake of the elect those days will be shortened. 23 At that time if anyone says to you, 'Look, here is the Christ!' or, 'There he is!' do not believe it. 24 For false Christs and false prophets will appear and perform great signs and miracles to deceive even the elect—if that were possible. 25 See, I have told you ahead of time.

26 "So if anyone tells you, 'There he is, out in the desert,' do not go out; or, 'Here he is, in the inner rooms,' do not believe it. 27 For as lightning that comes from the east is visible even in the west, so will be the coming of the Son of Man.

29 "Immediately after the distress (tribulation) of those days "'the sun will be darkened, and the moon will not give its light; the stars will fall from the sky, and the heavenly bodies will be shaken.'

30 "At that time the sign of the Son of Man will appear in the sky, and all the nations of the earth will mourn. They will see the Son of Man coming on the clouds of the sky, with power and great glory. 31 And he will send his angels with a loud trumpet call, and they will gather his elect from the four winds, from one end of the heavens to the other.

32 "Now learn this lesson from the fig tree: As soon as its twigs get tender and its leaves come out, you know that summer is near. 33 Even so, when you see all these things, you know that it is near, right at the door. 34 I tell you the truth, this generation will certainly not pass away until all these things have happened. 35 Heaven and earth will pass away, but my words will never pass away.

36 "No one knows about that day or hour, not even the angels in heaven, nor the Son, but only the Father. 37 As it was in the days of Noah, so it will be at the coming of the Son of Man. 38 For in the days before the flood, people were eating and drinking, marrying and giving in marriage, up to the day Noah entered the ark; 39 and they knew nothing about what would happen until the flood came and took them all away. That is how it will be at the coming of the Son of Man. 40 Two men will be in the field; one will be taken and the other left. 41 Two women will be grinding with a hand mill; one will be taken and the other left.

42 "Therefore keep watch, because you do not know on what day your Lord will come. 43 But understand this: If the owner of the house had known at what time of night the thief was coming, he would have kept watch and would not have let his house be broken into. 44 So you also must be ready, because the Son of Man will come at an hour when you do not expect him.

45 "Who then is the faithful and wise servant, whom the master has put in charge of the servants in his household to give them their food at the proper time? 46 It will be good for that servant whose master finds him doing so when he returns. 47 I tell you the truth, he will put him in charge of all his possessions. 48 But suppose that servant is wicked and says to himself, 'My master is staying away a long time,' 49 and he then begins to beat his fellow servants and to eat and drink with drunkards. 50 The master of that servant will come on a day when he does not expect him and at an hour he is not aware of. 51 He will cut him to pieces and assign him a place with the hypocrites, where there will be weeping and gnashing of teeth.

Luke 21:5-36 5 Some of his disciples were remarking about how the temple was adorned with beautiful stones and with gifts dedicated to God. But Jesus said, 6 "As for what you see here, the time will come when not one stone will be left on another; every one of them will be thrown down."

7 "Teacher," they asked, "when will these things happen? And what will be the sign that they are about to take place?"

8 He replied: "Watch out that you are not deceived. For many will come in my name, claiming, 'I am he,' and, 'The time is near.' Do not follow them. 9 When you hear of wars and revolutions, do not be frightened. These things must happen first, but the end will not come right away."

10 Then he said to them: "Nation will rise against nation, and kingdom against kingdom. 11 There will be great earthquakes, famines and pestilences in various places, and fearful events and great signs from heaven.

12 "But before all this, they will lay hands on you and persecute you. They will deliver you to synagogues and prisons, and you will be brought before kings and governors, and all on account of my name. 13 This will result in your being witnesses to them. 14 But make up your mind not to worry beforehand how you will defend yourselves. 15 For I will give you words and wisdom that none of your adversaries will be able to resist or contradict. 16 You will be betrayed even by parents, brothers, relatives and friends, and they will put some of you to death. 17 All men will hate you because of me. 18 But not a hair of your head will perish. 19 By standing firm you will gain your lives.

20 "When you see Jerusalem surrounded by armies, you will know that its desolation is near. 21 Then let those who are in Judea flee to the mountains, let those in the city get out, and let those in the country not enter the city. 22 For this is the time of punishment in fulfillment of all

that has been written. 23 How dreadful it will be in those days for pregnant women and nursing mothers! There will be great distress in the land and wrath against this people. 24 They will fall by the sword and will be taken as prisoners to all the nations. jerusalem will be trampled on by the Gentiles until the times of the Gentiles are fulfilled."

25 "There will be signs in the sun, moon and stars. On the earth, nations will be in anguish and perplexity at the roaring and tossing of the sea. 26 Men will faint from terror, apprehensive of what is coming on the world, for the heavenly bodies will be shaken. 27 At that time they will see the Son of Man coming in a cloud with power and great glory. 28 When these things begin to take place, stand up and lift up your heads, because your redemption is drawing near."

29 He told them this parable: "Look at the fig tree and all the trees. 30 When they sprout leaves, you can see for yourselves and know that summer is near. 31 Even so, when you see these things happening, you know that the kingdom of God is near."

32 "I tell you the truth, this generation will certainly not pass away until all these things have happened. 33 Heaven and earth will pass away, but my words will never pass away."

34 "Be careful, or your hearts will be weighed down with dissipation, drunkenness and the anxieties of life, and that day will close on you unexpectedly like a trap. 35 For it will come upon all those who live on the face of the whole earth. 36 Be always on the watch, and pray that you may be able to escape all that is about to happen, and that you may be able to stand before the Son of Man."

Christ's Chronology:

The Exile and the Return of the Jews to their Land

Isaiah 11:10 - 12:6 In that day the Root of Jesse will stand as a banner for the peoples; the nations will rally to him, and his place of rest will be glorious. 11 In that day the Lord will reach out his hand a second time to reclaim the remnant that is left of his people from Assyria, from Lower Egypt, from Upper Egypt, from Cush, from Elam, from Babylonia, from Hamath and from the islands of the sea.

12 He will raise a banner for the nations and gather the exiles of Israel; he will assemble the scattered people of Judah from the four quarters of the earth.

13 Ephraim's jealousy will vanish, and Judah's enemies will be cut off; Ephraim will not be jealous of Judah, nor Judah hostile toward Ephraim. 14 They will swoop down on the slopes of Philistia to the

west; together they will plunder the people to the east. They will lay hands on Edom and Moab, and the Ammonites will be subject to them. 15 The LORD will dry up the gulf of the Egyptian sea; with a scorching wind he will sweep his hand over the Euphrates River. He will break it up into seven streams so that men can cross over in sandals. 16 There will be a highway for the remnant of his people that is left from Assyria, as there was for Israel when they came up from Egypt.

Isaiah 12:1 In that day you will say: "I will praise you, O LORD. Although you were angry with me, your anger has turned away and you have comforted me. 2 Surely God is my salvation; I will trust and not be afraid. The LORD, the LORD, is my strength and my song; he has become my salvation." 3 With joy you will draw water from the wells of salvation.

4 In that day you will say: "Give thanks to the LORD, call on his name; make known among the nations what he has done, and proclaim that his name is exalted. 5 Sing to the LORD, for he has done glorious things; let this be known to all the world. 6 Shout aloud and sing for joy, people of Zion, for great is the Holy One of Israel among you."

Isaiah 27:6 In days to come Jacob will take root, Israel will bud and blossom and fill all the world with fruit.

Isaiah 43:1-13 But now, this is what the LORD says—he who created you, O Jacob, he who formed you, O Israel: "Fear not, for I have redeemed you; I have summoned you by name; you are mine. 2 When you pass through the waters, I will be with you; and when you pass through the rivers, they will not sweep over you. When you walk through the fire, you will not be burned; the flames will not set you ablaze. 3 For I am the LORD, your God, the Holy One of Israel, your Savior; I give Egypt for your ransom, Cush and Seba in your stead. 4 Since you are precious and honored in my sight, and because I love you, I will give men in exchange for you, and people in exchange for your life. 5 Do not be afraid, for I am with you; I will bring your children from the east and gather you from the west. 6 I will say to the north, 'Give them up!' and to the south, 'Do not hold them back.' Bring my sons from afar and my daughters from the ends of the earth—7 everyone who is called by my name, whom I created for my glory, whom I formed and made."

8 Lead out those who have eyes but are blind, who have ears but are deaf. 9 All the nations gather together and the peoples assemble. Which of them foretold this and proclaimed to us the former things? Let them

bring in their witnesses to prove they were right, so that others may hear and say, "It is true."

10 "You are my witnesses," declares the LORD, "and my servant whom I have chosen, so that you may know and believe me and understand that I am he. Before me no god was formed, nor will there be one after me. 11 I, even I, am the LORD, and apart from me there is no savior. 12 I have revealed and saved and proclaimed—I, and not some foreign god among you. You are my witnesses," declares the LORD, "that I am God. 13 Yes, and from ancient days I am he. No one can deliver out of my hand. When I act, who can reverse it?"

Isaiah 66:7-9 "Before she goes into labor, she gives birth; before the pains come upon her, she delivers a son. 8 Who has ever heard of such a thing? Who has ever seen such things? <u>Can a country be born in a day or a nation be brought forth in a moment?</u> Yet no sooner is Zion in labor than she gives birth to her children. 9 Do I bring to the moment of birth and not give delivery?" says the LORD. "Do I close up the womb when I bring to delivery?" says your God.

Jeremiah 3:15-18 Then I will give you shepherds after my own heart, who will lead you with knowledge and understanding. 16 In those days, when your numbers have increased greatly in the land," declares the LORD, "men will no longer say, 'The ark of the covenant of the LORD.' It will never enter their minds or be remembered; it will not be missed, nor will another one be made. 17 At that time they will call Jerusalem The Throne of the LORD, and all nations will gather in Jerusalem to honor the name of the LORD. No longer will they follow the stubbornness of their evil hearts. 18 In those days the house of Judah will join the house of Israel, and together they will come from a northern land to the land I gave your forefathers as an inheritance.

Ezekiel 28:25-26 "'This is what the Sovereign LORD says: When I gather the people of Israel from the nations where they have been scattered, I will show myself holy among them in the sight of the nations. Then they will live in their own land, which I gave to my servant Jacob. 26 They will live there in safety and will build houses and plant vineyards; they will live in safety when I inflict punishment on all their neighbors who maligned them. Then they will know that I am the LORD their God.'"

Ezekiel 37:1-27 The hand of the LORD was upon me, and he brought me out by the Spirit of the LORD and set me in the middle of a valley; it was full of bones. 2 He led me back and forth among them, and I saw a great many bones on the floor of the valley, bones that were very dry. 3 He asked me, "Son of man, can these bones live?" I said, "O Sovereign LORD, you alone know."

4 Then he said to me, "Prophesy to these bones and say to them, 'Dry bones, hear the word of the LORD! 5 This is what the Sovereign LORD says to these bones: I will make breath enter you, and you will come to life. 6 I will attach tendons to you and make flesh come upon you and cover you with skin; I will put breath in you, and you will come to life. Then you will know that I am the LORD.'"

7 So I prophesied as I was commanded. And as I was prophesying, there was a noise, a rattling sound, and the bones came together, bone to bone. 8 I looked, and tendons and flesh appeared on them and skin covered them, but there was no breath in them.

9 Then he said to me, "Prophesy to the breath; prophesy, son of man, and say to it, 'This is what the Sovereign LORD says: Come from the four winds, O breath, and breathe into these slain, that they may live.'" 10 So I prophesied as he commanded me, and breath entered them; they came to life and stood up on their feet—a vast army.

11 Then he said to me: "Son of man, these bones are the whole house of Israel. They say, 'Our bones are dried up and our hope is gone; we are cut off.' 12 Therefore prophesy and say to them: 'This is what the Sovereign LORD says: O my people, I am going to open your graves and bring you up from them; I will bring you back to the land of Israel. 13 Then you, my people, will know that I am the LORD, when I open your graves and bring you up from them. 14 I will put my Spirit in you and you will live, and I will settle you in your own land. Then you will know that I the LORD have spoken, and I have done it, declares the LORD.'"

15 The word of the LORD came to me: 16 "Son of man, take a stick of wood and write on it, 'Belonging to Judah and the Israelites associated with him.' Then take another stick of wood, and write on it, 'Ephraim's stick, belonging to Joseph and all the house of Israel associated with him.' 17 Join them together into one stick so that they will become one in your hand.

18 "When your countrymen ask you, 'Won't you tell us what you mean by this?' 19 say to them, 'This is what the Sovereign LORD says: I am going to take the stick of Joseph—which is in Ephraim's hand—and of the Israelite tribes associated with him, and join it to Judah's stick, making them a single stick of wood, and they will become one in my hand.' 20 Hold before their eyes the sticks you have written on 21 and say to them, 'This is what the Sovereign LORD says: I will take the

Israelites out of the nations where they have gone. I will gather them from all around and bring them back into their own land. 22 I will make them one nation in the land, on the mountains of Israel. There will be one king over all of them and they will never again be two nations or be divided into two kingdoms. 23 They will no longer defile themselves with their idols and vile images or with any of their offenses, for I will save them from all their sinful backsliding, and I will cleanse them. They will be my people, and I will be their God.

24 "'<u>My servant David will be king over them</u>, and they will all have one shepherd. They will follow my laws and be careful to keep my decrees. 25 They will live in the land I gave to my servant Jacob, the land where your fathers lived. They and their children and their children's children will live there forever, and David my servant will be their prince forever. 26 I will make a covenant of peace with them; it will be an everlasting covenant. I will establish them and increase their numbers, and I will put my sanctuary among them forever. 27 My dwelling place will be with them; I will be their God, and they will be my people. 28 Then the nations will know that I the LORD make Israel holy, when my sanctuary is among them forever.'"

Ezekiel 38:1-23 The word of the LORD came to me: 2 "Son of man, set your face against Gog, of the land of Magog, the chief prince of Meshech and Tubal; prophesy against him 3 and say: 'This is what the Sovereign LORD says: I am against you, O Gog, chief prince of Meshech and Tubal. 4 I will turn you around, put hooks in your jaws and bring you out with your whole army—your horses, your horsemen fully armed, and a great horde with large and small shields, all of them brandishing their swords. 5 Persia, Cush and Put will be with them, all with shields and helmets, 6 also Gomer with all its troops, and Beth Togarmah from the far north with all its troops—the many nations with you.

7 "'Get ready; be prepared, you and all the hordes gathered about you, and take command of them. 8 After many days you will be called to arms. <u>In future years you will invade a land that has recovered from war, whose people were gathered from many nations to the mountains of Israel, which had long been desolate. They had been brought out from the nations, and now all of them live in safety</u>. 9 You and all your troops and the many nations with you will go up, advancing like a storm; you will be like a cloud covering the land.

10 "'This is what the Sovereign LORD says: On that day thoughts will come into your mind and you will devise an evil scheme. 11 You will say, "I will invade a land of unwalled villages; I will attack a

peaceful and unsuspecting people—all of them living without walls and without gates and bars. 12 I will plunder and loot and turn my hand against the resettled ruins and the people gathered from the nations, rich in livestock and goods, living at the center of the land." 13 Sheba and Dedan and the merchants of Tarshish and all her villages will say to you, "Have you come to plunder? Have you gathered your hordes to loot, to carry off silver and gold, to take away livestock and goods and to seize much plunder?"'

14 "Therefore, son of man, prophesy and say to Gog: 'This is what the Sovereign LORD says: In that day, when my people Israel are living in safety, will you not take notice of it? 15 You will come from your place in the far north, you and many nations with you, all of them riding on horses, a great horde, a mighty army. 16 You will advance against my people Israel like a cloud that covers the land. In days to come, O Gog, I will bring you against my land, so that the nations may know me when I show myself holy through you before their eyes.

17 "'This is what the Sovereign LORD says: Are you not the one I spoke of in former days by my servants the prophets of Israel? At that time they prophesied for years that I would bring you against them. 18 This is what will happen in that day: When Gog attacks the land of Israel, my hot anger will be aroused, declares the Sovereign LORD. 19 In my zeal and fiery wrath I declare that at that time there shall be a great earthquake in the land of Israel. 20 The fish of the sea, the birds of the air, the beasts of the field, every creature that moves along the ground, and all the people on the face of the earth will tremble at my presence. The mountains will be overturned, the cliffs will crumble and every wall will fall to the ground. 21 I will summon a sword against Gog on all my mountains, declares the Sovereign LORD. Every man's sword will be against his brother. 22 I will execute judgment upon him with plague and bloodshed; I will pour down torrents of rain, hailstones and burning sulfur on him and on his troops and on the many nations with him. 23 <u>And so I will show my greatness and my holiness, and I will make myself known in the sight of many nations. Then they will know that I am the LORD.</u>'

Ezekiel 39:1-29 "Son of man, prophesy against Gog and say: 'This is what the Sovereign LORD says: I am against you, O Gog, chief prince of Meshech and Tubal. 2 I will turn you around and drag you along. I will bring you from the far north and send you against the mountains of Israel. 3 Then I will strike your bow from your left hand and make your arrows drop from your right hand. 4 On the mountains of Israel you will fall, you and all your troops and the nations with you. I will give you as food to all kinds of carrion birds and to the wild animals. 5 You will fall in the open field, for I have spoken, declares the Sovereign LORD. 6 I will send fire on Magog and on those who live in safety in the coastlands, and they will know that I am the LORD.

7 "'I will make known my holy name among my people Israel. I will no longer let my holy name be profaned, and the nations will know that I the LORD am the Holy One in Israel. 8 It is coming! It will surely take place, declares the Sovereign LORD. This is the day I have spoken of.

9 "'Then those who live in the towns of Israel will go out and use the weapons for fuel and burn them up—the small and large shields, the bows and arrows, the war clubs and spears. For seven years they will use them for fuel. 10 They will not need to gather wood from the fields or cut it from the forests, because they will use the weapons for fuel. And they will plunder those who plundered them and loot those who looted them, declares the Sovereign LORD.

11 "'On that day I will give Gog a burial place in Israel, in the valley of those who travel east toward the Sea. It will block the way of travelers, because Gog and all his hordes will be buried there. So it will be called the Valley of Hamon Gog.

12 "'For seven months the house of Israel will be burying them in order to cleanse the land. 13 All the people of the land will bury them, and the day I am glorified will be a memorable day for them, declares the Sovereign LORD.

14 "'Men will be regularly employed to cleanse the land. Some will go throughout the land and, in addition to them, others will bury those that remain on the ground. At the end of the seven months they will begin their search. 15 As they go through the land and one of them sees a human bone, he will set up a marker beside it until the gravediggers have buried it in the Valley of Hamon Gog. 16 (Also a town called Hamonah will be there.) And so they will cleanse the land.'

17 "Son of man, this is what the Sovereign LORD says: Call out to every kind of bird and all the wild animals: 'Assemble and come together from all around to the sacrifice I am preparing for you, the great sacrifice on the mountains of Israel. There you will eat flesh and drink blood. 18 You will eat the flesh of mighty men and drink the blood of the princes of the earth as if they were rams and lambs, goats and bulls— all of them fattened animals from Bashan. 19 At the sacrifice I am preparing for you, you will eat fat till you are glutted and drink blood till you are drunk. 20 At my table you will eat your fill of horses and riders, mighty men and soldiers of every kind,' declares the Sovereign LORD.

21 "I will display my glory among the nations, and all the nations will see the punishment I inflict and the hand I lay upon them. 22 From that day forward the house of Israel will know that I am the LORD their God. 23 And the nations will know that the people of Israel went into exile for their sin, because they were unfaithful to me. So I hid my face from them and handed them over to their enemies, and they all fell by the sword. 24 I dealt with them according to their uncleanness and their offenses, and I hid my face from them.

25 "Therefore this is what the Sovereign LORD says: I will now bring Jacob back from captivity and will have compassion on all the people of Israel, and I will be zealous for my holy name. 26 They will forget their shame and all the unfaithfulness they showed toward me when they lived in safety in their land with no one to make them afraid. 27 When I have brought them back from the nations and have gathered them from the countries of their enemies, I will show myself holy through them in the sight of many nations. 28 Then they will know that I am the LORD their God, for though I sent them into exile among the nations, I will gather them to their own land, not leaving any behind. 29 I will no longer hide my face from them, for I will pour out my Spirit on the house of Israel, declares the Sovereign LORD."

The Gospel to the Gentiles

Matthew 24:14 And this gospel of the kingdom will be preached in the whole world as a testimony to all nations, and then the end will come.

Romans 11:25-29 I do not want you to be ignorant of this mystery, brothers, so that you may not be conceited: Israel has experienced a hardening in part until the full number of the Gentiles has come in. 26 And so all Israel will be saved, as it is written: "The deliverer will come from Zion; he will turn godlessness away from Jacob. 27 And this is my covenant with them when I take away their sins." 28 As far as the gospel is concerned, they are enemies on your account; but as far as election is concerned, they are loved on account of the patriarchs, 29 for God's gifts and his call are irrevocable.

Romans 11:11-15 Again I ask: Did they stumble so as to fall beyond recovery? Not at all! Rather, because of their transgression, salvation has come to the Gentiles to make Israel envious. 12 But <u>if</u> their transgression means riches for the world, and <u>their loss means riches for the Gentiles, how much greater riches will their fullness bring!</u>

13 I am talking to you Gentiles. Inasmuch as I am the apostle to the Gentiles, I make much of my ministry 14 in the hope that I may somehow arouse my own people to envy and save some of them. 15 For if their rejection is the reconciliation of the world, <u>what will their acceptance be but life from the dead</u>? [allusion to the resurrection?]

Birth Pangs: Wars, Famines, Earthquakes, Pestilences, etc.

Matthew 24:1-8 1 Jesus left the temple and was walking away when his disciples came up to him to call his attention to its buildings. 2 "Do you see all these things?" he asked. "I tell you the truth, not one stone here will be left on another; every one will be thrown down.

3 As Jesus was sitting on the Mount of Olives, the disciples came to him privately. "Tell us," they said, "when will this happen, and what will be the sign of your coming and of the end of the age.?"

4 Jesus answered: "Watch out that no one deceives you. 5 For many will come in my name, claiming, 'I am the Christ,' and will deceive many. 6 You will hear of wars and rumors of wars, but see to it that you are not alarmed. Such things must happen, but the end is still to come. 7 Nation will rise against nation, and kingdom against kingdom. There will be famines and earthquakes in various places. 8 <u>All these are the beginning of birth pains</u>.

Antichrist and the Abomination of Desolation

Acts 2:1-4, 14-21 When the day of Pentecost came, they were all together in one place. 2 Suddenly a sound like the blowing of a violent wind came from heaven and filled the whole house where they were sitting. 3 They saw what seemed to be tongues of fire that separated and came to rest on each of them. 4 All of them were filled with the Holy Spirit and began to speak in other tongues as the Spirit enabled them.

Acts 2:14 Then Peter stood up with the Eleven, raised his voice and addressed the crowd: "Fellow Jews and all of you who live in Jerusalem, let me explain this to you; listen carefully to what I say. 15 These men are not drunk, as you ";suppose. It's only nine in the morning! 16 No, this is what was spoken by the prophet Joel:

17 "'In the last days, God says, I will pour out my Spirit on all people. Your sons and daughters will prophesy, your young men will see visions, your old men will dream dreams. 18 Even on my servants, both men and women, I will pour out my Spirit in those days, and they will prophesy. 19 I will show wonders in the heaven above and signs on the earth below, blood and fire and billows of smoke. 20 The sun will be

turned to darkness and the moon to blood before the coming of the great and glorious day of the Lord. 21 And everyone who calls on the name of the Lord will be saved.'

Matthew 24:9-14 "Then you will be handed over to be persecuted and put to death, and you will be hated by all nations because of me. 10 At that time many will turn away from the faith and will betray and hate each other, 11 and many false prophets will appear and deceive many people. 12 Because of the increase of wickedness, the love of most will grow cold, 13 but he who stands firm to the end will be saved.

Joel 2:28-32 'And afterward, I will pour out my Spirit on all people. Your sons and daughters will prophesy, your old men will dream dreams, your young men will see visions. 29 Even on my servants, both men and women, I will pour out my Spirit in those days. 30 I will show wonders in the heavens and on the earth, blood and fire and billows of smoke. 31 The sun will be turned to darkness and the moon to blood before the coming of the great and dreadful day of the LORD. 32 And everyone who calls on the name of the LORD will be saved; for on Mount Zion and in Jerusalem there will be deliverance, as the LORD has said, among the survivors whom the LORD calls.

Matthew 7:15-23 "Watch out for false prophets. They come to you in sheep's clothing, but inwardly they are ferocious wolves. 16 By their fruit you will recognize them. Do people pick grapes from thornbushes, or figs from thistles? 17 Likewise every good tree bears good fruit, but a bad tree bears bad fruit. 18 A good tree cannot bear bad fruit, and a bad tree cannot bear good fruit. 19 Every tree that does not bear good fruit is cut down and thrown into the fire. 20 Thus, by their fruit you will recognize them.
21 "Not everyone who says to me, 'Lord, Lord,' will enter the kingdom of heaven, but only he who does the will of my Father who is in heaven. 22 Many will say to me on that day, 'Lord, Lord, did we not prophesy in your name, and in your name drive out demons and perform many miracles?' 23 Then I will tell them plainly, 'I never knew you. Away from me, you evildoers!'

John 9:4 As long as it is day, we must do the work of him who sent me. Night is coming, when no one can work.

Luke 18:8 I tell you, he will see that they get justice, and quickly. However, when the Son of Man comes, will he find faith on the earth?

2 Thessalonians 2:1-12 Concerning the coming of our Lord Jesus Christ and our being gathered to him, we ask you, brothers, 2 not to become easily unsettled or alarmed by some prophecy, report or letter supposed to have come from us, saying that the day of the Lord has already come. 3 Don't let anyone deceive you in any way, for that day will not come until the rebellion occurs and the man of lawlessness is revealed, the man doomed to destruction. 4 He will oppose and will exalt himself over everything that is called God or is worshiped, so that he sets himself up in God's temple, proclaiming himself to be God.

5 Don't you remember that when I was with you I used to tell you these things? 6 And now you know what is holding him back, so that he may be revealed at the proper time. 7 For the secret power of lawlessness is already at work; but the one who now holds it back will continue to do so till he is taken out of the way. 8 And then the lawless one will be revealed, whom the Lord Jesus will overthrow with the breath of his mouth and destroy by the splendor of his coming. 9 The coming of the lawless one will be in accordance with the work of Satan displayed in all kinds of counterfeit miracles, signs and wonders, 10 and in every sort of evil that deceives those who are perishing. They perish because they refused to love the truth and so be saved. 11 For this reason God sends them a powerful delusion so that they will believe the lie 12 and so that all will be condemned who have not believed the truth but have delighted in wickedness.

Signs in the Sun, Moon, Stars

Luke 21:25-28 25"There will be signs in the sun, moon and stars. On the earth, nations will be in anguish and perplexity at the roaring and tossing of the sea. 26 Men will faint from terror, apprehensive of what is coming on the world, for the heavenly bodies will be shaken. 27 At that time they will see the Son of Man coming in a cloud with power and great glory. 28 When these things begin to take place, stand up and lift up your heads, because your redemption is drawing near."

5/6 The Antichrist and his Kingdom

Peace and Prosperity

1 Thesalonians 5:1-11 Now, brothers, about times and dates we do not need to write to you, 2 for you know very well that the day of the

Lord will come like a thief in the night. 3 While people are saying, "Peace and safety," destruction will come on them suddenly, as labor pains on a pregnant woman, and they will not escape.

4 But you, brothers, are not in darkness so that this day should surprise you like a thief. 5 You are all sons of the light and sons of the day. We do not belong to the night or to the darkness. 6 So then, let us not be like others, who are asleep, but let us be alert and self-controlled. 7 For those who sleep, sleep at night, and those who get drunk, get drunk at night. 8 But since we belong to the day, let us be self-controlled, putting on faith and love as a breastplate, and the hope of salvation as a helmet.

9 For God did not appoint us to suffer wrath but to receive salvation through our Lord Jesus Christ. 10 He died for us so that, whether we are awake or asleep, we may live together with him. 11 Therefore encourage one another and build each other up, just as in fact you are doing.

Deception of the Lawless One

2 Thessalonians 2:1-12 Concerning the coming of our Lord Jesus Christ and our being gathered to him, we ask you, brothers, 2 not to become easily unsettled or alarmed by some prophecy, report or letter supposed to have come from us, saying that the day of the Lord has already come. 3 Don't let anyone deceive you in any way, for that day will not come until the rebellion occurs and the man of lawlessness is revealed, the man doomed to destruction. 4 He will oppose and will exalt himself over everything that is called God or is worshiped, so that he sets himself up in God's temple, proclaiming himself to be God.

5 Don't you remember that when I was with you I used to tell you these things? 6 And now you know what is holding him back, so that he may be revealed at the proper time. 7 For the secret power of lawlessness is already at work; but the one who now holds it back will continue to do so till he is taken out of the way. 8 And then the lawless one will be revealed, whom the Lord Jesus will overthrow with the breath of his mouth and destroy by the splendor of his coming. 9 The coming of the lawless one will be in accordance with the work of Satan displayed in all kinds of counterfeit miracles, signs and wonders, 10 and in every sort of evil that deceives those who are perishing. They perish because they refused to love the truth and so be saved. 11 For this reason God sends them a powerful delusion so that they will believe the lie 12 and so that all will be condemned who have not believed the truth but have delighted in wickedness.

1 Timothy 4:1-3 The Spirit clearly says that in later times some will abandon the faith and follow deceiving spirits and things taught by demons. 2 Such teachings come through hypocritical liars, whose consciences have been seared as with a hot iron. 3 They forbid people to marry and order them to abstain from certain foods, which God created to be received with thanksgiving by those who believe and who know the truth.

2 Timothy 3:1-5 But mark this: There will be terrible times in the last days. 2 People will be lovers of themselves, lovers of money, boastful, proud, abusive, disobedient to their parents, ungrateful, unholy, 3 without love, unforgiving, slanderous, without self-control, brutal, not lovers of the good, 4 treacherous, rash, conceited, lovers of pleasure rather than lovers of God—5 having a form of godliness but denying its power. Have nothing to do with them.

Revelation 3:14-20 "To the angel of the church in Laodicea write: These are the words of the Amen, the faithful and true witness, the ruler of God's creation. 15 I know your deeds, that you are neither cold nor hot. I wish you were either one or the other! 16 So, because you are lukewarm—neither hot nor cold—I am about to spit you out of my mouth.
17 You say, 'I am rich; I have acquired wealth and do not need a thing.' But you do not realize that you are wretched, pitiful, poor, blind and naked.
18 I counsel you to buy from me gold refined in the fire, so you can become rich; and white clothes to wear, so you can cover your shameful nakedness; and salve to put on your eyes, so you can see.
19 Those whom I love I rebuke and discipline. So be earnest, and repent.
20 Here I am! I stand at the door and knock. If anyone hears my voice and opens the door, I will come in and eat with him, and he with me.

The Abomination of Desolation

Matthew 24:15-27 "So when you see standing in the holy place 'the abomination that causes desolation,' spoken of through the prophet Daniel—let the reader understand—16 then let those who are in Judea flee to the mountains. 17 Let no one on the roof of his house go down to take anything out of the house. 18 Let no one in the field go back to get his cloak.   19   How dreadful it will be in those days for pregnant women and nursing mothers!   20   Pray that your flight will not take place in winter or on the Sabbath.

21   "For then there will be great distress, unequaled from the beginning of the world until now—and never to be equaled again.   22   If those days had not been cut short, no one would survive, but for the sake of the elect those days will be shortened.   23   At that time if anyone says to you, 'Look, here is the Christ!' or, 'There he is!' do not believe it.   24   For false Christs and false prophets will appear and perform great signs and miracles to deceive even the elect—if that were possible.   25   See, I have told you ahead of time.

26   "So if anyone tells you, 'There he is, out in the desert,' do not go out; or, 'Here he is, in the inner rooms,' do not believe it.   27   For as lightning that comes from the east is visible even in the west, so will be the coming of the Son of Man.

Daniel 9:21-27   while I was still in prayer, Gabriel, the man I had seen in the earlier vision, came to me in swift flight about the time of the evening sacrifice.   22   He instructed me and said to me, "Daniel, I have now come to give you insight and understanding.   23   As soon as you began to pray, an answer was given, which I have come to tell you, for you are highly esteemed. Therefore, consider the message and understand the vision:

24   "Seventy 'sevens' are decreed for your people and your holy city to finish transgression, to put an end to sin, to atone for wickedness, to bring in everlasting righteousness, to seal up vision and prophecy and to anoint the most holy.

25   "Know and understand this: From the issuing of the decree to restore and rebuild Jerusalem until the Anointed One [greek, "Christ"], the ruler, comes, there will be seven 'sevens,' and sixty-two 'sevens.' It will be rebuilt with streets and a trench, but in times of trouble.   26   After the sixty-two 'sevens,' the Anointed One will be cut off and will have nothing. The people of the ruler who will come will destroy the city and the sanctuary. The end will come like a flood: War will continue until the end, and desolations have been decreed.   27   He will confirm a covenant with many for one 'seven.' In the middle of the 'seven' he will put an end to sacrifice and offering. And on a wing [of the temple] he will set up an abomination that causes desolation, until the end that is decreed is poured out on him."

7.   God's Judgments of the Past

2 Peter 2:1-9 But there were also false prophets among the people, just as there will be false teachers among you. They will secretly introduce destructive heresies, even denying the sovereign Lord who bought them—bringing swift destruction on themselves. 2 Many will follow their shameful ways and will bring the way of truth into disrepute. 3 In their greed these teachers will exploit you with stories they have made up. Their condemnation has long been hanging over them, and their destruction has not been sleeping.

4 For if God did not spare angels when they sinned, but sent them to hell, putting them into gloomy dungeons to be held for judgment; 5 if he did not spare the ancient world when he brought the flood on its ungodly people, but protected Noah, a preacher of righteousness, and seven others; 6 if he condemned the cities of Sodom and Gomorrah by burning them to ashes, and made them an example of what is going to happen to the ungodly; 7   and if he rescued Lot, a righteous man, who was distressed by the filthy lives of lawless men 8 (for that righteous man, living among them day after day, was tormented in his righteous soul by the lawless deeds he saw and heard)—9 if this is so, then the Lord knows how to rescue godly men from trials and to hold the unrighteous for the day of judgment, while continuing their punishment.

Noah and the Flood

Luke 17:26-37 "Just as it was in the days of Noah, so also will it be in the days of the Son of Man. 27   People were eating, drinking, marrying and being given in marriage up to the day Noah entered the ark. Then the flood came and destroyed them all.

28   "It was the same in the days of Lot. People were eating and drinking, buying and selling, planting and building. 29 But the day Lot left Sodom, fire and sulfur rained down from heaven and destroyed them all.

30   "It will be just like this on the day the Son of Man is revealed. 31 On that day no one who is on the roof of his house, with his goods inside, should go down to get them. Likewise, no one in the field should go back for anything. 32 Remember Lot's wife! 33 Whoever tries to keep his life will lose it, and whoever loses his life will preserve it. 34 I tell you, on that night two people will be in one bed; one will be taken and the other left. 35 Two women will be grinding grain together; one will be taken and the other left."

37 "Where, Lord?" they asked. He replied, "Where there is a dead body, there the vultures will gather."

Genesis 6:5 The LORD saw how great man's wickedness on the earth had become, and that every inclination of the thoughts of his heart was only evil all the time.

Genesis 8:21 The LORD smelled the pleasing aroma and said in his heart: "Never again will I curse the ground because of man, even though every inclination of his heart is evil from childhood. And never again will I destroy all living creatures, as I have done.

The Tower of Babel

Genesis 11:1-9 Now the whole world had one language and a common speech. 2 As men moved eastward, they found a plain in Shinar and settled there.
3 They said to each other, "Come, let's make bricks and bake them thoroughly." They used brick instead of stone, and tar for mortar. 4 Then they said, "Come, let us build ourselves a city, with a tower that reaches to the heavens, so that we may make a name for ourselves and not be scattered over the face of the whole earth."
5 But the LORD came down to see the city and the tower that the men were building. 6 The LORD said, "If as one people speaking the same language they have begun to do this, then nothing they plan to do will be impossible for them. 7 Come, let us go down and confuse their language so they will not understand each other."
8 So the LORD scattered them from there over all the earth, and they stopped building the city. 9 That is why it was called Babel—because there the LORD confused the language of the whole world. From there the LORD scattered them over the face of the whole earth.

Sodom and Gomorrah

Matthew 10:14-15; 20-24 14 If anyone will not welcome you or listen to your words, shake the dust off your feet when you leave that home or town. 15 I tell you the truth, it will be more bearable for Sodom and Gomorrah on the day of judgment than for that town.
20 Then Jesus began to denounce the cities in which most of his miracles had been performed, because they did not repent. 21 "Woe to you, Korazin! Woe to you, Bethsaida! If the miracles that were performed in you had been performed in Tyre and Sidon, they would

have repented long ago in sackcloth and ashes. 22 But I tell you, it will be more bearable for Tyre and Sidon on the day of judgment than for you. 23 And you, Capernaum, will you be lifted up to the skies? No, you will go down to the depths. If the miracles that were performed in you had been performed in Sodom, it would have remained to this day. 24 But I tell you that it will be more bearable for Sodom on the day of judgment than for you."

Jude 7 In a similar way, Sodom and Gomorrah and the surrounding towns gave themselves up to sexual immorality and perversion. They serve as an example of those who suffer the punishment of eternal fire.

Genesis 18:16-32 When the men got up to leave, they looked down toward Sodom, and Abraham walked along with them to see them on their way. 17 Then the LORD said, "Shall I hide from Abraham what I am about to do? 18 Abraham will surely become a great and powerful nation, and all nations on earth will be blessed through him. 19 For I have chosen him, so that he will direct his children and his household after him to keep the way of the LORD by doing what is right and just, so that the LORD will bring about for Abraham what he has promised him."

20 Then the LORD said, "The outcry against Sodom and Gomorrah is so great and their sin so grievous 21 that I will go down and see if what they have done is as bad as the outcry that has reached me. If not, I will know."

22 The men turned away and went toward Sodom, but Abraham remained standing before the LORD. 23 Then Abraham approached him and said: "Will you sweep away the righteous with the wicked? 24 What if there are fifty righteous people in the city? Will you really sweep it away and not spare the place for the sake of the fifty righteous people in it? 25 Far be it from you to do such a thing—to kill the righteous with the wicked, treating the righteous and the wicked alike. Far be it from you! Will not the Judge of all the earth do right?"

26 The LORD said, "If I find fifty righteous people in the city of Sodom, I will spare the whole place for their sake."

27 Then Abraham spoke up again: "Now that I have been so bold as to speak to the Lord, though I am nothing but dust and ashes, 28 what if the number of the righteous is five less than fifty? Will you destroy the whole city because of five people?" "If I find forty-five there," he said, "I will not destroy it."

29 Once again he spoke to him, "What if only forty are found there?" He said, "For the sake of forty, I will not do it."

30   Then he said, "May the Lord not be angry, but let me speak. What if only thirty can be found there?" He answered, "I will not do it if I find thirty there."

31   Abraham said, "Now that I have been so bold as to speak to the Lord, what if only twenty can be found there?" He said, "For the sake of twenty, I will not destroy it."

32   Then he said, "May the Lord not be angry, but let me speak just once more. What if only ten can be found there?" He answered, "For the sake of ten, I will not destroy it."

Genesis 19:1-29   The two angels arrived at Sodom in the evening, and Lot was sitting in the gateway of the city. When he saw them, he got up to meet them and bowed down with his face to the ground. 2 "My lords," he said, "please turn aside to your servant's house. You can wash your feet and spend the night and then go on your way early in the morning."

"No," they answered, "we will spend the night in the square."

3   But he insisted so strongly that they did go with him and entered his house. He prepared a meal for them, baking bread without yeast, and they ate. 4 Before they had gone to bed, all the men from every part of the city of Sodom—both young and old—surrounded the house. 5 They called to Lot, "Where are the men who came to you tonight? Bring them out to us so that we can have sex with them."

6   Lot went outside to meet them and shut the door behind him 7 and said, "No, my friends. Don't do this wicked thing. 8 Look, I have two daughters who have never slept with a man. Let me bring them out to you, and you can do what you like with them. But don't do anything to these men, for they have come under the protection of my roof."

9   "Get out of our way," they replied. And they said, "This fellow came here as an alien, and now he wants to play the judge! We'll treat you worse than them." They kept bringing pressure on Lot and moved forward to break down the door.

10   But the men inside reached out and pulled Lot back into the house and shut the door. 11 Then they struck the men who were at the door of the house, young and old, with blindness so that they could not find the door.

12   The two men said to Lot, "Do you have anyone else here—sons-in-law, sons or daughters, or anyone else in the city who belongs to you? Get them out of here, 13 because we are going to destroy this place. The outcry to the LORD against its people is so great that he has sent us to destroy it."

14 So Lot went out and spoke to his sons-in-law, who were pledged to marry his daughters. He said, "Hurry and get out of this place, because the LORD is about to destroy the city!" But his sons-in-law thought he was joking.

15 With the coming of dawn, the angels urged Lot, saying, "Hurry! Take your wife and your two daughters who are here, or you will be swept away when the city is punished."

16 When he hesitated, the men grasped his hand and the hands of his wife and of his two daughters and led them safely out of the city, for the LORD was merciful to them. 17 As soon as they had brought them out, one of them said, "Flee for your lives! Don't look back, and don't stop anywhere in the plain! Flee to the mountains or you will be swept away!"

18 But Lot said to them, "No, my lords, please! 19 Your servant has found favor in your eyes, and you have shown great kindness to me in sparing my life. But I can't flee to the mountains; this disaster will overtake me, and I'll die. 20 Look, here is a town near enough to run to, and it is small. Let me flee to it—it is very small, isn't it? Then my life will be spared."

21 He said to him, "Very well, I will grant this request too; I will not overthrow the town you speak of. 22 But flee there quickly, because I cannot do anything until you reach it." (That is why the town was called Zoar.)

23 By the time Lot reached Zoar, the sun had risen over the land. 24   Then the LORD rained down burning sulfur on Sodom and Gomorrah—from the LORD out of the heavens. 25 Thus he overthrew those cities and the entire plain, including all those living in the cities— and also the vegetation in the land. 26 But Lot's wife looked back, and she became a pillar of salt.

27 Early the next morning Abraham got up and returned to the place where he had stood before the LORD. 28 He looked down toward Sodom and Gomorrah, toward all the land of the plain, and he saw dense smoke rising from the land, like smoke from a furnace.

29 So when God destroyed the cities of the plain, he remembered Abraham, and he brought Lot out of the catastrophe that overthrew the cities where Lot had lived.

Isaiah 3:1-9 See now, the Lord, the LORD Almighty, is about to take from Jerusalem and Judah both supply and support: all supplies of food and all supplies of water, 2 the hero and warrior, the judge and prophet, the soothsayer and elder, 3 the captain of fifty and man of rank, the counselor, skilled craftsman and clever enchanter. 4 I will make boys their officials; mere children will govern them. 5 People will oppress each other—man against man, neighbor against neighbor. The young will rise up against the old, the base against the honorable. 6 A man will seize one of his brothers at his father's home, and say, "You have a cloak, you be our leader; take charge of this heap of ruins!" 7 But in that day he will cry out, "I have no remedy. I have no food or clothing in my house; do not make me the leader of the people." 8 Jerusalem staggers, Judah is falling; their words and deeds are against the LORD, defying his glorious presence. 9 The look on their faces testifies against them; <u>they parade their sin like Sodom</u>; they do not hide it. Woe to them! They have brought disaster upon themselves.

Ezekiel 16:45-50 You are a true daughter of your mother, who despised her husband and her children; and you are a true sister of your sisters, who despised their husbands and their children. Your mother was a Hittite and your father an Amorite. 46 Your older sister was Samaria, who lived to the north of you with her daughters; and your younger sister, who lived to the south of you with her daughters, was Sodom. 47 You not only walked in their ways and copied their detestable practices, but in all your ways you soon became more depraved than they. 48 As surely as I live, declares the Sovereign LORD, your sister Sodom and her daughters never did what you and your daughters have done.

49 "'Now this was the sin of your sister Sodom: She and her daughters were arrogant, overfed and unconcerned; they did not help the poor and needy. 50 They were haughty and did detestable things before me. Therefore I did away with them as you have seen.

Babylon

Isaiah 13:1-22 An oracle concerning Babylon that Isaiah son of Amoz saw:

2 Raise a banner on a bare hilltop, shout to them; beckon to them to enter the gates of the nobles. 3 I have commanded my holy ones; I have summoned my warriors to carry out my wrath—those who rejoice in my triumph.

4 Listen, a noise on the mountains, like that of a great multitude! Listen, an uproar among the kingdoms, like nations massing together! The LORD Almighty is mustering an army for war. 5 They come from faraway lands, from the ends of the heavens—the LORD and the weapons of his wrath—to destroy the whole country.

6 Wail, for the day of the LORD is near; it will come like destruction from the Almighty. 7 Because of this, all hands will go

limp, every man's heart will melt. 8 Terror will seize them, pain and anguish will grip them; they will writhe like a woman in labor. They will look aghast at each other, their faces aflame.

9 See, the day of the LORD is coming—a cruel day, with wrath and fierce anger—to make the land desolate and destroy the sinners within it. 10 The stars of heaven and their constellations will not show their light. The rising sun will be darkened and the moon will not give its light. 11 I will punish the world for its evil, the wicked for their sins. I will put an end to the arrogance of the haughty and will humble the pride of the ruthless. 12 I will make man scarcer than pure gold, more rare than the gold of Ophir. 13 Therefore I will make the heavens tremble; and the earth will shake from its place at the wrath of the LORD Almighty, in the day of his burning anger.

14 Like a hunted gazelle, like sheep without a shepherd, each will return to his own people, each will flee to his native land. 15 Whoever is captured will be thrust through; all who are caught will fall by the sword. 16 Their infants will be dashed to pieces before their eyes; their houses will be looted and their wives ravished. 17 See, I will stir up against them the Medes, who do not care for silver and have no delight in gold. 18 Their bows will strike down the young men; they will have no mercy on infants nor will they look with compassion on children. 19 Babylon, the jewel of kingdoms, the glory of the Babylonians' pride, will be overthrown by God like Sodom and Gomorrah. 20 She will never be inhabited or lived in through all generations; no Arab will pitch his tent there, no shepherd will rest his flocks there. 21 But desert creatures will lie there, jackals will fill her houses; there the owls will dwell, and there the wild goats will leap about. 22 Hyenas will howl in her strongholds, jackals in her luxurious palaces. Her time is at hand, and her days will not be prolonged.

Isaiah 14:1-24 The LORD will have compassion on Jacob; once again he will choose Israel and will settle them in their own land. Aliens will join them and unite with the house of Jacob. 2 Nations will take them and bring them to their own place. And the house of Israel will possess the nations as menservants and maidservants in the LORD's land. They will make captives of their captors and rule over their oppressors.

l3 On the day the LORD gives you relief from suffering and turmoil and cruel bondage, 4 you will take up this taunt against the king of Babylon: How the oppressor has come to an end! How his fury has ended!

5 The LORD has broken the rod of the wicked, the scepter of the rulers, 6 which in anger struck down peoples with unceasing blows, and in fury subdued nations with relentless aggression.

7 All the lands are at rest and at peace; they break into singing. 8 Even the pine trees and the cedars of Lebanon exult over you and say, "Now that you have been laid low, no woodsman comes to cut us down."

9 The grave below is all astir to meet you at your coming; it rouses the spirits of the departed to greet you—all those who were leaders in the world; it makes them rise from their thrones—all those who were kings over the nations. 10 They will all respond, they will say to you, "You also have become weak, as we are; you have become like us."

11 All your pomp has been brought down to the grave, along with the noise of your harps; maggots are spread out beneath you and worms cover you.

12 How you have fallen from heaven, O morning star, son of the dawn! You have been cast down to the earth, you who once laid low the nations! 13 You said in your heart, "I will ascend to heaven; I will raise my throne above the stars of God; I will sit enthroned on the mount of assembly, on the utmost heights of the sacred mountain. 14 I will ascend above the tops of the clouds; I will make myself like the Most High."

15 But you are brought down to the grave, to the depths of the pit. 16 Those who see you stare at you, they ponder your fate: "Is this the man who shook the earth and made kingdoms tremble, 17 the man who made the world a desert, who overthrew its cities and would not let his captives go home?"

18 All the kings of the nations lie in state, each in his own tomb. 19 But you are cast out of your tomb like a rejected branch; you are covered with the slain, with those pierced by the sword, those who descend to the stones of the pit. Like a corpse trampled underfoot, 20 you will not join them in burial, for you have destroyed your land and killed your people. The offspring of the wicked will never be mentioned again. 21 Prepare a place to slaughter his sons for the sins of their forefathers; they are not to rise to inherit the land and cover the earth with their cities.

22 "I will rise up against them," declares the LORD Almighty. "I will cut off from Babylon her name and survivors, her offspring and descendants," declares the LORD. 23 "I will turn her into a place for owls and into swampland; I will sweep her with the broom of destruction," declares the LORD Almighty. 24 The LORD Almighty has sworn, "Surely, as I have planned, so it will be, and as I have purposed, so it will stand.

Isaiah 47:1-15 "Go down, sit in the dust, Virgin Daughter of Babylon; sit on the ground without a throne, Daughter of the Babylonians. No more will you be called tender or delicate. 2 Take millstones and grind flour; take off your veil. Lift up your skirts, bare your legs, and wade through the streams. 3 Your nakedness will be exposed and your shame uncovered. I will take vengeance; I will spare no one."

4 Our Redeemer—the LORD Almighty is his name—is the Holy One of Israel. 5 "Sit in silence, go into darkness, Daughter of the Babylonians; no more will you be called queen of kingdoms. 6 I was angry with my people and desecrated my inheritance; I gave them into your hand, and you showed them no mercy. Even on the aged you laid a very heavy yoke. 7 You said, 'I will continue forever—the eternal queen!' But you did not consider these things or reflect on what might happen.

8 "Now then, listen, you wanton creature, lounging in your security and saying to yourself, 'I am, and there is none besides me. I will never be a widow or suffer the loss of children.' 9 Both of these will overtake you in a moment, on a single day: loss of children and widowhood. They will come upon you in full measure, in spite of your many sorceries and all your potent spells. 10 You have trusted in your wickedness and have said, 'No one sees me.' Your wisdom and knowledge mislead you when you say to yourself, 'I am, and there is none besides me.' 11 Disaster will come upon you, and you will not know how to conjure it away. A calamity will fall upon you that you cannot ward off with a ransom; a catastrophe you cannot foresee will suddenly come upon you.

12 "Keep on, then, with your magic spells and with your many sorceries, which you have labored at since childhood. Perhaps you will succeed, perhaps you will cause terror. 13 All the counsel you have received has only worn you out! Let your astrologers come forward, those stargazers who make predictions month by month, let them save you from what is coming upon you. 14 Surely they are like stubble; the fire will burn them up. They cannot even save themselves from the power of the flame. Here are no coals to warm anyone; here is no fire to sit by. 15 That is all they can do for you—these you have labored with and trafficked with since childhood. Each of them goes on in his error; there is not one that can save you.

Ezek. 30:1-5 The word of the LORD came to me: 2 "Son of man, prophesy and say: 'This is what the Sovereign LORD says: "'Wail and say, "Alas for that day!" 3 For the day is near, the day of the LORD is near—a day of clouds, a time of doom for the nations.

4   A sword will come against Egypt, and anguish will come upon Cush. When the slain fall in Egypt, her wealth will be carried away and her foundations torn down. 5 Cush and Put, Lydia and all Arabia, Libya and the people of the covenant land will fall by the sword along with Egypt.

The Judgments against Israel and Judah

For Apostasy, False Prophets, and False Religion

Isaiah 1:9-18   Unless the LORD Almighty had left us some survivors, we would have become like Sodom, we would have been like Gomorrah. 10 Hear the word of the LORD, you rulers of Sodom; listen to the law of our God, you people of Gomorrah!

11 "The multitude of your sacrifices—what are they to me?" says the LORD. "I have more than enough of burnt offerings, of rams and the fat of fattened animals; I have no pleasure in the blood of bulls and lambs and goats. 12 When you come to appear before me, who has asked this of you, this trampling of my courts? 13 Stop bringing meaningless offerings! Your incense is detestable to me. New Moons, Sabbaths and convocations—I cannot bear your evil assemblies. 14 Your New Moon festivals and your appointed feasts my soul hates. They have become a burden to me; I am weary of bearing them. 15 When you spread out your hands in prayer, I will hide my eyes from you; even if you offer many prayers, I will not listen. Your hands are full of blood; 16 wash and make yourselves clean. Take your evil deeds out of my sight! Stop doing wrong, 17 learn to do right! Seek justice, encourage the oppressed. Defend the cause of the fatherless, plead the case of the widow.

18 "Come now, let us reason together," says the LORD. "Though your sins are like scarlet, they shall be as white as snow; though they are red as crimson, they shall be like wool."

Jeremiah 2:4-13; 19-37   Hear the word of the LORD, O house of Jacob, all you clans of the house of Israel.

5 This is what the LORD says: "What fault did your fathers find in me, that they strayed so far from me? They followed worthless idols and became worthless themselves. 6 They did not ask, 'Where is the LORD, who brought us up out of Egypt and led us through the barren wilderness, through a land of deserts and rifts, a land of drought and darkness, a land where no one travels and no one lives?' 7 I brought you into a fertile land to eat its fruit and rich produce. But you came and

defiled my land and made my inheritance detestable. 8 The priests did not ask, 'Where is the LORD?' Those who deal with the law did not know me; the leaders rebelled against me. The prophets prophesied by Baal, following worthless idols.

9 "Therefore I bring charges against you again," declares the LORD. "And I will bring charges against your children's children. 10 Cross over to the coasts of Kittim and look, send to Kedar and observe closely; see if there has ever been anything like this: 11 Has a nation ever changed its gods? (Yet they are not gods at all.) But my people have exchanged their Glory for worthless idols.

12 Be appalled at this, O heavens, and shudder with great horror," declares the LORD. 13 "My people have committed two sins: They have forsaken me, the spring of living water, and have dug their own cisterns, broken cisterns that cannot hold water.

19 Your wickedness will punish you; your backsliding will rebuke you. Consider then and realize how evil and bitter it is for you when you forsake the LORD your God and have no awe of me," declares the Lord, the LORD Almighty.

20 "Long ago you broke off your yoke and tore off your bonds; you said, 'I will not serve you!' Indeed, on every high hill and under every spreading tree you lay down as a prostitute. 21 I had planted you like a choice vine of sound and reliable stock. How then did you turn against me into a corrupt, wild vine? 22 Although you wash yourself with soda and use an abundance of soap, the stain of your guilt is still before me," declares the Sovereign LORD.

23 "How can you say, 'I am not defiled; I have not run after the Baals'? See how you behaved in the valley; consider what you have done. You are a swift she-camel running here and there, 24 a wild donkey accustomed to the desert, sniffing the wind in her craving—in her heat who can restrain her? Any males that pursue her need not tire themselves; at mating time they will find her. 25 Do not run until your feet are bare and your throat is dry. But you said, 'It's no use! I love foreign gods, and I must go after them.'

26 "As a thief is disgraced when he is caught, so the house of Israel is disgraced—they, their kings and their officials, their priests and their prophets. 27 They say to wood, 'You are my father,' and to stone, 'You gave me birth.' They have turned their backs to me and not their faces; yet when they are in trouble, they say, 'Come and save us!' 28 Where then are the gods you made for yourselves? Let them come if they can save you when you are in trouble! For you have as many gods as you have towns, O Judah.

29 "Why do you bring charges against me? You have all rebelled against me," declares the LORD.

30 "In vain I punished your people; they did not respond to correction. Your sword has devoured your prophets like a ravening lion.

31 "You of this generation, consider the word of the LORD: "Have I been a desert to Israel or a land of great darkness? Why do my people say, 'We are free to roam; we will come to you no more'? 32 Does a maiden forget her jewelry, a bride her wedding ornaments? Yet my people have forgotten me, days without number. 33 How skilled you are at pursuing love! Even the worst of women can learn from your ways. 34 On your clothes men find the lifeblood of the innocent poor, though you did not catch them breaking in. Yet in spite of all this 35 you say, 'I am innocent; he is not angry with me.' But I will pass judgment on you because you say, 'I have not sinned.' 36 Why do you go about so much, changing your ways? You will be disappointed by Egypt as you were by Assyria. 37 You will also leave that place with your hands on your head, for the LORD has rejected those you trust; you will not be helped by them.

(also a Dualistic Prophecy, describing God's immediate judgment in terms of the final judgment)

Jeremiah 4:10-14, 19-26 Then I said, "Ah, Sovereign LORD, how completely you have deceived this people and Jerusalem by saying, 'You will have peace,' when the sword is at our throats."

11 At that time this people and Jerusalem will be told, "A scorching wind from the barren heights in the desert blows toward my people, but not to winnow or cleanse; 12 a wind too strong for that comes from me. Now I pronounce my judgments against them."

13 Look! He advances like the clouds, his chariots come like a whirlwind, his horses are swifter than eagles. Woe to us! We are ruined!

14 O Jerusalem, wash the evil from your heart and be saved. How long will you harbor wicked thoughts?

19 Oh, my anguish, my anguish! I writhe in pain. Oh, the agony of my heart! My heart pounds within me, I cannot keep silent. For I have heard the sound of the trumpet; I have heard the battle cry. 20 Disaster follows disaster; the whole land lies in ruins. In an instant my tents are destroyed, my shelter in a moment. 21 How long must I see the battle standard and hear the sound of the trumpet?

22 "My people are fools; they do not know me. They are senseless children; they have no understanding. They are skilled in doing evil; they know not how to do good."

23 I looked at the earth, and it was formless and empty; and at the heavens, and their light was gone. 24 I looked at the mountains, and they were quaking; all the hills were swaying. 25 I looked, and there were no people; every bird in the sky had flown away. 26 I looked, and the fruitful land was a desert; all its towns lay in ruins before the LORD, before his fierce anger.

Jeremiah 5:4-9, 12-13, 21-31 I thought, "These are only the poor; they are foolish, for they do not know the way of the LORD, the requirements of their God. 5 So I will go to the leaders and speak to them; surely they know the way of the LORD, the requirements of their God." But with one accord they too had broken off the yoke and torn off the bonds. 6 Therefore a lion from the forest will attack them, a wolf from the desert will ravage them, a leopard will lie in wait near their towns to tear to pieces any who venture out, for their rebellion is great and their backslidings many.

7 "Why should I forgive you? Your children have forsaken me and sworn by gods that are not gods. I supplied all their needs, yet they committed adultery and thronged to the houses of prostitutes. 8 They are well-fed, lusty stallions, each neighing for another man's wife. 9 Should I not punish them for this?" declares the LORD. "Should I not avenge myself on such a nation as this?

12 They have lied about the LORD; they said, "He will do nothing! No harm will come to us; we will never see sword or famine. 13 The prophets are but wind and the word is not in them; so let what they say be done to them."

21 Hear this, you foolish and senseless people, who have eyes but do not see, who have ears but do not hear: 22 Should you not fear me?" declares the LORD. "Should you not tremble in my presence? I made the sand a boundary for the sea, an everlasting barrier it cannot cross. The waves may roll, but they cannot prevail; they may roar, but they cannot cross it. 23 But these people have stubborn and rebellious hearts; they have turned aside and gone away. 24 They do not say to themselves, 'Let us fear the LORD our God, who gives autumn and spring rains in season, who assures us of the regular weeks of harvest.' 25 Your wrongdoings have kept these away; your sins have deprived you of good.

26 "Among my people are wicked men who lie in wait like men who snare birds and like those who set traps to catch men. 27 Like cages full of birds, their houses are full of deceit; they have become rich and powerful 28 and have grown fat and sleek. Their evil deeds have no limit; they do not plead the case of the fatherless to win it, they do not

defend the rights of the poor. 29 Should I not punish them for this?" declares the LORD. "Should I not avenge myself on such a nation as this?

30 "A horrible and shocking thing has happened in the land: 31 The prophets prophesy lies, the priests rule by their own authority, and my people love it this way. But what will you do in the end?

Jeremiah 7:4-11, 4 Do not trust in deceptive words and say, "This is the temple of the LORD, the temple of the LORD, the temple of the LORD!" 5 If you really change your ways and your actions and deal with each other justly, 6 if you do not oppress the alien, the fatherless or the widow and do not shed innocent blood in this place, and if you do not follow other gods to your own harm, 7 then I will let you live in this place, in the land I gave your forefathers for ever and ever. 8 But look, you are trusting in deceptive words that are worthless.

9 "'Will you steal and murder, commit adultery and perjury, burn incense to Baal and follow other gods you have not known, 10 and then come and stand before me in this house, which bears my Name, and say, "We are safe "—safe to do all these detestable things? 11 Has this house, which bears my Name, become a den of robbers to you? But I have been watching! declares the LORD.

Jeremiah 13:12-13 "Say to them: 'This is what the LORD, the God of Israel, says: Every wineskin should be filled with wine.' And if they say to you, 'Don't we know that every wineskin should be filled with wine?' 13 then tell them, 'This is what the LORD says: I am going to fill with drunkenness all who live in this land, including the kings who sit on David's throne, the priests, the prophets and all those living in Jerusalem.

Jeremiah 23:9-32 Concerning the prophets: My heart is broken within me; all my bones tremble. I am like a drunken man, like a man overcome by wine, because of the LORD and his holy words. 10 The land is full of adulterers; because of the curse the land lies parched and the pastures in the desert are withered. The [prophets] follow an evil course and use their power unjustly.

11 "Both prophet and priest are godless; even in my temple I find their wickedness," declares the LORD.

12 "Therefore their path will become slippery; they will be banished to darkness and there they will fall. I will bring disaster on them in the year they are punished," declares the LORD.

13 "Among the prophets of Samaria I saw this repulsive thing: They prophesied by Baal and led my people Israel astray. 14 And among the prophets of Jerusalem I have seen something horrible: They commit adultery and live a lie. They strengthen the hands of evildoers, so that no one turns from his wickedness. <u>They are all like Sodom to me; the people of Jerusalem are like Gomorrah.</u>"

15 Therefore, this is what the LORD Almighty says concerning the prophets: "I will make them eat bitter food and drink poisoned water, because from the prophets of Jerusalem ungodliness has spread throughout the land."

16 This is what the LORD Almighty says: "Do not listen to what the prophets are prophesying to you; they fill you with false hopes. They speak visions from their own minds, not from the mouth of the LORD. 17 They keep saying to those who despise me, 'The LORD says: You will have peace.' And to all who follow the stubbornness of their hearts they say, 'No harm will come to you.' 18 But which of them has stood in the council of the LORD to see or to hear his word? Who has listened and heard his word?

19 "See, the storm of the LORD will burst out in wrath, a whirlwind swirling down on the heads of the wicked. 20 The anger of the LORD will not turn back until he fully accomplishes the purposes of his heart. In days to come you will understand it clearly.

21 "I did not send these prophets, yet they have run with their message; I did not speak to them, yet they have prophesied. 22 But if they had stood in my council, they would have proclaimed my words to my people and would have turned them from their evil ways and from their evil deeds.

23 "Am I only a God nearby," declares the LORD, "and not a God far away?

24 Can anyone hide in secret places so that I cannot see him?" declares the LORD. "Do not I fill heaven and earth?" declares the LORD.

25 "I have heard what the prophets say who prophesy lies in my name. They say, 'I had a dream! I had a dream!' 26 How long will this continue in the hearts of these lying prophets, who prophesy the delusions of their own minds? 27 They think the dreams they tell one another will make my people forget my name, just as their fathers forgot my name through Baal worship. 28 Let the prophet who has a dream tell his dream, but let the one who has my word speak it faithfully. For what has straw to do with grain?" declares the LORD. 29 "Is not my word like fire," declares the LORD, "and like a hammer that breaks a rock in pieces?

30 "Therefore," declares the LORD, "I am against the prophets who steal from one another words supposedly from me. 31 Yes," declares the LORD, "I am against the prophets who wag their own tongues and yet declare, 'The LORD declares.' 32 Indeed, I am against those who prophesy false dreams," declares the LORD. "They tell them and lead my people astray with their reckless lies, yet I did not send or appoint them. They do not benefit these people in the least," declares the LORD.

Ezekiel 22:26-31 Her priests do violence to my law and profane my holy things; they do not distinguish between the holy and the common; they teach that there is no difference between the unclean and the clean; and they shut their eyes to the keeping of my Sabbaths, so that I am profaned among them. 27 Her officials within her are like wolves tearing their prey; they shed blood and kill people to make unjust gain. 28 Her prophets whitewash these deeds for them by false visions and lying divinations. They say, 'This is what the Sovereign LORD says '— when the LORD has not spoken. 29 The people of the land practice extortion and commit robbery; they oppress the poor and needy and mistreat the alien, denying them justice.

30 "I looked for a man among them who would build up the wall and stand before me in the gap on behalf of the land so I would not have to destroy it, but I found none. 31 So I will pour out my wrath on them and consume them with my fiery anger, bringing down on their own heads all they have done, declares the Sovereign LORD."

For Rebellion and Defiant Sin

Isaiah 3:1-26 See now, the Lord, the LORD Almighty, is about to take from Jerusalem and Judah both supply and support: all supplies of food and all supplies of water, 2 the hero and warrior, the judge and prophet, the soothsayer and elder, 3 the captain of fifty and man of rank, the counselor, skilled craftsman and clever enchanter. 4 I will make boys their officials; mere children will govern them. 5 People will oppress each other—man against man, neighbor against neighbor. The young will rise up against the old, the base against the honorable.

6 A man will seize one of his brothers at his father's home, and say, "You have a cloak, you be our leader; take charge of this heap of ruins!" 7 But in that day he will cry out, "I have no remedy. I have no food or clothing in my house; do not make me the leader of the people."

8 Jerusalem staggers, Judah is falling; their words and deeds are against the LORD, defying his glorious presence. 9 The look on their

faces testifies against them; they parade their sin like Sodom; they do not hide it. Woe to them! They have brought disaster upon themselves.

10 Tell the righteous it will be well with them, for they will enjoy the fruit of their deeds.

11 Woe to the wicked! Disaster is upon them! They will be paid back for what their hands have done. 12 Youths oppress my people, women rule over them. O my people, your guides lead you astray; they turn you from the path.

13 The LORD takes his place in court; he rises to judge the people. 14 The LORD enters into judgment against the elders and leaders of his people: "It is you who have ruined my vineyard; the plunder from the poor is in your houses. 15 What do you mean by crushing my people and grinding the faces of the poor?" declares the Lord, the LORD Almighty.

16 The LORD says, "The women of Zion are haughty, walking along with outstretched necks, flirting with their eyes, tripping along with mincing steps, with ornaments jingling on their ankles. 17 Therefore the Lord will bring sores on the heads of the women of Zion; the LORD will make their scalps bald." 18 In that day the Lord will snatch away their finery: the bangles and headbands and crescent necklaces, 19 the earrings and bracelets and veils, 20 the headdresses and ankle chains and sashes, the perfume bottles and charms, 21 the signet rings and nose rings, 22 the fine robes and the capes and cloaks, the purses 23 and mirrors, and the linen garments and tiaras and shawls. 24 Instead of fragrance there will be a stench; instead of a sash, a rope; instead of well-dressed hair, baldness; instead of fine clothing, sackcloth; instead of beauty, branding.

25 Your men will fall by the sword, your warriors in battle. 26 The gates of Zion will lament and mourn; destitute, she will sit on the ground.

Jeremiah 8:5-8 Why then have these people turned away? Why does Jerusalem always turn away? They cling to deceit; they refuse to return. 6 I have listened attentively, but they do not say what is right. No one repents of his wickedness, saying, "What have I done?" Each pursues his own course like a horse charging into battle. 7 Even the stork in the sky knows her appointed seasons, and the dove, the swift and the thrush observe the time of their migration. But my people do not know the requirements of the LORD.

8 "'How can you say, "We are wise, for we have the law of the LORD," when actually the lying pen of the scribes has handled it falsely?

Jeremiah 18:12 But they will reply, 'It's no use. We will continue with our own plans; each of us will follow the stubbornness of his evil heart.'"

For the Rejection of Truth and Justice

Isaiah 10:1-4 Woe to those who make unjust laws, to those who issue oppressive decrees, 2 to deprive the poor of their rights and withhold justice from the oppressed of my people, making widows their prey and robbing the fatherless.
3 What will you do on the day of reckoning, when disaster comes from afar? To whom will you run for help? Where will you leave your riches? 4 Nothing will remain but to cringe among the captives or fall among the slain. Yet for all this, his anger is not turned away, his hand is still upraised.

Jeremiah 6:10 10 To whom can I speak and give warning? Who will listen to me? Their ears are closed so they cannot hear. The word of the LORD is offensive to them; they find no pleasure in it.

Jeremiah 7:23-28 but I gave them this command: Obey me, and I will be your God and you will be my people. Walk in all the ways I command you, that it may go well with you. 24 But they did not listen or pay attention; instead, they followed the stubborn inclinations of their evil hearts. They went backward and not forward. 25 From the time your forefathers left Egypt until now, day after day, again and again I sent you my servants the prophets. 26 But they did not listen to me or pay attention. They were stiff-necked and did more evil than their forefathers.'
27 "When you tell them all this, they will not listen to you; when you call to them, they will not answer. 28 Therefore say to them, 'This is the nation that has not obeyed the LORD its God or responded to correction. Truth has perished; it has vanished from their lips.

When God Gives the People over to Judgment

Jeremiah 5:21-31 Hear this, you foolish and senseless people, who have eyes but do not see, who have ears but do not hear: 22 Should you not fear me?" declares the LORD. "Should you not tremble in my presence? I made the sand a boundary for the sea, an everlasting barrier it cannot cross. The waves may roll, but they cannot prevail; they may roar, but they cannot cross it. 23 But these people have stubborn and rebellious hearts; they have turned aside and gone away. 24 They do not say to themselves, 'Let us fear the LORD our God, who gives autumn and spring rains in season, who assures us of the regular weeks of harvest.' 25 Your wrongdoings have kept these away; your sins have deprived you of good.

26 "Among my people are wicked men who lie in wait like men who snare birds and like those who set traps to catch men. 27 Like cages full of birds, their houses are full of deceit; they have become rich and powerful 28 and have grown fat and sleek. Their evil deeds have no limit; they do not plead the case of the fatherless to win it, they do not defend the rights of the poor. 29 Should I not punish them for this?" declares the LORD. "Should I not avenge myself on such a nation as this? 30 A horrible and shocking thing has happened in the land: 31 The prophets prophesy lies, the priests rule by their own authority, and my people love it this way. But what will you do in the end?"

Amos 4:1-13 Hear this word, you cows of Bashan on Mount Samaria, you women who oppress the poor and crush the needy and say to your husbands, "Bring us some drinks!" 2 The Sovereign LORD has sworn by his holiness: "The time will surely come when you will be taken away with hooks, the last of you with fishhooks. 3 You will each go straight out through breaks in the wall, and you will be cast out toward Harmon," declares the LORD.

4 "Go to Bethel and sin; go to Gilgal and sin yet more. Bring your sacrifices every morning, your tithes every three years. 5 Burn leavened bread as a thank offering and brag about your freewill offerings—boast about them, you Israelites, for this is what you love to do," declares the Sovereign LORD.

6 "I gave you empty stomachs in every city and lack of bread in every town, yet you have not returned to me," declares the LORD.

7 "I also withheld rain from you when the harvest was still three months away. I sent rain on one town, but withheld it from another. One field had rain; another had none and dried up. 8 People staggered from town to town for water but did not get enough to drink, yet you have not returned to me," declares the LORD.

9 "Many times I struck your gardens and vineyards, I struck them with blight and mildew. Locusts devoured your fig and olive trees, yet you have not returned to me," declares the LORD.

10 "I sent plagues among you as I did to Egypt. I killed your young men with the sword, along with your captured horses. I filled your

nostrils with the stench of your camps, yet you have not returned to me," declares the LORD.

11 "I overthrew some of you as I overthrew Sodom and Gomorrah. You were like a burning stick snatched from the fire, yet you have not returned to me," declares the LORD.

12 "Therefore this is what I will do to you, Israel, and because I will do this to you, <u>prepare to meet your God</u>, O Israel."

13 He who forms the mountains, creates the wind, and reveals his thoughts to man, he who turns dawn to darkness, and treads the high places of the earth—the LORD God Almighty is his name.

Amos 5:12-24 For I know how many are your offenses and how great your sins. You oppress the righteous and take bribes and you deprive the poor of justice in the courts. 13 Therefore the prudent man keeps quiet in such times, for the times are evil.

14 Seek good, not evil, that you may live. Then the LORD God Almighty will be with you, just as you say he is. 15 Hate evil, love good; maintain justice in the courts. Perhaps the LORD God Almighty will have mercy on the remnant of Joseph.

16 Therefore this is what the Lord, the LORD God Almighty, says: "There will be wailing in all the streets and cries of anguish in every public square. The farmers will be summoned to weep and the mourners to wail. 17 There will be wailing in all the vineyards, for I will pass through your midst," says the LORD.

18 Woe to you who long for the day of the LORD! Why do you long for the day of the LORD? That day will be darkness, not light. 19 It will be as though a man fled from a lion only to meet a bear, as though he entered his house and rested his hand on the wall only to have a snake bite him. 20 Will not the day of the LORD be darkness, not light— pitch-dark, without a ray of brightness?

21 "I hate, I despise your religious feasts; I cannot stand your assemblies. 22 Even though you bring me burnt offerings and grain offerings, I will not accept them. Though you bring choice fellowship offerings, I will have no regard for them. 23 Away with the noise of your songs! I will not listen to the music of your harps. 24 But let justice roll on like a river, righteousness like a never-failing stream!

(a dualistic prophecy, describing the present judgment in terms of the "last days" judgment)

Zephaniah 1:1-18 The word of the LORD that came to Zephaniah son of Cushi, the son of Gedaliah, the son of Amariah, the son of Hezekiah, during the reign of Josiah son of Amon king of Judah:

2 "I will sweep away everything from the face of the earth," declares the LORD.

3 "I will sweep away both men and animals; I will sweep away the birds of the air and the fish of the sea. The wicked will have only heaps of rubble when I cut off man from the face of the earth," declares the LORD.

4 "I will stretch out my hand against Judah and against all who live in Jerusalem. I will cut off from this place every remnant of Baal, the names of the pagan and the idolatrous priests—5 those who bow down on the roofs to worship the starry host, those who bow down and swear by the LORD and who also swear by Molech, 6 those who turn back from following the LORD and neither seek the LORD nor inquire of him. 7 Be silent before the Sovereign LORD, for the day of the LORD is near. The LORD has prepared a sacrifice; he has consecrated those he has invited. 8 On the day of the LORD's sacrifice I will punish the princes and the king's sons and all those clad in foreign clothes. 9 On that day I will punish all who avoid stepping on the threshold, who fill the temple of their gods with violence and deceit. 10 "On that day," declares the LORD, "a cry will go up from the Fish Gate, wailing from the New Quarter, and a loud crash from the hills. 11 Wail, you who live in the market district; all your merchants will be wiped out, all who trade with silver will be ruined. 12 At that time I will search Jerusalem with lamps and punish those who are complacent, who are like wine left on its dregs, who think, 'The LORD will do nothing, either good or bad.' 13 Their wealth will be plundered, their houses demolished. They will build houses but not live in them; they will plant vineyards but not drink the wine.

14 "The great day of the LORD is near—near and coming quickly. Listen! The cry on the day of the LORD will be bitter, the shouting of the warrior there. 15 That day will be a day of wrath, a day of distress and anguish, a day of trouble and ruin, a day of darkness and gloom, a day of clouds and blackness, 16 a day of trumpet and battle cry against the fortified cities and against the corner towers. 17 I will bring distress on the people and they will walk like blind men, because they have sinned against the LORD. Their blood will be poured out like dust and their entrails like filth. 18 Neither their silver nor their gold will be able to save them on the day of the LORD's wrath. In the fire of his jealousy the whole world will be consumed, for he will make a sudden end of all who live in the earth."

The "Jeremiah Ministry" of the Church

Jeremiah 6:10-19, 26-30   10   To whom can I speak and give warning? Who will listen to me? Their ears are closed so they cannot hear. The word of the LORD is offensive to them; they find no pleasure in it.   11   But I am full of the wrath of the LORD, and I cannot hold it in. "Pour it out on the children in the street and on the young men gathered together; both husband and wife will be caught in it, and the old, those weighed down with years.

13   "From the least to the greatest, all are greedy for gain; prophets and priests alike, all practice deceit.   14   They dress the wound of my people as though it were not serious. 'Peace, peace,' they say, when there is no peace.   15   Are they ashamed of their loathsome conduct? No, they have no shame at all; they do not even know how to blush. So they will fall among the fallen; they will be brought down when I punish them," says the LORD.

16   This is what the LORD says: "Stand at the crossroads and look; ask for the ancient paths, ask where the good way is, and walk in it, and you will find rest for your souls. But you said, 'We will not walk in it.'   17   I appointed watchmen over you and said, 'Listen to the sound of the trumpet!' But you said, 'We will not listen.'   18   Therefore hear, O nations; observe, O witnesses, what will happen to them.   19   Hear, O earth: I am bringing disaster on this people, the fruit of their schemes, because they have not listened to my words and have rejected my law.

26   O my people, put on sackcloth and roll in ashes; mourn with bitter wailing as for an only son, for suddenly the destroyer will come upon us.

27   <u>"I have made you a tester of metals and my people the ore, that you may observe and test their ways.</u>   28   They are all hardened rebels, going about to slander. They are bronze and iron; they all act corruptly.   29   The bellows blow fiercely to burn away the lead with fire, but the refining goes on in vain; the wicked are not purged out.   30   They are called rejected silver, because the LORD has rejected them."

Jeremiah 7:16   "So do not pray for this people nor offer any plea or petition for them; do not plead with me, for I will not listen to you.

Jeremiah 9:1-9   Oh, that my head were a spring of water and my eyes a fountain of tears! I would weep day and night for the slain of my people.   2   Oh, that I had in the desert a lodging place for travelers, so that I might leave my people and go away from them; for they are all adulterers, a crowd of unfaithful people.

3 "They make ready their tongue like a bow, to shoot lies; it is not by truth that they triumph in the land. They go from one sin to another; they do not acknowledge me," declares the LORD.

4 "Beware of your friends; do not trust your brothers. For every brother is a deceiver, and every friend a slanderer. 5 Friend deceives friend, and no one speaks the truth. They have taught their tongues to lie; they weary themselves with sinning.

6 You live in the midst of deception; in their deceit they refuse to acknowledge me," declares the LORD.

7 Therefore this is what the LORD Almighty says: "See, I will refine and test them, for what else can I do because of the sin of my people? 8 Their tongue is a deadly arrow; it speaks with deceit. With his mouth each speaks cordially to his neighbor, but in his heart he sets a trap for him. 9 Should I not punish them for this?" declares the LORD. "Should I not avenge myself on such a nation as this?"

Jeremiah 14:9-22; Jeremiah 15: 1-7 Why are you like a man taken by surprise, like a warrior powerless to save? You are among us, O LORD, and we bear your name; do not forsake us!

10 This is what the LORD says about this people: "They greatly love to wander; they do not restrain their feet. So the LORD does not accept them; he will now remember their wickedness and punish them for their sins."

11 Then the LORD said to me, "Do not pray for the well-being of this people. 12 Although they fast, I will not listen to their cry; though they offer burnt offerings and grain offerings, I will not accept them. Instead, I will destroy them with the sword, famine and plague."

13 But I said, "Ah, Sovereign LORD, the prophets keep telling them, 'You will not see the sword or suffer famine. Indeed, I will give you lasting peace in this place.'"

14 Then the LORD said to me, "The prophets are prophesying lies in my name. I have not sent them or appointed them or spoken to them. They are prophesying to you false visions, divinations, idolatries and the delusions of their own minds. 15 Therefore, this is what the LORD says about the prophets who are prophesying in my name: I did not send them, yet they are saying, 'No sword or famine will touch this land.' Those same prophets will perish by sword and famine. 16 And the people they are prophesying to will be thrown out into the streets of Jerusalem because of the famine and sword. There will be no one to bury

them or their wives, their sons or their daughters. I will pour out on them the calamity they deserve.

17 "Speak this word to them: "'Let my eyes overflow with tears night and day without ceasing; for my virgin daughter—my people—has suffered a grievous wound, a crushing blow. 18 If I go into the country, I see those slain by the sword; if I go into the city, I see the ravages of famine. Both prophet and priest have gone to a land they know not.'"

19 Have you rejected Judah completely? Do you despise Zion? Why have you afflicted us so that we cannot be healed? We hoped for peace but no good has come, for a time of healing but there is only terror. 20 O LORD, we acknowledge our wickedness and the guilt of our fathers; we have indeed sinned against you. 21 For the sake of your name do not despise us; do not dishonor your glorious throne. Remember your covenant with us and do not break it. 22 Do any of the worthless idols of the nations bring rain? Do the skies themselves send down showers? No, it is you, O LORD our God. Therefore our hope is in you, for you are the one who does all this.

Jeremiah 15:1-7 Then the LORD said to me: "Even if Moses and Samuel were to stand before me, my heart would not go out to this people. Send them away from my presence! Let them go!

2 And if they ask you, 'Where shall we go?' tell them, 'This is what the LORD says: "'Those destined for death, to death; those for the sword, to the sword; those for starvation, to starvation; those for captivity, to captivity.'

3 "I will send four kinds of destroyers against them," declares the LORD, "the sword to kill and the dogs to drag away and the birds of the air and the beasts of the earth to devour and destroy. 4 I will make them abhorrent to all the kingdoms of the earth because of what Manasseh son of Hezekiah king of Judah did in Jerusalem.

5 "Who will have pity on you, O Jerusalem? Who will mourn for you? Who will stop to ask how you are? 6 You have rejected me," declares the LORD. "You keep on backsliding. So I will lay hands on you and destroy you; I can no longer show compassion. 7 I will winnow them with a winnowing fork at the city gates of the land. I will bring bereavement and destruction on my people, for they have not changed their ways.

Jeremiah 15:15-21 You understand, O LORD; remember me and care for me. Avenge me on my persecutors. You are long-suffering—do not take me away; think of how I suffer reproach for your sake. 16 When your words came, I ate them; they were my joy and my heart's delight, for I bear your name, O LORD God Almighty. 17 I never sat in the company of revelers, never made merry with them; I sat alone because your hand was on me and you had filled me with indignation. 18 Why is my pain unending and my wound grievous and incurable? Will you be to me like a deceptive brook, like a spring that fails?

19 Therefore this is what the LORD says: "If you repent, I will restore you that you may serve me; if you utter worthy, not worthless, words, you will be my spokesman. Let this people turn to you, but you must not turn to them. 20 I will make you a wall to this people, a fortified wall of bronze; they will fight against you but will not overcome you, for I am with you to rescue and save you," declares the LORD.

21 "I will save you from the hands of the wicked and redeem you from the grasp of the cruel."

Jeremiah 17:15-18 They keep saying to me, "Where is the word of the LORD? Let it now be fulfilled!" 16 I have not run away from being your shepherd; you know I have not desired the day of despair. What passes my lips is open before you. 17 Do not be a terror to me; you are my refuge in the day of disaster. 18 Let my persecutors be put to shame, but keep me from shame; let them be terrified, but keep me from terror. Bring on them the day of disaster; destroy them with double destruction.

Ezekiel 2:1-10 He said to me, "Son of man, stand up on your feet and I will speak to you." 2 As he spoke, the Spirit came into me and raised me to my feet, and I heard him speaking to me.

3 He said: "Son of man, I am sending you to the Israelites, to a rebellious nation that has rebelled against me; they and their fathers have been in revolt against me to this very day. 4 The people to whom I am sending you are obstinate and stubborn. Say to them, 'This is what the Sovereign LORD says.' 5 And whether they listen or fail to listen—for they are a rebellious house—they will know that a prophet has been among them. 6 And you, son of man, do not be afraid of them or their words. Do not be afraid, though briers and thorns are all around you and you live among scorpions. Do not be afraid of what they say or terrified by them, though they are a rebellious house. 7 You must speak my words to them, whether they listen or fail to listen, for they are rebellious. 8 But you, son of man, listen to what I say to you. Do not rebel like that rebellious house; open your mouth and eat what I give you."

9 Then I looked, and I saw a hand stretched out to me. In it was a scroll, 10 which he unrolled before me. On both sides of it were written words of lament and mourning and woe.

Ezekiel 3:1-21 And he said to me, "Son of man, eat what is before you, eat this scroll; then go and speak to the house of Israel." 2 So I opened my mouth, and he gave me the scroll to eat.

3 Then he said to me, "Son of man, eat this scroll I am giving you and fill your stomach with it." So I ate it, and it tasted as sweet as honey in my mouth. 4 He then said to me: "Son of man, go now to the house of Israel and speak my words to them. 5 You are not being sent to a people of obscure speech and difficult language, but to the house of Israel—6 not to many peoples of obscure speech and difficult language, whose words you cannot understand. Surely if I had sent you to them, they would have listened to you. 7 But the house of Israel is not willing to listen to you because they are not willing to listen to me, for the whole house of Israel is hardened and obstinate. 8 But I will make you as unyielding and hardened as they are. 9 I will make your forehead like the hardest stone, harder than flint. Do not be afraid of them or terrified by them, though they are a rebellious house."

17 "Son of man, I have made you a watchman for the house of Israel; so hear the word I speak and give them warning from me. 18 When I say to a wicked man, 'You will surely die,' and you do not warn him or speak out to dissuade him from his evil ways in order to save his life, that wicked man will die for his sin, and I will hold you accountable for his blood. 19 But if you do warn the wicked man and he does not turn from his wickedness or from his evil ways, he will die for his sin; but you will have saved yourself.

20 "Again, when a righteous man turns from his righteousness and does evil, and I put a stumbling block before him, he will die. Since you did not warn him, he will die for his sin. The righteous things he did will not be remembered, and I will hold you accountable for his blood. 21 But if you do warn the righteous man not to sin and he does not sin, he will surely live because he took warning, and you will have saved yourself."

Judgment and Hope for the Jews

Isaiah 29:1-8 Woe to you, Ariel, Ariel, the city where David settled! Add year to year and let your cycle of festivals go on. 2 Yet I will besiege Ariel; she will mourn and lament, she will be to me like an altar hearth. 3 I will encamp against you all around; I will encircle you with towers and set up my siege works against you. 4 Brought low, you will speak from the ground; your speech will mumble out of the dust. Your voice will come ghostlike from the earth; out of the dust your speech will whisper.

5 But your many enemies will become like fine dust, the ruthless hordes like blown chaff. Suddenly, in an instant, 6 the LORD Almighty will come with thunder and earthquake and great noise, with windstorm and tempest and flames of a devouring fire. 7 Then the hordes of all the nations that fight against Ariel, that attack her and her fortress and besiege her, will be as it is with a dream, with a vision in the night—8 as when a hungry man dreams that he is eating, but he awakens, and his hunger remains; as when a thirsty man dreams that he is drinking, but he awakens faint, with his thirst unquenched. So will it be with the hordes of all the nations that fight against Mount Zion.

Isaiah 29:9-30 Be stunned and amazed, blind yourselves and be sightless; be drunk, but not from wine, stagger, but not from beer. 10 The LORD has brought over you a deep sleep: He has sealed your eyes (the prophets); he has covered your heads (the seers). 11 For you this whole vision is nothing but words sealed in a scroll. And if you give the scroll to someone who can read, and say to him, "Read this, please," he will answer, "I can't; it is sealed." 12 Or if you give the scroll to someone who cannot read, and say, "Read this, please," he will answer, "I don't know how to read."

13 The Lord says: "These people come near to me with their mouth and honor me with their lips, but their hearts are far from me. Their worship of me is made up only of rules taught by men.

14 Therefore once more I will astound these people with wonder upon wonder; the wisdom of the wise will perish, the intelligence of the intelligent will vanish."

15 Woe to those who go to great depths to hide their plans from the LORD, who do their work in darkness and think, "Who sees us? Who will know?" 16 You turn things upside down, as if the potter were thought to be like the clay! Shall what is formed say to him who formed it, "He did not make me"? Can the pot say of the potter, "He knows nothing"?

17 In a very short time, will not Lebanon be turned into a fertile field and the fertile field seem like a forest?

18 In that day the deaf will hear the words of the scroll, and out of gloom and darkness the eyes of the blind will see. 19 Once more the humble will rejoice in the LORD; the needy will rejoice in the Holy One of Israel. 20 The ruthless will vanish, the mockers will disappear, and

all who have an eye for evil will be cut down—21 those who with a word make a man out to be guilty, who ensnare the defender in court and with false testimony deprive the innocent of justice.

22 Therefore this is what the LORD, who redeemed Abraham, says to the house of Jacob: "No longer will Jacob be ashamed; no longer will their faces grow pale. 23 When they see among them their children, the work of my hands, they will keep my name holy; they will acknowledge the holiness of the Holy One of Jacob, and will stand in awe of the God of Israel. 24 Those who are wayward in spirit will gain understanding; those who complain will accept instruction."

25 In the day of great slaughter, when the towers fall, streams of water will flow on every high mountain and every lofty hill. 26 The moon will shine like the sun, and the sunlight will be seven times brighter, like the light of seven full days, when the LORD binds up the bruises of his people and heals the wounds he inflicted.

27 See, the Name of the LORD comes from afar, with burning anger and dense clouds of smoke; his lips are full of wrath, and his tongue is a consuming fire. 28 His breath is like a rushing torrent, rising up to the neck. He shakes the nations in the sieve of destruction; he places in the jaws of the peoples a bit that leads them astray.

29 And you will sing as on the night you celebrate a holy festival; your hearts will rejoice as when people go up with flutes to the mountain of the LORD, to the Rock of Israel. 30 The LORD will cause men to hear his majestic voice and will make them see his arm coming down with raging anger and consuming fire, with cloudburst, thunderstorm and hail.

8.   The Day of the Lord

Luke 21:25-28 25"There will be signs in the sun, moon and stars. On the earth, nations will be in anguish and perplexity at the roaring and tossing of the sea. 26 Men will faint from terror, apprehensive of what is coming on the world, for the heavenly bodies will be shaken. 27 At that time they will see the Son of Man coming in a cloud with power and great glory. 28 When these things begin to take place, stand up and lift up your heads, because your redemption is drawing near."

Isaiah 2:1-22   This is what Isaiah son of Amoz saw concerning Judah and Jerusalem:

2   In the last days the mountain of the LORD's temple will be established as chief among the mountains; it will be raised above the hills, and all nations will stream to it.

3   Many peoples will come and say, "Come, let us go up to the mountain of the LORD, to the house of the God of Jacob. He will teach us his ways, so that we may walk in his paths." The law will go out from Zion, the word of the LORD from Jerusalem. 4 He will judge between the nations and will settle disputes for many peoples. They will beat their swords into plowshares and their spears into pruning hooks. Nation will not take up sword against nation, nor will they train for war anymore.

5   Come, O house of Jacob, let us walk in the light of the LORD.

6   You have abandoned your people, the house of Jacob. They are full of superstitions from the East; they practice divination like the Philistines and clasp hands with pagans. 7 Their land is full of silver and gold; there is no end to their treasures. Their land is full of horses; there is no end to their chariots. 8 Their land is full of idols; they bow down to the work of their hands, to what their fingers have made. 9 So man will be brought low and mankind humbled—do not forgive them.

10   Go into the rocks, hide in the ground from dread of the LORD and the splendor of his majesty! 11 The eyes of the arrogant man will be humbled and the pride of men brought low; the LORD alone will be exalted in that day. 12 The LORD Almighty has a day in store for all the proud and lofty, for all that is exalted (and they will be humbled), 13 for all the cedars of Lebanon, tall and lofty, and all the oaks of Bashan, 14 for all the towering mountains and all the high hills, 15 for every lofty tower and every fortified wall, 16 for every trading ship and every stately vessel.

17   The arrogance of man will be brought low and the pride of men humbled; the LORD alone will be exalted in that day, 18 and the idols will totally disappear.

19   Men will flee to caves in the rocks and to holes in the ground from dread of the LORD and the splendor of his majesty, when he rises to shake the earth. 20 In that day men will throw away to the rodents and bats their idols of silver and idols of gold, which they made to worship. 21   They will flee to caverns in the rocks and to the overhanging crags from dread of the LORD and the splendor of his majesty, when he rises to shake the earth.

22   Stop trusting in man, who has but a breath in his nostrils. Of what account is he?

Isaiah 24:1-23 See, the LORD is going to lay waste the earth and devastate it; he will ruin its face and scatter its inhabitants—2 it will be the same for priest as for people, for master as for servant, for mistress as for maid, for seller as for buyer, for borrower as for lender, for debtor as for creditor. 3 The earth will be completely laid waste and totally plundered. The LORD has spoken this word.

4 The earth dries up and withers, the world languishes and withers, the exalted of the earth languish. 5 The earth is defiled by its people; they have disobeyed the laws, violated the statutes and broken the everlasting covenant. 6 Therefore a curse consumes the earth; its people must bear their guilt. Therefore earth's inhabitants are burned up, and very few are left.

7 The new wine dries up and the vine withers; all the merrymakers groan. 8 The gaiety of the tambourines is stilled, the noise of the revelers has stopped, the joyful harp is silent. 9 No longer do they drink wine with a song; the beer is bitter to its drinkers. 10 The ruined city lies desolate; the entrance to every house is barred. 11 In the streets they cry out for wine; all joy turns to gloom, all gaiety is banished from the earth. 12 The city is left in ruins, its gate is battered to pieces.

13 So will it be on the earth and among the nations, as when an olive tree is beaten, or as when gleanings are left after the grape harvest. 14 They raise their voices, they shout for joy; from the west they acclaim the LORD's majesty. 15 Therefore in the east give glory to the LORD; exalt the name of the LORD, the God of Israel, in the islands of the sea. 16 From the ends of the earth we hear singing: "Glory to the Righteous One." But I said, "I waste away, I waste away! Woe to me! The treacherous betray! With treachery the treacherous betray!"

17 Terror and pit and snare await you, O people of the earth. 18 Whoever flees at the sound of terror will fall into a pit; whoever climbs out of the pit will be caught in a snare. The floodgates of the heavens are opened, the foundations of the earth shake.

19 The earth is broken up, the earth is split asunder, the earth is thoroughly shaken. 20 The earth reels like a drunkard, it sways like a hut in the wind; so heavy upon it is the guilt of its rebellion that it falls— never to rise again.

21 In that day the LORD will punish the powers in the heavens above and the kings on the earth below. 22 They will be herded together like prisoners bound in a dungeon; they will be shut up in prison and be punished after many days.

23 The moon will be abashed, the sun ashamed; for the LORD Almighty will reign on Mount Zion and in Jerusalem, and before its elders, gloriously.

Isaiah 27:1 <u>In that day</u>, the LORD will punish with his sword, his fierce, great and powerful sword, Leviathan the gliding serpent, Leviathan the coiling serpent; he will slay the monster of the sea.

Isaiah 34:1-10 Come near, you nations, and listen; pay attention, you peoples! Let the earth hear, and all that is in it, the world, and all that comes out of it! 2 The LORD is angry with all nations; his wrath is upon all their armies. He will totally destroy them, he will give them over to slaughter. 3 Their slain will be thrown out, their dead bodies will send up a stench; the mountains will be soaked with their blood. 4 All the stars of the heavens will be dissolved and the <u>sky rolled up like a scroll</u>; all the starry host will fall like withered leaves from the vine, like shriveled figs from the fig tree. 5 My sword has drunk its fill in the heavens; see, it descends in judgment on Edom, the people I have totally destroyed. 6 The sword of the LORD is bathed in blood, it is covered with fat—the blood of lambs and goats, fat from the kidneys of rams. For the LORD has a sacrifice in Bozrah and a great slaughter in Edom. 7 And the wild oxen will fall with them, the bull calves and the great bulls. Their land will be drenched with blood, and the dust will be soaked with fat.
8 For the LORD has a day of vengeance, a year of retribution, to uphold Zion's cause. 9 Edom's streams will be turned into pitch, her dust into burning sulfur; her land will become blazing pitch! 10 It will not be quenched night and day; its smoke will rise forever. From generation to generation it will lie desolate; no one will ever pass through it again.

Isaiah 51:4-6 "Listen to me, my people; hear me, my nation: The law will go out from me; my justice will become a light to the nations. 5 My righteousness draws near speedily, my salvation is on the way, and my arm will bring justice to the nations. The islands will look to me and wait in hope for my arm. 6 Lift up your eyes to the heavens, look at the earth beneath; the heavens will vanish like smoke, the earth will wear out like a garment and its inhabitants die like flies. But my salvation will last forever, my righteousness will never fail.

Isaiah 63:1-6 Who is this coming from Edom, from Bozrah, with his garments stained crimson? Who is this, robed in splendor, striding forward in the greatness of his strength? "It is I, speaking in righteousness, mighty to save."
2 Why are your garments red, like those of one treading the winepress?

3 "I have trodden the winepress alone; from the nations no one was with me. I trampled them in my anger and trod them down in my wrath; their blood spattered my garments, and I stained all my clothing. 4 For the day of vengeance was in my heart, and the year of my redemption has come.

5 I looked, but there was no one to help, I was appalled that no one gave support; so my own arm worked salvation for me, and my own wrath sustained me. 6 I trampled the nations in my anger; in my wrath I made them drunk and poured their blood on the ground."

Joel 2:1-32 Blow the trumpet in Zion; sound the alarm on my holy hill. Let all who live in the land tremble, <u>for the day of the LORD is coming</u>. It is close at hand—2 a day of darkness and gloom, a day of clouds and blackness. Like dawn spreading across the mountains a large and mighty army comes, such as never was of old nor ever will be in ages to come.

3 Before them fire devours, behind them a flame blazes. Before them the land is like the garden of Eden, behind them, a desert waste—nothing escapes them. 4 They have the appearance of horses; they gallop along like cavalry. 5 With a noise like that of chariots they leap over the mountaintops, like a crackling fire consuming stubble, like a mighty army drawn up for battle. 6 At the sight of them, nations are in anguish; every face turns pale. 7 They charge like warriors; they scale walls like soldiers. They all march in line, not swerving from their course. 8 They do not jostle each other; each marches straight ahead. They plunge through defenses without breaking ranks. 9 They rush upon the city; they run along the wall. They climb into the houses; like thieves they enter through the windows. 10 Before them the earth shakes, the sky trembles, the sun and moon are darkened, and the stars no longer shine. 11 The LORD thunders at the head of his army; his forces are beyond number, and mighty are those who obey his command. The day of the LORD is great; it is dreadful. Who can endure it?

12 'Even now,' declares the LORD, 'return to me with all your heart, with fasting and weeping and mourning.' 13 Rend your heart and not your garments. Return to the LORD your God, for he is gracious and compassionate, slow to anger and abounding in love, and he relents from sending calamity. 14 Who knows? He may turn and have pity and leave behind a blessing—grain offerings and drink offerings for the LORD your God.

15 Blow the trumpet in Zion, declare a holy fast, call a sacred assembly. 16 Gather the people, consecrate the assembly; bring together the elders, gather the children, those nursing at the breast. Let

the bridegroom leave his room and the bride her chamber. 17 Let the priests, who minister before the LORD, weep between the temple porch and the altar. Let them say, 'Spare your people, O LORD. Do not make your inheritance an object of scorn, a byword among the nations. Why should they say among the peoples, 'Where is their God?''

18 Then the LORD will be jealous for his land and take pity on his people. 19 The LORD will reply to them: 'I am sending you grain, new wine and oil, enough to satisfy you fully; never again will I make you an object of scorn to the nations.

20 'I will drive the northern army far from you, pushing it into a parched and barren land, with its front columns going into the eastern sea and those in the rear into the western sea. And its stench will go up; its smell will rise.' Surely he has done great things.

21 Be not afraid, O land; be glad and rejoice. Surely the LORD has done great things. 22 Be not afraid, O wild animals, for the open pastures are becoming green. The trees are bearing their fruit; the fig tree and the vine yield their riches. 23 Be glad, O people of Zion, rejoice in the LORD your God, for he has given you the autumn rains in righteousness. He sends you abundant showers, both autumn and spring rains, as before. 24 The threshing floors will be filled with grain; the vats will overflow with new wine and oil.

25 'I will repay you for the years the locusts have eaten—the great locust and the young locust, the other locusts and the locust swarm—my great army that I sent among you. 26 You will have plenty to eat, until you are full, and you will praise the name of the LORD your God, who has worked wonders for you; never again will my people be shamed. 27 Then you will know that I am in Israel, that I am the LORD your God, and that there is no other; never again will my people be shamed.

28 'And afterward, I will pour out my Spirit on all people. Your sons and daughters will prophesy, your old men will dream dreams, your young men will see visions. 29 Even on my servants, both men and women, I will pour out my Spirit in those days. 30 I will show wonders in the heavens and on the earth, blood and fire and billows of smoke. 31 The sun will be turned to darkness and the moon to blood before the coming of the great and dreadful day of the LORD. 32 And everyone who calls on the name of the LORD will be saved; for on Mount Zion and in Jerusalem there will be deliverance, as the LORD has said, among the survivors whom the LORD calls.

Joel 3:1-2, 9-21 'In those days and at that time, when I restore the fortunes of Judah and Jerusalem, 2 I will gather all nations and bring them down to the Valley of Jehoshaphat. There I will enter into judgment against them concerning my inheritance, my people Israel, for they scattered my people among the nations and divided up my land.

9 Proclaim this among the nations: Prepare for war! Rouse the warriors! Let all the fighting men draw near and attack. 10 Beat your plowshares into swords and your pruning hooks into spears. Let the weakling say, 'I am strong!' 11 Come quickly, all you nations from every side, and assemble there. Bring down your warriors, O LORD!

12 'Let the nations be roused; let them advance into the Valley of Jehoshaphat, for there I will sit to judge all the nations on every side. 13 Swing the sickle, for the harvest is ripe. Come, trample the grapes, for the winepress is full and the vats overflow—so great is their wickedness!'

14 Multitudes, multitudes in the valley of decision! For the day of the LORD is near in the valley of decision. 15 The sun and moon will be darkened, and the stars no longer shine. 16 The LORD will roar from Zion and thunder from Jerusalem; the earth and the sky will tremble. But the LORD will be a refuge for his people, a stronghold for the people of Israel.

17 'Then you will know that I, the LORD your God, dwell in Zion, my holy hill. Jerusalem will be holy; never again will foreigners invade her.

18 'In that day the mountains will drip new wine, and the hills will flow with milk; all the ravines of Judah will run with water. A fountain will flow out of the LORD's house and will water the valley of acacias. 19 But Egypt will be desolate, Edom a desert waste, because of violence done to the people of Judah, in whose land they shed innocent blood. 20 Judah will be inhabited forever and Jerusalem through all generations. 21 Their bloodguilt, which I have not pardoned, I will pardon.' The LORD dwells in Zion!

Obadiah 15-21 "The day of the LORD is near for all nations. As you have done, it will be done to you; your deeds will return upon your own head. 16 Just as you drank on my holy hill, so all the nations will drink continually; they will drink and drink and be as if they had never been. 17 But on Mount Zion will be deliverance; it will be holy, and the house of Jacob will possess its inheritance. 18 The house of Jacob will be a fire and the house of Joseph a flame; the house of Esau will be stubble, and they will set it on fire and consume it. There will be no survivors from the house of Esau." The LORD has spoken.

19 People from the Negev will occupy the mountains of Esau, and people from the foothills will possess the land of the Philistines. They will occupy the fields of Ephraim and Samaria, and Benjamin will

possess Gilead. 20 This company of Israelite exiles who are in Canaan will possess [the land] as far as Zarephath; the exiles from Jerusalem who are in Sepharad will possess the towns of the Negev.

21 Deliverers will go up on Mount Zion to govern the mountains of Esau. And the kingdom will be the LORD's.

Micah 1:1-5 The word of the LORD that came to Micah of Moresheth during the reigns of Jotham, Ahaz and Hezekiah, kings of Judah—the vision he saw concerning Samaria and Jerusalem.

2 Hear, O peoples, all of you, listen, O earth and all who are in it, that the Sovereign LORD may witness against you, the Lord from his holy temple. 3 Look! The LORD is coming from his dwelling place; he comes down and treads the high places of the earth. 4 The mountains melt beneath him and the valleys split apart, like wax before the fire, like water rushing down a slope. 5 All this is because of Jacob's transgression, because of the sins of the house of Israel. What is Jacob's transgression? Is it not Samaria? What is Judah's high place? Is it not Jerusalem?

Nahum 1:1-15 An oracle concerning Nineveh. The book of the vision of Nahum the Elkoshite.

2 The LORD is a jealous and avenging God; the LORD takes vengeance and is filled with wrath. The LORD takes vengeance on his foes and maintains his wrath against his enemies. 3 The LORD is slow to anger and great in power; the LORD will not leave the guilty unpunished. His way is in the whirlwind and the storm, and clouds are the dust of his feet. 4 He rebukes the sea and dries it up; he makes all the rivers run dry. Bashan and Carmel wither and the blossoms of Lebanon fade. 5 The mountains quake before him and the hills melt away. The earth trembles at his presence, the world and all who live in it. 6 Who can withstand his indignation? Who can endure his fierce anger? His wrath is poured out like fire; the rocks are shattered before him.

7 The LORD is good, a refuge in times of trouble. He cares for those who trust in him, 8 but with an overwhelming flood he will make an end of [Nineveh]; he will pursue his foes into darkness.

9 Whatever they plot against the LORD he will bring to an end; trouble will not come a second time. 10 They will be entangled among thorns and drunk from their wine; they will be consumed like dry stubble. 11 From you, [O Nineveh,] has one come forth who plots evil against the LORD and counsels wickedness.

12 This is what the LORD says: "Although they have allies and are numerous, they will be cut off and pass away. Although I have afflicted

you, [O Judah,] I will afflict you no more. 13 Now I will break their yoke from your neck and tear your shackles away."

14 The LORD has given a command concerning you, [Nineveh]: "You will have no descendants to bear your name. I will destroy the carved images and cast idols that are in the temple of your gods. I will prepare your grave, for you are vile."

15 Look, there on the mountains, the feet of one who brings good news, who proclaims peace! Celebrate your festivals, O Judah, and fulfill your vows. No more will the wicked invade you; they will be completely destroyed.

Zephaniah 2:1-3 Gather together, gather together, O shameful nation, 2 before the appointed time arrives and that day sweeps on like chaff, before the fierce anger of the LORD comes upon you, before the day of the LORD's wrath comes upon you. 3 Seek the LORD, all you humble of the land, you who do what he commands. Seek righteousness, seek humility; perhaps you will be sheltered on the day of the LORD's anger.

Zephaniah 3:1-20 Woe to the city of oppressors, rebellious and defiled! 2 She obeys no one, she accepts no correction. She does not trust in the LORD, she does not draw near to her God. 3 Her officials are roaring lions, her rulers are evening wolves, who leave nothing for the morning. 4 Her prophets are arrogant; they are treacherous men. Her priests profane the sanctuary and do violence to the law. 5 The LORD within her is righteous; he does no wrong. Morning by morning he dispenses his justice, and every new day he does not fail, yet the unrighteous know no shame.

6 "I have cut off nations; their strongholds are demolished. I have left their streets deserted, with no one passing through. Their cities are destroyed; no one will be left—no one at all. 7 I said to the city, 'Surely you will fear me and accept correction!' Then her dwelling would not be cut off, nor all my punishments come upon her. But they were still eager to act corruptly in all they did. 8 Therefore wait for me," declares the LORD, "for the day I will stand up to testify. I have decided to assemble the nations, to gather the kingdoms and to pour out my wrath on them— all my fierce anger. The whole world will be consumed by the fire of my jealous anger. 9 "Then will I purify the lips of the peoples, that all of them may call on the name of the LORD and serve him shoulder to shoulder. 10 From beyond the rivers of Cush my worshipers, my scattered people, will bring me offerings. 11 On that day you will not be put to shame for all the wrongs you have done to me, because I will

remove from this city those who rejoice in their pride. Never again will you be haughty on my holy hill. 12 But I will leave within you the meek and humble, who trust in the name of the LORD. 13 The remnant of Israel will do no wrong; they will speak no lies, nor will deceit be found in their mouths. They will eat and lie down and no one will make them afraid."

14 Sing, O Daughter of Zion; shout aloud, O Israel! Be glad and rejoice with all your heart, O Daughter of Jerusalem! 15 The LORD has taken away your punishment, he has turned back your enemy. The LORD, the King of Israel, is with you; never again will you fear any harm. 16 On that day they will say to Jerusalem, "Do not fear, O Zion; do not let your hands hang limp. 17 The LORD your God is with you, he is mighty to save. He will take great delight in you, he will quiet you with his love, he will rejoice over you with singing."

18 "The sorrows for the appointed feasts I will remove from you; they are a burden and a reproach to you. 19 At that time I will deal with all who oppressed you; I will rescue the lame and gather those who have been scattered. I will give them praise and honor in every land where they were put to shame. 20 At that time I will gather you; at that time I will bring you home. I will give you honor and praise among all the peoples of the earth when I restore your fortunes before your very eyes," says the LORD.

Hagai. 2:6-9 "This is what the LORD Almighty says: 'In a little while I will once more shake the heavens and the earth, the sea and the dry land. 7 I will shake all nations, and the desired of all nations will come, and I will fill this house with glory,' says the LORD Almighty. 8 'The silver is mine and the gold is mine,' declares the LORD Almighty. 9 'The glory of this present house will be greater than the glory of the former house,' says the LORD Almighty. 'And in this place I will grant peace,' declares the LORD Almighty."

Zechariah 9:9-17 Rejoice greatly, O Daughter of Zion! Shout, Daughter of Jerusalem! See, your king comes to you, righteous and having salvation, gentle and riding on a donkey, on a colt, the foal of a donkey.

10 I will take away the chariots from Ephraim and the war-horses from Jerusalem, and the battle bow will be broken. He will proclaim peace to the nations. His rule will extend from sea to sea and from the River to the ends of the earth. 11 As for you, because of the blood of my covenant with you, I will free your prisoners from the waterless pit. 12 Return to your fortress, O prisoners of hope; even now I announce

that I will restore twice as much to you. 13 I will bend Judah as I bend my bow and fill it with Ephraim. I will rouse your sons, O Zion, against your sons, O Greece, and make you like a warrior's sword.

14 Then the LORD will appear over them; his arrow will flash like lightning. The Sovereign LORD will sound the trumpet; he will march in the storms of the south, 15 and the LORD Almighty will shield them. They will destroy and overcome with slingstones. They will drink and roar as with wine; they will be full like a bowl used for sprinkling the corners of the altar. 16 The LORD their God will save them on that day as the flock of his people. They will sparkle in his land like jewels in a crown. 17 How attractive and beautiful they will be! Grain will make the young men thrive, and new wine the young women.

Zechariah 10:6-12 "I will strengthen the house of Judah and save the house of Joseph. I will restore them because I have compassion on them. They will be as though I had not rejected them, for I am the LORD their God and I will answer them. 7 The Ephraimites will become like mighty men, and their hearts will be glad as with wine. Their children will see it and be joyful; their hearts will rejoice in the LORD. 8 I will signal for them and gather them in. Surely I will redeem them; they will be as numerous as before. 9 Though I scatter them among the peoples, yet in distant lands they will remember me. They and their children will survive, and they will return. 10 I will bring them back from Egypt and gather them from Assyria. I will bring them to Gilead and Lebanon, and there will not be room enough for them. 11 They will pass through the sea of trouble; the surging sea will be subdued and all the depths of the Nile will dry up. Assyria's pride will be brought down and Egypt's scepter will pass away. 12 I will strengthen them in the LORD and in his name they will walk," declares the LORD.

Zechariah 12:2-14 "I am going to make Jerusalem a cup that sends all the surrounding peoples reeling. Judah will be besieged as well as Jerusalem. 3 On that day, when all the nations of the earth are gathered against her, I will make Jerusalem an immovable rock for all the nations. All who try to move it will injure themselves. 4 On that day I will strike every horse with panic and its rider with madness," declares the LORD. "I will keep a watchful eye over the house of Judah, but I will blind all the horses of the nations. 5 Then the leaders of Judah will say in their hearts, 'The people of Jerusalem are strong, because the LORD Almighty is their God.'

6 "On that day I will make the leaders of Judah like a firepot in a woodpile, like a flaming torch among sheaves. They will consume right

and left all the surrounding peoples, but Jerusalem will remain intact in her place. 7 "The LORD will save the dwellings of Judah first, so that the honor of the house of David and of Jerusalem's inhabitants may not be greater than that of Judah. 8 On that day the LORD will shield those who live in Jerusalem, so that the feeblest among them will be like David, and the house of David will be like God, like the Angel of the LORD going before them. 9 On that day I will set out to destroy all the nations that attack Jerusalem.

10 "And I will pour out on the house of David and the inhabitants of Jerusalem a spirit of grace and supplication. They will look on me, the one they have pierced, and they will mourn for him as one mourns for an only child, and grieve bitterly for him as one grieves for a firstborn son. 11 On that day the weeping in Jerusalem will be great, like the weeping of Hadad Rimmon in the plain of Megiddo. 12 The land will mourn, each clan by itself, with their wives by themselves: the clan of the house of David and their wives, the clan of the house of Nathan and their wives, 13 the clan of the house of Levi and their wives, the clan of Shimei and their wives, 14 and all the rest of the clans and their wives.

Zechariah 13:1-8 "On that day a fountain will be opened to the house of David and the inhabitants of Jerusalem, to cleanse them from sin and impurity.

2 "On that day, I will banish the names of the idols from the land, and they will be remembered no more," declares the LORD Almighty. "I will remove both the prophets and the spirit of impurity from the land. 3 And if anyone still prophesies, his father and mother, to whom he was born, will say to him, 'You must die, because you have told lies in the LORD's name.' When he prophesies, his own parents will stab him.

4 "On that day every prophet will be ashamed of his prophetic vision. He will not put on a prophet's garment of hair in order to deceive. 5 He will say, 'I am not a prophet. I am a farmer; the land has been my livelihood since my youth.' 6 If someone asks him, 'What are these wounds on your body?' he will answer, 'The wounds I was given at the house of my friends.'

7 "Awake, O sword, against my shepherd, against the man who is close to me!" declares the LORD Almighty. "Strike the shepherd, and the sheep will be scattered, and I will turn my hand against the little ones. 8 In the whole land," declares the LORD, "two-thirds will be struck down and perish; yet one-third will be left in it. 9 This third I will bring into the fire; I will refine them like silver and test them like gold. They will call on my name and I will answer them; I will say, 'They are my people,' and they will say, 'The LORD is our God.'"

Zechariah 14:1-21   A day of the LORD is coming when your plunder will be divided among you. 2 I will gather all the nations to Jerusalem to fight against it; the city will be captured, the houses ransacked, and the women raped. Half of the city will go into exile, but the rest of the people will not be taken from the city.

3 Then the LORD will go out and fight against those nations, as he fights in the day of battle. 4 On that day his feet will stand on the Mount of Olives, east of Jerusalem, and the Mount of Olives will be split in two from east to west, forming a great valley, with half of the mountain moving north and half moving south. 5 You will flee by my mountain valley, for it will extend to Azel. You will flee as you fled from the earthquake in the days of Uzziah king of Judah. Then the LORD my God will come, and all the holy ones with him.

6 On that day there will be no light, no cold or frost. 7 It will be a unique day, without daytime or nighttime—a day known to the LORD. When evening comes, there will be light.

8 On that day living water will flow out from Jerusalem, half to the eastern sea and half to the western sea, in summer and in winter.

9 The LORD will be king over the whole earth. On that day there will be one LORD, and his name the only name.

10 The whole land, from Geba to Rimmon, south of Jerusalem, will become like the Arabah. But Jerusalem will be raised up and remain in its place, from the Benjamin Gate to the site of the First Gate, to the Corner Gate, and from the Tower of Hananel to the royal winepresses. 11 It will be inhabited; never again will it be destroyed. Jerusalem will be secure.

12 This is the plague with which the LORD will strike all the nations that fought against Jerusalem: Their flesh will rot while they are still standing on their feet, their eyes will rot in their sockets, and their tongues will rot in their mouths. 13 On that day men will be stricken by the LORD with great panic. Each man will seize the hand of another, and they will attack each other. 14 Judah too will fight at Jerusalem. The wealth of all the surrounding nations will be collected—great quantities of gold and silver and clothing. 15 A similar plague will strike the horses and mules, the camels and donkeys, and all the animals in those camps.

16 Then the survivors from all the nations that have attacked Jerusalem will go up year after year to worship the King, the LORD Almighty, and to celebrate the Feast of Tabernacles. 17 If any of the peoples of the earth do not go up to Jerusalem to worship the King, the LORD Almighty, they will have no rain. 18 If the Egyptian people do

not go up and take part, they will have no rain. The LORD will bring on them the plague he inflicts on the nations that do not go up to celebrate the Feast of Tabernacles. 19 This will be the punishment of Egypt and the punishment of all the nations that do not go up to celebrate the Feast of Tabernacles.

20 On that day HOLY TO THE LORD will be inscribed on the bells of the horses, and the cooking pots in the LORD's house will be like the sacred bowls in front of the altar. 21 Every pot in Jerusalem and Judah will be holy to the LORD Almighty, and all who come to sacrifice will take some of the pots and cook in them. And on that day there will no longer be a Canaanite in the house of the LORD Almighty.

Malachi 4:1-6 "Surely the day is coming; it will burn like a furnace. All the arrogant and every evildoer will be stubble, and that day that is coming will set them on fire," says the LORD Almighty. "Not a root or a branch will be left to them. 2 But for you who revere my name, the sun of righteousness will rise with healing in its wings. And you will go out and leap like calves released from the stall. 3 Then you will trample down the wicked; they will be ashes under the soles of your feet on the day when I do these things," says the LORD Almighty.

4 "Remember the law of my servant Moses, the decrees and laws I gave him at Horeb for all Israel.

5 "See, I will send you the prophet Elijah before that great and dreadful day of the LORD comes. 6 He will turn the hearts of the fathers to their children, and the hearts of the children to their fathers; or else I will come and strike the land with a curse."

9. The Resurrection and the Rapture

1 Thessalonians 4:13-18 Brothers, we do not want you to be ignorant about those who fall asleep, or to grieve like the rest of men, who have no hope. 14 We believe that Jesus died and rose again and so we believe that God will bring with Jesus those who have fallen asleep in him. 15 According to the Lord's own word, we tell you that we who are still alive, who are left till the coming of the Lord, will certainly not precede those who have fallen asleep. 16 For the Lord himself will come down from heaven, with a loud command, with the voice of the archangel and with the trumpet call of God, and the dead in Christ will rise first. 17 After that, we who are still alive and are left will be caught up together with them in the clouds to meet the Lord in the air. And so we will be with the Lord forever. 18 Therefore encourage each other with these words.

1 Corinthians 15:1-58 Now, brothers, I want to remind you of the gospel I preached to you, which you received and on which you have taken your stand. 2 By this gospel you are saved, if you hold firmly to the word I preached to you. Otherwise, you have believed in vain.

3 For what I received I passed on to you as of first importance: that Christ died for our sins according to the Scriptures, 4 that he was buried, that he was raised on the third day according to the Scriptures, 5 and that he appeared to Peter, and then to the Twelve. 6 After that, he appeared to more than five hundred of the brothers at the same time, most of whom are still living, though some have fallen asleep. 7 Then he appeared to James, then to all the apostles, 8 and last of all he appeared to me also, as to one abnormally born. 9 For I am the least of the apostles and do not even deserve to be called an apostle, because I persecuted the church of God. 10 But by the grace of God I am what I am, and his grace to me was not without effect. No, I worked harder than all of them—yet not I, but the grace of God that was with me. 11 Whether, then, it was I or they, this is what we preach, and this is what you believed.

12 But if it is preached that Christ has been raised from the dead, how can some of you say that there is no resurrection of the dead? 13 If there is no resurrection of the dead, then not even Christ has been raised. 14 And if Christ has not been raised, our preaching is useless and so is your faith. 15 More than that, we are then found to be false witnesses about God, for we have testified about God that he raised Christ from the dead. But he did not raise him if in fact the dead are not raised. 16 For if the dead are not raised, then Christ has not been raised either. 17 And if Christ has not been raised, your faith is futile; you are still in your sins. 18 Then those also who have fallen asleep in Christ are lost. 19 If only for this life we have hope in Christ, we are to be pitied more than all men.

20 But Christ has indeed been raised from the dead, the firstfruits of those who have fallen asleep. 21 For since death came through a man, the resurrection of the dead comes also through a man. 22 For as in Adam all die, so in Christ all will be made alive. 23 But each in his own turn: Christ, the firstfruits; then, when he comes, those who belong to him. 24 Then the end will come, when he hands over the kingdom to God the Father after he has destroyed all dominion, authority and power. 25 For he must reign until he has put all his enemies under his feet. 26 The last enemy to be destroyed is death. 27 For he "has put everything

under his feet." Now when it says that "everything" has been put under him, it is clear that this does not include God himself, who put everything under Christ. 28 When he has done this, then the Son himself will be made subject to him who put everything under him, so that God may be all in all.

29 Now if there is no resurrection, what will those do who are baptized for the dead? If the dead are not raised at all, why are people baptized for them? 30 And as for us, why do we endanger ourselves every hour? 31 I die every day—I mean that, brothers—just as surely as I glory over you in Christ Jesus our Lord. 32 If I fought wild beasts in Ephesus for merely human reasons, what have I gained? If the dead are not raised, "Let us eat and drink, for tomorrow we die."

33 Do not be misled: "Bad company corrupts good character." 34 Come back to your senses as you ought, and stop sinning; for there are some who are ignorant of God—I say this to your shame.

35 But someone may ask, "How are the dead raised? With what kind of body will they come?" 36 How foolish! What you sow does not come to life unless it dies. 37 When you sow, you do not plant the body that will be, but just a seed, perhaps of wheat or of something else. 38 But God gives it a body as he has determined, and to each kind of seed he gives its own body. 39 All flesh is not the same: Men have one kind of flesh, animals have another, birds another and fish another. 40 There are also heavenly bodies and there are earthly bodies; but the splendor of the heavenly bodies is one kind, and the splendor of the earthly bodies is another. 41 The sun has one kind of splendor, the moon another and the stars another; and star differs from star in splendor.

42 So will it be with the resurrection of the dead. The body that is sown is perishable, it is raised imperishable; 43 it is sown in dishonor, it is raised in glory; it is sown in weakness, it is raised in power; 44 it is sown a natural body, it is raised a spiritual body. If there is a natural body, there is also a spiritual body.

45 So it is written: "The first man Adam became a living being"; the last Adam, a life-giving spirit. 46 The spiritual did not come first, but the natural, and after that the spiritual. 47 The first man was of the dust of the earth, the second man from heaven. 48 As was the earthly man, so are those who are of the earth; and as is the man from heaven, so also are those who are of heaven. 49 And just as we have borne the likeness of the earthly man, so shall we bear the likeness of the man from heaven.

50 I declare to you, brothers, that flesh and blood cannot inherit the kingdom of God, nor does the perishable inherit the imperishable. 51 Listen, I tell you a mystery: We will not all sleep, but we will all be changed—52 in a flash, in the twinkling of an eye, at the last trumpet.

For the trumpet will sound, the dead will be raised imperishable, and we will be changed. 53 For the perishable must clothe itself with the imperishable, and the mortal with immortality. 54 When the perishable has been clothed with the imperishable, and the mortal with immortality, then the saying that is written will come true: "Death has been swallowed up in victory."

55 "Where, O death, is your victory? Where, O death, is your sting?"

56 The sting of death is sin, and the power of sin is the law. 57 But thanks be to God! He gives us the victory through our Lord Jesus Christ.

58 Therefore, my dear brothers, stand firm. Let nothing move you. Always give yourselves fully to the work of the Lord, because you know that your labor in the Lord is not in vain.

Matthew 24:29-31 "Immediately after the distress (tribulation) of those days "'the sun will be darkened, and the moon will not give its light; the stars will fall from the sky, and the heavenly bodies will be shaken.'

30 "At that time the sign of the Son of Man will appear in the sky, and all the nations of the earth will mourn. They will see the Son of Man coming on the clouds of the sky, with power and great glory. 31 And he will send his angels with a loud trumpet call, and they will gather his elect from the four winds, from one end of the heavens to the other.

The Resurrection

John 5:21-29 For just as the Father raises the dead and gives them life, even so the Son gives life to whom he is pleased to give it. 22 Moreover, the Father judges no one, but has entrusted all judgment to the Son, 23 that all may honor the Son just as they honor the Father. He who does not honor the Son does not honor the Father, who sent him.

24 "I tell you the truth, whoever hears my word and believes him who sent me has eternal life and will not be condemned; he has crossed over from death to life. 25 I tell you the truth, a time is coming and has now come when the dead will hear the voice of the Son of God and those who hear will live. 26 For as the Father has life in himself, so he has granted the Son to have life in himself. 27 And he has given him authority to judge because he is the Son of Man.

28 "Do not be amazed at this, for a time is coming when all who are in their graves will hear his voice 29 and come out—those who have done good will rise to live, and those who have done evil will rise to be condemned.

John 14:1-3 "Do not let your hearts be troubled. Trust in God; trust also in me. 2 In my Father's house are many rooms; if it were not so, I would have told you. I am going there to prepare a place for you. 3 And if I go and prepare a place for you, I will come back and take you to be with me that you also may be where I am.

1 Corinthians 2:9 However, as it is written: "No eye has seen, no ear has heard, no mind has conceived what God has prepared for those who love him"—

Job 19:25 I know that my Redeemer lives, and that in the end he will stand upon the earth.

Psalms 16:9-11 Therefore my heart is glad and my tongue rejoices; my body also will rest secure,
10 because you will not abandon me to the grave, nor will you let your Holy One see decay.
11 You have made known to me the path of life; you will fill me with joy in your presence, with eternal pleasures at your right hand.

Psalms 17:13-15 Rise up, O LORD, confront them, bring them down; rescue me from the wicked by your sword.
14 O LORD, by your hand save me from such men, from men of this world whose reward is in this life. You still the hunger of those you cherish; their sons have plenty, and they store up wealth for their children.
15 And I—in righteousness I will see your face; when I awake, I will be satisfied with seeing your likeness.

Daniel 12:2 Multitudes who sleep in the dust of the earth will awake: some to everlasting life, others to shame and everlasting contempt.

Hosea 13:14 "I will ransom them from the power of the grave; I will redeem them from death. Where, O death, are your plagues? Where, O grave, is your destruction? "I will have no compassion,

Isaiah 25:6-9 On this mountain the LORD Almighty will prepare a feast of rich food for all peoples, a banquet of aged wine—the best of meats and the finest of wines. 7 On this mountain he will destroy the shroud that enfolds all peoples, the sheet that covers all nations; 8 he will swallow up death forever. The Sovereign LORD will wipe away the tears from all faces; he will remove the disgrace of his people from all the earth. The LORD has spoken.

9 In that day they will say, "Surely this is our God; we trusted in him, and he saved us. This is the LORD, we trusted in him; let us rejoice and be glad in his salvation."

Isaiah 26:17-21   As a woman with child and about to give birth writhes and cries out in her pain, so were we in your presence, O LORD. 18 We were with child, we writhed in pain, but we gave birth to wind. We have not brought salvation to the earth; we have not given birth to people of the world.

19 But your dead will live; their bodies will rise. You who dwell in the dust, wake up and shout for joy. Your dew is like the dew of the morning; the earth will give birth to her dead. 20 Go, my people, enter your rooms and shut the doors behind you; hide yourselves for a little while until his wrath has passed by.

21 See, the LORD is coming out of his dwelling to punish the people of the earth for their sins. The earth will disclose the blood shed upon her; she will conceal her slain no longer.

Matthew 22:29-32   Jesus replied, "You are in error because you do not know the Scriptures or the power of God. 30 At the resurrection people will neither marry nor be given in marriage; they will be like the angels in heaven. 31 But about the resurrection of the dead—have you not read what God said to you, 32 'I am the God of Abraham, the God of Isaac, and the God of Jacob'? He is not the God of the dead but of the living."

Luke 24:36-43   While they were still talking about this, Jesus himself stood among them and said to them, "Peace be with you."

37 They were startled and frightened, thinking they saw a ghost. 38 He said to them, "Why are you troubled, and why do doubts rise in your minds? 39 Look at my hands and my feet. It is I myself! Touch me and see; a ghost does not have flesh and bones, as you see I have."

40 When he had said this, he showed them his hands and feet. 41 And while they still did not believe it because of joy and amazement, he asked them, "Do you have anything here to eat?" 42 They gave him a piece of broiled fish, 43 and he took it and ate it in their presence.

The Rapture

Isaiah 27:12-13 In that day the LORD will thresh from the flowing Euphrates to the Wadi of Egypt, and you, O Israelites, will be gathered up one by one. 13 And <u>in that day a great trumpet will sound</u>. Those who were perishing in Assyria and those who were exiled in Egypt will come and worship the LORD on the holy mountain in Jerusalem.

10. The Millennium and Beyond

Ps. 2:1-12 Why do the nations conspire and the peoples plot in vain?

2 The kings of the earth take their stand and the rulers gather together against the LORD and against his Anointed One.

3 "Let us break their chains," they say, "and throw off their fetters."

4 The One enthroned in heaven laughs; the Lord scoffs at them.

5 Then he rebukes them in his anger and terrifies them in his wrath, saying,

6 "I have installed my King on Zion, my holy hill."

7 I will proclaim the decree of the LORD: He said to me, "You are my Son; today I have become your Father.

8 Ask of me, and I will make the nations your inheritance, the ends of the earth your possession.

9 <u>You will rule them with an iron scepter</u>; you will dash them to pieces like pottery."

10 Therefore, you kings, be wise; be warned, you rulers of the earth.

11 Serve the LORD with fear and rejoice with trembling.

12 Kiss the Son, lest he be angry and you be destroyed in your way, for his wrath can flare up in a moment. Blessed are all who take refuge in him.

Isaiah 4:1-6 In that day seven women will take hold of one man and say, "We will eat our own food and provide our own clothes; only let us be called by your name. Take away our disgrace!"

2 In that day the Branch of the LORD will be beautiful and glorious, and the fruit of the land will be the pride and glory of the survivors in Israel. 3 Those who are left in Zion, who remain in Jerusalem, will be called holy, all who are recorded among the living in Jerusalem.

4 The Lord will wash away the filth of the women of Zion; he will cleanse the bloodstains from Jerusalem by a spirit of judgment and a spirit of fire.

5 Then the LORD will create over all of Mount Zion and over those who assemble there a cloud of smoke by day and a glow of flaming fire by night; over all the glory will be a canopy. 6 It will be a shelter and shade from the heat of the day, and a refuge and hiding place from the storm and rain.

Isaiah 11:1-9 A shoot will come up from the stump of Jesse; from his roots a Branch will bear fruit. 2 The Spirit of the LORD will rest on him—the Spirit of wisdom and of understanding, the Spirit of counsel and of power, the Spirit of knowledge and of the fear of the LORD—3 and he will delight in the fear of the LORD. He will not judge by what he sees with his eyes, or decide by what he hears with his ears; 4 but with righteousness he will judge the needy, with justice he will give decisions for the poor of the earth. He will strike the earth with the rod of his mouth; with the breath of his lips he will slay the wicked. 5 Righteousness will be his belt and faithfulness the sash around his waist.
6 The wolf will live with the lamb, the leopard will lie down with the goat, the calf and the lion and the yearling together; and a little child will lead them. 7 The cow will feed with the bear, their young will lie down together, and the lion will eat straw like the ox. 8 The infant will play near the hole of the cobra, and the young child put his hand into the viper's nest. 9 They will neither harm nor destroy on all my holy mountain, for the earth will be full of the knowledge of the LORD as the waters cover the sea.

Isaiah 25:6-9 On this mountain the LORD Almighty will prepare a feast of rich food for all peoples, a banquet of aged wine—the best of meats and the finest of wines. 7 On this mountain he will destroy the shroud that enfolds all peoples, the sheet that covers all nations; 8 he will swallow up death forever. The Sovereign LORD will wipe away the tears from all faces; he will remove the disgrace of his people from all the earth. The LORD has spoken.
9 In that day they will say, "Surely this is our God; we trusted in him, and he saved us. This is the LORD, we trusted in him; let us rejoice and be glad in his salvation."

Isaiah 33:17-24 Your eyes will see the king in his beauty and view a land that stretches afar. 18 In your thoughts you will ponder the former terror: "Where is that chief officer? Where is the one who took the revenue? Where is the officer in charge of the towers?" 19 You will see those arrogant people no more, those people of an obscure speech, with their strange, incomprehensible tongue.

20   Look upon Zion, the city of our festivals; your eyes will see Jerusalem, a peaceful abode, a tent that will not be moved; its stakes will never be pulled up, nor any of its ropes broken.   21   There the LORD will be our Mighty One. It will be like a place of broad rivers and streams. No galley with oars will ride them, no mighty ship will sail them.   22   For the LORD is our judge, the LORD is our lawgiver, the LORD is our king; it is he who will save us.

23   Your rigging hangs loose: The mast is not held secure, the sail is not spread. Then an abundance of spoils will be divided and even the lame will carry off plunder.   24   No one living in Zion will say, "I am ill"; and the sins of those who dwell there will be forgiven.

Isaiah 35:1-10   The desert and the parched land will be glad; the wilderness will rejoice and blossom. Like the crocus, 2   it will burst into bloom; it will rejoice greatly and shout for joy. The glory of Lebanon will be given to it, the splendor of Carmel and Sharon; they will see the glory of the LORD, the splendor of our God.

3   Strengthen the feeble hands, steady the knees that give way; 4   say to those with fearful hearts, "Be strong, do not fear; your God will come, he will come with vengeance; with divine retribution he will come to save you."

5   Then will the eyes of the blind be opened and the ears of the deaf unstopped.   6   Then will the lame leap like a deer, and the mute tongue shout for joy. Water will gush forth in the wilderness and streams in the desert.   7   The burning sand will become a pool, the thirsty ground bubbling springs. In the haunts where jackals once lay, grass and reeds and papyrus will grow.

8   And a highway will be there; it will be called the Way of Holiness. The unclean will not journey on it; it will be for those who walk in that Way; wicked fools will not go about on it.   9   No lion will be there, nor will any ferocious beast get up on it; they will not be found there. But only the redeemed will walk there, 10   and the ransomed of the LORD will return. They will enter Zion with singing; everlasting joy will crown their heads. Gladness and joy will overtake them, and sorrow and sighing will flee away.

Isaiah 65:17-25   "Behold, I will create new heavens and a new earth. The former things will not be remembered, nor will they come to mind. 18 But be glad and rejoice forever in what I will create, for I will create Jerusalem to be a delight and its people a joy. 19 I will rejoice over Jerusalem and take delight in my people; the sound of weeping and of crying will be heard in it no more.

20 "Never again will there be in it an infant who lives but a few days, or an old man who does not live out his years; he who dies at a hundred will be thought a mere youth; he who fails to reach a hundred will be considered accursed. 21 They will build houses and dwell in them; they will plant vineyards and eat their fruit. 22 No longer will they build houses and others live in them, or plant and others eat. For as the days of a tree, so will be the days of my people; my chosen ones will long enjoy the works of their hands. 23 They will not toil in vain or bear children doomed to misfortune; for they will be a people blessed by the LORD, they and their descendants with them. 24 Before they call I will answer; while they are still speaking I will hear. 25 The wolf and the lamb will feed together, and the lion will eat straw like the ox, but dust will be the serpent's food. They will neither harm nor destroy on all my holy mountain," says the LORD.

Micah 4:1-8 In the last days the mountain of the LORD's temple will be established as chief among the mountains; it will be raised above the hills, and peoples will stream to it.

2 Many nations will come and say, "Come, let us go up to the mountain of the LORD, to the house of the God of Jacob. He will teach us his ways, so that we may walk in his paths." The law will go out from Zion, the word of the LORD from Jerusalem. 3 He will judge between many peoples and will settle disputes for strong nations far and wide. They will beat their swords into plowshares and their spears into pruning hooks. Nation will not take up sword against nation, nor will they train for war anymore. 4 Every man will sit under his own vine and under his own fig tree, and no one will make them afraid, for the LORD Almighty has spoken. 5 All the nations may walk in the name of their gods; we will walk in the name of the LORD our God for ever and ever.

6 "In that day," declares the LORD, "I will gather the lame; I will assemble the exiles and those I have brought to grief. 7 I will make the lame a remnant, those driven away a strong nation. The LORD will rule over them in Mount Zion from that day and forever. 8 As for you, O watchtower of the flock, O stronghold of the Daughter of Zion, the former dominion will be restored to you; kingship will come to the Daughter of Jerusalem."

Zechariah 14:1-21 A day of the LORD is coming when your plunder will be divided among you. 2 I will gather all the nations to Jerusalem to fight against it; the city will be captured, the houses ransacked, and the women raped. Half of the city will go into exile, but the rest of the people will not be taken from the city.

3 Then the LORD will go out and fight against those nations, as he fights in the day of battle. 4 <u>On that day his feet will stand on the Mount of Olives</u>, east of Jerusalem, and the Mount of Olives will be split in two from east to west, forming a great valley, with half of the mountain moving north and half moving south. 5 You will flee by my mountain valley, for it will extend to Azel. You will flee as you fled from the earthquake in the days of Uzziah king of Judah. <u>Then the LORD my God will come, and all the holy ones with him.</u>

6 On that day there will be no light, no cold or frost. 7 It will be a unique day, without daytime or nighttime—a day known to the LORD. When evening comes, there will be light.

8 On that day living water will flow out from Jerusalem, half to the eastern sea and half to the western sea, in summer and in winter.

9 The LORD will be king over the whole earth. On that day there will be one LORD, and his name the only name.

10 The whole land, from Geba to Rimmon, south of Jerusalem, will become like the Arabah. But Jerusalem will be raised up and remain in its place, from the Benjamin Gate to the site of the First Gate, to the Corner Gate, and from the Tower of Hananel to the royal winepresses. 11 It will be inhabited; never again will it be destroyed. Jerusalem will be secure.

12 This is the plague with which the LORD will strike all the nations that fought against Jerusalem: Their flesh will rot while they are still standing on their feet, their eyes will rot in their sockets, and their tongues will rot in their mouths. 13 On that day men will be stricken by the LORD with great panic. Each man will seize the hand of another, and they will attack each other. 14 Judah too will fight at Jerusalem. The wealth of all the surrounding nations will be collected—great quantities of gold and silver and clothing. 15 A similar plague will strike the horses and mules, the camels and donkeys, and all the animals in those camps.

16 Then the survivors from all the nations that have attacked Jerusalem will go up year after year to worship the King, the LORD Almighty, and to celebrate the Feast of Tabernacles. 17 If any of the peoples of the earth do not go up to Jerusalem to worship the King, the LORD Almighty, they will have no rain. 18 If the Egyptian people do not go up and take part, they will have no rain. The LORD will bring on them the plague he inflicts on the nations that do not go up to celebrate the Feast of Tabernacles. 19 This will be the punishment of Egypt and the punishment of all the nations that do not go up to celebrate the Feast of Tabernacles.

20 On that day HOLY TO THE LORD will be inscribed on the bells of the horses, and the cooking pots in the LORD's house will be like the sacred bowls in front of the altar. 21 Every pot in Jerusalem and Judah will be holy to the LORD Almighty, and all who come to sacrifice will take some of the pots and cook in them. And on that day there will no longer be a Canaanite in the house of the LORD Almighty.

11. Our Blessed Hope

Titus 2:11-14 For the grace of God that brings salvation has appeared to all men. 12 It teaches us to say "No" to ungodliness and worldly passions, and to live self-controlled, upright and godly lives in this present age, 13 while we wait for the blessed hope—the glorious appearing of our great God and Savior, Jesus Christ, 14 who gave himself for us to redeem us from all wickedness and to purify for himself a people that are his very own, eager to do what is good.

1 Corinthians 1:7-8 Therefore you do not lack any spiritual gift as you eagerly wait for our Lord Jesus Christ to be revealed. 8 He will keep you strong to the end, so that you will be blameless on the day of our Lord Jesus Christ.

1 Corinthians 13:8-13 Love never fails. But where there are prophecies, they will cease; where there are tongues, they will be stilled; where there is knowledge, it will pass away. 9 For we know in part and we prophesy in part, 10 but when perfection comes, the imperfect disappears.
11 When I was a child, I talked like a child, I thought like a child, I reasoned like a child. When I became a man, I put childish ways behind me. 12 Now we see but a poor reflection as in a mirror; then we shall see face to face. Now I know in part; then I shall know fully, even as I am fully known.
13 And now these three remain: faith, hope and love. But the greatest of these is love.

James 5:7-11 Be patient, then, brothers, until the Lord's coming. See how the farmer waits for the land to yield its valuable crop and how patient he is for the autumn and spring rains. 8 You too, be patient and stand firm, because the Lord's coming is near. 9 Don't grumble against each other, brothers, or you will be judged. The Judge is standing at the door!

10 Brothers, as an example of patience in the face of suffering, take the prophets who spoke in the name of the Lord. 11 As you know, we consider blessed those who have persevered. You have heard of Job's perseverance and have seen what the Lord finally brought about. The Lord is full of compassion and mercy.

1 Peter 4:7-10 The end of all things is near. Therefore be clear minded and self-controlled so that you can pray. 8 Above all, love each other deeply, because love covers over a multitude of sins. 9 Offer hospitality to one another without grumbling. 10 Each one should use whatever gift he has received to serve others, faithfully administering God's grace in its various forms.

Appendix 2

Times, Dates, and other Such Conjecture

Since this book is attempting to offer a complete picture of the Second Coming of Christ, we might as well look at some puzzle pieces that are not really in the Bible. Oh, people may think they see them there. And, to be sure, God may be hinting at their existence - as we shall see. However, we cannot in good conscience teach or preach these concepts in the same context as biblical truth. At best, we can only wonder about the interesting possibilities they may present us! At worst, we must be careful about teaching them as gospel truth lest people "throw the baby out with the bath water" and lose their faith if they do not come to pass.

The area where prophetic speculation is most common is over the timing of our Lord's return. After all, Jesus did give us plenty of signs to look for. It is too tempting for some people not to try to find hidden dating systems in the Bible. They quickly ignore His admonition not to engage in such futility: "But of that day or hour no one knows, not even the angels in heaven, nor the Son, but the Father alone" (Mark 13:32; NASB).

For instance, Jesus said, "Truly I say to you, this generation will not pass away until all things take place" (Luke 21:32; NASB). So, when Israel became a nation in 1948, many people began to expect Christ to return no later than 1988 - 40 years later (a biblical generation). There were books and seminars whose purpose was to get Christians excited about the coming rapture of the church. I guarantee that we will see the same resurgence of speculation as the year 2007 approaches - 40 years after Jerusalem fell into Jewish hands during the 1967 Six-Day War. Who knows, that may be the time Jesus was referring to. But the problem with using "this generation" as a date-setting device is that we do not know when its actual starting point is. Obviously it wasn't 1948, but I suppose it could be 1967. However, it could also be calculated from the rebuilding of the temple! So, if you are still reading this book after 2007 you will know why it is so foolish to seriously believe things that ought to be understood as only speculation!

With all the dangers in mind, let's have some fun and discover two other areas of conjecture, one having to do with the advent of the year 2000 and the other concerning the time of the year when Christ will return. Why not? You might as well read it here first!

Millennium Fever is Rising

Many people were deeply concerned about the problems the so-called "millennium bug" was supposed to cause during the change of years from 1999 to 2000. But far fewer people are aware of the possible prophetic significance that the advent of this new millennium brings. While our society was fortunate that the computer bug did not bite in the year 2000, we will not be out of the woods for the next few years if some early church fathers were right about prophecy!

One of the Apostle Paul's ministry partners (and an apostle in his own right) was a Hellenistic Jew called Barnabas. His original name was Joseph, but he was commonly called by his nickname that meant, "Son of Encouragement." He was a Levite born on the island of Cyprus (Acts 4:36). It was Barnabas who first introduced Paul to the apostles in Jerusalem after Paul's conversion. He was also the one instrumental in bringing Paul out of obscurity and putting him into full-time ministry in Antioch (Acts 11:26). And it was he who led Paul on his first missionary journey to, naturally, the island of Cyprus. Church tradition tells us that Barnabas was later martyred by his Jewish countrymen on his native island. However, sometime during his ministry Barnabas wrote a letter that is known as *The Epistle of Barnabas*.

When the New Testament was being compiled, the church presbyters did not choose to include *The Epistle of Barnabas* in the canon. Even though many of the early church fathers, including Origen and Eusebius, considered it as having been written by the apostle Barnabas, others, such as Jerome, reckoned it among the Apocryphal books of the period. For our purposes, however, it does not matter whether *The Epistle of Barnabas* was really written by Barnabas or not. What is important for us is simply to recognize that the ideas about the Second Coming presented in the book were taught and understood by the early church.

The *Epistle of Barnabas* was written to the Hellenistic Jews in a style that would appeal to their particular allegorical approach to interpreting scripture. I have referred to this style earlier in this book as the same method used by some of the New Testament authors to show that Jesus was the fulfillment of Old Testament prophetic typologies. In chapter thirteen of the *Epistle of Barnabas*, an interesting allegory is found:

> 1 Furthermore, it is written concerning the sabbath, in the Ten Commandments, which God spake in the Mount Sinai to Moses, face to face: Sanctify the sabbath of the Lord with pure hands, and with a clean heart. 2 And elsewhere he saith, "If thy children shall deep my sabbaths, then will I put my mercy upon them." 3 And even in the beginning of the creation he makes mention of the sabbath. "And god

made in six days the works of his hands; and he finished them on the seventh day, and he rested the seventh day, and sanctified it."

4 Consider, my children, what that signifies, "he finished them in six days." The meaning of it is this; that in six thousand years the Lord God will bring all things to an end. 5 For with him one day is as a thousand years, as himself testifieth, saying, "Behold this day shall be as a thousand years." Therefore, children, in six days, that is, in six thousand years, shall all things be accomplished. 6 And what is that he saith, "And he rested the seventh day:" he meaneth this, that when his Son shall come, and abolish ehe season of the Wicked One, and judge the ungodly; and shall change the sun and the moon, and the stars; then he shall gloriously rest in that seventh day. (*The Genuine Epistles of the Apostolic Fathers*, translated by William, Lord Archbishop of Canterbury, Hartford, CT: Parsons and Hills, 1836.)

In other words, Barnabas was making an allegorical link between the six days of Creation, followed by the Sabbath rest, and an expected six thousand years of human history, followed by the Millennial Kingdom of Christ. Just how widespread was Barnabas' teaching about the six thousand years until the end of the age? We don't know. All we are certain of is the fact that the *Epistle of Barnabas* was generally well known during the first few hundred years of church history. I am not making the case for either its canonicity or accuracy, but only to show that such an expectation existed in the early church.

What does this mean for prophecy buffs today? According to the infamous dating system developed from the Bible's genealogies by Bishop Usher, Adam and Eve were created by God in 4004 BC. Some two thousand years later, around the year 2000 BC, God founded the Jewish nation through their father, Abraham. Then, two thousand years later, God sent His Son to save both Jews and Gentiles who would believe in His work on the cross. In other words, God has been working in this world to save mankind for *six thousand years!* Could it be that the time of man (signified by man's mystical number, six) is now about to come to an end? Will the Millennium sabbath rest begin soon?

Conjecture or coincidence???

The Timing of the Lord's Return

All right. We recognize that Jesus said we wouldn't know the day or the hour of His return. Why should that stop us from trying to figure out the general time of the year He might come back? Here is an interesting speculation that will put a new anticipation in your heart every year!

We know that God instituted the temple and sacrificial systems through Moses. We read in the Book of Hebrews how these holy ordinances pointed to

Christ as their perfect fulfillment. In addition to the Law and the sacrifices, God also told the Jewish people to gather together before the Him at His tabernacle three times a year for commemorative feasts, whereby they would celebrate God's acts of salvation.

The first feast was The Feast of Passover, also known as the Feast of Unleavened Bread. It was held on the 14th day of Nisan, the first month in the Jewish religious calendar. (The Jewish calendar had two concurrent years, the religious year, beginning in the month of Nisan, and the civic year, beginning in the month of Tishri - the seventh month of the religious year.) The Passover was held to remember God's great work of salvation from slavery in Egypt. Every Jewish family would celebrate the Passover with a ritual meal known as the Passover Supper, where every element had historical and prophetic significance.

When Jesus and the disciples celebrated the Passover, Jesus pointed out many prophetic elements in the Passover Sedar service. In doing so, He was claiming to be the fulfillment of the perfect Passover. For instance, when Jesus held up the bread during dinner and spoke, "This is my body which is broken for you," He was not suggesting that the bread would literally become His flesh (as our Roman Catholic friends believe). Nor, for that matter, was He saying that the meal was supposed to be only a "memorial meal" whereby His disciples would simply eat it in order to "remember" what Jesus did for them. Rather, He was showing His disciples that the Passover Meal was actually a prophetic picture that was fulfilled by His death on their behalf! At a certain point in the meal, a flat matzo was to be taken out of a cloth that wrapped up three matzos. The cloth was known as the "Unity." The matzo was to be broken and a piece of it was to be hidden somewhere in the house. At a certain point in the ceremony, the youngest child would go find the hidden bread. So, when Jesus pulled out the second of three matzos from where they were wrapped in the "Unity" cloth, He was showing His disciples that "What you have been doing for centuries in the Passover meal all points to Me as its fulfillment. I am the second Person of the Trinity. I have come to be broken in death, hidden in burial, and discovered alive by rising again! Likewise, the cups of wine that were drunk also pointed to the prophetic fulfillment in Jesus.

Jesus is the "Lamb of God that takes away the sin of the world." He was the sacrificial lamb "slain before the foundations of the world." Jesus was the complete fulfillment of the Passover Feast!

The second Jewish feast, called the Feast of Weeks, was held fifty days after Passover. This feast was also known by its Greek name, Pentecost. It was also called the Feast of Harvest (Exodus 23:16), or the Day of First Fruits (Numbers 28:26). The feast lasted only one day, and marked the completion of the wheat harvest when the first fruits of the harvest would be offered to God. It was on this very feast day when the gift of the Baptism of the Holy Spirit was given to the first Christians. "When the day of Pentecost 'was being fulfilled' [literal

Greek], they were all together in one place" (Acts 2:1). We can conclude that this feast, too, had a prophetic significance in the plan of God for salvation. It was on the exact day of the feast when the "first fruits" of the salvation of Jesus Christ were consecrated and anointed by God, through the powerful Baptism of the Holy Spirit!

The third time the Jews were commanded to appear before the Lord was in the fall - for the Feast of Trumpets, followed by the Day of Atonement, and finally, the Feast of Tabernacles. The Feast of Trumpets was held on the first day of the seventh month (Tishri), which was the beginning of the civil year. The Day of Atonement was observed ten days later as the day of national repentance and mourning. The high priest would confess the sins of the nation and then enter the Most Holy Place with the blood of the offering to make atonement for the people (Leviticus 23:26-32). Five days later, the Feast of Tabernacles began. It was celebrated by erecting "booths" or "tabernacles" in which the people camped during the eight days of the feast. Its purpose was to commemorate the entrance into the Promised Land after the wandering in the wilderness.

What is significant about these feasts? The first, Passover, was held in order to commemorate the great deliverance from bondage. It had a significant prophetic fulfillment. The second, the Feast of Weeks, was held in order to celebrate the first fruits of the harvest. It, too, had a significant prophetic fulfillment. Could the last set of feasts have prophetic significance, as well? And, just as the first two feasts had their prophetic fulfillment at the exact same time the feasts were being celebrated, can we then conclude that whatever prophetic fulfillment the last feast has will be accomplished at the same time of year - namely, the month of Tishri?

There are numerous hints from Scripture that this may be the case!

Let's first look at an interesting passage in the Book of Zechariah. We have seen from our study that Zechariah 14 is a description of the actual physical return of Christ to Jerusalem during the last battle. He will come down from above (with all of His holy ones accompanying Him) and will land on the Mount of Olives. From there He will defeat all His enemies on earth and then set up the promised Millennial Kingdom of God on earth. There truly will be "peace on earth; good will toward men" at that time!

However, notice what Zechariah says about a certain annual celebration that all the nations *must* observe: "Then it will come about that any who are left of all the nations that went against Jerusalem will go up from year to year to worship the King, the Lord of hosts, and to celebrate the Feast of Booths" (Zechariah 14:16; NASB). In fact, Zechariah emphasizes that if certain nations disobey this heavenly edict they will be severely punished: "And it will be that whichever of the families of the earth does not go up to Jerusalem to worship the King, the Lord of hosts, there will be no rain on them. If the family of Egypt does not go up or enter, then no rain will fall on them; it will be the plague with which the Lord smites the nations who do not go up to celebrate the Feast of Booths. This will be the punishment of Egypt, and the punishment of all the nations who do not go up to celebrate the Feast of Booths" (Zechariah 14:17-19; NASB).

Why would God insist that *this* feast still be observed during the Millennium? Could it be that it will become the most important date on the calendar - even surpassing the importance of Easter or Christmas? Could it be that it will be most important in the Millennium because it will celebrate the time of the Second Coming? (Notice that I am *not* speculating on when during this month of Tishri that Jesus will return! We still cannot know the "day or the hour.")

It is important to understand the symbolism of the Feast of Booths. The Israelites were commanded to celebrate it in order to remember their time of wandering in the Wilderness before they entered the Promised Land. Likewise, the Feast of Booths will continue to be celebrated throughout the Millennium period in order to remember what it was we were delivered from, and what we have received through Christ our King: the Promised Land!

If we understand the significant nature the Feast of Booths will have during the Millennium kingdom reign of Christ, we can better understand a confusing passage in the New Testament. At one time during His ministry, Jesus told His disciples, "...I say to you truthfully, there are some of those standing here who will not taste death until they see the kingdom of God (Luke 9:27; NASB). What happened next is intended to show the reader that Jesus words were fulfilled soon afterwards: "Some eight days after these sayings, He took along Peter and John and James, and went up on the mountain to pray. And while He was praying, the appearance of His face became different, and His clothing became white and gleaming. And behold, two men were talking with Him; and they were Moses and Elijah, who, appearing in glory, were speaking of His departure which He was about to accomplish at Jerusalem" (Luke 9:28-31; NASB). Peter, James, and John were witnessing a prophetic picture of the kingdom of God coming in glory! Matthew describes the scene in all of its radiant splendor: "He was transfigured before them; and His face shone like the sun, and His garments became as white as light" (Matthew 17:2). These three disciples were witnessing a little bit of the glory of the Second Coming of Christ!

At that moment the three began to experience what the powers of the age to come will be like. For instance, how did they know whom Jesus was talking to? Jesus did not introduce them. Even though they had no pictures of Moses or Elijah, they immediately recognized them. How did they suddenly know who they were? Probably in the same way we will all know one another in the heavenly kingdom, as Paul writes in First Corinthians: "...now I know in part, but then [when Christ returns] I will know fully just as I also have been fully known" (1 Corinthians 13:12). In other words, they just *knew* who the people were. No explanation or introductions were needed.

Something else happened that has befuddled commentators for centuries. Peter made another one of his famous "spoken without thinking" statements: "Master, it is good for us to be here; let us make three tabernacles: one for You, and one for Moses, and one for Elijah" (Luke 9:33; NASB). Most people assume that Peter was so excited to be in the presence of these holy men of old that he did not want to leave the mountain. He wanted to build shelters for them all to stay in. But Luke's comments tell us that this could not be the case, because he spoke these words "not realizing what he was saying" (Luke 9:33). In other words, Peter did not even know *why* he said it! Just as the powers of the Age to Come were so powerfully manifested before Peter, James, and John that they immediately knew Moses and Elijah were the ones with Jesus, Peter also spoke prophetically about the Kingdom of God! Peter said that he wanted to build three "sacred booths," using the same term used to describe the shelters built during the Feast of Tabernacles. Could he have inadvertently identified the approximate time of the year when Christ will come in glory with the heavenly armies?

Another curious passage concerning the Feast of Tabernacles is found in a conversation between Jesus and, this time, His brothers as recorded in John 7:1-10:

> 1 After this, Jesus went around in Galilee, purposely staying away from Judea because the Jews there were waiting to take his life. 2 But when the Jewish Feast of Tabernacles was near, 3 Jesus' brothers said to him, "You ought to leave here and go to Judea, so that your disciples may see the miracles you do. 4 No one who wants to become a public figure acts in secret. Since you are doing these things, show yourself to the world."
>
> 5 For even his own brothers did not believe in him. 6 Therefore Jesus told them, "The right time for me has not yet come; for you any time is right. 7 The world cannot hate you, but it hates me because I testify that what it does is evil. 8 You go to the Feast. I am not yet going up to this Feast, because for me the right time has not yet come." 9 Having said this, he stayed in Galilee.
>
> 10 However, after his brothers had left for the Feast, he went also, not publicly, but in secret.

Jesus' brothers wanted Him to "go public" with His message and His miracles. They figured that the Feast of Tabernacles would make a great springboard for notoriety. Jesus' response is intriguing. He would not go to this feast to make a public show of His power and glory (although He did later attend it secretly). He said that He would not yet go up to this Feast with His brothers.

He was not going to reveal Himself to the world at this particular Feast of Tabernacles because "the *right* time for Me has not yet come." The right time for revealing Himself as the Christ was going to be during the Passover, when He would be lifted up on the Cross-for all to behold. However, there will be a right time for the Feast of Tabernacles, too. Perhaps he may have also been hinting at His revelation to the world when He will return in glory at the Second Coming!

Finally, it is an strange fact that the Jewish calendar had two systems for counting the months of the year - the religious calendar which was used by the priests, where Nisan was the first month (and when they celebrated Passover), and the secular calendar (used by the kings of Judah and Israel) where Tishri is the first month (and when the Day of Atonement, Feast of Trumpets, and the Feast of Tabernacles occurred). These two calendars may point prophetically to the two advents of the Messiah.

Isn't it interesting that Christ died for our sins so that we can be reconciled to God during the first month of the religious calendar? He is our perfect sacrifice. Now, clothed in His righteousness, we can boldly approach the throne of God. And He has sent the Holy Spirit to us so we can worship Him in Spirit and Truth. All of these directly affect our spiritual, or religious, nature.

When Christ returns again, He will come to rule the nations "with a rod of iron" (Psalm 2:9). He alone will be king on that day. He will set up His kingdom to reign in peace and righteousness. In other words, Christ's Second Coming will be characterized by a peaceful, benevolent government! Isn't it a coincidence that the Jewish calendar also numbers its months according to a second, secular standard for use by the government officials! And isn't it interesting that the first month of Tishri is begun by the blowing of seven trumpets, followed by the day when all Israel confesses their sins and receives forgiveness, and is concluded by the Feast of Booths!

We will just have to wait and see if God completes the pattern of the prophetic fulfillment of the Feasts of Israel!

Bibliography

General Prophetic Books

Clouse, Robert G., *The Meaning of the Millennium.* Downers Grove: Inter-Varsity Press, 1977.

Graham, Billy, *The Approaching Hoofbeats.* Waco: Word Books, 1983.

Hocking, David, *The Coming World Leader.* Portland: Multnomah Press, 1988.

LaSor, William S., *The Truth About Armageddon.* Grand Rapids: Baker Book House, 1987.

Leightner, Robert P., *The Last Days Handbook.* Nashville: Thomas Nelson Publishers, 1990.

Lindsey, Hal, *The Late Great Planet Earth.* Grand Rapids: Zondervan Publishing House, 1970.

Amillennial View

Adams, Jay, *The Time is at Hand.* Presbyterian and Reformed Publishing Co., 1974.

Allis, O.T., *Prophecy and the Church.* Presbyterian and Reformed Publishing Co.,
 1945.

Postmillenial View

Boettner, Loraine, *The Millennium.* Presbyterian and Reformed Publishing Co., 1964.

Premillennial View

McClain, Alva J., *The Greatness of the Kingdom.* Chicago: Moody Press, 1968.

Pentecost, J. Dwight, *Things to Come.* Grand Rapids: Zondervan Publishing House, 1958.

Pentecost, J. Dwight, *Thy Kingdom Come.* Grand Rapids: Zondervan Publishing House, 1990.

Ryrie, Charles, *The Basis of Premillennial Faith.* New York: Loizeaux Brothers, 1953.

Pre-tribulation Rapture View

DeHahn, M.R., *Coming Events in Prophecy.* Lamplighter, 1962.

Stanton, Gerald B., *Kept From the Hour.* Grand Rapids: Zondervan Publishing House, 1964.

Walvoord, John F., *The Church in Prophecy.* Grand Rapids: Zondervan Publishing House, 1964.

Post-tribulation Rapture View

Gundry, Robert H., *The Church and the Tribulation.* Grand Rapids: Zondervan Publishing House, 1973.

Ladd, George E., *The Blessed Hope.* Grand Rapids: Zondervan Publishing House, 1956.

MacPherson, Dave, *The Incredible Cover-up.* Medford: Omega Publications, 1991.

Mid-tribulation Rapture View

Archer, Gleason L., Paul D. Feinberg, Douglas J. Moo, and Richard Reiter, *The Rapture: Pre-, Mid-, or Post-?.* Grand Rapids: Zondervan Publishing House, 1984.

Rosenthal, Marvin, *The Prewrath Rapture of the Church.* Nashville: Thomas Nelson Publishers, 1990.

About the Author

Chip Crosby graduated from Fuller Theological Seminary in 1979 (M.Div.). His writing style reflects his calling as both a pastor and a teacher. He began his ministry as a missions researcher for World Vision International, writing books and articles concerning the identification of unreached people groups, as well as the status of Christianity. Since 1991, he has served as an adjunct professor at LIFE Bible College, where he teaches courses in Homiletics, Systematic Theology, and Eschatology. In addition, he has been a pastor since 1986. Currently, he is the senior pastor of Harbor Light Foursquare Church, PO Box 10128, Costa Mesa, California, 92627. Email: cm4square@earthlink.net.

Printed in the United States
71278LV00004B/79-87

9 780759 686823